Additional Books by the Editors

Berg, I., & Miller, S. D. (1992). *Working with the problem drinker: A solution-focused approach.* New York: W. W. Norton.

Duncan, B. L., Hubble, M. A., & Miller, S. D. (in press). *Psychotherapy with impossible cases: Efficient and effective treatment of therapy veterans.* New York: Guilford.

Duncan, B. L., & Rock, J. W. (1991). *Overcoming relationship impasses: Ways to initiate change without your partner's help.* New Orleans: Insight Press.

Duncan, B. L., Solovey, A. D., & Rusk, G. (1992). *Changing the rules: A client-directed approach to therapy.* New York: Guilford.

McFarland, B., & Miller, S. D. (1995). *Finding the adult within: A solution-focused self-help guide.* Cincinnati: Brief Therapy Center Press.

Miller, S. D., & Berg, I. (1995). *The miracle method: A radically new approach to problem drinking.* New York: W. W. Norton.

Miller, S. D., Duncan, B. L., & Hubble, M. A. (in press). *Escape from Babel: Toward a unifying language of psychotherapy practice.* New York: W. W. Norton

HANDBOOK OF
SOLUTION-FOCUSED BRIEF THERAPY

HANDBOOK OF SOLUTION-FOCUSED BRIEF THERAPY

Scott D. Miller,
Mark A. Hubble,
Barry L. Duncan,
Editors

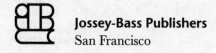

Jossey-Bass Publishers
San Francisco

The extract in Chapter Three, page 56, from Steve de Shazer, "Post-Mortem: Mark Twain *Did* Die in 1910," *Family Process*, 1984, *23*, 20–21, is used here with permission of the publisher.

The extract in Chapter Three, page 56, from William Burroughs, *The Job*, published in 1970 by Grove/Atlantic, © 1969, 1970, 1974 by William Burroughs and Daniel Odier, is reprinted with the permission of Wylie, Aitken & Stone, Inc.

The quote from "Northern Exposure" at the beginning of Chapter Six is copyrighted © 1995 by Universal City Studios, Inc. Used courtesy of MCA Publishing Rights, a Division of MCA Inc. All rights reserved.

The epigraph at the beginning of Chapter Ten is from *Paula*, by Isabel Allende, Copyright © 1994 by Isabel Allende. Translation copyright © 1995 by HarperCollins Publishers. Reprinted by permission of HarperCollins Publishers, Inc..

The results in Chapter Twelve are reprinted from *How to Interview for Client Strengths and Solutions*, by Peter De Jong and Insoo Kim Berg. Copyright 1995 by Brooks/Cole Publishing Company, a Division of International Thomson Publishing Inc. Used with the permission of Brooks/Cole Publishing Company, Pacific Grove, CA 93950.

Substantial discounts on bulk quantities of Jossey-Bass books are available to corporations, professional associations, and other organizations. For details and discount information, contact the special sales department at Jossey-Bass Inc., Publishers (415) 433–1740; Fax (800) 605–2665.

For sales outside the United States, please contact your local Simon & Schuster International Office.

 Manufactured in the United States of America on Lyons Falls Pathfinder Tradebook. This paper is acid-free and 100 percent totally chlorine-free.

Library of Congress Cataloging-in-Publication Data
Handbook of solution-focused brief therapy / Scott D. Miller, Mark
   Hubble, Barry Duncan, editors.
      p.   cm.—(The Jossey-Bass psychology series)
   Includes bibliographical references and index.
   ISBN 0-7879-0217-9 (alk. paper)
   1. Solution-focused therapy. 2. Brief psychotherapy. I. Miller,
Scott D. II. Hubble, Mark, date. III. Duncan, Barry L.
IV. Series.
RC489.S65H36   1996
616.89′14—dc20   95-48252
                                                   CIP

HB Printing 10 9 8 7 6 5 4 3 2 1   FIRST EDITION

CONTENTS

PART THREE: RESEARCH ON SOLUTION-FOCUSED THERAPY

HANDBOOK OF SOLUTION-FOCUSED
BRIEF THERAPY

To our families

INTRODUCTION

Ten years have passed since the publication of "Brief Therapy: Focused Solution Development," the first article to set forth the principles and techniques of what is now known as *solution-focused brief therapy* (de Shazer and others, 1986). From its humble beginnings in the Brief Family Therapy Center, a not-for-profit treatment center in Milwaukee, Wisconsin, the solution-focused model has spread in popularity and use throughout the United States and abroad. Books by the model's originators and other leading thinkers in the field have been translated into Swedish, Danish, Finnish, German, Korean, and Mandarin, to name but a few of the languages. The popularity of the model is such that the editor of the influential *Family Therapy Networker*, Richard Simon, recently remarked that the solution-focused approach has virtually become synonymous with the practice of brief therapy (Simon, personal communication, October 4, 1995).

Another indication of the popularity of the approach is the annual gathering of mental health professionals in Virginia for the East Coast Conference on Solution-Focused Therapy. Each year since 1993, during the first weeks of May, practitioners from around the globe gather to share their knowledge and learn from others who are experimenting with the approach. No other conference offers—or has offered—such a rich diversity of theoretical and practical information unified around the theme of solution-focused therapy. This explains, perhaps, why attendance at the conference has grown steadily since its inception.

In fact, it was during the 1995 East Coast Conference that the idea for this book began to take shape. Clinicians well-trained in the basics of solution-focused brief therapy had gathered together once again to share how they had changed, modified, and adapted the model to fit the needs of different clients, presenting problems, treatment contexts, and cultures. Unfortunately, with few exceptions the information they were presenting did not exist in published form. Indeed, a major shortcoming of most existing books and publications on solution-focused brief therapy is that they are often basic, introductory texts that focus on a single theme. While exceptional articles on specific topics are scattered throughout the professional literature, no single collection exists that gives explicit suggestions for applying the approach to a variety of presenting problems and across a number of different treatment settings.

The same could be said of research on solution-focused therapy. Not only does no single collection of studies exist, but for the most part there simply are no research studies to report! In fact, in spite of having been around for ten years, no well-controlled, scientifically sound outcome studies on solution-focused therapy have ever been conducted or published in any peer-reviewed professional journal (Miller, 1994). Indeed, the majority of information about the efficacy of the approach continues to come from anecdotal reports, subjective clinical experience, and several demographic studies that for the most part consist of stories about successful cases, statistical averages of client characteristics, client ratings of satisfaction, and the average number of therapy sessions (see de Shazer, 1991).

The history of the field of psychotherapy makes it clear that research is the key to preventing the solution-focused approach from becoming just one more in a long list of therapy fads to sweep into the field and quickly fade into obscurity (Lask, 1987; Miller, Hubble, and Duncan, 1995). Several presenters at the 1995 conference reported the results of research they had conducted over the previous year or so on various aspects of the model. Having these and any other available research studies appear in a common source, these presenters thought, would help establish what *is* known about the efficacy and applicability of the approach, as well as direct researchers to those areas in need of further assessment.

Several presenters at the 1995 conference also added their voices to the burgeoning discussion on solution-focused theory. Clearly, over the last several years postmodern philosophy has emerged as the "dominant discourse" in most discussions and writing about solution-focused theory (see de Shazer, 1991, 1994). The ascendance of postmodern theory, however, may say more about the lack of alternative views than about any necessary theoretical connection with solution-focused therapy. The sheer diversity of the presentations made at the conference clearly indicated that no one, single, accepted theory of solution-focused therapy exists. Again, as with clinical issues and research studies, the presenters thought that combining these unique views with any other existing perspectives on theory that could be found would benefit the evolving discussion on solution-focused theory.

The publishers at Jossey-Bass were immediately supportive of the idea and pushed the proposal for the book through their review process in record time. The chapters that appear in *The Handbook of Solution-Focused Brief Therapy* were contributed by many of the conference's presenters. In addition, a number of chapters were solicited from practitioners, theoreticians, and researchers doing innovative work in the United States and abroad. With a few notable exceptions, most of the chapters have been written by solution-focused therapists working in the trenches of the day-to-day clinical world, *not* by the established voices of the solution-focused movement. The work of this second generation of clinicians is, perhaps more than anything else, a testament to the success of the original ideas that the small group of iconoclastic pioneers in Milwaukee set forth ten years ago.

Overview of the Contents

The chapters in the *The Handbook of Solution-Focused Brief Therapy* are divided into three main sections: (1) foundations, (2) applications, and (3) research. The foundations section offers three chapters on the state of solution-focused theory. The second section contains seven chapters on various applications of the solution-focused model. This section is the largest in the book because of the historical and current emphasis on practical skills in solution-focused therapy. Here the reader will learn how to adapt the basic elements of the solution-focused model for use in a variety of contexts and with many presenting problems. The last section of the book contains four chapters on research about solution-focused work that have direct implications for improving clinical work.

Aside from this basic organization, the chapters in this book do not appear in any particular order. Furthermore, each chapter stands on its own and does not build on the ideas contained in previous chapters (except in the most general fashion). For this reason, readers can feel comfortable skipping around and reading those chapters that interest them most. To facilitate this approach, a brief description of each chapter follows.

Foundations

Postmodernism, narrative therapy, and language theory are at the leading edge of the topics currently being discussed among solution-focused thinkers. In the first chapter of this section, John L. Walter and Jane E. Peller, the authors of *Becoming*

Solution-Focused in Brief Therapy (1992), describe how postmodern theory has come to inform their clinical practice. They put forth their reconsideration of the assumptions that are at the base of their work. The shift in their thinking since the publication of their earlier book represents their movement away from an instrumental therapy, with the practitioner enacting the role of expert, to one established in conversation and mutual meaning making.

In Chapter Two, Barbara Held critiques the growing interest in and application of postmodern theory to psychotherapy practice in general and solution-focused therapy in particular. Building on her groundbreaking book, *Back to Reality* (1995), Held points out the contradictions in most of the writing that associates solution-focused therapy with postmodernism, while simultaneously helping readers develop a theory of clinical practice that is both individualized and empirically based.

Dvorah Simon speaks personally and poetically in Chapter Three about her experience of solution-focused therapy as a spiritual path. She shows how the assumptions of solution-focused work are similar to the core values of many different spiritual traditions. Furthermore, she makes the point that many of the techniques of solution-focused therapy can be understood as practices aimed at helping therapists learn the spiritual values inherent in all therapeutic work. For anyone who has ever heard that the model is only about technique, Dvorah's chapter exposes the very heart of solution-focused work.

Applications

In Chapter Four, which is likely to be one of the most controversial chapters in the book, Eve Lipchik and Tony Kubicki present their ideas for utilizing solution-focused therapy in cases of domestic violence. It is a courageous piece that identifies, addresses, and actually bridges the differences in an area fraught with rigid pronouncements and gloomy predictions. The chapter's format of a conversation between the authors allows the richness of their experience, as well as the depth of their commitment, to be expressed. Their dialogue also models a collaborative, solution-oriented approach for bridging differences. Lipchik and Kubicki respect and validate the traditional view while simultaneously offering an exciting alternative perspective.

In Chapter Five, Kay Vaughn, Bonnie Cox Young, Denise Webster, and Marshall R. Thomas present a model for utilizing solution-focused therapy in inpatient psychiatric settings. The authors bring their years of experience to bear on providing quality services while simultaneously managing the usually high costs associated with inpatient care. As they point out, the key to efficient and effective care is to tailor the approach to the needs of clients across the continuum of care—from admission through discharge and follow-up. Their results are some of the most convincing being reported for solution-focused therapy.

In Chapter Six, Frank N. Thomas presents a model and method for clinical supervision based on the principles and practice of solution-focused therapy. Thomas's chapter provides a way for supervisors to step out of the traditional, hierarchical, expert mode for providing clinical supervision and into a relationship with supervisees that highlights strengths and builds on competence.

In Chapter Seven, Susan Lee Tohn and Jordan A. Oshlag present a step-by-step process for developing cooperative and therapeutic relationships with mandated clients based on the principles and techniques of solution-focused therapy. Readers who work with clients who are forced to be in therapy will especially enjoy the many case examples and explicit therapy dialogue that Tohn and Oshlag use to illustrate the process they present.

In Chapter Eight, John J. Murphy brings the solution focus to the arena in which brief therapy has perhaps been practiced more than any other modality—the school. He describes how the model is ideally suited for the day-to-day exigencies of a school-based practice. With accompanying commentary, he also provides clear examples of intervention strategies for working with both individuals and schoolwide programs.

Judi Booker's overview of hospital diversion, in Chapter Nine, provides an informative description of how solution-focused therapy can assist in this growing area of clinical practice. Criticized in some quarters as the therapy of the walking well and the normally neurotic, the solution-focused model has been regarded as ill-equipped to handle tough clinical problems, particularly those involving questions of life and death and psychotic regression. Booker convincingly shows with case examples that a solution-focus may be the approach of first resort for steering patients to less restrictive and expensive modalities of treatment.

Chapter Ten, by Bill Butler and Keith Powers, shows how to use the solution-focused approach with clients who are grieving. Butler and Powers respond to the criticism that solution-focused therapy is contraindicated in cases of grief and loss, and they use numerous case examples and dramatic dialogue to show how the model can be applied in a sensitive and thoughtful manner. Their chapter is proof that solution-focused therapy is more than technique.

Research

The first chapter in this section, Chapter Eleven, is by A. Jay McKeel. It presents a long overdue review of the existing research on solution-focused brief therapy. Written in a "clinician-friendly" style, McKeel's chapter summarizes the data and "bottom-lines" the practical implications for practitioners. It presents research that affirms many of the assumptions and techniques of solution-focused brief therapy while also providing a provocative discussion of the relationships among innovation, research, and the future growth of the approach.

In Chapter Twelve, researchers and clinicians Peter De Jong and Larry Hopwood present their findings from an extensive study of cases seen at the Brief Family Therapy Center in Milwaukee. The data presented in this chapter not only provide evidence for the utility of solution-focused therapy in addressing a wide range of presenting problems but also show that the effectiveness of the model cuts across economic, gender, and racial lines.

In Chapter Thirteen, Mark Beyebach and his associates in Salamanca, Spain, present an overview of their process research on solution-focused research. More than any other chapter in the book, this chapter points to the importance of conducting systematic and ongoing research for furthering the development and understanding of solution-focused work. Though supportive of the model in general, the research presented by Beyebach and his colleagues shows how some specific practices and concepts of solution-focused therapy need to be modified.

In Chapter Fourteen, the book's final chapter, Linda Metcalf and associates present a provocative qualitative study that addresses client and therapist perceptions of solution-focused brief therapy. This exploratory investigation, conducted at the Brief Family Therapy Center, confronts the critical issue of whether practitioners of solution-focused brief therapy do what they say they do, and more importantly, what their clients perceive as helpful about what they do. While affirming many of the assumptions of solution-focused brief therapy, this interesting study also provides a surprising perspective that challenges prevailing accounts of how it is practiced and what makes it effective.

References

De Shazer, S. (1991). *Putting difference to work.* New York: W. W. Norton.

De Shazer, S. (1994). *Words were originally magic.* New York: W. W. Norton.

De Shazer, S., Berg, I., Lipchik, E., Nunnally, E., Molnar, A., Gingerich, W., and Weiner-Davis, M. (1986). Brief therapy: Focused solution development. *Family Process, 25,* 207–222.

Held, B. (1995). *Back to reality: A critique of postmodern theory in psychotherapy.* New York: W. W. Norton.

Lask, B. (1987). Editorial: From honeymoon to reality, or how to survive a plague in our house. *Journal of Family Therapy, 8,* 303–305.

Miller, S. D. (1994). The solution conspiracy: A mystery in three installments. *Journal of Systemic Therapies, 13*(1), 18–37.

Miller, S. D., Hubble, M. A., & Duncan, B. (1995). No more bells and whistles. *Family Therapy Networker, 19*(2), 52–63.

Walter, J. L., & Peller, J. E. (1992). *Becoming solution-focused in brief therapy.* New York: Brunner-Mazel.

PART ONE

FOUNDATIONS OF SOLUTION-FOCUSED BRIEF THERAPY

CHAPTER ONE

RETHINKING OUR ASSUMPTIONS

Assuming Anew in a Postmodern World

John L. Walter and Jane E. Peller

When we first considered writing this chapter, we thought of the title, "Rethinking Our Assumptions." We considered this writing project an opportunity to offer a revision of our thinking about personal consultation (that is, therapy).[1] However, as our work on the chapter progressed, we discovered that what we were writing was not just a reconsideration of the assumptions we had written about in *Becoming Solution-Focused in Brief Therapy* (1992) but a new way of thinking with a different set of assumptions. In essence, this chapter marks a maturation of our work and a shift from reliance on information theory and cybernetics to a focus on postmodernism, language, and narrative.

What we have written is a fundamental assumption about language, followed by eight pragmatic assumptions relating to personal consulting. This chapter is not a complete philosophical description of these assumptions, as that task would be well beyond the scope of this chapter. Scholars such as Wittgenstein (1958, 1965), Rorty (1979), and Maturana and Varela (1987), and thinkers in the fields of psychotherapy and family therapy such as Andersen (1991), Anderson and Goolishian (1988), de Shazer (1994), Gergen (1992), Gergen and Kaye (1992), Shotter (1993), White and Epston (1990), and others have already spoken rather extensively about the philosophy that underlies our approach to personal consulting. Our purpose in this chapter is not to describe postmodernism, social constructionism, or the new paradigm within social science, but to describe some of the assumptions within this philosophy that are applicable to our personal consulting, to explain what those assumptions mean to us, and to talk about how they inform our work.

Recent Background

The background for this current evolution in our thinking began in the early eighties. At that time, we were using the *brief strategic therapy model,* the brief problem-focused therapy model of the Mental Research Institute (Weakland, Fisch, Watzlawick, and Bodin, 1974). We thought of *problem-maintaining patterns* as consisting of the client's definition of the problem as well as his or her attempted solution. We also subscribed to the philosophy of *radical constructivism* proposed by von Glaserfeld (1984), von Foerster (1984), Watzlawick (1984), and Maturana and Varela (1987). We believed, as that philosophy proclaims, that individuals construct their own realities based on the lenses they use and the distinctions they make. We also believed that the individual observer could never be separated from what she observed.[2]

Yet, while we believed these notions, we struggled. Radical constructivism and second-order cybernetics did not talk about observed systems. Rather, they talked about "self-observing systems," in which the observer was seen as never apart from what she observed. Our difficulty was with the word "observing," which always implies a distance or separation between observer and observed. We struggled with how we could be observers of ourselves and others at the same time. While we said to ourselves that the observation of problem patterns and attempted solutions were our constructions, we somehow gave these constructions a significance, as if they were "real."

We also thought that as long as we stayed within the visual language of observation, we would perpetuate the distance between observer and observed, subject and object. As we began to think of personal consultation as involving two subjects, the personal consultant and the client, who are mutually influencing each other, we also struggled with how cybernetics could continue to be a suitable metaphor. While cybernetics made sense when talking about observers and observed, subject and object, it had no language for talking about two subjects talking with each other. We felt muddled.

What began to make sense was a criticism of Gregory Bateson's thought by Paul Dell (1985). While Bateson spoke of a new epistemology in which people create their worlds out of the distinctions they make, he also spoke of information as "news of *difference*" (Bateson, 1979, p. 29), implying that this difference is objective in the real world of objective reality. He treated information as though it were a real object, as real data, talking about it perhaps as one might talk about data in a computer. Bateson's cybernetics and information theory seemed to carry the notion that information represented something besides the influence of people, that it had a life of its own. In Bateson's thinking, reality was a creation, but somehow information had a special status. In his talk about information, he implied that it had a realism that everything else did not. Dell pointed out this inconsistency and concluded that treating information as data that represented some real difference was an attitude left over from objective realism.

What began to look more consistent to us was the ontology of Maturana and Varela (1987), and the idea that personal consulting is at least two subjects involved in mutual meaning making rather than exchange of information. Thinking of language as representational perpetuated the notion of realism that ideas (language) were signs of what was real, of what was outside the observer.

The language of conversation, narrative, reflections, and text has become more relevant to our approach than the language of observation, interview, information, and feedback. This different philosophy of language has provided the hinge of change for us as we have made many fundamental shifts in our assumptions.

A Fundamental Assumption

We live in a world of meaning and language that is creational, social, and active.

In the early eighties, we used the words "language" and "information" synonymously. Although we subscribed to radical constructivism and the belief that people create their own realities, we used language as though it represented objects apart from us (information) and as if information were a real entity. As we mentioned above, this was a strong incongruity in our work. While on the one hand we believed that as observers we could not be divorced from what we were observing, we treated the observations, the information that was created, as though it were a real entity.

An example is in our early use of the notion of "exceptions." Early on in our work within a solution-focused approach, we thought of exceptions as exceptions to problem patterns. While we said, on the one hand, that as solution-focused therapists we could not be apart from our observations, on the other hand we talked of problem patterns and exceptions as though they existed apart from our observations. We spoke of exceptions as real events rather than as events we created by making distinctions. In workshops, participants continually asked us what we did if there were no exceptions. Participants believed as we did that exceptions were real events. When they heard their clients say there were no exceptions, they heard that assertion as a statement about reality—there were no times in the real world when the problem pattern did not exist. So, we suggested that participants put aside the exceptions question and use "the miracle question."[3] This answer was our acknowledgment that we too believed that exceptions were real events. By responding with that answer we were participating in the presupposition of the participant's question that exceptions were somehow real events.

What became apparent over time was the inconsistency between saying that we create our reality and saying that problem patterns or exceptions somehow have an existence apart from our observations. We were treating the existence or nonexistence of exceptions as difference in the Bateson sense and therefore as information. We were treating this difference as though it were real. While in our heads we were saying that we invented reality, we were treating information as though it still had a special status close to an objective reality.

What was more consistent with a created reality was to rethink language as creational rather than as representational. Rather than thinking of words as representing something outside of us or as representing our experience, we began to think of words as drawing forth and creating our experience rather than the other way around.

In everyday conversation, most people think of words as representing objects apart from themselves. They think of words as symbols that represent as close as possible an observable world. They assume that everybody who uses the word "tree" means the same thing because there is an object out there that the word refers to. When language is thought of as creational, however, the implication is that the word "tree" draws forth the experience of tree. The word "tree" does not take on meaning until it is used. This means that people make meaning of their lives through language. (For a more extensive explanation of language as creational, as well as a presentation of the supporting research, see Maturana and Varela's *The Tree of Knowledge*, 1987.)

For example, if a parent uses the terms of morality to describe her son's behavior, the parent is creating a world of good and bad son behavior. The parent experiences her son as good and bad, an experience that is different from the parent describing her son's behavior in mental health terms. If the parent were to use the language of mental health, she would experience her son as a functional or dysfunctional boy.

When we were using a brief strategic therapy model, we commonly thought of words and distinctions as *frames*. We spoke of behaviors being defined by the meaning or frame we placed around them. We considered words like "good" or "bad" to be the meaning surrounding the behaviors. The implication of separating behavior and meaning is that the behavior is somehow more real and the meaning is subjective. However, that is not the implication of language as creational. Language as creational includes more than interpretation and framing.

Language *creates* the experience of bad behavior. The behavior is not separated from the interpretation of "badness."

When teaching reframing, we would use the example of a raised right hand to demonstrate the significance of framing. We would talk about how this same behavior—a raised right hand—could be framed very differently in different contexts. For example, in a classroom a teacher would assume that such a gesture by a student meant the student had a comment or question and was requesting permission to speak. At a curbside, a raised hand could be interpreted as a request for a cab. On a boat, the gesture could be framed as a greeting to passengers on other boats. In using this example, we were subtly implying that the behavior was somehow observable and describable, but the meaning or frame was subjective. With the notion of language as creational we are saying that it is not just the interpretation or meaning that is subjective but the whole experience. Both the gesture and the meaning are created.

Experience is one with and the same as the meaning and language of that experience. Language does not represent experience—it is inseparable from it. In changing our view of meaning and language, we are not just reversing a cause and effect. Thinking of language as representational leads one to believe that experience comes first and then words are used to represent it. Thinking of language as creational might lead one to think instead that words come first. But this is not what we mean. Language and experience are simultaneous.

The assumption that language is creational goes beyond the idea of an individual creating her world, however. Language is social. If we were to end our explanation of language as creational here we could be giving you the impression that everyone has and creates her own individual reality. The example of the parent making her world about her son could lead you to believe that we are speaking only about an individual subjectivism. Our limited explanation would lead you to believe that our assumption is no more than what philosophers over the years have labeled *naive solipsism*, a philosophy that assumes that what is real is contained within our individual heads. This philosophy maintains that each person creates her own reality and that there are as many realities as there are people.

However, what would be left out if we were to stop here is that the individual parent, the subjective "I" in our example, exists in a world of others, a social world, and she is making meaning of her situation by using a language that has been developed and used socially. So, the parent's moral distinctions of good and bad behavior on the part of her son have been used over time by many people in interaction. These are not the private words of the "I" and this is not a private language. The meaning of the words "good and bad son behavior" are the result of a social consensus—an agreement over time about what the words mean. Wittgenstein (1958) discusses meaning more extensively; he says we cannot find the meaning of a word in a private language or in the speaker's intention. He concludes that the meaning of a word is in its use.

In everyday conversation in this culture, the words "good and bad son behavior" are used as though they refer to identifiable objective behavior. Again, the reverse is the case. By using these words with their socially created meaning, the experience of that behavior is drawn forth. The question of whether the son's actions exist apart from the parent's observations and her talking about them is not relevant. By making the distinction of good or bad behavior, the parent creates the experience.

What we have also left out in the earlier example is that the words the parent uses in thinking about her son's behavior take place in an interaction. That interaction may be a conversation with herself or with someone else. In thinking about the parent making conversation with herself or someone else about her son, the above example becomes a "we" event rather than an "I" creating a subjective world. The meaning making takes place in an interaction, a social event.

Looking at meaning making as an interaction, between either the parent and herself, the parent and someone else, or the parent and an author through a written text, we reach the conclusion that meaning making involves at least two selves, two views, two constructions. The implications of seeing meaning making as a social event of at least two selves while at the same time realizing that language is not tied to an objective reality are that in a conversation there are at least two stories, at least two constructions, and a mutual, coordinated construction process.

When we say that language creates our experience, we do not mean that meaning making is just passive use of certain terms. Language is active and language is a verb. The parent's use of the terms "good and bad son's behavior" is a choice. The parent has the option of using other words and thereby creating a different meaning or story for herself. This means that each person is responsible for the language she uses and for the "reality" she creates. This means that each person bears the ethical responsibility for the language she uses.

Language is also not just a tool. While one may choose one's language and create the story or experience one wants, it is not a matter of using or not using language. Language is not something one can step outside of. While people may be selective in the words they speak, they have no choice but to be in language. It is inescapable. Both alone and with others, people are always thinking, talking, and being in language.

We agree with Maturana and Varela's (1987) use of the word "language" as a verb, because it emphasizes that language is an action. Language is something people do. "Languaging," as used by Maturana and Varela, is a social action that everyone is immersed in. Languaging is also creational in the sense that in talking with others, people are sharing their experiences in language. As people talk with each other, they mutually create the experience; they answer other people's questions, they respond to others' experience, or they mirror to others what they hear. As this mutual languaging continues, the experience changes. People use additional words, they tell the story differently, they elaborate, and they even create new parts. Meaning evolves through the languaging.

While the meaning of a word is in its use or the social consensus about its use, what a word means is never a finished fact. The consensus is forever changing and evolving, as is the use of the word. The constant revision of dictionaries are a testament to this. In addition, while words say some things, they also leave out or are open to even further interpretation or inquiry. Languaging is not just the sharing of experience; it is also the sharing of what has not yet been said, and of what more can be said. Languaging is always becoming, and in that sense it always invites more conversation in a search for understanding. Languaging is contextual. People never "language" in a vacuum. They language in a relationship. As Lax (1992) has stated, "Clients are not passively inscribed texts waiting to be interpreted by a reader. . . . Each reading is different, given the interaction between the client and therapist. The client, in essence, does not have a singular 'true' story independent of a 'reader' to whom she is telling that particular story (p. 73)." Each client's languaging will be different with each consultant. Languaging takes place in interaction, and each interaction is different or unique.

Implications for Personal Consulting

What does all this mean to us, for how we do consulting? This shift in our thinking about language has resulted in a maturation of our solution-focused mind-set. We would now like to discuss eight of the pragmatic implications of the assumption we have just considered.

1. *The personal consulting group is a languaging group that is self-defining. The definition or purpose is unique and defined by the participants.*

A personal consulting group is defined by the members of that group and the membership is defined by the declaring of a shared purpose. The membership and purpose are declared from within. The group's organization is created by the declaring of a goal that everyone is concerned about, even if they do not agree on the particulars. This includes the consultant, who agrees to work with the client(s) on the stated goal.

An example is a man who came to see us because of his concern about a recent incident in which he had struck his two young daughters with a plastic baseball bat.

He said he was very frightened and concerned about his loss of control and he wanted to figure out what he could do to make sure that this never happened again. He also related that his wife had called the police during this incident and that child protective services had become involved. While he knew his wife was very angry with him and his daughters were frightened, he was sure they wanted him to return home.

The consulting group in this case consisted of those who were stating that they wanted a change. This included the father, his wife, the probation officer who became involved after the man's court appearance, and us as consultants. The father attended all the sessions, the wife attended some sessions, and the probation officer was involved by phone.

All of the participants became involved as each of them stated that they wanted something to be different. Each of them became involved by their own initiation rather than by our asking or insisting. The group became defined by their mutual concern about what had happened and by each person's desire to change the situation. The group was defined by their languaging about the goal.

When clients ask, "Who should attend?" we say that everyone should come who is concerned about the situation. This is different from therapy models that determine the membership and purpose of the therapy according to some authority or criteria established outside the therapy session. Traditional therapy models assume that the problem results from some deficiency in a socially defined unit such as an individual psyche, a family, or a couple. These models then assume that the therapist's role is to treat the disorder or dysfunction within these structures. They also assume that the membership of the therapy system should be the therapist and whatever unit the therapist determines is the source of the problem. For us, the reverse is true. The languaging about a goal determines who will participate, who will be the membership of the personal consulting group.

This approach is similar to Anderson, Goolishian, and Winderman's (1984) problem-determined system. They state that the therapy system is determined within language by those who state there is a problem. The treatment system is a problem-organizing and problem-dissolving system.

While we share the notion that the personal consulting group is determined and defined from within, we prefer to speak of the group as a goal-determined system. The personal consultant and the client form this group as they language around the purpose or goal for their meeting. We make the assumption that people coming to us for personal consultation are coming for some reason or purpose. Even if clients cannot state that purpose very clearly or have not thought through all the reasons for their coming, we assume they are coming for some reason. We also assume that the purpose in their coming may and probably will change over time. The purpose or goal may change through talking and conversing about it. This means that while the consultant and client are conversing, this conversation is not ordinary or casual. The meeting is purposeful and the purpose is determined by those who join the conversation and declare a mutual concern or goal.

This conversation may be about what the clients want or how they want their experience to be, and about how they will know they are having a new experience or making progress toward it. We believe that focusing on these areas facilitates the generation of new meaning and experience. This conversing generates a goal-oriented and pragmatic meaning pertinent to the created purpose of the meeting. We call this goal-oriented conversing "goaling."

2. *Goaling is the evolution of meaning about what the client wants to experience or what her life may be like beyond the problem.*

Because we believe that personal consulting is a purposeful meeting, we organize the conversation around the stated and evolving purpose. Further, we assume that we can facilitate the evolution of meaning by conversing about what the client wants, as opposed to conversing about problems or about what she does not want. We believe that focusing on what the client wants takes her beyond the limits that may arise from her problem/solution narrative. Goaling takes the conversation beyond the problem/solution distinction altogether to a hypothetical narrative in which the client's life is free of the problem and that area of the client's life is the way she wants it.

Metaphorically, goaling is the mutual creation of a story alternative to what the client is experiencing as problematic. Goaling is conversational and creational, not problem solving or goal oriented. Problem solving more than likely stays within the language of the problem. For example, if a man came into a therapist's office and complained of being excessively shy, a problem-solving approach would be to try to find out the causes of the shyness or to problem solve around what he would have to do to become less shy. The therapist might direct the man to explore in his past where he learned or decided to withdraw. Even a solution focus within problem solving might be just the flip side of the problem and not an alternative. The therapist might assume that the shy man needs more self-esteem or some other resource to overcome his shyness. Both of these approaches stay within the language of the problem and solution—in this case, shyness and increased self-esteem. What we are focusing on is "storying" life beyond the problem, to a time when the problem/solution distinction is no longer relevant.

Goaling is also not traditional goal-oriented therapy. In that approach, the therapist thinks of a goal as representing a real event that must be reached or accomplished. If we were to think in those objective-realistic terms, we would imagine that the word "goal" would mark some real event that was an end point. An example is someone coming into a therapist's office who wants to lose weight. A traditional goal-oriented approach would define the end point, say a thirty-pound weight loss, from 205 to 175, and then develop strategies for reaching the end point of 175. The therapist might even assume the responsibility of developing motivational strategies for getting the client to take the next step toward the end point.

Problem-solving therapies and goal-as-end-point therapies are usually built on a language-as-representation assumption. The therapists think of the shyness and the weight loss as real events for which resources must be developed to change the objectively real events.

Goaling is not about changing "reality." It is about evolving meaning, about creating different or alternative experiences. Traditional goal-oriented therapy uses a goal as an end point. Therapy then becomes the devising of strategies and motivation for doing what it takes to reach that goal.

Using goal as a verb, however, highlights that we are talking about a process and about developing possibilities, not about an end point. We are talking about conversation by which meaning evolves and the client begins to have a different experience and to envision alternatives for her life outside the session.

A goaling conversation with the man complaining about shyness might evolve into a conversation about what he wants rather than the shyness—say assertiveness—and how he will know when assertiveness is happening. More generally, the goaling conversation might evolve into a discussion of what will be signs to him that either the problem is solved or his life is going more the way he wants it to. He may say that he will be thinking about where he wants his career to go and how that will make a difference to him rather than thinking about what is holding him back. His thinking of where he wants his career to go may lead to a conversation about how that would lead him to think differently about himself as well.

We might think that the client's choice of assertiveness is just the solution side of the shyness distinction and therefore not that much different than the results of the other approaches. However, the conversation and meaning might further evolve with our asking him, "How would this assertiveness make a difference to you?" He might then say that he would feel he was moving on with his life, making plans, thinking about what he wants and what is important for his career, rather than just reacting to what others might think. As consultants we would be very curious about this moving on with his life, this making of plans, and this thinking about what he wants rather than being reactive. The meaning of his goal would have evolved from a lack of shyness to assertiveness to thinking of what he wants in his future versus being reactive to what others might think. In this process, we are mutually constructing with the client possible meanings, possible stories, and possible experiences of the future.

With the weight-loss example, we might find that in response to the miracle question the client states the obvious, that he would be at 175 pounds. In addition, he might say that he would be wearing different clothes, newer and more stylish. He might say that the difference this would make would be that he would feel more proud of himself, that he would have more variety in what he could wear. He might also say that he would be working out again, getting back into running, and thinking about his health.

It is these signs and meanings that would be intriguing to us. The man would be proud of himself if he had more options and were thinking about his health. We would not only find these new meanings intriguing, but we would also be hopeful that as he continued to talk about his health, his new story would evolve even further. We would hope that his conversing about his health would open more possibilities for him than thinking only about losing thirty pounds.

As with the shyness example, the goaling evolved from conversing about losing weight and reaching a 175-pound end point to having more and different clothes, having a different feeling about himself, getting into working out, and thinking more about his health. We would not treat any of these notions as end points but rather as points of departure for an even further evolving conversation.

The signs of goaling on the consultants' part are that the conversing is centered on the more creational questions, How will the person know the problem is solved or that she is experiencing her goal? and How will this make a difference to her? The focus in the session is on a goaling conversation, not on a problem or solution or fixed end point.

3.   *Goaling is facilitated through questions asked from a position of curiosity and not-yet-understanding.*

This position of curiosity and not-yet-understanding has been discussed as part of Anderson and Goolishian's (1988) collaborative language systems approach to personal consulting. From this point of view, consultants do not ask questions to

- Gather information
- Make an assessment
- Validate a hypothesis
- Get the client to do something, or to do something different
- Solve a problem
- To be helpful

Consultants do not ask questions because they have some expertise about a client's particular problem or because they know the solution. Consultants ask questions from a position of curiosity about what may be created. Consultants never ask questions if they already know the answers. They do not ask questions to get the client to say something the consultants already have in mind.

Because we assume that focusing on what clients want facilitates the evolution of meaning, we ask questions generated from four general areas. These are:

1. What does the client say she *wants* from consulting?
2. How will what she wants make a *difference* to her?
3. *How will the client know* that she is experiencing her goal or that the problem is solved? How will she know she is "*on track*"?
4. How is she *experiencing some* of what she wants *now*?

    4.   *The generic purpose of consulting is to promote the evolution of meaning or experience relevant to the unique purpose of the meeting.*

Our broadest hope is that as a result of our meeting, the client will leave with a different experience, a different meaning, or a different story that is germane to her purpose in coming.

An example is a woman who came to consulting and reported that her three children had turned against her and that her new husband of a year was against her as well. Her husband had spent and lost all her savings and her children were telling her that not only should she leave him but she should move in with them. She was very frustrated with them and their telling her what to do.

Our understanding of our goaling conversation was that we had talked about her frustration with her family. In response to the question, "If a miracle happened tonight while you were sleeping and you woke up tomorrow and the problems were solved, how would you know the problems were solved or that your life was going more the way you want?" the woman said she realized that she was better off on her own now and that she wanted to get back to experiencing "composure." We did not assess the relationships in her family, we did not try to develop strategies for how she could deal with her family, and we did not attempt to get her to *do* anything outside of the session. We merely let the conversation evolve around how she would know the problem was solved, how she would know that her goal was happening, and how any of the matters she mentioned would make a difference to her.

When we asked what was helpful to her from the session, she said that it was helpful to have someone to tell all this to, and it was helpful to realize that she wanted to be back in control of herself—that is, to have "composure."

This process is very different from what we would do in more strategic therapy, when we thought the meeting with the client was primarily to gather information about the problem and the attempted solution pattern, as well as any exceptions to that pattern. With that accomplished, we would design a homework assignment. We assumed that change came about through the reframing of the problem and through the client doing the task.

Now we are primarily focused on the conversation and the evolution within the session of new possibilities for the client. In the case just presented, the new meaning or possibility was the notion of "composure."

5.   *The role of the consultant is to establish and create a setting of mutual respect, of dialogue, of inquiry, of affirmation, and of goaling.*

This assumption contrasts with the notion that therapists have expert knowledge based on scientific research on what is good, normal, and to be valued. Within that paradigm, the therapist assumes the responsibility of gathering information about the presenting complaint as well as other information applicable to the therapist's metaphor of normality; the therapist then, in an expert fashion, prescribes a course of treatment to correct the abnormality. Within such models, the concept of therapy is consistent with the role of the therapist as treating the disorder or source of the problem. The notion of therapy is consistent with a pathological orientation.

In our way of thinking, "therapy" does not make sense. Because we do not conceptualize problems as located in or caused by dysfunctional structures, we do not think of ourselves as "treating" anything dysfunctional. We do not think it is possible to be objective about someone else's experience or that we have a privileged position about how the person's life should be. We do assume that by approaching each person's telling of her experience with respect and curiosity we can contribute to the creation of a setting of respect and curiosity. We also believe that by asking questions that invite exploration and by presupposing that meetings are purposeful we can contribute to a setting of evolving purpose. We further assume that by asking questions related to the four areas presented in the third assumption we can facilitate a process of goaling.

In the consulting role, we do assume the responsibility of directing the process of the conversation, a process of goaling. While we are not experts about the client's experience, we do claim as our role the facilitation of a conversation that can lead to different possibilities for the client. This is why we call ourselves personal consultants.

6.   *The role of the client is to explore, create, and coauthor the evolving story in relation to the declared and evolving purpose of the consultation.*

The client's expertise is in her own experience, which she helps the consultant to understand. In the postmodern perspective, there is no objective truth or correct way. As consultants, we do not claim expertise or to know the truth about what is good or healthy. Each person's experience is her own and is valid. Therefore, in this approach the client is the expert on her experience and has the right to and responsibility for that experience and for her choices of what she wants to do. This is a consumer-oriented approach, with the client being the expert about both her experience and what she wants from the consultation.

We trust that the pragmatic result of this assumption will be that the client will be much more interested and invested in what she says she wants from the consultation than she would be in what some expert said she should want or be concerned about. We assume that a client is much more likely to participate in a consultation if she perceives herself as determining the direction and purpose of the conversation.

We do not, as in some models, expect clients to change or do something different. The goal of a meeting is to facilitate alternative possibilities and experiences. The client still has the choice of declaring what has been helpful and what she will do.

For example, many models assume the responsibility of assessing the extent of a client's alcohol abuse before prescribing a treatment plan. The therapists within these models assume expertise about the client's experience. In a solution-focused approach, we assume that the client is the expert about what she is experiencing as problematic and about why she is coming to consultation. We assume that she is also the co-participant in the goaling conversation, sharing what she wants and creating how she will know the problem is solved.

7. *The focus is on the consulting meeting and the evolution of meaning.*

The focus of the consulting meeting is not on a client system but on the conversation. Because we believe we have no expert knowledge about what happens outside the consulting room and because we do not claim a position of objective observer, our focus is on the consulting system. De Shazer (1993) has talked about how all consultants have in the meeting is talk: "There are no wet beds, no voices without people, no depressions. There is only *talk* about wet beds, *talk* about voices without people, *talk* about depression. There are no family systems, no family structures, no psyches: just talk about systems, structures, and psyches" (p. 89). Therefore, as consultants we cannot assume that we know or have any expertise about anything that happened or will happen outside the session.

Even as we speak of focusing on the consulting conversation, we are not talking about focusing in the scientific sense of client-consultant patterns or transference and countertransference. We are speaking of focusing on the evolution of meaning, the evolution of a goal or solution story, and how we can further facilitate that evolution.

8.   *The focus is on the evolving meaning, the storying versus the story.*

No story is ever complete or totally understood. What is relevant to the consulting meeting is what happens between the people participating, the mutual exploration and creation of new meaning. What becomes most important is the *becoming* of the conversation, the unfolding of what is said. The focus is on continuing the conversation, and on the potential hypothetical experience of life beyond the problem, when the client's goal is happening, the times of some success, or the times of more personal agency.

By talking about consulting as a mutual creation of a goal movie or story, we are not suggesting that our focus is on the problem story or on the solution or goal story. The focus is not on the content but on a *process* or the possibilities of storying or creating. Thus, personal consulting is goaling oriented.

An example is a client who says that she is depressed and confused, a state that she explains is the result of being sexually abused. In a content-focused approach we would become concerned with how the client was abused, the identity of the abuser, and even whether the abuse is a repressed memory. In a process-focused approach we are concerned with the client's experience, with what the client wants to tell us about her experience, and then with moving into the process of goaling.

While this approach could be described as narrative therapy, our focus is not on problem-saturated stories, solution stories, goal stories, or any other kind of stories as content. We are focused on the storying, the creating of new meaning together.

Conclusion

Many changes have occurred for us as our thinking has moved from radical constructivism and strategic therapy in the early eighties to a more collaborative consulting approach now, and we have centered our discussion here on a different way of thinking about language. Thinking about language as languaging makes it easier for us (1) to place language as an action among and shared by consultants and clients, and (2) to think of personal consulting as a collaborative conversation between equals, mutually creating an evolving goal.

Pragmatically, this change of thinking has enabled us to shift our focus within a session away from gathering information and attempting to get the client to do something or do something different toward focusing on facilitating the evolution of a conversation about what the client wants and about new possibilities related to an evolving goal. This change of thinking has also allowed for more respect for client determination by focusing on what a client wants rather than on what is wrong as determined by some expert criteria. Finally, we experience ourselves as more present to our clients by asking questions from a position of curiosity rather than by strategizing, and by making statements to the clients based on our experience of them rather than on some objective knowledge.

Questions from the Editors

1. *If there is no objective reality and all views are equally valid, why propose any structure for therapy at all? That is, why have any questions to ask or an agenda to follow?*

The question seems to suggest that if we assume there is no way of objectively knowing a world apart from our observing, then there is no way of making choices for how to work. We believe that we make choices in personal consultation all the time based on values and criteria of our own choosing, not based on objective truths. For example, we choose to call our activity "personal consultation" because we choose not to be in an evaluative position with regard to our client's experience. For that reason and for others, we choose not to conceptualize our work as evaluating structural deficiencies but rather as consulting clients about achieving what they want. This definition is a choice based on values we hold that seem to make sense relative to our personal styles and other values. We assume that defining our work and choosing a way of working that is consistent with our personal styles will make us more congruent with our clients. While we choose goaling and purposive conversation as key distinctions in our way of working, these choices do not mean we are suggesting a structure or agenda in a prescriptive fashion. By suggesting hypothetical goals and success-oriented questions as tools for developing a goaling conversation, we are moving away from the formats and decision trees (de Shazer, 1988) of our earlier solution-focused work.

2. *If therapy has become mainly a matter of conversation and creation of meaning, on what basis should postmodern therapists be reimbursed for their services?*

We use the word conversation to highlight the flattening of hierarchy in this collaborative postmodern approach, and to highlight that personal consultation is talk interchange or discussion between equals, with neither participant in an evaluative position of the other. We also use "conversation" in contrast to "interview." For us, an interview is a meeting in which one person seeks information from the other. As we have stated, we conceptualize personal consultation as a purposive conversation facilitating an evolving meaning and goal. Personal consultation is not casual conversation but rather a meeting in which purpose and meaning evolve. This evolving meaning may mean that the client now has possibilities she did not realize before, that what she thought was a problem is not one now because she has other choices or meanings, or that she recognizes how she is on track to getting what she wants.

Personal consultants are reimbursed for the service they provide—that is, for consulting with clients about getting what the clients want in their experience. Clients should and do decide whether personal consultants should be hired.

3.   *In the postmodern perspective, how can one assert that there is no objective truth or correct way? Is that not an assertion of truth?*

Saying that there is no objective truth or correct way is a statement of *belief.* We do not believe there is any way we can stand outside our observations in a totally objective fashion and know what is apart from us. We believe and act as if there are many experiences, many creations, many potentials, many languages, many possibilities within language. Our curiosity with our clients and our not-yet-understanding position come from our belief that we cannot know. We also believe that when we think we know what our client's experience is, we are probably cutting ourselves off from the client and from further possibilities of experience.

Notes

1. Throughout this chapter we will refer to our work as *personal consultation*. We first published our use of this term in *Becoming Solution-Focused in Brief Therapy* in 1992. Although at that time we said we would prefer to use "personal consultation" when referring to what we do, we nevertheless continued to use the term "therapy" because it seemed to be the term most commonly used in the field and we wanted to use a term that most people could relate to. Now, however, we want to take a more assertive stand in initiating a change within the language of the field. We prefer the term *personal consultation* because it more accurately reflects the nonpathological approach we are talking about. Later in the text we will discuss more of our reasons for choosing this term. When referring to other models, we will still use the term "therapy," as used by those models.
2. Throughout this text we will use the female pronoun for persons not otherwise specified.
3. The use of this question is quite common within a solution-focused approach. It is intended to invite clients to create possible signs of how they will know the problem is solved or the goal reached. We generally ask the question as, "If a miracle happened tonight while you were sleeping and you woke up tomorrow and the problems that you are coming in about

were totally solved, what would be signs to you that this miracle had occurred and the problems were solved?" This is a variation of de Shazer's phrasing (de Shazer, 1988, p. 5).

References

Andersen, T. (1991). *The reflecting team*. New York: W. W. Norton.

Anderson, H., & Goolishian, H. (1988). Human systems as linguistic systems: Preliminary and evolving ideas about the implications of clinical theory. *Family Process, 27*, 371–398.

Anderson, H., Goolishian, H., & Winderman, L. (1984). Problem-determined systems: Towards transformation in family therapy. *Journal of Strategic and Systemic Therapies, 5*(4), 1–13.

Bateson, G. (1979). *Mind and nature: A necessary unity*. New York: Dutton.

De Shazer, S. (1988). *Clues: Investigating solutions in brief therapy*. New York: W. W. Norton.

De Shazer, S. (1993). Creative misunderstanding: There is no escape from language. In S. Gilligan & R. Price (Eds.), *Therapeutic conversations*. New York: W. W. Norton.

De Shazer, S. (1994). *Words were originally magic*. New York: W. W. Norton.

Dell, P. (1985). Understanding Bateson and Maturana: Toward a biological foundation for the social sciences. *Journal of Marital and Family Therapy, 11*, 1–20.

Gergen, K. (1992). Toward a postmodern psychology. In S. Kvale (Ed.), *Psychology and postmodernism*. Newbury Park, CA: Sage.

Gergen, K., & Kaye, J. (1992). Beyond narrative in the negotiation of therapeutic meaning. In S. McNamee & K. Gergen (Eds.), *Therapy as social construction*. Newbury Park, CA: Sage.

Lax, W. (1992). Postmodern thinking in a clinical practice. In S. McNamee & K. J. Gergen (Eds.), *Therapy as social construction*. Newbury Park, CA: Sage.

Maturana, H., & Varela, F. (1987). *The tree of knowledge*. Boston: New Science Library.

Rorty, R. (1979). Philosophy and the mirror of nature. Princeton, NJ: Princeton University Press.

Shotter, J. (1993). *Conversational realities: Constructing life through language*. London: Sage.

Von Foerster, H. (1984). On constructing reality. In P. Watzlawick (Ed.), *The invented reality: How do we know what we believe we know? Contributions to constructivism*. New York: W. W. Norton.

Von Glaserfeld, E. (1984). An introduction to radical constructivism. In P. Watzlawick (Ed.), *The invented reality: How do we know what we believe we know? Contributions to constructivism*. New York: W. W. Norton.

Walter, J., & Peller, J. (1992). *Becoming solution-focused in brief therapy*. New York: Brunner/Mazel.

Watzlawick, P. (Ed.). (1984). *The invented reality: How do we know what we believe we know? Contributions to constructivism*. New York: W. W. Norton.

Weakland, J., Fisch, R., Watzlawick, P., & Bodin, A. (1974). Brief therapy: Focused problem resolution. *Family Process, 13*, 141–168.

White, M., & Epston, D. (1990). *Narrative means to therapeutic ends*. New York: W. W. Norton.

Wittgenstein, L. (1958). *Philosophical investigations* (3rd ed.). (G.E.M. Anscombe, Trans.). New York: Macmillan.

Wittgenstein, L. (1965). *Blue and brown books*. New York: HarperCollins.

CHAPTER TWO

SOLUTION-FOCUSED THERAPY AND THE POSTMODERN

A Critical Analysis

Barbara S. Held

Solution-focused therapy, the roots of which lie within the brief strategic therapy movement (Watzlawick, Weakland, & Fisch, 1974), has, like its predecessor, founded itself upon the shaky rock of antirealism. Usually called "constructivism" or "social constructionism" outside the context of philosophy proper, antirealism is an epistemological doctrine that currently enjoys immense popularity in the social sciences and the humanities. Its core claim about knowing is that the knower does not—indeed cannot—under any circumstances attain knowledge of a reality that is objective or independent of the knower—knowledge of how the world really is. The ability to attain such knowledge is, after all, a claim about knowing that is typical of the doctrine of realism. According to antirealism, all knowers instead make or construct their own biased or subjective "realities" in language.[1]

Antirealism can hardly be said to lurk in some harmless philosophical background, with no practical implications for the actual doing of therapy. For instance, reframing (or redefining) the meaning of the client's problem,[2] the most prominent intervention of strategic therapy, has always been based more or less explicitly on an antirealist or constructivist epistemology (see, for example, Cade & O'Hanlon, 1993; Coyne, 1985; Eron & Lund, 1993; Reamy-Stephenson,1983; Watzlawick, 1984; Watzlawick, Weakland, & Fisch, 1974). Indeed, the antirealism of strategic therapy is, according to some within the strategic therapy movement, what allegedly gives therapists license to alter quite liberally the meanings clients may be encouraged by their therapists to place upon their problematic experiences. Thus, the practical effect of the adoption of antirealism seems to those therapists to consist in reducing the constraints placed upon the actual practice of therapy. This supposed effect of antirealism on therapeutic practice is prized by strategic therapists (as it is by solution-focused therapists in particular and postmodern therapists in general), but it is not an effect that is properly attributed to antirealism. I will reassess the real cause of that effect at the end of this chapter.

Antirealism plays an even more profound role in the new and increasingly popular postmodern narrative therapies, which, like strategic therapy, also strive to alleviate clients' difficulties by giving them new stories or narratives of their life circumstances through the (linguistic) act of "restorying."[3] Like the earlier "reframes" constructed by strategic therapists through the act of reframing, these new stories, narratives, and meanings cannot reflect the objective reality to which none of us supposedly has any access; they are therefore alleged to be subjective, or as I prefer to put it, antirealist. The evermore explicit and extreme antirealism of the postmodern narrative therapy movement should come as no surprise, since that movement has adopted the pervasive postmodern mind-set that is itself defined by nothing short of a thoroughgoing antirealism (see Held, 1995a).

In the following pages I intend to demonstrate how the use of antirealism within solution-focused therapy is ill-conceived and, speaking more practically, perfectly unnecessary given the mission of solution-focused therapists as I understand it. By the end of this chapter I hope to have convinced the reader that solution-focused therapists have burdened themselves with a philosophical doctrine they neither can adhere to with any consistency nor must adhere to in order to fulfill their mission. To accomplish my own mission, I will first document the antirealism found within solution-focused therapy; then I will discuss the problems caused by that antirealism and the reasons for its adoption. In my conclusion I will suggest a more realistic alternative to it.

The Endorsement of Antirealism Within Solution-Focused Therapy

The easiest way to prove that antirealism (of a postmodern variety) pervades solution-focused therapy would be to ask the reader to turn to Chapter One in this book, by John L. Walter and Jane E. Peller, entitled "Rethinking Our Assumptions: Assuming Anew in a Postmodern World." Since that move would indeed let me off the hook too easily, I shall start elsewhere and return to that chapter later.

I will begin by discussing one who may rightly claim the title of founder (and ongoing innovator) of solution-focused therapy, namely, Steve de Shazer. De

Shazer has made no secret of his allegiance to antirealism, beginning with his en-
dorsement of constructivism (see de Shazer & Berg, 1988) and moving steadfastly
into the antirealist terrain of postmodern literary theory and philosophy (see de
Shazer, 1991, 1993, & 1994). Here are some of his own words that make his antirealism apparent:

> Post-structuralists [another term for "postmodernists"], in fact, question the op-
> position of the subject and the object upon which the possibility of objectivity
> depends [de Shazer, 1991, p. 50].

> There are no wet beds, no voices without people, no depressions. There is only
> *talk* about wet beds, *talk* about voices without people, *talk* about depression [ital-
> ics in original] [de Shazer, 1993, p. 89].

> In contemporary post-structuralist thought, our world—our social, interac-
> tional context—is seen as created by language, by words. . . . Language consti-
> tutes 'the human world and the human world constitutes the whole world' [de
> Shazer & Berg, 1992, p. 73].

In these quotations, de Shazer tells us not only that we can never *know* a reality that exists independent of us or outside of or beyond our language/sto-
ries/talk (that is, an extralinguistic reality), but also that no such reality even *exists*.
This is an example of one of the more radical or extreme versions of antirealism or constructivism.[4]

William O'Hanlon and Michele Weiner-Davis also deserve credit for ad-
vancing the theory and practice of solution-focused therapy. Although the anti-
realism/constructivism that informs their therapy is of a less radical sort than that
of de Shazer, such philosophy can be found in their writing nonetheless (see also
Cade & O'Hanlon, 1993). In their book *In Search of Solutions,* O'Hanlon and
Weiner-Davis (1989) give their own nod to antirealism:

> *There Is No One "Right" Way to View Things; Different Views May Be Just as Valid and
> May Fit the Facts Just as Well*

> There is no way to ascertain which of the views is most "correct"; rather, it is
> evident that each view is merely a small portion of the total picture and is col-
> ored by each person's biases and assumptions. . . . As the different views are de-
> scribed, rather than thinking of each as "right" or "wrong," we assume that
> each person's perception represents an equally valid, integral part of the situa-
> tion. While we do not think that there are any correct or incorrect points of
> view, we do believe there are more or less *useful* [italics added] viewpoints. That

is, the views that people hold about their problems enhance or diminish the likelihood of solution [pp. 46–47].

Notice the use of what have been called "scare quotes" around terms such as "right," "correct," and "wrong," terms that without the scare quotes would imply knowledge of an objective reality and, thus, the adoption of a realist epistemology (or realism), which is what these authors evidently want to avoid. Also notice the nod to pragmatism conveyed by the use of the term "useful." Pragmatism is an antirealist philosophical doctrine that has been adopted by many constructivists/postmodernists, including postmodern narrative therapists. I shall have more to say about this in due course.

Although Michael White and David Epston are known more as postmodern narrative therapists than as solution-focused therapists per se, the common features of the two therapy movements—namely, a minimalist theory and an antirealist epistemology—create a convergence (see Eron & Lund, 1993) that makes the two movements increasingly indistinguishable for me. I therefore now provide evidence of White and Epston's antirealism.

Since we cannot know objective reality, all knowing requires an act of interpretation [White & Epston, 1990, p. 2].

Therapists can undermine the idea that they have privileged access to the truth by consistently encouraging persons to assist them in the quest for understanding. . . . The therapist can call into question the idea that s/he possesses an objective and unbiased account of reality. . . [White, 1993, p. 57].

These knowledges [that shape clients' stories] are not about discoveries regarding the "nature" of persons and of relationships, but are *constructed* [italics added] knowledges that are specifying of a particular strain of personhood and relationship [White, 1993, p. 38].

Notice again the telling use of scare quotes to undermine the normal use of the term "nature," namely, to refer to something real. Also note that I italicized the word "constructed." I will discuss my reasons for doing so in the second part of the next section.

How the Adoption of Antirealism in Therapy is Problematic

For the past ten years I have worked to call attention to the problems therapists face when they adopt antirealism as their core, or even a peripheral, theoretical construct (see Held, 1995a, for a complete account). Here I limit my comments to two concerns.

Reality or Truth Claims: A Logical Problem

Despite their professed antirealism, the solution-focused therapists I quoted above inevitably make—as they should—general truth claims about the effectiveness of their own particular therapeutic interventions. Indeed, without those claims the ethicality of taking payment for their services could be called into question.

Traditionally—which in the context of solution-focused circles means before the postmodern "revolution" of the early 1990s—claims about the effectiveness of solution-focused interventions emphasized how techniques designed to get the client to notice "exceptions" to the problem state—that is, occasions or circumstances when the problem did *not* occur—caused solutions to emerge. The term "solution" was originally defined in the traditional way—namely, as a desirable change, or a new way of *being*, that precluded the existence of the problem. The new way of being could include new thoughts, feelings, and/or behaviors; but certainly the effect of solution-focused interventions—just like the effect of the strategic interventions that preceded them—on the *real* or *actual* behavioral interactions of clients was never in question in the early days of the solution-focused movement. This prerevolutionary quotation of de Shazer and Berg (1988, p. 43) makes that realism apparent: "We consider talking about change during therapy as a map of the client's reality and thus as a *representation of change in real life* [italics added]."

The postmodern revolution changed all that. With its antirealist epistemology—its emphasis on language/stories/narrative that could not even in principle reflect or represent reality as it exists objectively, extralinguistically, or independent of our language—postmodernism paved the way for the emphasis on "therapy talk" that is, as de Shazer says, the only reality. Thus, for de Shazer and others in the solution-focused movement who have followed his postmodern/antirealist lead, "There are no wet beds . . . there is only *talk* about wet beds" (de Shazer, 1993, p. 89).[5]

Of course, how we can presume to know that there really are clients (and therapists) in the act of talking—and talking about wet beds at that, or whatever we claim to know the topic of conversation to be—is a logical problem that even the most ardent antirealists have trouble circumventing. Most people within the postmodern narrative therapy movement do not bother to deal with this contradiction but are content simply to defend their professed antirealism by arguing that therapeutic interventions—solution-focused or otherwise—change nothing more than the way clients talk about, or narrate, the events of their lives—events about which none of us supposedly has any objective knowledge. (Here they are of course inadvertently making a causal claim about reality, to which I shall return later.) However, when it is convenient to have solution "talk" refer to or represent some real events, that reference to reality is made. Hence, we find an oscillation between realism and antirealism within all so-called postmodern therapies; this is the contradiction that I have tried over the years to make explicit (Held, 1990, 1995a; Held & Pols, 1985, 1987).[6]

Chapter One, by Walter and Peller, in the present book is unusual in that it takes as seriously as I have the contradiction I have tried to point out; for that reason these authors should, in my opinion, be commended. But I could not rejoice about their solution to the contradiction: instead of adopting a more realistic position to resolve it (my obvious preference), they have become even more stridently antirealist than they say they have been in the past. Although I found their argument difficult to follow, I think it can be reduced to their claim that "solutions" and "exceptions" have heretofore been given too much reality status within solution-focused therapy, and so to maintain a consistent antirealist position, even solutions and exceptions must be seen as having no objective truth or reality—that is, none independent of the knower or knower's theory/language[7] (see Chapter One, pp. 11–15). Thus, for Walter and Peller the language of therapy—therapy talk—causes nothing more than solution talk or the experience in language of something new and desirable. So far, this is nothing new. The alleged leap (for them) occurs when they argue that even if the something new and desirable appears to be behavior itself, that behavior has no independent reality status, no real existence, since we supposedly create, bring into being, even behavior within language. (I do not think they are making the less radical and therefore less debatable claim that the way we think, feel, and talk about life affects the way we actually behave in life—behavior that can be known as it objectively exists.)[8] To quote Walter and Peller, "Language *creates* the experience of bad [and hence also, as they later say, good] behavior" (p. 13). (This causal assertion is problematic, since these authors also say that "thinking of language as creational might lead one to think . . . that words come first. But this is not what we mean. Language and experience are simultaneous" [p. 13].)

The word "experience" is tricky, and I will not even attempt to disentangle its many meanings here, except to say that unless one is hallucinating, there is surely at least some real/objective reality to be found within one's experience of the world. Instead, I want to make a simpler point: even if solution-focused interventions are alleged to change nothing more than the client's meanings/language (if that limited sense is what Walter and Peller actually mean when they use the word "experience" to discuss therapy/change), those interventions are still alleged to have a causal effect that is real—albeit, admittedly, in only a particular aspect of reality, namely, the linguistic aspect. Put differently, to make the pragmatic claim, as O'Hanlon and Weiner-Davis do above, that some viewpoints are not true but merely useful for purposes of enhancing solution, is also to claim that such viewpoints are truly useful for that purpose: they make a real difference in the client's life, that is, in the client's real experience, even if that experiential difference is limited to the real experience of new meanings or ways of talking about life (that is, limited to a new linguistic reality) and does not extend to the way life actually or really gets lived in any extralinguistic or nonlinguistic/behavioral reality. If even the more limited claim were not true, solution-focused therapy would make no difference in any domain or aspect of reality whatsoever, linguistic or extralinguistic, and hence it should not be promoted as a real path to real solutions of any sort.

Limiting oneself to affecting or changing only a linguistic domain/reality (that is, the client's story or narrative) is, however, exceedingly problematic for any therapist. Would any postmodern or solution-focused therapist want to accept this scenario: that as a result of successful solution-focused therapy a battered wife *says* she is no longer beaten, but we cannot take her story as giving us any extralinguistic, objective, behaviorally-based truth or reality about her battered status? That is, she may, despite her story, still be battered, and all we and she have is the story, or linguistic construction of reality. Yet that is what the antirealism of the solution-focused therapists I have quoted calls upon us to accept.

Of course, these authors, like all the others I have examined who have taken the antirealist/postmodern "turn" (see Held, 1995a, pp. 143–146), cannot avoid at least some minimal reference to actual behaviors and the whole of real life itself when they want to persuade us of the truth, the reality, of the effectiveness of their methods. So, it seems in the final analysis that solution-focused talk or narrative intervention in therapy has—fortunately—two real effects: (a) it really causes the client to experience new meanings or new talk—new language—and (b) that new linguistic experience is somehow related to new extralinguistic (or more than linguistic) experience in real (that is, extratherapy) life. (Again, this second effect is of course what makes therapy talk truly worthy of real payment.) "We are talking about conversing in language by which meaning evolves and the client begins to have a different experience and to envision alternatives for her life outside the session" (Walter & Peller, p. 18).

The Word "Construct" and the Confusion About Active Versus Passive Knowing

The word "construct" (noun or verb), and by extension "construction," is, in my experience, behind much of the confusion about knowledge and knowing. In short, the idea of an active rather than a passive knower is falsely assumed to imply antirealism. Since the term "constructivism" (or "constructionism") is typically used by postmodern (including some solution-focused) therapists to convey or promote antirealism as well as active knowing, the terminological basis of the confusion becomes obvious. This problem is important; let me elaborate.

We all sometimes construct (or create) theories about how the world works, both in science and in life. The fact that knowing involves an active process on the part of the knower does not make all knowers antirealists and all knowledge subjective. Put differently, all theories are themselves linguistic constructions. The active constructing of theories is the business of science, all science. But that fact does not make all scientists constructivists/antirealists. Those participating in the realism/antirealism debate take it for granted that all theories are constructions, an assumption that does not automatically assign anyone to one or the other side of the controversy.

However, to then say that the theory we have just constructed is the only reality we have (as when antirealist therapists say "we create [or invent] our reality"[9] [see Walter & Peller, p. 12]) is to confuse two things: (1) the linguistic status of the theory itself with (2) the extralinguistic or extratheoretic reality that the theory is attempting to approximate indirectly. That is, the reality under investigation is not itself a mere linguistic construction—a nonreality, if we take seriously the proclamations of postmodern/constructivist therapists, either in itself or as it is known to the investigator.[10] And no therapist I know of—solution focused or otherwise—treats it as such, despite his or her antirealist epistemological declarations.

Reasons for the Adoption of Antirealism in Solution-Focused Therapy

I have previously divided reasons for the antirealist turn in many therapy systems, including solution-focused therapy, into those that to me seem cynical and those that do not (Held, 1995a, 1995b). A cynical reason focuses upon the inherent trendiness of therapy as a discipline. In short, antirealism pervades the late twentieth-century humanities, sometimes in the form of so-called postmodernism. That therapy has actively cultivated this latest trend should come as no surprise, since therapists have a long history of adopting popular trends. The reason for this tendency may be less frivolous than the tendency itself. I think that reason has in part to do with the discomfort or difficulty therapists have in maintaining their own disciplinary traditions. By this I mean that therapists have tended to look beyond therapy for legitimate paradigms—indeed, for legitimation itself. Consider, for example, the turn to physical sciences that began at least as early as Freud and that has continued more recently by way of an appeal to quantum physics to support antirealist leanings (see, for example, Doherty, 1986). Now, in the last few years, there has been an appeal to the postmodern "humanities" to support those same leanings. However intellectually captivating these exercises may be, I am not convinced that either the scientific world of subatomic physics or the humanistic world of postmodern literary theory and linguistic/antirealistic philosophy has much to tell us about how to do good therapy.

Nonetheless, I do find reasons for this turn to antirealism that do not have cynical overtones. These have to do with what I consider to be sincere attempts to solve the eternal problem of achieving a system of therapy that maintains the unique individuality of each client. In looking carefully at the writings of many postmodern/antirealist therapists, I have found a pervasive mission, one that strikes me as more fundamental than antirealism: how to preserve in therapy the client's unique individuality—including personal views of unique life experience. This mission is no less prominent in solution-focused therapy than in other therapies that have adopted a postmodern/antirealist philosophy;[11] indeed, it is to this mission that I referred at the start of this chapter. Let us again consider some statements made by prominent solution-focused therapists as evidence of that mission.

Even when de Shazer (1985, 1988) was just emerging from the tradition of strategic therapy, he worked, consistent with that tradition, to eliminate the general, predetermined notions about problems that are still typically found in psychological and psychiatric theories of psychopathology. In more recent writings (de Shazer, 1991, 1993, 1994), he has reinforced his antipathology position and tied it to antirealism. He has deepened his dedication to the uniqueness of the meanings that emerge in each and every therapeutic/linguistic encounter, as evidenced by the following:

> The therapy system can be seen as a set of "language games," a self-contained linguistic system that creates meanings through negotiation between therapist and client. . . . What a therapist and client do during the interview is akin to writing or coauthoring and reading text. . . . Thus, a therapeutic interview is a putting together of various misunderstandings (misreadings) and whatever is meant is a result of how therapist and client agree to misunderstand (or misread) what is said: "Nymphomania" becomes misunderstood as "insomnia" . . . and the misreading becomes useful to the client. Again, following Wittgenstein, we can only know what a word means by how the participants in the conversation use it [de Shazer, 1991, pp. 68–69].

Not only are there no predetermined categories of problems and pathology, but words themselves are always alleged to have different meanings in different conversational moments. We can count on no generality or stability, not even of meaning itself.

> In some ways client problems are, however, more different than similar when we take a "person in his context" approach to describing the situation, rather than a formal "problem" approach. That is, any two "phobia" cases or two "depression" cases will differ widely when it comes to the language games involving the client's description of his life circumstances, family history, problem onset, failed solution attempts, goals for therapy, etc. [de Shazer, 1991, p. 83].

The use of scare quotes around the terms "problem," "phobia," and "depression" says it all. (Then again, there is that problematic—that is, reality-alluding—reference to life circumstances, family history, and so on.)

O'Hanlon and Weiner-Davis (1989) reveal their adherence to the unique (and also hint at their antirealism) in a section entitled "Clients Define the Goal":

> Since we do not believe that there is such a thing as "the real problem" underlying the complaint, nor do we believe that therapists are better equipped to decide how their clients should live their lives, we ask our people seeking our help to establish their own goals for treatment. Only in rare circumstances do we make alternate suggestions to our clients' goals. The establishment of illegal goals, such as child abuse, is one obvious exception [Here I am compelled to ask: Is that particular "problem" too real?] [pp. 44–45].

White and Epston (1990) contrast their preferred "narrative mode of thought" with the traditional "logico-scientific mode," which

> prescribe[s] . . . the production of universal rather than particular "truth conditions," and a theory that is "testably right." . . . The narrative mode of thought, on the other hand, is characterized by good stories that gain credence through their lifelikeness. They are not concerned with procedures and conventions for the generation of abstract and general theories but with the particulars of experience. They do not establish universal truth conditions but a connectedness of events across time. The narrative mode leads, not to certainties, but to varying perspectives. In this world of narrative, the subjunctive mood prevails rather than the indicative mood [p. 78].

Notice the antigeneral stance and, once again, the use of scare quotes to convey antirealism, which is linked, especially in the last two sentences, to particularity or nongenerality.

The goal of individualizing therapy found in solution-focused therapy (and in the broader postmodern narrative therapy movement) is, then, typically pursued by rejecting the use of general, predetermined theories, meanings, and contents. But what most theorists fail to realize is that this goal is confounded with antirealism, as the quotations just provided reveal. The conflation of the doctrine of antirealism with the intent to individualize therapy is, moreover, completely unnecessary. Working it the other way around, Solovey and Duncan (1992) convey this connection between the adoption of antirealism and the quest for uniqueness/individuality when they define constructivism, which is after all an antirealist doctrine about knowing, in terms of client individuality:

> Constructivism elevates the client's view of reality . . . to paramount importance in the therapeutic process. The application of constructivism to therapy makes the client's meaning system hierarchically superior to the therapist's theoretical orientation and/or personal beliefs. Constructivism, therefore, provides a strong rationale for respecting the preeminence of the client's world view. In practical terms, it emphasizes the client's idiosyncratic meaning system as the impetus for therapy [p. 55].

It is my claim that the realism/antirealism distinction is irrelevant to the pursuit of an individualized therapy practice. That is because—and this may well be considered radical in some circles—there is no need to assume that either the client's awareness (that is, experience) or interpretation of unique personal events is antirealist. Most fundamental to my argument is this: it is the composition of the therapy system that guides one's practice that is relevant to that pursuit. Consideration of a generic model of therapy systems will make my point clearer.

Let us begin by assuming that therapy systems, when complete, can be characterized by the following three predetermined component parts (Held, 1991, 1995a):

1. One or more descriptions of what constitutes problems, pain, or, put less neutrally, pathology—for instance, depression, anxiety, or chronic indecision.
2. One or more theories about what causes problems, pain, or pathology—such as a neurotransmitter defect, an early emotional trauma, or a failure to notice "exceptions" to the problem state. These I call theories of problem causation, and they, along with the descriptions themselves, constitute the content of therapy—what must be considered and discussed, indeed changed, in the course of therapy.
3. One or more theories (with attendant methods) about how to alleviate problems, pain, or pathology—for example, by challenging irrational beliefs, teaching new

skills for coping, or helping clients to "restory" or "renarrate" their life experience by incorporating neglected aspects of that life experience into their life narratives. These I call theories-cum-methods of problem resolution, and they constitute the process of therapy—how therapy, or change, occurs, whatever its content.

We are now in a position to see just how those solution-focused therapists who propound antirealism are attempting to individualize practice by eliminating predetermined content—that is, problem categories and their theorized causes—from the theoretical systems they construct and use. They seek to replace that generalized content with unique, client-determined views, understandings, meanings, and goals. But all they have done—the real consequence of their activity—is make the therapy system they use less complete, and so the practice guided by that minimalist system is less systematic, rule governed, and replicable; hence, I have elsewhere called their aspirations antisystematic (Held, 1995a). Moreover, they have not made the system that remains—namely, the general, predetermined method of problem resolution, that is, the therapeutic process of "solution talk"— more open to an antirealist interpretation. (Nor are the solutions that allegedly emerge from that "solution talk" any less real just because those who write about solution-focused therapy also like on occasion to claim that what they do is neither about nor based in reality.) And, again, the client's personal meanings/ views/understandings need not be given an antirealist interpretation (recall the battered wife, whose *particular* battered experience is completely unique to her), certainly not any more than general, predetermined theories of problem causation and problem resolution need to be taken as realist, or extratheoretically true; they could simply be bad/wrong theories. Thus, what we have is a confusing of the problem of individualizing therapy (and the related problem of systematizing it) with antirealism, or subjectivity.

To reiterate: the individualization (and systematization) of therapy is not a function of the realism or antirealism of the theoretical system used to guide one's practice. It is a function of the completeness of that system in terms of the three component parts I outlined earlier. This is true even for those systems of therapy that are taken to be completely antirealist, by design or otherwise.

A Real Solution

I hope that, in the final analysis, solution-focused therapists—actually, all therapists with a postmodern/antirealist inclination—will spend more of their time reconsidering the nature and composition—the completeness—of the theoretical systems that guide their practice, and less time extolling the virtues of antirealism as a foundation for therapy. If such therapists want to go the route of endorsing a theoretical system that takes minimalism to new heights—namely, the therapist does something in language (which is unspecified other than its ambiguous relation to what Walter and Peller call "not-yet-understanding" and "goaling") and this linguistic act causes the client to undergo a new experience/"solution" (also unspecified)—then two realities are inevitable: (1) the practice of therapy guided by such a minimalist theoretical system will itself be highly individualized, but always at the expense of also being highly antisystematic; and (2) there will be a causal claim about change itself within that minimalist theoretical system, even though the change is supposed to be limited exclusively to the domain of language itself, which I obviously think it is not and cannot be.

Elsewhere (Held, 1992) I have argued that there is—or at least there used to be—a claim about what causes problems (or maybe, better stated, a claim about what impedes solutions) within the solution-focused literature, but that that causal claim (namely, not noticing exceptions) has itself escaped notice, perhaps because it is so very general or abstract in its articulation. In any case, I hope that the other chapters in this book (I have seen only the one by Walter and Peller) have more to say about (1) what constitutes problems or impediments to solutions/goals, (2) what causes those problems/impediments to occur, and (3) what methods help clients to solve their problems, overcome those impediments, or attain their goals.

Whether the language in those theoretical systems is about solving problems, overcoming impediments, or attaining goals does not matter to me. What does matter to me is that the therapists who develop such systems, in addition to making them as complete as possible given the goal of an individualized practice, devote a good portion of their time to making them as extratheoretically (or extralinguistically) true as possible, an activity that must include the systematic empirical evaluation of the effectiveness of those systems. After all, as therapists we have no business turning our backs on the all-too-harsh realities that our clients have not invented but nonetheless must face in their quests for better lives. Need it be said that we have an obligation to get hold of as much knowledge about those aspects of reality as we possibly can?

Questions from the Editors

1. *What do you see as the real-world consequences of adopting the strong antirealist stance for the practicing clinician?*

Because therapists who promote postmodernism/social constructionism have conflated their antirealist epistemology with their minimalist (or antisystematic) aspirations, I cannot discuss one without the other. Therefore, in the final chapter of *Back to Reality* (1995a), "Ethical and Other Practical Implications of Postmodern Antirealism in Therapy," I give extensive consideration to the way both of these trends together can affect the answers to three important questions, namely:

1. What, within postmodern, therapies constitutes help, and what constitutes harm?
2. What constitutes truth, and what constitutes lies?
3. What constitutes therapist expertise?

Just let me make two quick points here: First, if there is no real reality to be known, there can be no truth and no lies. There also can be no real therapist expertise, especially if there is a simultaneous repudiation of any theoretical system used to guide therapeutic practice. The ethical implications of those outcomes should be immediately apparent. Second, in my opinion the point of therapy is to help people cope with reality; surely one must know something about reality in order to cope with it.

2.   *How can theoreticians and researchers contribute, as you say in your chapter, to the legitimation of psychotherapy itself rather than to the continued search beyond psychotherapy for a paradigm that legitimates psychotherapy?*

For a discipline—any discipline—to be legitimate it must function with some constraints and replicability, and so it must devise and utilize a system of its own. The minimalist or antisystematic aspirations of the postmodern therapists lead them to denounce the construction and use of theoretical systems of therapy, but they have not been completely successful in that regard, just as they have failed to adhere consistently to their own antirealism. If they were successful in eliminating the use of theory in practice, therapists would naively start each and every case from scratch, with nothing—no expertise—to guide their practice. These are problems to which I give considerable attention in *Back to Reality.* To be very brief here, I suggest that therapists collect evidence from their therapy experiences so that they can construct the best theories possible about the nature of human problems, their causes, and their remedies. Such theory building has of course been seen in solution-focused therapy; if that were not the case, then solution-focused therapy could not be described coherently and replicated successfully by solution-focused therapists. All theoretical systems of therapy should be subjected to continual empirical tests. I am of course advocating nothing more than a return to an empirical method that tests the validity of theory in real experience. To individualize therapy, we should individualize or tailor our *applications* of theory rather than call for an *abandonment* of theory.

3.   *What sources, in addition to your book, do you recommend for clinicians interested in thinking critically about postmodernism?*

The book that has given me the most helpful critical overview of postmodernism in the social sciences is *Postmodernism and the Social Sciences: Insights, Inroads, and Intrusions,* by Pauline Marie Rosenau (1992). For philosophical background on realism versus antirealism/relativism, I recommend *Radical Realism: Direct Knowing in Science and Philosophy,* by Edward Pols (1992), and *Evidence and Inquiry,* by Susan Haack (1993). I refer readers interested in the recent (postmodernist) attacks on science to *Higher Superstition: The Academic Left and Its Quarrels with Science,* by Paul R. Gross and Norman Levitt (1994), and *Science and Anti-Science,* by Gerald Holton (1993). For critiques of the postmodernist renunciation of truth and rationality in the humanities as well as in science and social science, I recommend *The Flight from Science and Reason (Annals of the New York Academy of Sciences)* edited by Paul R. Gross, Norman Levitt, and Martin W. Lewis (in press).

Notes

1. See Held (1995a) and Held and Pols (1985) for more complete descriptions of realism and antirealism, including descriptions of constructivism and social constructionism.
2. An example of reframing provided by Eron and Lund (1993) is a wife whose nagging behavior is relabeled as protectiveness toward her withdrawn husband; a noble, self-sacrificing, positive meaning is thus given to what had previously been seen as a negative or problematic behavior.
3. The words "story" and "narrative" are nothing more than new (narrative therapy) jargon for "meaning," and so the new term "restorying" supplants the old strategic therapy term "reframing." Despite Eron and Lund's (1993, p. 294) perception of differences between strategic and narrative therapies based on what content gets reframed or restoried, I find these therapies to be remarkably similar.
4. See Held (1995a, 1995b) and Held and Pols (1985) for elaboration of the distinction between more radical and less radical forms of antirealism/constructivism.
5. See Chapter One in this volume, by Walter and Peller, p. 22, for a restatement of this quotation.
6. See Held (1995a, pp. 96–101) for a comprehensive listing of antirealist statements made by postmodern (including some solution-focused) therapists, and Held (1995a, pp. 143–146) for a listing of truth/reality claims made by those same therapists about what causes problems and the way therapy works to resolve them.
7. See Held (1995a, pp. 37–38, 267, note 7) and Pols (1992) for discussions of the conflation of theory and language in antirealist/linguistic philosophy.

8. Cade and O'Hanlon (1993) make that less radical claim in this statement: "Also typical of most brief/strategic therapists is the belief that, in terms of the meanings that can be attributed to events, no absolute reality exists. . . . They operate from the assumption that if the way that the world is viewed can be questioned and modified, then meaning can be changed, and thus also the experiential and the behavioral consequences of meaning" (p. 15). Notice that unlike Walter and Peller, Cade and O'Hanlon draw an unequivocal distinction between a cause—in this case, meaning—on the one hand and an effect—in this case, experience and behavior—on the other. Also note the distinction they make between experience and behavior.

9. In the next paragraph, Walter and Peller also speak of "creating our experience." The two statements together—that we create both reality and our experience—lead me to conclude that they equate reality itself with the experience of reality, so that no reality independent of the knower can be said to exist. If my conclusion is correct, theirs is indeed a most radical form of antirealism.

10. As I suggested earlier, to call the linguistic construction itself a nonreality is misleading in one sense. Even if the linguistic construction were the only reality, this would still pose a problem for antirealists: the construction would then have a real existence in language as the linguistic construction it was formed to be, regardless of its truth status, that is, even if it gave us no knowledge of extralinguistic reality. How, then, can we know that (linguistic) reality? See Pols (1992) and Held (1995a) for extensive discussions of that problem.

11. See Held (1995a, pp. 82–89) for additional evidence of this concern.

References

Cade, B., & O'Hanlon, W. H. (1993). *A brief guide to brief therapy.* New York: W. W. Norton.

Coyne, J. C. (1985). Toward a theory of frames and reframing: The social nature of frames. *Journal of Marital and Family Therapy, 11,* 337–344.

De Shazer, S. (1985). *Keys to solution in brief therapy.* New York: W. W. Norton.

De Shazer, S. (1988). *Clues: Investigating solutions in brief therapy.* New York: W. W. Norton.

De Shazer, S. (1991). *Putting difference to work.* New York: W. W. Norton.

De Shazer, S. (1993). Creative misunderstanding: There is no escape from language. In S. Gilligan & R. Price (Eds.), *Therapeutic conversations* (pp. 81–90). New York: W. W. Norton.

De Shazer, S. (1994). *Words were originally magic.* New York: W. W. Norton.

De Shazer, S., & Berg, I. K. (1988). Constructing solutions. *Family Therapy Networker, 12*(5), 42–43.

De Shazer, S., & Berg, I. K. (1992). Doing therapy: A post-structural re-vision. *Journal of Marital and Family Therapy, 18,* 71–81.

Doherty, W. J. (1986). Quanta, quarks, and families: Implications of quantum physics for family research. *Family Process, 25,* 249–263.

Eron, J. B., & Lund, T. W. (1993). How problems evolve and dissolve: Integrating narrative and strategic concepts. *Family Process, 32,* 291–309.

Gross, P. R., & Levitt, N. (1994). *Higher superstition: The academic left and its quarrels with science.* Baltimore, MD: The Johns Hopkins University Press.

Gross, P. R., Levitt, N., & Lewis, M. L. (Eds.). (in press). *The flight from science and reason (Annals of the New York Academy of Sciences).* New York: New York Academy of Sciences.

Haack, S. (1993). *Evidence and inquiry.* Cambridge: Blackwell.

Held, B. S. (1990). What's in a name? Some confusions and concerns about constructivism. *Journal of Marital and Family Therapy, 16,* 179–186.

Held, B. S. (1991). The process/content distinction in psychotherapy revisited. *Psychotherapy, 28,* 207–217.

Held, B. S. (1992). The problem of strategy within the systemic therapies. *Journal of Marital and Family Therapy, 18,* 25–34.

Held, B. S. (1995a). *Back to reality: A critique of postmodern theory in psychotherapy.* New York: W. W. Norton.

Held, B. S. (1995b). The real meaning of constructivism. *Journal of Constructivist Psychology, 8,* 305–315.

Held, B. S., & Pols, E. (1985). The confusion about epistemology and "epistemology"—and what to do about it. *Family Process, 24,* 509–517.

Held, B. S., & Pols, E. (1987). Dell on Maturana: A real foundation for family therapy? *Psychotherapy, 24,* 455–461.

Holton, G. (1993). *Science and anti-science.* Cambridge, MA: Harvard University Press.

O'Hanlon, W. H., & Weiner-Davis, M. (1989). *In search of solutions: A new direction in psychotherapy.* New York: W. W. Norton.

Pols, E. (1992). *Radical realism: Direct knowing in science and philosophy.* Ithaca: Cornell University Press.

Reamy-Stephenson, M. (1983). The assumption of non-objective reality: A missing link in the training of strategic family therapists. *Journal of Strategic and Systemic Therapies, 2,* 51–67.

Rosenau, P. M. (1992). *Postmodernism and the social sciences: Insights, inroads, and intrusions.* Princeton, N.J.: Princeton University Press.

Solovey, A. D., & Duncan, B. L. (1992). Ethics and strategic therapy: A proposed ethical direction. *Journal of Marital and Family Therapy, 18,* 53–61.

Walter, J. L., & Peller, J. E. (1996). Rethinking our assumptions: Assuming anew in a postmodern world. In S. D. Miller, M. A. Hubble, & B. L. Duncan (Eds.), *Handbook of solution-focused brief therapy.* San Francisco: Jossey-Bass.

Watzlawick, P. (Ed.). (1984). *The invented reality.* New York: W. W. Norton.

Watzlawick, P., Weakland, J. H., & Fisch, R. (1974). *Change: Principles of problem formation and problem resolution.* New York: W. W. Norton.

White, M. (1993). Deconstruction and therapy. In S. Gilligan & R. Price (Eds.), *Therapeutic conversations* (pp. 22–61). New York: W. W. Norton.

White, M., & Epston, D. (1990). *Narrative means to therapeutic ends.* New York: W. W. Norton.

CHAPTER THREE

CRAFTING CONSCIOUSNESS THROUGH FORM

Solution-Focused Therapy as a Spiritual Path

Dvorah Simon

Steve de Shazer was once asked if he took it as an assumption that clients have the resources they need to solve their problems. He replied, "It isn't an assumption; it's absolute knowledge."

From the very beginning of my training in solution-focused therapy, I've been touched by and heard comments from others about a "spiritual dimension" to this work. These comments have not been part of formal discussions but have related to such things as belief in the client's resourcefulness, appreciation for the "miraculous" nature of changes that happened or were reported in sessions, and the willingness of the therapist to give up the "ego gratification" of taking credit for "making" change happen. These conversations have been intriguing to me, but somehow unsatisfying; I have wanted to define this spiritual dimension and to understand what it is about solution-focused therapy that makes people talk about the spiritual being present in their work. While both Weakland, of the Men-

Note: I want to thank the following people for having been part of the conversation that has gotten me to this point: Steve de Shazer, Insoo Berg, Eve Lipchik, John Weakland, Dan Gallagher, Ray Gurney, Rich McLaughlin, Hans Skott-Myhre, Linda Bailey-Martiniere, James Armantage, Bill Whedbee, Judith Claremon, Allen Mumper, Susan Egelko and Stephen Gilligan. A very special thank you to Patricia Casamo, friend and fellow enquirer in the solution-focused "spiritual" thing. Thanks also to Yvonne Dolan for encouraging me to write, and Scott Miller who asked me to develop the original article into this chapter.

tal Research Institute school of thought, and de Shazer, of the solution-focused school, have at times referred to Buddhist influences on their thinking (de Shazer, 1985; Watzlawick, Weakland, and Fisch, 1974), both have avoided using anything suggestive of religious language in describing their work. At the second Thera-peutic Conversations conference held in Reston, Virginia, in 1994, de Shazer went so far as to argue against the ascription of anything spiritual to solution-focused therapy's "miracle question." And yet, the conversations keep happening (see, for example, "Letters to the Editor," 1995). What is so compelling about this work that evokes this kind of conversation?

This question has stayed in the back of my mind over the years since I was first exposed to solution-focused therapy in 1986 and 1987. I have continued to have conversations with various colleagues on this topic, and I have still reached no formal conclusions. Meanwhile, solution-focused therapy was gaining wider exposure and was beginning to be marketed as an answer to managed care's emphasis on brief treatment. This led to an inevitable backlash as therapists who had never been "customers" for learning brief treatment were sent to work-shops to learn the way of the future.

The latter point was brought home to me earlier this year when I was asked to do a seminar on solution-focused and Ericksonian therapies for the psychology interns at the hospital where I work. I asked the person arranging the seminar to ask the interns if they had any particular questions or concerns they wanted me to address during the seminar. The following list of questions came back:

"Was solution-focused therapy developed to meet the needs of managed care?"

"Is there any place in solution-focused therapy for the unconscious?"

"How do you keep solution-focused therapy from being mechanical?"

When I met the students who had posed these questions, I discovered that they had been exposed to solution-focused therapy before and had been left with the impression that it was gimmicky, technique driven, and dismissive of emo-tions and any discussion of an inner life. I was dismayed by their responses be-cause they seemed so at odds with the values and spiritual dimension that solution-focused therapy has always had for me. I was similarly disturbed by pub-lished critiques that characterized solution-focused therapy as prone to becom-ing "solution-forced" (Efron, 1994a; Miller, 1994; Nylund & Corsiglia, 1994) because of a perceived tendency to pressure clients into only discussing the positive, or to "invalidat[e] a client's perceptions" by "whitewashing anything negative" (Efran & Schenker, 1993).

The solution-focused therapy I learned from de Shazer, Berg, and Lipchik is never about denying the negative; rather, it is about expanding the focus of treatment to include that which is *not* the problem—the ground as well as the figure, the exception as well as the rule. Reminiscent of Erickson's, Weakland's, and the Palo Alto group's attention to the structure of language in therapy (see Watzlawick, 1978; Watzlawick, Beavin, & Jackson, 1967; Watzlawick, Weakland, & Fisch, 1974), solution-focused therapy as I learned it is an attempt to replace the "either/or" logic of traditional therapy with a "both/and" logic (Lipchik, 1993)—to focus on both the problem *and* the solution or, even more generally, nonproblem life. Also, within the Ericksonian framework, solution-focused therapy is an embodiment of the belief that an understanding of the problem does not necessarily lead to its solution. As Jay Haley once stated, "You need one theory to understand a problem but a different one to solve it" (J. Haley, personal communication, 1986).

An even more radical aspect of solution-focused therapy is that it is not, in spite of its name, about solutions. The word "solution" implies the need to "fix" the "problem," and solutions are therefore driven by the problem. Rather, solution-focused therapy is about shifting attention to the life the client would prefer to lead (Gilligan, 1993)—a viewpoint that Casamo (personal communication, May 1987) had earlier described as one in which "the future determines the past." This emphasis on the preferred life—an emphasis that could be misconstrued or misapplied by therapists as squelching discussion of the problem—seems to me to be at the spiritual heart of this work—placing longing, desire, and the belief that a better life is not only possible but available in a central position around which everything else can flow.

My dilemma has been how to communicate what I take to be this spiritual heart. Any technique, any description, can be misconstrued. Spiritual matters are especially difficult to discuss, involving as they do particularly loaded and slippery language. Knowing that there is no hope, I nevertheless persist and offer here a scheme for understanding what I have referred to as the spiritual dimension of solution-focused therapy. The intent of this scheme is to show that by centering in the "spiritual," the solution-focused therapist can avoid the pitfalls of both solution-forced therapy and the larger cultural trance of pathology and medically oriented thinking.

Spirituality and Spiritual Paths

First, it is important to define "spiritual." While the word itself implies a dichotomy or split between matter and spirit, I am using it here to point, for want of a better term, to a way of thinking and viewing that is nonjudgmental and inclusive. To be spiritual, in this usage, is to embrace both/and logic, that is, to endeavor to train perception beyond the limitations of dichotomous thinking and fixed categories. In conventional reasoning (the logic of either/or), if one thing is true, its opposite must be false. Both/and logic means that many things, even apparently contradictory things, can be true simultaneously. Similarly, in spiritual practice, both familiar realities—as we have been taught to perceive them—and unfamiliar experiences, such as altered states of consciousness, can be valid and "true." The inclusive logic of spirituality gains a beating heart when compassion is compounded into the equation—compassion being the emotional correlate of both/and logic.

Spirituality may also be defined as an intense awareness of being alive, of breathing, of being present in this moment of all moments and this place of all places. Simultaneously, the particularity of this moment is perceived, in the spiritual vision, in perspective with larger frames of reality and possibility. There is a story of a certain rabbi who kept in each of two pockets a piece of paper on which was written a biblical quote. On one paper was written, "Man comes from dust and to dust he will return," and on the other, "Man is created in the image of God." The rabbi would pull out each paper as needed, one when he needed to remember humility, the other when he needed to lift his spirits. As this story illustrates, there is no one fixed spiritual vantage point. Rather, spirituality implies a fluidity of perspectives and positions.

A spiritual path is a set of practices that work, serendipitously or by design, to promote particular attitudes, values, beliefs, states of consciousness, and patterns of behavior. In this respect, and more central to the subject of this paper, solution-focused therapy can be viewed or understood as analogous to a spiritual path, for several reasons. First, the solution-focused approach reflects values common to many spiritual paths. Second, as is true of other spiritual paths, the values of the solution-focused approach work to engender a new consciousness or way of looking at and experiencing the world. Finally (again, akin to other spiritual paths), the learning takes place by *naming* (the creation of new words or new usages to define new concepts), *enactment* (prescribed behaviors), and *talking to colleagues* (participation in a language community that shares ways of describing a set of ideas).

The analogy of solution-focused therapy as a spiritual path proposed here centers on the stance of the therapist. Other aspects of psychotherapy also fall within the purview of spirituality, including consideration of the spiritual condition of the client, as in pastoral counseling or Jungian-influenced approaches; spiritual practices of the therapist that originate outside the therapy but that have an impact on clinical work (such as meditation practice, church attendance, prayer, and so forth); and awareness of and sensitivity to the religio-cultural traditions of the individual client. While there has been a burgeoning interest in the intersection of spirituality and psychotherapy among practitioners of many kinds of therapy (see, for example, issues of *Common Boundary* and the *Journal of Systemic Therapies*, especially Efron, 1994b), this chapter focuses solely on the consideration of solution-focused therapy itself as a spiritual path.

Spiritual Elements of Solution-Focused Therapy

Solution-focused therapy reflects values and attitudes common to many spiritual paths (including the Hindu, Buddhist, Jewish, Moslem, and Christian traditions). While ideologies and sociological identifications may separate adherents into different religions, spiritual values and ideas can cross religious lines. Some of these common values or attitudes are reverence, gratitude, receptivity, "the fear of heaven," service, and compassion or love. I define these terms here, using illustrations from different religious and spiritual traditions. While I have tried to draw from a variety of sources, I am most conversant with Jewish ideas. This bias does not imply a privileged position for these ideas; they are merely the ones with which I am most familiar.

Reverence

Reverence is about honoring existence; it is the awareness that one exists in relationship to a larger frame, an "Other" who is worthy of respect. The "Other" can be construed as life, other beings, nature, the universe, or "God." Reverence can be seen in terms of Bateson's (1972) conception of consciousness as interpersonal, that is, one cannot have reverence without an awareness of the contextual field of consciousness—there must be a universe out there to revere. Reverence is therefore about bringing awareness to the interpersonal or contextual nature of one's own consciousness and existence, about the realization that there is no individual mind apart from the whole.

Traditional religious paths teach and express reverence in many ways—for example, the edict, common to many religions, to honor one's parents, or the Hindu greeting "namaste," which literally means, "I salute the God within you." Other expressions of reverence include the Sufi (Moslem) practice of "Zikr," a contemplative practice for "remembering" God; the Jewish custom of covering the bread while blessing the wine so the bread won't be embarrassed about not being blessed first; and the Talmudic declaration that to shame someone publicly is worse than making that person walk through fire.

Reverence can also be seen in the domain of therapy. In particular, reverence is most apparent in the Rogerian injunction to respect the client (Rogers, 1951). Respecting the client is also the sine qua non of good solution-focused work. While therapists of every school believe in respecting the client, solution-focused therapy has mapped out particular ways in which respect translates into behavior. For example, respecting the client means trusting in the client's resourcefulness by eliciting his or her ways of solving problems rather than suggesting new approaches. Similarly, the client is treated as the one who most appropriately defines the complaint and who knows how and when things can be defined as "better." Respecting the client means seeing him or her as one who is and always has been essentially OK, whose repertoire of "nonproblem" life patterns provides infinite opportunities for learning and solution development, and whose words and ways are the best tools for having the conversation.

Gratitude

Gratitude is an attitude of appreciation or thankfulness for life, both one's own life and life in general. Gratitude is a way of taking the universe personally, so to speak, a way of feeling honored by life. Implicit in the concept of gratitude, however, is the recognition that life in this universe is precarious—that good things are never a given and therefore should not be taken for granted. Gratitude is not Pollyannaish. Rather, gratitude is deepened by a mature recognition of the possibility that bad things can happen.

Traditional religious paths give form to gratitude in many ways, most often in blessings, prayers of thanksgiving, and psalms of praise. In solution-focused therapy, gratitude is expressed as appreciation—for the client, for small steps, and for change. Solution-focused practitioners are particularly well known for expressing appreciation through compliments, by asking clients the question, "How did you do that?" and by telling clients how impressed they are with them. Gratitude is expressed when any word or deed serves to acknowledge a client's ideas, resources, experience, and solutions—especially in the face of difficulties, trials, and pain.

Receptivity

Receptivity is openness and curiosity; it means losing one's sense of self-importance—giving up both the illusion of and the ambition for control. Receptivity also means knowing that you don't know it all and that you therefore are open to surprise, to the universe as it shows up, without demanding that it fit some preconceived framework or idea. In particular, receptivity means surrendering the security of dichotomies as a way of parsing reality and choosing instead the uncertain terrain of unpredictable, chaotic life. To be receptive is to be nonjudgmental; it is to invite all aspects of the situation into awareness, into the conversation, without prejudice. Receptivity also means playfulness, trying on different ways of being, as no one position is "the truth." Like reverence, receptivity invites connection to the larger contexts in which one finds oneself.

Receptivity is traditionally cultivated by such concepts as the Buddhist idea of nonattachment and by such practices as meditation and mystical contemplation. For example, in Yoga meditation, the goal is to identify without judgment, reactivity, or attachment the thoughts and sensations that emerge while one is meditating. The practitioner is directed to receive these thoughts and sensations into awareness without fixing the experience into a conceptual box.

Similarly, in solution-focused work, receptivity to the client's way of describing the universe of the client's experience means the therapist must be open, curious, and nonjudgmentally attentive without reactivity or attachment. Cultivating both/and logic means hearing "black" without assuming that "black" rules out the possibility of "white," or grey, turquoise, or pink, for that matter. Receptivity also means losing self-importance—that is, recognizing that the client's values and solutions matter more than the therapist's. This is not meant to devalue either the therapist or the therapist's contribution to treatment, but rather to restore some semblance of balance to the inherently hierarchical relationship that exists between therapist and client. Receptivity allows the therapist to know that not only is it alright not to know the answers but that is how it should be. At the same time, the therapist can know that knowledge is available from all around, whether it is understood as coming from the client, from the brilliance of the unconscious, from God, or from the emergent wisdom of the therapist-client system. The therapist's task is precisely to cultivate receptivity to that knowledge, whatever its name, to tap into the listening spirit of the work, the aliveness of the silence in which the client's definitions and descriptions of his or her experience and desires are repeatedly invited and cherished. This is not necessarily a literal silence, but rather an opening up of the space of communication by the therapist's restraint in imposing definitions, criteria, and agendas.

The Fear of Heaven

"The fear of heaven" is a term from the Jewish tradition that means "behave yourself." Do the right thing. Don't do to anyone else what you wouldn't want them to do to you (according to Hillel). Or do unto others as you would have them do unto you (according to Jesus). How you treat others, how you behave in community, matters—you are living in a witnessed universe. Actions have consequences, karmic or otherwise. In Jewish lore, the first question you will be asked when you get to heaven relates not to piety or faith but to how you treated others in the marketplace. Literally, the question is, "Did you keep honest weights?"

In his book *The Mind of Clover*, Robert Aitken (1984) discusses the meaning of "karma": "Affinity and coincidence are surface manifestations of the organic nature of the universe, in which nothing occurs independently or from a specific set of causes, but rather everything is related to everything else, and things happen by the tendencies of the whole in the context of particular circumstances. The Law of Karma expresses the fact that the entire universe is in equilibrium" (p. 8).

Aitken goes further to draw the implication of interconnectedness for human relationships: "Saving others is saving ourselves. . . . I and all beings perfectly reflect and indeed *are* all people, animals, plants, and so on. The metaphor is the 'Net of Indra,' a model of the universe in which each point of the net is a jewel that perfectly reflects all other jewels" (p. 9). This elucidation of the Buddhist concept of karma highlights the relationship of the fear of heaven, or "doing the right thing," to connectedness.

In solution-focused work, the fear of heaven translates into attention to ethics, boundaries, and advocacy on various social, political, and cultural issues. The idea of doing the right thing raises questions about the role of advocacy and political action, both within and outside the formal therapeutic relationship. While there is considerable debate over whether therapy is the proper venue for such advocacy (especially if clients have not raised these issues), therapists in fact live in society and cannot isolate the therapy room from it. At a minimum, the emphasis on client competence in solution-focused therapy leads naturally to the idea of empowering disenfranchised populations (Bailey-Martiniere, 1993). How far a solution-focused therapist goes in seeking out or creating opportunities to address social issues such as gender and race/class inequities, sexual or physical abuse, or homelessness will in all likelihood depend on the particular therapist and therapist/client relationship. Finally, the "fear of heaven" raises the question of ethical behavior within the therapist community—challenging therapists to inquire of themselves whether they show colleagues, students, and teachers the same respect and spirit of collaborative learning that they advocate showing clients.

Service and Compassion/Love

Ideals of service and love or compassion are a part of most spiritual traditions. For many traditions, service is the answer to the existential question, "Why am I here?" For example, in answering this question Mother Theresa spoke not only of serving "the poorest of the poor" but of seeing Christ in each person she served—even the most degraded and defiled. The Jewish tradition outlines specific obligations of service: visiting the sick, caring for the disenfranchised (such as widows, orphans, and the poor), and providing dowries for brides who need them. In the Buddhist tradition, the ideals of love and compassion are represented by bodhisatvas, enlightened beings who refrain from attaining nirvana in order to work for the enlightenment of all sentient beings.

Ideals of service and compassion drive most therapists, not just solution-focused therapists. In solution-focused therapy, the extreme focus on the client's agenda (rather than on the therapist's interpretation or recasting of that agenda) conforms to the service ideal. This focus means being willing to take a back seat to the client and the client's process, to become invisible as needed. Being invisible can be hard on one's sense of importance; doing solution-focused therapy can become spiritual work for the therapist as he or she works to maintain respect for and acknowledgment of the client while putting his or her own needs for attention and credit on hold. As de Shazer (personal communication, May 1987) has said, solution-focused therapists do not get Christmas cards thanking them for all they have done (as Milton Erickson was said to). As Nowitz (1995) so poignantly described, this can be a bit disconcerting to professionals who have not been trained to serve clients in this way. After using the method with a family, she noted: "I had mixed feelings when this family left. Initially I had felt their need for me to be their problem solver and now I felt I had helped them solve their problems themselves. While I believe strongly in this method of practice, my ego felt a little strange. I actually missed feeling acknowledged. The family members' initial pull for me to solve their problem still had a hold on me despite what I believed" (p. 9).

Doing this work can be a challenge to the ego, but it has its own rewards. For example, if I do not have the answers and do not make solutions happen, then with my intentions and craft in hand I can relax into wonder as the work the client and I need to do unfolds. The ideal of love is less explicit: perhaps one can do this work without compassion, but what a tiresome task it would be. Compassion and love are the unspoken heart of service.

Solution-Focused Techniques as Spiritual Practice

Berg (1994) calls solution-focused questions "expressions of an attitude, a posture and a philosophy," saying that "no amount of technique will disguise the therapist's lack of listening skills, lack of faith in the client's ability to know what is good for him, and miscomprehension of the philosophical thinking that generates questions" (p. 14). I would go further and propose that the techniques (such as questions and interventions) of solution-focused therapy are not only expressions of "an attitude, a posture and a philosophy" but are also a way for the therapist to learn that attitude, posture, and philosophy. That is, technique can be a practice that teaches the therapist—through naming, enactment, and talking to colleagues—the attitudes and values from which solution-focused therapy is generated. Seen this way, solution-focused therapy is a spiritual path, according to the definition provided earlier of "spiritual path" as a set of practices that work, whether serendipitously or by design, to induce or evoke attitudes, a philosophical stance, or a state of consciousness.

I got the idea of seeing methods as practice from a story told at a conference by Garry Lane about Gregory Bateson's experiences as an anthropologist in Japan (G. Lane, personal communication, 1993). Bateson had told Lane about observing the members of a Japanese family as they made great efforts to show respect to the father of the family by bowing and making a fuss when he came home. Bateson had asked one of the daughters why she respected her father so much. "Oh no," she said, "it's not that we respect him. We *practice* showing him respect so that if we ever meet anyone we really respect we will know how to show it." After relating Bateson's story, Lane then introduced the idea that our techniques as brief therapists can be seen as a practice, designed to induce in the therapist the attitude of respect for the client. From a position of true respect, techniques per se become superfluous, as action appropriate to the situation is generated from the simple act of paying attention to what is needed.

In the solution-focused tradition, solution-focused questions can be seen not as rigid prescriptions to follow but rather as extremely valuable tools for learning to respect the client, appreciate what works, and keep a sense of perspective in the work. De Shazer (personal communication, 1994) has observed that what is referred to as "the model" of solution-focused therapy was originally intended as a *description* of what the Brief Family Therapy Center team found themselves doing, not as a *prescription* for fixed behaviors, which is how it may have been taken. Mostert (1995) stated the same idea in more operational terms when she wrote the following:

> Solution-focused therapy provides me with a framework for correcting errors in my practice of psychotherapy. Am I hearing what the client wants? What goals are we working on, mine or the client's? Am I getting ahead of my client? Am I noticing small changes? Am I presuming I know best for my client or am I acknowledging that they are the best expert on their own lives? If these are things I once knew but forgot, then solution-focused therapy makes it easier to remember. It also reminds me to be hopeful, not, as some have claimed, relentlessly (and disrespectfully) cheerful" [p. 80].

Some Solution-Focused Practices

I am aware of five different solution-focused activities that could be considered practices: (1) the questions we ask, (2) the questions we don't ask, (3) the things we say, (4) the things we don't say, and (5) the things we do. In the paragraphs that follow, I give examples of each of these five practices and attempt to show the impact that each may have on the consciousness of the practitioner.

The Questions We Ask. Solution-focused therapy has been called the "model of questions" (Miller, 1995). In fact, questions do play a major role in the model. Some types of questions familiar to most solution-focused practitioners follow, with one or two examples of each type.

- Exception questions
  "What's different when the problem is not occurring?"
- Coping questions
  "With all the terrible things you've been going through, what has kept you from becoming a stark raving lunatic?"
- Scaling questions
  "On a scale from one to ten, with one being the way you felt when you called to make this appointment and ten being feeling great, how are you doing right now?"
- The miracle question
  "Suppose tonight while you are sleeping a miracle occurs, and the problem you came here to deal with is no longer a problem. But because the miracle happened while you were sleeping, you didn't know it happened. What would be the first thing you would notice after you woke up that would tell you the miracle happened?"
- Future-oriented questions
  "What will you do with all the time you save when you no longer have this problem?
- Competence and/or resource questions
  "How did you do that?"
  "How did you figure that out?"

All of these questions help craft a certain kind of awareness or consciousness on the part of the therapist, related to the values I discussed earlier (reverence, gratitude, receptivity, the fear of heaven, service, and compassion or love). For example, *exception questions* remind therapists to be reverent in the presence of the client by providing evidence that there is more to the client than the client's problem.

In addition, exception questions are perhaps the most reliable way to work with both/and consciousness—an aspect, as noted earlier, of receptivity. By asking questions about times when the problem is not a problem, the therapist is inducted into considering both figure and ground, both problem and nonproblem life.

Coping questions also help to engender a new consciousness in the therapist. By asking and being curious about how clients manage, how they survive in spite of their difficulties, therapists are reminded that clients have resources and skills regardless of their experience of suffering. Coping questions also teach therapists that human suffering is not a problem they can fix—or even that human suffering is not a problem. Suffering may just be, as the Buddha taught, the nature of life. Coping questions remind the therapist to see the dignity and competence of the client's coping: no matter how much "shit happens," there is always an element of agency, even poignant beauty, in the way people respond to it.

By introducing gradations and shades of grey, *scaling questions* increase receptivity by working on either/or, all-or-nothing thinking. Scaling questions remind the therapist to set small goals and to help the client set small goals. They also remind the therapist to keep looking for exceptions, for elements of the nonproblem pattern, even when the initial descriptions of the client's functioning are problem saturated. The *miracle question* also enhances receptivity by teaching the therapist to be curious, to be open to being surprised by the client's response. In addition, it puts the focus of the therapy on the client's vision of a good life rather than on the therapist's concept of a solution to the stated problem. This focus is in keeping with the value of reverence. *Future-oriented questions*—such as "What will you do with all the time you save when you no longer have this problem?"—serve a similar purpose, but they also remind the therapist that the client has better things to do than be in therapy.

The Questions We Don't Ask. Part of doing solution-focused therapy is restraining from following certain lines of inquiry—remembering not to get too impressed with stories of pathology, too entranced by exploration of history, or too engaged in questions of etiology. While practicing restraint in no way prevents the solution-focused therapist from responding to a client's interest in such areas, it does serve to remind the therapist both that the purpose of therapy is not to satisfy the therapist's intellectual curiosity and that one need not understand the problem in order to solve it.

The Things We Say. Solution-focused therapists not only pose questions; they also give feedback in the form of compliments and exclamations of being impressed by change, difference, exceptions, success, and resourcefulness (for example, "Wow!" and "How did you do that?"). These statements function, for the most part, as validations of some aspect of the client's functioning.

Related to validating statements are normalizing frames. These provide the client with a context in which behaviors and feelings the client presents as problematic or pathological can be seen as part of a normal reaction or stage of life. For example, a client who complains of "depression" and feelings of derealization or confusion after suffering a loss may find it a relief to learn that such reactions are a normal part of the grieving process. Normalizing frames counteract, for therapist as well as client, the pathologization of human feeling and behavior that is endemic in our culture.

Things We Don't Say. Just as solution-focused therapists don't ask questions about the causes of problems, they also avoid exclamations of being impressed by problem descriptions. In addition, they avoid "interpretations," that is, statements that imply that the therapist understands the client better than the client does. These latter types of statements include describing client behavior as pathological, suggesting that the client's goal is not the "right" one, or recommending that the client needs "more therapy." Avoiding the implication that the therapist understands the client better than the client understands himself or herself helps the therapist remember to respect the client as the best authority on the client's own life.

Things We Do. Client assignments developed from strategic, Ericksonian, and solution-focused traditions (for instance, odd-even day tasks, coin-flipping tasks, observational assignments, and so on) are part of the behavioral repertoire of solution-focused therapists. Also included are ways of structuring the session, such as taking a break before giving compliments and interventions, and the use of the visitor/complainer/customer framework in determining which kind of homework assignment to give. Taking breaks is a practice that can teach therapists to relinquish the rush to appear clever by having "the answer." Similarly, giving homework is a good reminder that the hour spent together comprises a small portion of the client's life—the most important part has nothing to do with therapy.

The Benefits of Practice

We all know that the earth circles the sun, and the moon circles the earth, and we have known this for centuries. But the language still reflects another worldview: the sun rises and sets and so does the moon" [de Shazer, 1984, pp. 20–21].

Language is a virus from outer space [Burroughs, 1970].

Therapists need practices for several reasons. One is to avoid using methods and techniques as devices or gimmicks to operate on the client or on the clinical process. Such use only leads to therapy that is "solution-forced" because it ulti- mately fails to see the client as the source of the solution. When therapists use methods as practice they can avoid this problem by relating to each method or technique as one of many that express an attitude. Ultimately, it is the attitude rather than the technique that generates the work, or rather the context in which the work can occur.

A second reason that therapists need practices is that for all the commit- ment one may have to the philosophy of solution-focused therapy as outlined in this chapter, moods or feelings may vary. Whether distracted, having a bad day, or irritated by something about the client, any therapist can be in the position of not feeling respectful, appreciative, or receptive. Practices can guide behavior as a last resort when one's mood is not cooperating with one's philosophy.

The third reason that therapists need practices is because of the tendency to speak in ways that are not in accord with one's beliefs. Solution-focused therapists live and practice in a culture that often supports the use of problem-focused rather than solution-focused terms. Most therapists have been trained in problem-focused, pathology-based models, and many continue to work in settings that favor these models. One cannot bill for services without putting a diagnosis from the *Diagnostic and Statistical Manual* (DSM) on an insurance form, thereby conforming one's language to the medical model. While solution-focused therapists conceptualize problems and solutions differently than the dominant culture, it is hard *not* to be affected by the language we hear all around us. After all, most solution-focused therapists accept that language and the assumptions embedded in that language "create" reality, or at the very least predispose the listener to a state of mind. As Weakland (1993) has trenchantly pointed out, even terms that are commonly used "by old habit" and because they are "familiar to clients," such as "therapy" or "psychotherapy," are "too closely tied to the medical idea of 'mental illness,' with its concept of specific 'pathology' on the one hand, and 'normality' on the other, and the implication that there is some right way—but where is there any con- sensus?—for an individual or a family to think and act" (p. 142). And yet we continue to use these words, and others like them, that are incongruent with our philosophy, for the reasons Weakland pointed out: familiarity and habit.

The problem with language habits is not in the language itself but in the way language can slip into consciousness and change it. It is as if when we hear our- selves say something there is a part of us that thinks, "I must have meant that." Our culture has long since adopted the Freudian notion that if a person says some- thing with which he or she does not consciously agree, then the statement is evi- dence of unconscious intent—"If I didn't think I meant that, I must have meant it at a level of my being of which I am not aware."

Even if the Freudian assumption of unconscious intent is rejected, cognitive dissonance resolution (Festinger, 1967) works to promote reconciliation of what we have said with what we take to be the meaning of what we have said. Cognitive dissonance resolution occurs when one of two apparently contradictory statements or perceptions that have created a "dissonance" is altered so that the dissonance is "resolved." Cognitive dissonance resolution is based on either/or logic. Either statement A is correct or statement B is correct. Both cannot be correct. Therefore either A or B is altered to resolve the dissonance. Using cognitive dissonance resolution can subtly alter one's beliefs as one participates in pathology-based language usage. For example, if the two statements creating dissonance are "Pathology is not a useful concept" and "This patient has obsessive compulsive disorder," the dissonance may be resolved by weakening the therapist's conviction in the first statement.

Both/and logic offers another way not merely of thinking about things but of experiencing the world. With both/and logic, contradictory experiences do not need to be resolved but can coexist (Gilligan, in press); a client can both have problems and be OK. The practice of both/and logic is a way to pay attention to the persistence of language habits.

The tradition of brief therapy has always been hip to language. To say that language is a virus—to borrow Burroughs's locution—offers a way of thinking about language as an entity with its own existence and rules. Words are then seen as the contents of a free-floating cultural soup of potential but not inevitable meaning. Treating language as an entity to be respected helps break the automatic association of language habits with meaning. For solution-focused therapists, pathology language is akin to racist or sexist language—something we do not agree with but that keeps showing up nevertheless, and that can affect our consciousness if we are not paying close attention.

How Practices Work

As I noted earlier, practices foster learning in three ways: by *naming, enactment,* and *talking to colleagues. Naming* is the process of creating and using new words or special usages of words to parse experience or observed phenomena in new ways—for example, "customer" is a nonmedical way to describe a client, with its echo of "the customer is always right" (Watzlawick, Weakland, & Fisch, 1974). Similarly, the word "exception" takes on special resonance as a shorthand way to describe all the ways in which the client's life is not a problem (de Shazer, 1988). Using new words, or old words in special ways, creates a break in the automatic language patterns usually used in conversations about therapy.

Enactment is the performance of prescribed behaviors (for instance, taking a break, giving homework, or using speech in particular ways, such as to ask "What's better?" "How did you do that?" and so on). Enactment and naming both work by taking advantage of the propensity for cognitive dissonance resolution: as one observes oneself using new language and behavior, feelings can come into alignment with the values inherent in that language and behavior.

The third way practices work is by *talking to colleagues*—participating in a language community that shares ways of describing the work. By talking to each other with deliberate use of new language, therapists build new language patterns and habits that then become resources in the face of the larger cultural patterns of language usage. Thus, these conversations can offset conversations held outside the language community that reflect or create a different point of view (such as those that use the pathology/medical model).

Another communal element of practices is the use of ritual. When I ask the miracle question, I include myself in the tradition and community of all the people who have ever asked the miracle question. As with conversations, the enactment of behaviors that link the therapist to a like-minded community supports the cultivation of the desired attitudes from which the work of solution-focused therapy is generated. The deliberate cultivation of these attitudes is advanced by observing one's own reactions to the effects of asking an exception question, taking a break, and so on.

The Spiritual Heart of Solution-Focused Therapy

Taking psychotherapy as a spiritual path means, ultimately, that as the therapist I take responsibility for the way I craft my presence in the interaction in terms of language, silence, attention, intention, imagination, curiosity, playfulness, and respect. Therapy is an improvisatory art that is improved by craft. Presence is crafted by engagement in specific practices for the purpose of learning from and working with the values, attitudes, and philosophy of solution-focused therapy. Reverence, gratitude, receptivity, the fear of heaven, service, and compassion or love are the metaphors useful to me personally, through which I make my artistic choices and through which my individuality is expressed within the demands of those values, that attitude, and that philosophy. I offer these metaphors not as the last word on spirituality and psychotherapy but as a framework in which further discussion is invited and welcomed.

This discussion is important because now more than ever it is important to remember that solution-focused therapy was not developed to meet the needs of managed care. While the solution-focused approach may in fact prove to have a beneficial influence on market-driven policies, the issue of whether to use this approach has always been, first and foremost, a matter of values. Solution-focused therapy and other collaborative approaches such as narrative therapy (White &

Epston, 1990) and self-relations therapy (Gilligan, in press) are important because they provide languages and technologies with which a therapist can work in congruence with those values. The question of whether to use the solution-focused approach has *always* been a spiritual issue, in which spirituality is defined as the practices that teach reverence, gratitude, receptivity, the fear of heaven, service, and compassion or love. One does not become a solution-focused therapist simply by learning to ask an exception question or take a break before giving an intervention. Rather, becoming solution-focused is a process of cultivating a worldview and a consciousness from which respectful, effective behaviors can flow and that invite and invoke the context in which clients can discover and recover who they are.

Questions from the Editors

1. *What do you make of scientific literature that suggests that other treatment approaches based on different—even opposite—practices and values achieve roughly equivalent results?*

I have two responses to this question. One is a cautionary note about psychotherapy outcome research. Such research demands a standardized treatment protocol, usually formulated in a manual. Generally, clients are included in such studies on the basis of standardized, nomothetic, pathology-based diagnostic criteria. Obviously, this kind of standardization is anathema to a solution-focused approach, which must always key itself to the particulars of the client. So, I am not convinced that such research, as it is usually practiced, is the most appropriate paradigm for assessing and comparing solution-focused therapy and other approaches. My other response is that I am not searching for the holy grail. It is quite believable to me that other people have discovered ways of doing therapy that are helpful to their clients. This is not a competition. Rather, it is a question of what best facilitates each individual therapist's ability to come into the moment, listen to and respect the client, and be open to possibilities for solution. Doing solution-focused therapy, and more recently, Gilligan's self-relations therapy, has meshed best with my own constitution, values, and style such that the combination of me plus these methods seems to result in my best work (as determined by attainment of stated goals, client expressions of satisfaction, and client-generated referrals).

2. *In a way, your view of solution-focused therapy as a practice implies that the approach may have more to do with therapists than with clients. Could you please comment?*

This *chapter* is about the therapist's stance and about how she or he may best cultivate it. The therapy is still about the client.

3.   *In your opinion, are the values of managed care either similar to or different from the values of solution-focused work, and if so, how?*

I cannot speak to the values of managed care because in all my dealings with managed care companies (as an assessor/provider for three of them) they have never indicated to me what these values might be. I can say that the practices of managed care are often in conflict with my values as a solution-focused therapist. Most pointedly, these practices include requiring me to use pathology-based language (to make a DSM diagnosis) in order to bill for payment, and taking decisions about therapist choice and treatment length away from the client.

References

Aitkin, R. (1984). *The mind of clover.* San Francisco: North Point Press.

Bailey-Martiniere, L. (1993). Solution oriented psychotherapy: The difference for female clients. *News of the Difference, 2*(2), 10–12.

Bateson, G. (1972). *Steps to an ecology of mind.* New York: Aronson.

Berg, I. K. (1994). A wolf in disguise is not a grandmother. *Journal of Systemic Therapies, 13*(1), 13–14.

Burroughs, W. (1970). *The job.* New York: Grove/Atlantic.

De Shazer, S. (1984). Post-mortem: Mark Twain *did* die in 1910. *Family Process, 23,* 20–21.

De Shazer, S. (1985). *Keys to solution in brief therapy.* New York: W. W. Norton.

De Shazer, S. (1988). *Clues: Investigating solutions in brief therapy.* New York: W. W. Norton.

Efran, J., & Schenker, M. (1993, May/June). A potpourri of solutions: How new and different is solution-focused therapy? *Family Therapy Networker, 17*(3), 71–74.

Efron, D. (1994a). Commentary. *Journal of Systemic Therapies,* 13(1), 38–41.

Efron, D. (Ed.). (1994b). Spirituality, religion, and world view. *Journal of Systemic Therapies,* 13(3).

Festinger, L. (1967). *Conflict, decision, and dissonance.* Stanford Studies in Psychology III. Stanford, CA: Stanford University Press.

Gilligan, S. (1993). [Commentary on "Creative misunderstanding: There is no escape from language," by Steve de Shazer, a chapter in the same book.] In S. Gilligan and R. Price (Eds.), *Therapeutic conversation.* New York: W. W. Norton.

Gilligan, S. (in press). The relational self: The expanding of love beyond desire. In Michael Hoyt (Ed.), *Constructive therapies* (Vol. 2). New York: Guilford Press.

Letters to the editor (1995, May). *News of the Difference, 4*(2), 6–8.

Lipchik, E. (1993). "Both/and" solutions. In S. Friedman (Ed.), *The new language of change: Constructive collaboration in psychotherapy* (pp. 25–49). New York: Guilford.

Miller, S. D. (1994). The solution-conspiracy: A mystery in three installments. *Journal of Systemic Therapies, 13*(1), 18–37.

Miller, S. D. (1995). Some questions (not answers) for the brief treatment of people with drug and alcohol problems. In M. Hoyt (Ed.), *Constructive therapies* (pp. 92–110). New York: Guilford.

Mostert, D. (1995). Letter to the editor. *Journal of Systemic Therapies, 14*(1), 80.

Nowitz, L. (1995). Letter to the editor. *News of the Difference,* 4(1), 8–9.

Nylund, D., & Corsiglia, V. (1994). Becoming solution-forced in brief therapy: Remembering something important we already knew. *Journal of Systemic Therapies, 13*(1), 5–12.

Rogers, C. (1951). *Client-centered therapy.* New York: Houghton-Mifflin.

Simon, D. (1993). First word: Discovering the future. *News of the Difference, 2*(1), 1–2.

Simon, D. (1994). First word: Random notes from de Shazer in Denver and Gilligan in Mattapoisett. *News of the Difference, 3*(2), 1–2.

Watzlawick, P. (1978). *The language of change.* New York: Basic Books.

Watzlawick, P., Beavin, J., & Jackson, D. (1967). *Pragmatics of human communication.* New York: W. W. Norton.

Watzlawick, P., Weakland, J., & Fisch, R. (1974). *Change.* New York: W. W. Norton.

Weakland, J. (1993). Conversation—but what kind? In S. Gilligan and R. Price (Eds.), *Therapeutic conversation.* New York: W. W. Norton.

White, M., & Epston, D. (1990). *Narrative means to therapeutic ends.* New York: W. W. Norton.

PART TWO

APPLICATIONS OF
SOLUTION-FOCUSED THERAPY

CHAPTER FOUR

SOLUTION-FOCUSED DOMESTIC VIOLENCE VIEWS

Bridges Toward a New Reality in Couples Therapy

Eve Lipchik and Anthony D. Kubicki

This chapter reflects the efforts of Eve Lipchik, a pioneer of solution-focused brief therapy (SFBT), and Tony Kubicki, a coordinator of a batterers program since 1984, to develop a treatment model for couples experiencing emotional and/or physical abuse in their relationship. This evolutionary effort attempts to integrate a SFBT point of view with the arguably irreconcilable perspective of the domestic violence field. As such, the chapter presents an integrative model that is a "work in progress" and proposes a bridge that unites the two disparate approaches. Issues of safety, ethics, personal responsibility, power and control, and therapy versus advocacy are addressed and fleshed out in the format of a conversation between the authors.

Since couples treatment faces considerable opposition in the domestic violence field, we hope that our dialogue will make it clear that we are fully aware of, and take very seriously, the arguments against it. However, our combined years of experience have resulted in views that we feel deserve consideration.

Historical Context

Through her experience in the domestic violence field, Eve Lipchik became increasingly aware that most women return to their partners in spite of what they say when they first come to shelters, and regardless of the earnest efforts of those dedicated to helping them leave abusive partners and start a new life. Consequently, it made sense that if couples stayed together, they needed help to eliminate physical and emotional abuse from their relationship as quickly as possible. Working with couples therefore seemed the most logical option. However, this option is contrary to the traditional belief among domestic violence advocates that working with abusive couples is both unsafe and unethical. Eve believed that the therapeutic approach she and her colleagues at the Brief Family Therapy Center were developing eliminated these safety and ethical objections.

In 1992, she sought out Tony Kubicki in hopes of interesting him in co-developing an outcome study that would compare men in a traditional batterers group with men treated along with their partners with her approach. She quickly discovered that Tony's batterers groups were also founded on humanistic, competency-based premises. She also found that he was in agreement with her about the need for safe couples treatment. This common ground formed the foundation for a bridge between the two views and led to their decision to collaborate.

What Is Domestic Violence and How Prevalent Is It?

Domestic violence is not confined to any socioeconomic, racial, ethnic, religious, sexual orientation, or age group (Hamberger & Hastings, 1986; Hotaling & Sugarman, 1986; Tolman & Bennett, 1990). We believe it can best be thought of as occurring on a continuum from very severe violence (kicking, punching, and stabbing) to less severe violence (pushing, shoving, and slapping). Anywhere from 4 percent (O'Leary et al., 1989; Straus, Gelles, & Steinmetz, 1980) to 6.8 percent (Dutton, 1988) of violence falls into the severe category. A recent study conducted in Colorado indicates that 11 percent of women who come to emergency rooms have sustained injuries as a result of domestic violence (Abbott, Johnson, Kazio-McLain, & Lowenstein, 1995).

Many people think of domestic violence as no more than physical abuse or threats of physical abuse by one family member against another. The American Medical Association's diagnostic and treatment guidelines on domestic violence (1992, p. 40) define it as "violence characterized as a pattern of coercive behaviors that may include repeated battering and injury, psychological abuse, sexual assault, progressive social isolation, deprivation, and intimidation. These behaviors are perpetrated by someone who is or was involved in an intimate relationship with the victim." One can readily see the pool of domestic violence recipients becoming a flood via this definition, and in response, the need for safe and effective professional interventions rising exponentially.

Existing Treatment Options

A review of the relevant literature about treatment options for battering points to a major deterrent to better outcomes: the polarization between the prevailing philosophy, which describes all domestic violence as men using power to control women, and the practical reality that men who batter and women who are battered are unique people in unique relationships, therefore making each case different. From a clinical point of view, the polarization between those who believe in mandatory, gender-separate treatment for men (Pence & Paymar, 1990; Walker, 1984; Yllo & Bograd, 1988) and those who are open to treating the relationship as well (Geffner, Mantooth, Franks, & Rao, 1989; Galdner, 1992; Lipchik, 1991; Neidig, Freedman, & Collins, 1985) has been practically irreconcilable. More specifically, the sociopolitical school asserts that the only safe, ethical option is for men to be seen in groups for "resocialization" and for women to be seen separately to be empowered. The other perspective believes that violence is at times relationship specific, and that in these cases, since such a great percentage of couples stay together, it is safer to help the couple improve their relationship.

Overall, mandatory arrest and court-ordered group meetings for men have become the most commonly accepted modes of civil intervention for batterers *in spite of* an absence of supporting research. As of 1993, relatively little research has been completed on batterers groups. A review by Hamberger and Hastings (1993, p. 229) of twenty-eight major studies evaluating treatment outcomes of mostly court-mandated batterers groups from 1984 to 1990 concluded that "it is discouraging that all of the effort and expense of the treatment themselves, as well as the research on them, have yielded so few conclusions, none of them firm. . . . As of this time we cannot confidently say whether treatment works. Actually, we should be well beyond that question, asking instead, 'what treatment works best on which type of client and under what circumstances?' "

The prototype for batterers group is the Duluth, Minnesota, program (Pence & Paymar, 1990). The program lasts twenty-six weeks and has been duplicated all over the world. In an interview (Hoffman, 1992), Pence expressed her disappointment in the results of her hard work. She estimates a 60 percent recidivism rate and urges women to leave men who batter because no program, even hers, can insure that a violent man will change his ways (Hoffman, 1992).

Lawrence Sherman, principal investigator of the most definitive U.S. study on arrest of batterers, is equally pessimistic about the overall effect of short-term arrest for battering (Sherman, 1992). His study, conducted in Minneapolis, shows that a night in jail for batterers cuts the risk of repeat violence against the same victim over a six-month follow-up period from 20 to 10 percent. Replication of that study in six major cities in the United States showed that arrest had different effects on different kinds of people within the same cities. For instance, in Milwaukee, Omaha, and Colorado Springs, unemployed persons were actually found to be more violent after the arrest. By contrast, arrest of employed persons in those cities achieved a deterrent effect. There were also clear distinctions between chronically and occasionally violent couples. As a result, Sherman beseeched communities not to use his research as a criterion for instituting domestic violence arrest policies.

These dismal results should encourage an outcry for efforts to develop new treatment methods and research to evaluate them. This has not been happening. In fact, on the national level, there is a strong movement against couples treatment; some states, like Colorado in 1993, have passed laws forbidding it for any court-ordered domestic violence perpetrator until he has completed twenty weeks in a batterers group (Colorado Standards, 1993).

It is common knowledge among people who work in the domestic violence field that in spite of all their interventional efforts, up to 75 percent of all women who seek shelter end up back with their abusive partners (Feazell, Mayers, & Deschner, 1984; Purdy & Nickle, 1981). Approximately half of married battered women who seek help from shelters decide to remain married (Giles-Sims, 1983; Strube, 1988). In fact, to do so, many of them must ignore the restraining orders for which they have asked. It is generally believed that most women end up not testifying against the men they had arrested, making this intervention a very impotent one at times.

While it is thought that some women go back to men who abuse them because they are being coerced to do so, many appear to go back because they still feel love for the man and would like the relationship to work out. In the light of these realities, we have felt compelled to develop a safe option for treating relationships in which physical and/or emotional violence has occurred. In keeping with our belief that every victim, perpetrator, and relationship is unique, we also believe that we must evaluate each couple to determine their appropriateness for treatment. Our work is dedicated to these goals.

Solution-Focused Therapy

The prohibitions in the field of domestic violence are, in a generic sense, against "couples counseling." No one has ever specifically defined what "couples counseling" actually means. If it is meant to imply individually oriented, problem-focused treatments that use techniques like confrontation and ventilation, the cautions are warranted. Any approach that requires the therapist to challenge one partner's position more than that of the other is likely to incite resistance and anger on the part of the challenged party and, in the case of spouse abuse, may be dangerous for the woman. It could inadvertently make the abuser seem to be the victim and the abused party collusive with the therapist. It is our contention that for couples treatment to be safe, therapists must be equally joined with and accepting of both partners. That will not mean that they condone physical or emotional abuse. It will mean that they accept the individuals and the stories they tell, but not the abusive behavior. ("I understand that from your point of view your wife's behavior is very hurtful, but violence is not acceptable. What other responses have you tried that work or do you imagine you could try instead?") Couples treatment must be approached from a competency-based, collaborative point of view as represented by therapies with constructivist underpinnings. SFBT as defined by Steve de Shazer (1985, 1988) and his colleagues (de Shazer et al., 1986) and by Eve Lipchik (1991) is one of these therapies and our model of choice.

SFBT is a nonpathology-oriented approach that assumes that people have the strengths and resources to find their own solutions but they have reached a point where they perceive themselves as stuck. SFBT considers individuals to be unique in their genetic heritage, social development, and perception of reality. It believes that language (verbal and nonverbal) is the source of personal and social reality and the means toward a future in which clients can perceive solutions. The therapist collaborates with clients to this end in a conversation characterized by therapist acceptance of, and curiosity about, the clients' present reality. The therapist asks questions about exceptions to the problem, existing and potential resources, and a future in which the problem does not exist. This conversation shifts the clients' reality toward one that includes both/and thinking and possible new options. It also promotes hope and motivation.

The Solution-Focused Domestic Violence Model

In our approach to the treatment of couples engaged in domestic violence, clients are seen for one hour per session. Before they enter the first session they are asked to complete a very detailed intake form covering demographics, an extensive family and personal history, and two psychological assessment forms, the Conflict Tactics Scale (Straus, 1979) and the Dyadic Adjustment Scale (Spanier & Thompson, 1982; Spanier, 1976). We work in a setting that has a one-way mirror, and sessions may be videotaped. Clients give their informed consent before they enter the session. The mirror and taping is explained again when they enter the room, and questions are encouraged. Clients have the option to work with only one therapist in a room without a mirror and not to be videotaped, or both therapists may come into the room to work with them.

We do not read records about clients until after the first session so we may form our own impressions. Both members of the couple are seen for the first session to observe how they interact and are then invited back for one individual session each. During the individual session, the woman's safety is assessed without the man present and a safety plan is developed, when necessary. In the individual session with the man, his safety from loss of control over his anger is discussed along with ideas for control, if necessary. These sessions join the therapist further with each partner.

After the conjoint and individual sessions and after we have looked at the intake data and psychological tests, we decide whether the couple is appropriate for work on their relationship. The conditions that guide our decision are:

1. The man says he really wants to stop being abusive in any way his partner experiences it.
2. The man takes responsibility for the abuse.
3. The man takes responsibility for contributing to the quality of the relationship.

The woman is not responsible for her partner's abuse but she must

1. Express the desire for emotional and physical violence to cease
2. Take responsibility for contributing to the quality of the relationship

If these conditions are not present, or if one partner seems less sure than the other about whether to stay in the relationship, we do not proceed with couples treatment but, rather, offer individual treatment or referral to groups, shelters, advocacy programs, and so forth.

Forty-five minutes into every session, the interviewing therapist joins the one behind the mirror for a conversation about what they both heard and experienced. (If there is no mirror or team, the therapist leaves the room by himself or herself.) Together, the therapists compose a summation message, which is read to the clients by the interviewing therapist. This message consists of:

1. What both therapists heard the clients say about why they are there and what their goals are.
2. The therapists' responses to what they heard (including compliments, reinforcement of strengths and positives, normalization statements, or psychoeducational comments).

3. A suggestion for something the clients can do until the next session. This suggestion is made tentatively to give clients a choice.

A Bridging Conversation Between Eve and Tony

In this section we discuss the major issues involved in developing a treatment model that can bridge the deep chasm between opponents of "couples treatment" and those who favor it under certain circumstances. Tony applies his knowledge of the field of domestic violence to point out the most salient arguments presented against couples treatment, as well as his reasons for or against them. Eve presents her clinical point of view. Short case material illustrates our major points. Eve's comments are in italics and Tony's are in regular type.

Safety

Tony: Safety is the first category of concern with regard to couples treatment. It is said that it is never safe to see a perpetrator and a victim together because all batterers are alike, that is, they all use power to control women.

Eve: *That premise is incongruent with the solution-focused perspective in particular and constructivist-informed therapies in general. One of the assumptions of these orientations is that each person's reality or worldview is unique in spite of basic similarities, such as gender or culture. So, lumping clients together for any reason, including for diagnostic purposes, is totally unfitting and unsafe. The goal of these therapies is to understand and accept individual realities and then talk with clients about how they can create a different one together that works for both of them. I believe that this accepting attitude toward a batterer is much less likely to incite further anger and violence.*

Tony: From the sociopolitical perspective, all men are potential abusers. This perspective presumes we live in a patriarchal society that is structured in such a way that men have power over women. If a man chooses to use that power in a physically violent way against his partner, this creates such a power imbalance that it cannot be reversed via couples counseling.

Eve: *That is one type of belief system. We all make decisions based on our belief systems. Let's look at that statement through two different lenses: the sociopolitical one and the solution-focused one. From the sociopolitical point of view, there is inequality in the society we live in and men have more power than women. That is true, and we should all continue to work to correct that. From the solution-focused, clinical point of view, I am guided by certain theoretical assumptions about everyone's unique reality and people's inherent strengths and resources. When a man and a woman come into my office and say they want to try to work out how to stay together even though violence has occurred in their relationship, I put on my clinician's hat and let my theoretical orientation guide me. If I were to put on the sociopolitical hat, I could only do individual therapy with the men and women, but that is not what they are asking for, nor is that what always works best* (Sirles, Lipchik, & Kowalski, 1992).

Tony: I agree. More than four thousand men who have been arrested for hitting their partners have taken part in my batterers groups for six months at a time, and I have come to the conclusion that there is no such thing as a generic batterer. I can no longer agree with the assumption that all men are alike, that they are all patriarchal oppressors, and that once a man has used violence against women he is the same as all other men. There are so many degrees of violence, so many different dynamics that go on between men and women. There are as many variables between people as there are people (Cantos, Neidig, & O'Leary, 1994; O'Leary, 1993; Rosenbaum & O'Leary, 1981). So, I can also no longer make a blanket statement that it is never safe to see some men and some women together in treatment as couples.

On the other hand, we should not ignore other arguments against safety, such as that batterers are also said to be two-faced. They will be pleasant during the session but then take it out on their partner afterward.

Eve: *That statement puts a universal label on batterers again and makes a presupposition about them. It ignores the fact that they are unique individuals.*

Tony: Yes, but anyone who would go so far as to actually strike his spouse may be capable of pretty outlandish behavior, in general. That is a betrayal of a high degree, and if a man can go that far, it would not be a big deal for him to come into a therapy session and act like a nice guy and then turn around and abuse his partner.

Eve: *True, but how do you think clients will respond to a therapist who is distrustful of their story and takes a skeptical or judgmental stance toward them?*

Tony: With defensiveness. I find the blending of therapy and domestic violence advocacy one of the greatest challenges in our work. For example, it is common for people in the domestic violence field to generalize that all batterers use denial and minimization. I have come to realize that as therapists, or as people who in any capacity try to help or control, how we approach clients creates an atmosphere that cultivates deceit or cooperation. In other words, my attitudes and intentions are instrumental in co-creating clinical outcomes. Since our culture demands punishment for guilt, a therapist can predispose clients to defensiveness by seeing them through a judgmental lens. I am encouraged by the openness and candor I often receive from clients after I use nonjudgmental (strength-searching rather than fault-finding) questions. For example, instead of asking, "Did you use any controlling behavior toward your wife this week?" I ask, "What are some ways that you collaborated with your wife on a decision this week?" I find that my expectation of positive change seems to encourage more of it.

Another safety issue is that batterers are believed to be sociopaths who can manipulate therapists into blaming the victim for "her part in the violence."

Eve: *What is generally described as a sociopathic personality would not be appropriate for couples treatment with solution-focused therapy whether there has been violence or not. In solution-focused therapy we do not see couples together when one person does not seem to have the capacity to take responsibility for his or her own behavior. This could also mean they are the type of person who has no capacity for empathy, who blames others for everything that happens in their life. This suggests they are poorly equipped to have a mutually satisfying relationship to begin with. Solution-focused therapists have always known that one cannot construct solutions with two people when one person says things are fine the way they are and/or that it's the other person who has to change. In those situations we suggest individual sessions. More often than not, the one who feels that he or she does not have a problem won't want to come in at all. Research findings are now providing typologies of batterers and their partners that are going to make the decision about appropriateness for couples treatment much easier and safer (Holzworth-Munroe & Stuart, 1994; O'Leary, Malone, & Tyree, 1994; Jacobson et al., 1994; Pan, Neidig, & O'Leary, 1994). While categorizing people is inconsistent with solution-focused thinking, the solution-focused assessment for seeing a couple together or separately correlates with these typologies.*

Tony: Another point frequently raised about couples treatment is that batterers cannot control their emotions and are therefore a safety hazard for the therapist.

Eve: *I must say that that has never been a problem for me in all the years I have worked in this area. When you treat people respectfully and listen to them, they do not attack you, no matter who they are.*

Tony: I feel the same way. In ten years I have never had a man who has battered attack me. But I have had some get up and get louder and more animated. I don't see that as a danger as long as I stay calm and don't escalate the tension by my behavior.

Here is another concern, though. Won't batterers use couples counseling as a way to keep their victims in an unsafe relationship, whereas a good domestic violence advocacy program may empower women to leave?

Eve: *In the first place, I don't believe that therapists or advocates have the power to make clients do anything they don't want to do. My work in shelters has convinced me of that. How many times have I worked with a shelter staff member who is devastated because she found out that a woman she spent hours with, and who seemed to be empowered, went back to her partner?*

The other piece of your statement implies that couples counseling will keep the unsafe relationship going. I think a safety feature of solution-focused therapy is that the therapist has no stake in either preserving the relationship or ending it. The relationship is a creation of the people who are in it, and they are each responsible for the actions and decisions they make in regard to it. So, one can actually think of the relationship, RATHER THAN THE PEOPLE WHO ARE IN IT, being the client. I think of myself as collaborating with the individual partners for the benefit of their relationship. I talk to them about that. For example, when they are talking about defensive behavior when they have conflict, I might ask them, "What choices do you have in this situation and which one do you think would be best for the relationship in the long run?" I try to help them recognize that if they make choices for themselves only, without also considering the effect on the relationship, those choices will not benefit them in the long run.

Couples have to decide separately and together whether the relationship can work for both of them. Helping a couple to make the decision to separate in a constructive manner is a major safety feature when one considers how many couples keep getting back together, again and again, without anything having changed in their interactional dynamics.

When couples seem to be stuck between wanting to be together but not knowing how to move ahead constructively, we suggest they work separately until they are clearer about a direction. Here is an example of the type of letter we send couples in this situation:

Dear Mary and Pat:

After careful consideration and consultation with each other about what we heard and observed in your joint and separate sessions so far, we would like to make the following recommendation.

Since both of you would rather save the relationship than lose it, we believe further therapy is necessary. However, given the anger and pain both of you are experiencing at present, and the fact that there is a realistic concern about emotional and physical safety, we recommend individual sessions for both of you rather than conjoint sessions. The more you each understand yourself and what you need and expect from a relationship, the more potential there is for a mutually satisfying relationship in the future.

We further suggest that Pat continue to see Tony individually and Mary consider seeing Eve, or someone else at our agency, so that we can keep evaluating individual progress, as well as the possibility for further conjoint sessions. We would understand, however, if one or both of you would like to make a different choice for your individual therapy.

Please think about this and let us know what your decision is.

Tony: Actually, research now shows that the most dangerous time for the woman
is not when she is living with the man but when she is leaving or has left the
relationship (U.S. Department of Justice, 1983).

Eve: *Here again, I feel that solution-focused therapy has a good chance of avoiding danger. The
goal in treatment, provided that the couple is appropriate for treatment, is for both of them
to be satisfied staying together or for both to accept separation. When they decide to split,
it should be because they have both come to realize that that is a better solution than
staying together. If the issue of whether or not to stay together arises during treatment,
we immediately begin to see them separately until they have a common goal again. Then,
if the woman decides to leave, the man is still joined with a therapist for support. That is
very different than when a man who is already prone to violence gets violent when the
woman leaves him when he does not think the relationship has had a fair chance. He may
think a therapist he does not know is encouraging her to leave. If he is part of the whole
discussion with an unblaming therapist, this danger will not be there.*

Tony: I do think that men who are afraid of losing their partners may use couples
counseling to keep the woman in the relationship. Particularly during the
"honeymoon stage," after he has been violent and wants to show how sincere he is about changing. But I don't see that as a bad thing. It is possible
that this is one of the major junctures at which one or both members of a
hurting relationship are most likely to be willing to seek outside help.

Overall, most women do not call the police, most do not go to a shelter, and most do not contact a batterers program. Furthermore, most therapists do not assess for or recognize domestic violence, or know how to
address it once it is recognized. Aldorondo and Straus (1994, p. 425) point
out that "over two thirds of clients in family therapy clinics have experienced
some form of physical violence against their partner within the year prior
to the initiation of therapy," so it is up to all therapists who work with couples to learn how to make it safe for clients to talk about emotional and physical abuse in their relationship. My goal is to maximize the benefit of that
window of opportunity. In fact, advocating to split some couples at that point
may be even more dangerous. O'Leary and Curley (1986) indicate that
women are safer if they get assertiveness training with the batterer in the
session, too.

I have come to believe that no one type of treatment can totally eliminate all future acts of violence. There may never be such a thing. When people ask me about the results of my program, I say it's a "take-home exam."
I don't get to grade the papers. I can try calling and getting evaluations filled
out, but realistically, recidivism of most types of abuse is difficult to measure
in any meaningful manner. However, I too have seen small changes disrupt

patterns that could have built up to an explosive incident. Small changes can actually bring about results. And a small change can lead to bigger ones.

Case Example 1: Staying Joined with Both Partners as a Way of Providing Safety

Tom, a successful business man in a managerial position, has been violent a number of times with Millie, a part-time nurse. Millie has never called the police because she does not want to jeopardize Tom's position at work and in the community and because, as she put it, "I am afraid he would kill me." They have been married about ten years and have two children, ages eight and six. This dialogue occurred in the fifth session, about two months after they were initially seen. (There had been no further reports of physical violence.)

At the start of the session, both partners said there had been improvement overall in meeting each other's needs and being closer. When the therapist tried to build on this, Millie replied that even though things were getting better, she was still afraid of the extreme sporadic blowups. She added, looking at Tom, "There was an incident this week, but I'm not supposed to talk about it." Tom then told a story about how Millie had made a decision about their garden that Tom disagreed with. He recounted what happened in a verbally abusive manner, calling Millie "stupid" and "idiotic."

Confrontation at this point would have shamed Tom and he might have chosen not to come back to therapy. This could have put Millie in great danger. But ethically, this behavior must be addressed because not doing so indirectly condones it and may make the victim feel unsupported. The solution-focused therapist must find a way to deal with this situation in a manner that allows him or her to stay joined with both partners.

In this example, the therapist found an opportune time when Millie and Tom resumed arguing about Millie's decision later in the session. Tom accused her of never admitting that she could be wrong. The therapist asked Tom how he lets Millie know when he feels he has made a mistake. This put Tom in a bind. He mumbled a little and said, "I would say, 'Maybe I acted too quickly or should have made another decision.'" Millie jumped in with, "He never admits he's wrong." The therapist's response was to ask Millie how she would react to Tom if she thought he had made a wrong decision. She answered that she wouldn't put him down and call him names that would only make him feel worse, but would ask him how he made his decision. Tom blushed at this point and was quiet for a moment. He attempted defensiveness again:

Tom: But, she doesn't listen to me, she's so busy defending herself she couldn't care less what I say.

Millie: He insults me right away.

Tom: You're insulting me by not listening.

The therapist joined them by drawing a parallel between feelings and needs.

Therapist: Tom, you are saying you don't want to be insulted by not being listened to. Millie, you are saying you don't want to be insulted by being called names. It sounds like both of you are wanting the same thing: not to be hurt by the other. What options do you have at times like that other than just hurting back?

It is difficult, if not impossible, to determine the outcome of a particular intervention. Yet, in the sessions that followed, Millie did not accuse Tom of further verbal abuse. (Later developments in the case are illustrated in Case Example 3.) This case exemplifies the importance of the therapist's staying joined with both partners to ensure continued safety and openness to possibilities for a better future.

Ethics

Tony: A major argument against couples counseling is that it is unethical because seeing the abused spouse together with the batterer connotes equal responsibility.

Eve: Relationships are the product of people in interaction. Their relationship belongs to both of them. But that doesn't mean that one partner is to blame for the other partner's violence.

Tony: Yes. Each person is responsible for how they choose to act. At no time is one person responsible for the other's behavior. In intimate relationships, people have a lot of influence on each other, but they still have individual choice.

Another argument against couples counseling is that it is unethical because domestic violence is a crime. Thus, conducting couples counseling is tantamount to aiding and abetting a criminal.

Eve: I have a difficult time with this argument since I believe couples counseling can offer a viable rehabilitation sooner than other options for certain cases.

Tony: But a common argument is that since domestic violence couples often have restraining orders, it is unethical to see them together.

Eve: Probation and parole cases I have seen usually get permission from their officer to go to couples counseling if they express the desire to stay together and work on their relationship. In my experience, probation and parole officers tend to believe that the best solution for abuse in relationships is for the couple to get help together. They say that except in very extreme cases in which the men are sociopathic, both partners need to do something different in the relationship.

Tony: The field is changing when it comes to restraining orders. Probation and parole officers, judges, and advocates are recognizing that restraining orders often don't work. They are moving more and more toward what is called a "no violence contact order." You can have contact and live together, but you can't have any violence.

Eve: *You just forbid the violence and then there isn't any?*

Tony: They are no longer thinking that they can separate the couple by a court order. Actually, we can think of our work with couples as helping with the no-violence portion of the no violence contact order. Even the coordinated community response has seen fit to make exceptions. What I often hear in conversations with people in the criminal justice system is that they believe at least three quarters of couples with restraining orders are living together anyway.

Eve: *Now that really doesn't make any sense to me unless they encourage some safe form of treatment to improve the relationship while the couple is living together.*

Tony: Part of me is still wrestling with the argument that couples counseling encourages cohabitation and women would be safer living separately.

Eve: *Solution-focused couples counseling does not aim to encourage or discourage. It tries to help people decide what is best for them individually and together. Couples are going to make their own decisions about how to live. We don't have any influence over that. My argument is that if they are going to live together anyway, let us try to help them do that more peacefully.*

Case Example 2: Working with Couples to Protect the Battered Woman When She and Her Partner Do Not Have the Same Goals

Sylvia and Frank are an attractive, unmarried couple in their mid thirties. Both were married previously and have children from their earlier relationships. They lived together for two years during which Frank was physically and verbally abusive. Sylvia took the initiative to move out and end their relationship six months prior to the initiation of counseling. Since then there had been a gradual resumption of contact. Frank was attending Tony's batterers group and Sylvia was seeing a therapist individually. At Frank's suggestion, Sylvia came for couples treatment to see if they could start over and build a good relationship, now that he was learning about anger management and personal responsibility.

It was apparent from the first session that Sylvia was reluctant about a possible reconciliation at that time, even though she admitted that Frank's behavior had changed drastically, and she indicated that she might want to consider a future together. Frank, conversely, was pushing for reconciliation while trying to appear sensitive to Sylvia.

This dialogue is from the second conjoint session. The separate sessions with this couple established that Sylvia was not afraid of any physical violence, that Frank was not being verbally abusive, and that Sylvia was ambivalent about the future but willing to keep talking about improving the relationship. We decided on one more conjoint session, since Sylvia seemed to be ambivalent but was not in danger.

The couple was talking about their relationship issues when Frank suddenly said:

Frank: What I would like to talk about next time we meet is Jimmy [*Sylvia's sixteen-year-old son*]. What can I do as his stepparent? Should I urge him to get a job, go to college? If we're going to get this family together, what role do I play? What can I expect?

Therapist: Yes, I see. I'm just a bit confused. My understanding is that we were going to focus on getting your relationship on a good track first.

Sylvia: Yes, Frank. We have other things to talk about first.

Frank: [*Persisting*] Sylvia has told me she may consider moving back in after this semester. I think this is of the essence. I have no problem with Sam [*the younger child*], but with Jimmy. He is sixteen, he's a pretty good boy, but there are a lot of things going on right now. We can't avoid this issue. For example, she doesn't want to go to dinner with me because, as she puts it, "I have another boy at home." This has a lot to do with our relationship.

Therapist: So, Frank, you are saying you need to talk about the choices Sylvia makes about being a mother and being your partner. What do you think about that, Sylvia?

Sylvia: We need to talk about us, you and me.

Frank: If, say, for instance, she didn't have to go home to feed Jimmy, she'd move back in with me now, I know.

Therapist: [*To Sylvia*] Is that right?

Sylvia: No. [*To Frank*] You're pressuring me.

Frank: [*To therapist*] I will probably get another roommate if she doesn't move back in. I don't mean to put pressure on her but I have to take care of my bills. I'm just trying to correct what I have power over and I'm doing a good job. So is Sylvia.

Sylvia: I feel he's threatening me.

Therapist: How do you think that will affect working on your relationship?

Sylvia: I don't know. I just feel it as a threat.

Therapist: How could Frank talk to you about this without making you feel threatened?

Sylvia: I don't know. I guess the whole thing of it is Frank depends on other people for money. I think he should depend on himself. He could get a part-time job and then he could cover the rent. He always asks for help financially. He wants me back so I can help him with the bills.

Frank: That's not true. I love you.

Sylvia: I don't want to go to Frank's place and have a stranger there and spend the night or have the kids there with me.

Frank: Are you saying if I get a roommate you won't stay overnight with me?

Sylvia: Yes.

Frank: Well, that would end our relationship.

Sylvia: See, that is how he pressures me.

Therapist: It seems that both of you have some choices about how to solve the financial problems, how to decide what to consider pressure or not.

Sylvia: He's rejecting me for someone else's money.

Frank: I see Jimmy as the stumbling block here, how I should react to Jimmy in our family structure. When he calls his mother names, what should I do?

Sylvia: That is not the issue.

Therapist: Sylvia, do you want to discuss this?

Sylvia: No, absolutely not.

Therapist: I feel caught in the middle. I want to respect what both of you want. I don't know in which direction to go without upsetting the other.

Sylvia: Why should I discuss Jimmy? You're talking about a roommate moving in.

This second conjoint session clearly demonstrates a lack of mutual goals, with Frank trying to pressure Sylvia into doing what he wants her to do and Sylvia trying to assert herself against it. In the summation message at the end of the session, the therapists agreed to affirm both partners' needs and goals and to reflect the view that they seem to have different time frames for what they both want from therapy right now. We suggested they take a break from couples treatment for a while until they could find themselves in synch again. Frank could continue in the batterers group with Tony, and Sylvia could continue her individual sessions. Frank became very angry at this suggestion and the therapists, in an attempt to model compromise for him, agreed to meet conjointly once a month to evaluate readiness for working on mutually agreed upon issues. Sylvia liked this suggestion very much. Frank agreed, but seemed reluctant. He cancelled their conjoint session a month later and proudly told Tony at the batterers group that Sylvia was moving back in with him. For a while he reported that things were totally changed and that they were doing wonderfully, as though to prove us wrong, but eventually they broke up again and Frank began to see another woman. There were no further reports of violence. Frank signed up for another six months in the batterers group because he said it taught him a lot about relationships.

It would not have been ethical to continue to see this couple together given Frank's attempts to pressure Sylvia to do what he wanted. Since she was seeing a therapist and reported no violence, safety was not an immediate concern. Had this couple been in a violent situation, we would have become advocates for both of them. We would have advocated for Sylvia to see someone on her own, and worked out a safety plan for her. We would also have advocated for Frank to go to a group, or to see Tony individually.

Tony: Another issue in the area of ethics is that some people believe that therapists in private practice, whose income is dependent upon payment from clients or insurance, won't hold batterers accountable as nonprofit workers would.

Eve: It is totally unethical to think of profit rather than outcome for clients. I guess there are always some unethical people in all professions. Some therapists even sexually abuse their clients.

Tony: Well, given the evidence about the prevalence of abuse among couples who seek family therapy (Aldorondo & Straus, 1994), I think there should be some standards for family therapists regarding domestic violence. Our inclusion criteria seem like a good start.

Eve: *Yes, but of course there will never be a surefire assessment for who is going to be violent and who will not be. Of course, if we believe a man is homicidal we must do everything we can to separate him from his wife and children. But we cannot control whether or not they live in the same house together. That is their business or the business of the judicial system. What is important about couples treatment from the ethical point of view is to have some standards for judging when it is appropriate and when it is not.*

Our conceptualization about appropriateness for couples work is based on the following points:

1. *Intensity and chronicity of abuse.* Early intervention is best. Couples in which there is less frequent and intense violence are usually more appropriate.
2. *Quality of relationship.* Both partners must be able to give some concrete examples of what they appreciate about each other and about their relationship. There should be some evidence of the capacity for empathy and mutuality.
3. *Mental status.* Clients who manifest signs of possible neurological or psychological impairment should be further evaluated before being assessed appropriate for couples counseling.
4. *Alcohol or Drug Abuse (AODA).* We try to ascertain whether drug or alcohol consumption precedes abusive or violent behavior. If the relationship is judged mutually satisfying and free of abuse except after substances are used, assessment for AODA treatment is indicated.
5. *Previous interventions.* We find out what has worked, or not worked, for this couple in past attempts to improve their relationship, including any professional interventions.
6. *Clients' goals.* Both partners must agree that

    They want no further violence.

    They want to preserve the relationship.

    There is one issue they will begin working on.

    They will do something different, not only expect the other to change.

Personal Responsibility

Tony: Another point frequently made is that if a battered woman is honest in couples treatment, it will serve as ammunition for the man to blame her and shirk his responsibility.

Eve: I have two responses: (1) a good solution-focused therapist would not allow that to hap-
pen; and (2) a good solution-focused therapist would be interested in both parties con-
tributing to change. If the couple is not constructing a solution but discovering increasing
differences they cannot resolve, they should be seen separately to talk that through. For cou-
ples therapy to continue to be warranted, there has to be movement toward new ways of
being together that satisfy both partners.

Tony: I have come to realize that there is a sanctity to relationships. They have a
life of their own that other people cannot understand. It seems logical that
people should split when they don't get along, but it isn't an either/or thing.
Bad relationships have good aspects to them, too. It takes a skilled person
either to relieve the relationship of its burdens so it can go on or to find a
way to help end it constructively.

What about the complaint that systemic therapy just confirms what the
batterers are saying all along—it takes two to tango?

Eve: That is true. It takes two people to have a relationship. That does not absolve the man
who batters from how he chooses to behave toward his partner.

Tony: Well, I have found that it is good to go along with the colloquialisms that
group members use. So, rather than argue, what I have said over the years
is, yes, it takes two to tango, but just one to change the dance.

Eve: So, you are saying that the man alone is responsible for the changes?

Tony: Yes and no. He is responsible for stopping his violence. The locus of responsibility is clearly on him and not on her, but there are other patterns
in the relationship that both partners have to be willing to work on.

Case Example 3: Dealing with a Partner Who Is Avoiding Responsibility

In the fourth session with Tom and Millie (introduced in Case Study 1), Tom described
what he called "the heart of the matter of their relationship." When he and Millie have
differences of opinion, he wants to talk about it at a later time, and she pursues him
to address it right away. This makes him lose control of his temper. The incident they
discussed in this session is what precipitated their call for therapy.

Tom had been exercising with the kids in the family room. They invited Millie to
join them and she refused. When the children started to tease her about not exercising
and being fat, Tom joined with them instead of telling the children not to tease their
mother. Millie asked Tom to step into another room with her so she could talk to him
about this, and he refused. Tom said he was not going to allow her to "scold" him.

Millie: I just wanted to tell him how I feel.

Tom: And I think I should have the opportunity to tell you I don't want to talk about
it at that point in time, but you stick to the point regardless of what I say.

Millie: Sometimes I can't back off. There are times I feel it is imperative that I explain my position, and that doesn't mean I'm going to get into a verbal war with you.

Therapist: Are you saying you just want to express your opinion rather than to scold him?

Millie: Yes.

Tom: Well, that's her opinion that it isn't a scolding. I think in light of why we are here [the violence], she should be more yielding, and when I ask her not to talk about it she should do that; it's not forever. She should respect that and bring it up at a different time.

Therapist: Tom, are you saying that you need this from Millie in order not to get violent?

Tom: I'm asking for a time out and she wants to do whatever she wants to do, damn my need; I think that this is pretty unyielding.

Therapist: Millie, what are you thinking about what Tom is saying?

Millie: It's always the same story—I should consider him—but there are times when I have to discuss what I have to discuss, at that time, and then he should yield to me.

Tom: Yes, if it is a matter of health or safety, I can see it. We've had this discussion a lot of times before. I ask you to back off and you pursue and want to make a point.

Millie: I don't see why you got violent that time.

Tom: Because there was no reason for you to make an issue out of something that was not an issue.

Millie: I thought it was a big issue.

Therapist: You are two different people and always will be—both of you have the right to your opinions, this is not a matter of right or wrong. We also cannot undo the past. Let's imagine for a moment that a similar situation comes up in the future when both of you feel very strongly that you are right and don't want to yield to the other, and those situations will come again. What can you do differently in the future?

When the couple continued to argue about the past and Tom insisted that Millie should not have been bothered about this incident, the therapist said:

Therapist: It is up to her to decide what bothers her and for you to decide what bothers you. But at those times when you are both bothered, how can you resolve it so you respect the differences?

At this point, Tom tried to divert by talking about how stressed he was at work at that time and that Millie should have known that and backed off at that particular time. Millie defended herself by saying she was aware of that and that is why she took the children out of the house all afternoon, so he could rest.

Tom: You didn't care at all that this was the first time in six days that I was re-
            laxing with the kids, you just had to have your way.

Therapist: [*Going back to Tom's earlier statement that he expected a scolding*] How can
            Millie ask for your attention at times like this in the future without you feel-
            ing scolded?

Tom: Maybe she could say what she has to say without dragging me into another
            room.

Millie: You are assuming you will be scolded. I don't want to scold you—just tell
            you what I think, and you don't want to listen.

Therapist: It sounds to me like both of you are saying you feel a lack of respect from
            the other. Millie doesn't feel respect for her need to express herself and Tom
            doesn't feel respect for his need to have some time out first. You both de-
            serve that respect. How can you learn to communicate at those times so
            you can respect the other without feeling put down?

Tom: I asked her to stop first.

Therapist: How will you make a decision in the future about whose needs are stronger
            at any point?

Both Tom and Millie looked perplexed.

Therapist: Are there times when you do that already?

Millie: Yes.

Therapist: What's different at those times?

Millie: One or the other doesn't feel so strongly about it.

Tom: This has always been a problem for us. We're at the heart of the matter here.
            [*Tom stops being defensive.*] Maybe I'm being too stubborn and one sided but
            when I ask her to back off, if she just would, there wouldn't be a problem.

Millie: There are times when I do that, but there are times when something is very
            important to me and he has to respect my needs, too.

Therapist: Absolutely. You should respect each other's needs.

Tom: [*Softening*] But how do you resolve conflict with all the emotion?

Therapist: Maybe the question isn't how to do it, but *whether* to?

Tom: What do you mean?

Therapist: Sometimes when people decide they want to do that, the "how" becomes
            easier.

This led to a discussion about how one has a choice about how to react to another person. Tom recognized that in situations like this he would have to take the
time to think about how to react before he let his emotions run away with him. In the
next few sessions, choosing how to react so that it benefits the relationship rather than
satisfies an emotional need of the moment became a theme that seemed to make a
big difference in Tom's behavior toward Millie. He began to take responsibility for his
choices rather than blaming Millie for not taking care of him.

Advocacy Versus Therapy

Tony: Another argument against couples treatment is that if insurance is used, the batterer will be given a diagnosis that supports medical need, and that will serve as an excuse for the batterer's behavior. It will make a medical problem out of a behavioral one.

Eve: *Since solution-focused therapy, like all the constructivist therapies, is not pathology oriented, theoretically this would not happen. However, all of us who take third-party payments have to conform with their regulation to give a diagnosis. In our approach, we usually discuss the diagnosis with clients and choose one that is congruent with the problem, like "impulse control disorder." In the therapy process itself, we treat each situation as unique, and we talk in terms of solutions rather than disorders.*

Tony: Do you think family therapists are willing to be held accountable to the courts, to report recidivism and missed meetings, and to have probation revoked for repeated acts of violence?

Eve: *The issue of therapy versus social control is a central one to this whole controversy of how to intervene in domestic violence. As part of a coordinated community response, therapists should provide another opportunity for change that is different from what probation officers and police officers have to offer. Therapy should help people rethink their choices. It requires a trusting relationship to be effective. Probation is a position of control and threat, a punitive stance. Both may be necessary, especially if one approach does not work alone. But as a therapist, I know that when people feel threatened, guilty or not, they use all their energy to defend themselves. In solution-focused therapy we believe that if you treat people with respect, regardless who they are, and listen to their story in an accepting manner, they will be more honest with themselves and take responsibility sooner.*

    In terms of reporting to probation officers, it would be nice if the therapist could be free of that obligation, but it is not realistic. Sometimes we have the obligation to report. My suggestion is to say to the person who battered, "Look, I have to report this, but I want to continue to see you and work with you." I suggest they report themselves. Many therapists say that if there is any recidivism, they stop therapy. Who is being punished by that attitude?

Tony: So, you are actually saying the model has to make room for advocacy?

Eve: *Yes,* under certain circumstances, *such as life threatening ones. We have to be flexible about theoretical purity. In solution-focused work with domestic violence, the first compromise I make is to refrain from asking why they have come and what they are hoping for. Instead, I ask the man whether he wants to stop being physically and emotionally abusive and the woman whether she wants him to stop. If he has any reservations about stopping totally or she is not emphatic about wanting it to stop, we won't go any further to treat their relationship. I cannot accept a man's belief that he has the right to be violent. I cannot accept a woman's belief that she deserves to be hit. Another compromise is that I will become an advocate for a woman who is afraid to go home with a man after they have begun fighting in a session. However, after doing that, I will advocate for the man to remain safe from his anger, as well.*

Tony: Another argument against conjoint treatment is that men will use a belief in male superiority to attempt to have a sense of control during the session.

Eve: *I actually think that is grist for the mill in solution-focused therapy because we accept both partners' realities and try to bridge them. This type of situation is addressed in a nonshaming, nonconfrontive manner so the therapist can stay joined with the man but offer him a different perspective at the same time* [see Case Example 3].

Tony: What about the idea that the batterer will use male bonding to enlist a male therapist into collusive abuse of his victim?

Eve: *That will not happen to a good solution-focused therapist who sees his job as joining with both partners. Aside from that, working with one therapist behind the mirror is a great safety feature for this. It helps maintain boundaries.*

Tony: This point is an important one. The issue of male bonding is a potential pitfall. That is why a male therapist will have to have insight into his own beliefs about male superiority, and about any way that he has been taught to have privilege in his life.

I encourage anyone who works with domestic violence to do three examinations. The first item to examine is intent: what is my intent when I discover that the person before me has been physically violent toward a spouse or partner, or has been abused by a loved one? The next item is attitude: what is my attitude toward each of these people? And the third item is my own experience of being abused and of being abusive in both my family of origin and in adult relationships. It is essential to ask oneself these three questions, to bring an answer into awareness, and to be willing to examine them with colleagues and supervisors. Without personal insight, one runs the risk of subliminally forcing one's own agenda onto others. Balance helps therapists to suspend prejudices and presuppositions long enough to really hear what the clients are saying.

Eve: *Women have to be aware of their preconceptions and intentions as well. If the woman automatically sides with the victim and is against the batterer, this also will not be useful in working with the relationship.*

Tony: Many people believe that victims get set up for more violence when they trust the therapist to protect them. They then risk saying things in front of the batterer that he will later use to fuel his rage against her and beat her.

Eve: *That's a valid point. Solution-focused therapy is present and future oriented. The therapist keeps questions focused on the future. He or she will remind clients that they cannot change the past, they can only do something different in the future. He or she will separate a couple that cannot stop ventilating anger about the past.*

Tony: This point continues to be a concern for me and is a particularly important awareness for anyone working with domestic violence. I know that people often ascribe more power to therapists than they actually have, such as believing the therapist can "fix" them or "tell them what to do." But then you see a tragic case like one we recently had here in Milwaukee, where police, advocates, restraining orders, and bodyguards did not protect a woman from being murdered by her estranged partner—right in the courthouse. I believe we all must be humbled regarding our abilities to protect one spouse from another. Yet, we don't give up trying. Since couples who have experienced domestic violence are seeking out family therapists, family therapists must keep trying to develop safer and more effective models of remediation. I see our blending of solution-focused therapy and domestic violence advocacy as serving that need.

Eve: *Yes, there is no guarantee ever, regardless of whether they get help or not, or regardless of what approach is used.*

Tony: What about the argument that a therapy model like SFBT gives false hope that small changes will endure. Isn't more severe violence likely after keeping the lid on for a while?

Eve: *This represents a misunderstanding of the approach. The goal of therapy is not small changes. The goal in working with couples who have experienced domestic violence and who are considered appropriate for this treatment is first to stop the physical and emotional abuse. Second, the goal is to deal with whatever relationship issues they feel are important to address. They are asked to describe progress toward these goals in small, concrete behavioral steps so they can experience success and so the success is easy to track. It is hard to track changes in feelings. One of the basic assumptions of the solution-focused approach is that a small change can lead to bigger changes. This is one reason that I believe this type of couples work would be so important as an early intervention. There is research that indicates that small acts of aggression increase toward more extreme violence. Emotional abuse grows into physical abuse* (Murphy & O'Leary, 1989; Pan, Neidig, & O'Leary, 1994).

Tony: Solution-focused therapy suggests that the clients should establish their own goals. Do you think you can allow people to establish their own goals when there may be a life in danger or goals set by the courts?

Eve: *That is a good point. But the goals we are talking about are around relationship issues after both partners have declared their desire to have a relationship free of physical and emotional abuse. Courts set goals to have clients go to therapy, or for them not to have contact.*

Tony: And this has been an important point for me in agreeing to do domestic violence couples work with you. I found that after ten years in a social change advocacy role that it was hard for me to feel comfortable without a level of advocacy included in the work. We have integrated therapy and advocacy quite well. We agree with the referral sources that we will notify them about the client's involvement in our program. We agree to a minimum of six months of not only counseling but also accountability to the community. We have become a part of a coordinated community response.

Eve: *One of the ways I think we deal with the therapy versus advocacy issue is the structure we have established to see the couple together first and then to see them separately.*

Power Imbalances

Tony: I have heard that once a woman has been betrayed by battering, she can't trust anything that comes out of conjoint sessions.

Eve: *A battered woman needs a long time to develop trust, but I am not sure I understand what part the conjoint session plays in that. I can only see it as an advantage if both partners are asked to work on a different future in which both get their needs met. If a woman and her partner are asking for some help to see if their relationship can be improved, we owe them the respect to try to see if that is possible. Since couples tend to stay together, imagine how horrible it could be for the woman to stay without trust, and not have the hope for change that solution-focused therapy offers. We have to make it clear that it will take a long time to build trust, but that is why we say that treatment will take at least six months, even if it is not every week but every few weeks or more.*

You are aware, as I am, that there is a certain pattern with couples who really are invested in staying together. At first there is hope and change, and then it usually plateaus after four or five sessions, after which they report tension and more arguing. What that tends to be about is that the man is trying very hard but the woman is still fearful and not trusting. The therapist then has to work with the man and woman around that issue. What does he need to be patient and to allow her time to build trust? What does she need as added evidence of safety, if anything?

Tony: I always warn men in groups who are attempting to eliminate their physically and emotionally abusive behavior that things may get worse before they get better. After an act of violence toward a loved one, forgiveness and trust must occur. Forgiveness and trust are not an event but a process that has stages that will be very difficult for the abuser to accept. These stages include:

1. *Disbelief:* "I've heard this remorse, promise, and so on before."
2. *Testing:* "I wonder if it's real?"
3. *Ventilating:* The partner starts to say and do things she was afraid to do before.

A common argument against couples treatment is that a batterer exercises power over the woman at all times. She'll never get a fair chance during therapy.

Eve: *Here we are dealing with generalities again. There are studies that suggest that men use violence because they are in a relationship with a woman they perceive as holding more power* (Babcock, Waltz, Jacobson, & Gottman, 1993; O'Leary & Curley, 1986; Rosenbaum & O'Leary, 1981).

Solution-focused therapists work very hard not to take sides and to help both partners to get their needs met. In the case of Tom and Millie, I had the opportunity to speak to her about a year and a half after they terminated treatment. She told me that things were going very well and that verbal and physical abuse is a thing of the past. I asked what she believed was the most helpful thing in therapy. She answered without hesitation that it was the fact that I never took sides with either one of them, even though they both tried to get me to do so. It appears that this was helpful because they both trusted me and it helped them to consider what the other person was saying. This would indicate that a therapist who is perceived to be on either partner's side would be met with anger and distrust by the other partner.

The other point is that nobody exerts power over someone totally except when they are holding a gun to them or have beaten them into unconsciousness. I believe there is a continuum of power imbalance just as there is a continuum of violence. While no violence is acceptable, each couple has their own power balance and that is OK as long as neither feels constrained or intimidated. Some couples alternate being powerful in different situations.

Tony: There is power other than just physical power. This is often said in relation to racial issues. There is a power imbalance between black and white society, but a black person can be prejudiced but not a racist. Only a white person can be a racist because you have to have power and be prejudiced to be a racist. The same thing applies to women and men in society. This power imbalance is a very important issue.

Eve: *It definitely needs consideration, but the context of all that depends on the particular couple—how these issues affect a particular couple is important, you can't generalize that it is a problem for every couple.*

Tony: This issue of power also does not exclude couples from couples counseling, from my point of view. Power too often is talked about as if it is all or nothing. Relationships have many levels. On each level the balance of power is different and often shifts. Relationships are very complex. What is balance for one couple is out of balance for another. I think it is important for people who are in the position of power not to use their power to control others—and that goes for therapists and domestic violence advocates as well. We must not foist our solutions on our clients.

Eve: *Power and control have a totally negative connotation in the field of domestic violence. A good balance between power and control for both partners can be thought of as positive for a relationship. However, each couple has their own definition of what constitutes a good balance for them. Rachel Hare-Mustin and Jeanne Marecek (1990) elegantly address the whole issue of gender and power issues in therapy. They recognize that neither exaggerating differences between men and women (which they call "alpha bias") or minimizing them ("beta bias") is a solution for women or men. They delineate how both approaches have the potential of inadvertently perpetuating stereotypical and restrictive roles and fostering further polarization between men and women. Duncan, Solovey, and Rusk (1992) suggest that to avoid alpha and beta bias, therapists should assume that the client is the ultimate judge of what is right. While gender sensitivity is critical, placing gender theory above the client's unique frame of reference is antithetical to empathy and respect. A solution is to evaluate whether gender difference seems relevant to clients by offering it for consideration. This may lead to a cogeneration of new directions, or it may fade away as irrelevant if the client indicates that it is not meaningful to pursue* (Duncan et al., 1992). *This way of thinking is truly congruent with the solution-focused approach.*

Tony: What do you think about the belief that since the victim is usually more willing to work for change than the perpetrator, family therapists often put a greater burden on her, leaving him in the power position again, free not to change?

Eve: Once again, I think the solution-focused approach eliminates that argument. Both parties have to agree that they are willing to take responsibility for looking at their relationship and what they can each do to become more sensitive to each other's needs.

Tony: That is one of the things I really like about this model—the balancing.

Eve: Yes, we are not condoning violence or psychological control when we talk with a couple about contributions to their relationship.

Tony: But I have heard the argument that a therapist might become frustrated by a woman's greater demand for change. Women, in general, may be more articulate about relationship issues and seem to think more about them. This may lead the therapist to think the woman is the problem.

Eve: It has not been my experience that women demand more change than men, generally. This is a generalization again. This goes back to therapists needing to be clear about how they feel about issues of domestic violence, victims, and perpetrators. A solution-focused therapist will not be thinking about who is causing the problem with demands, but will focus on the future and the possibilities for a better relationship.

Tony: Many argue that batterers use their intimidation skills to co-opt the therapist into working on changing the woman.

Eve: That is unlikely to happen in a therapeutic approach in which the therapist does not take sides in the first place.

Tony: Well, I have come to the conclusion that there isn't one perfect power balance for all relationships. I now respect that relationships are going to develop a balance that might work for them that does not look right to me. Some time ago a woman came to my office to thank me for all the work I had done with her husband, who had been arrested for battery. When I asked her what made the difference, she said he used to come home and scream at her, "Why don't you get off your lazy ass and clean up this house; it's a mess." She told me that now he comes home and yells, "This house is a mess." I asked her how that is better. "He's not calling me a fucking lazy bitch anymore," she said. I asked her what she does now when he yells. She answered that she yells right back at him, "'You're right, it is a mess, I don't like it either,' and then we pitch in together and straighten it up."

Eve: *Sounds like that couple learned some good relationship skills. He doesn't call her names, so she can express agreement with him and that interaction leads to better cooperation between them.*

Tony: Formerly I would not have accepted that—I would have thought it wrong for there to be any yelling at all, but *she* did not mind the yelling. The power balance that fits for her is for him not to call her names. What I think is a right balance is not what other people find OK. So, some domestic violence programs may be hurting themselves by saying they know what is right for everyone. Everyone has to establish a balance that works for them.

Eve: *In my opinion, that is the problem with some of the thinking in the domestic violence field today. There is a one-size-fits-all mentality, which is the opposite of the assumptions of the solution-focused and constructivist approaches. I think there is much good that can come from conversations between people like you and me, those in the domestic violence field and those who work clinically with the clients.*

Tony: I agree.

Summary and Conclusion

Eve: *In this conversation we have tried to address some of the major controversies in the field of domestic violence about couples treatment, and how we are trying to bridge those controversies. In thinking over our discussion, it is apparent that we are dealing with two very different belief systems:*

Domestic Violence	*Solution-Focused Therapy*
Advocate for the victim.	Accept both sides of the story and take a collaborative stance.
Confront the man's denial.	Motivate the man to accept responsibility by not making him more defensive.
Resocialize the man.	Identify positives in the relationship and amplify them in the future.
Separate the couple.	Help the couple set goals for themselves that satisfy both their needs.

These differences seem as difficult to bridge as some of the differences our couples are grappling with, but the solution is much like one in a good relationship: the willingness to see more than one point of view about a goal that is useful to everyone. I think that you and I work very hard to listen to each other and to try to find compromises that are ethical, safe, and as theoretically sound as possible.

It has become very clear to me that the two of us, just like our colleagues who work as advocates or as constructivist-oriented therapists, have a common goal of eliminating emotional and physical abuse from relationships. We must look to each other for solutions toward that common goal rather than be divided by our differences. You and I agree in many areas, particularly humanistic ones, yet I find it useful when you challenge my thinking from the domestic violence perspective. I listen because of the respectful way you do that, and I try to compromise wherever I can. Sometimes I have to stand firm when I feel these ideas are incongruent with my theoretical and clinical beliefs. Getting other people to consider my ideas about treating couples and to dialogue with me without discounting what I say has been one of the greatest challenges of all. I have learned that to get anyone to listen at all I must think the way I do when I collaborate with clients: join them in their reality and then ask them questions that make them expand that reality to include other options.

The major adjustment I have been willing to make is in terms of inclusion or assessment criteria. This suggests that I am evaluating and judging when I want to take an accepting, collaborative position. I am able to justify this with the belief that the evaluation is not that different from the decision I make in nonabusive marital cases about whether to see a couple together or not. With violence cases, I ask some more pointed questions, such as whether the abuser wants to stop emotional and physical abuse and whether the victim wants it to stop. I pursue more intensely information about the extent of the violence and about symptoms indicating drug and alcohol abuse or psychiatric problems because I feel I have the responsibility not to overlook anything that may contribute to the possibility of further violence. I feel that theoretical adaptations are justified if they keep only one person safer.

Conversely, I think that solution-focused thinking has much to offer the domestic violence field in terms of how to approach the defensive behaviors of abusive partners, such as denial or minimization. Confrontation and punishment have not proved so successful that we should not consider and welcome other options. The trick, of course, will be to learn how to identify what approach is best for whom. I also think that our focus on the relationship as something that belongs to both partners and that both want to enjoy is a useful perspective. It transcends the winner/loser mentality that contributes so greatly to keeping conflict alive not only for the couples but for some helping professionals as well. Finally, looking at the positives in the relationship, and at the commonalties rather than the differences, is also a valuable bridge to a better future.

Just a few words of caution! What I have been doing for fifteen years, and what we have been doing together the past few years, is work in progress and can only be thought of as our clinical opinion, so far. I look forward to our collaboration in the near future to demonstrate the validity of our work in more concrete terms.

    I would also like to suggest that only very experienced solution-focused therapists consider using this approach with domestic violence. A common misunderstanding is that solution-focused therapy consists of some techniques that can be "done sometimes" in conjunction with other techniques. Solution-focused therapy, as other constructivist approaches, is a way of thinking, a philosophy, and a set of assumptions that represent a framework within which techniques are applied. The techniques do not work by themselves. Their success is related to the context in which they are used, and the therapist's ability to establish, as nearly as possible, the clients' reality about their problems and their ideas about solutions. When life and death issues are involved, as they are in domestic violence, therapists need to be confident of their skills. In solution-focused therapy, that requires ongoing training over an extended period that includes intense supervision, preferably live, and more than a few years of experience.

Tony: Eve, I think that bridges not only *can* be built between those of us who work in the domestic violence field and mental health professionals like you but they *must* be built. It is dangerous if they are not built. For a decade I have sat around tables with people representing agencies to develop a coordinated community response to violence, and I have found clinicians grossly underrepresented. It is time that they be invited to the table to collaborate with us. Our conversation has proven to me the value of learning from each other. Our respective fields must share their knowledge so that safer and more effective methods of assessment, intervention, and prevention can continue to be developed.

    What domestic violence advocates have to offer systemic and constructivist thinkers is a heightened awareness of how to avoid inadvertently blaming the abused partner and of how to be attuned to the possible presence of domestic violence when it is not presented as part of the problem. Domestic violence advocates have developed an expertise in identifying a myriad of subtle forms of controlling and violent behaviors that are part of emotionally abusive patterns that clinicians not experienced in this area are prone to overlook. Domestic violence advocates can also contribute to a better understanding of how to emphasize personal responsibility (that is, the person who hits is always responsible for the hitting). Battering behavior should never be misunderstood as systemic in the sense that one person's behavior is caused by that of another. Finally, advocates can also assist clinicians in appropriate collaboration with the police, courts, probation and parole officers, and shelters and batterers groups, which are often involved in the case already or can be useful resources.

Constructivist-oriented clinicians can help the domestic violence field remember that "batterers" and "victims" are unique individuals and that all domestic violence is not the same. Therefore, neither are the solutions! They can help advocates ask questions in ways that co-create solutions instead of co-creating the resistance we call denial and minimization. They can help domestic violence advocates explore their attitudes, intentions, and personal experiences of domestic violence. Such self-awareness increases one's usefulness in helping clients find their own workable solutions. In other words, *constructivist-oriented clinicians can help domestic violence professionals recognize the benefits of a collaborative rather than an expert stance for dealing with difficult clients.*

Eve, I can see how we have built a bridge together. We're blending our domestic violence and solution-focused therapy knowledge to produce a hybrid form of assessment, intervention, and prevention of violence within couples. We have bridged advocacy with solution-focused therapy, resocialization with building a future for couples based on mutual satisfaction, and confronting denial with strength searching. We have utilized other domestic violence resources in town, and they are utilizing us. In spite of my vigilance about ethics and safety in domestic violence work, I find that I am comfortable with the attention and sensitivity the solution-focused approach offers for working with couples. But our work is far from over!

Our efforts to validate our work through research should guide us in the future development of this project. It is good that we go slowly and make safety a priority. I invite others working in the domestic violence field to venture out on this bridge with us to get a view from a variety of perspectives and to help seek new solutions.

Questions from the Editors

1. *In your discussion you mention mental status and psychiatric evaluating and testing. How do you reconcile using such instruments in a constructivist approach?*

There is no theoretical way of reconciling it. Conversely, we do not believe that use of medication is always inconsistent with constructivist therapy. What seems important to us is for clients not to abrogate responsibility for their behavior because they take medication.

We use the language of the medical model as a way of joining the collateral systems in the community involved with many of our clients and the people we address in our public presentations. The great majority of the people we speak to still share the dominate belief system in the domestic violence field that the batterer must be resocialized and the couple should be separated. We are trying to get people to hear us because we believe that we have an option that can provide safety for many women sooner than existing options. If we spoke about this in a language that is totally foreign to them, we would not be consistent with solution-focused thinking.

Theoretically, we see each client as unique. People's violence can be considered to be unique and so can solutions for it. For ethical reasons, we have to hear the batterer take responsibility for his abuse and say he really wants to stop it before we get into defining goals for his relationship with his partner. Once that has been established, we can be more theoretically pure. But sometimes we run into situations in which the batterer is trying to make some changes in how he responds to anger toward his partner and he does not seem to be able to recognize or experience warning signs. His history may be that he struck out so fast that he did not realize he had been violent until he saw his partner bleeding. This type of client can profit from neurological or psychiatric evaluation and medication. Some men who experience depression also often do better with medication and work on the relationship.

2.   *When you separate couples because of the lack of agreement of goals or because of ambivalence, if safety issues aren't relevant do you work on relationship issues or on how the batterer can get back with his partner?*

When the woman isn't certain about staying in the relationship and the batterer wants to work it out, we talk with him about two things: (1) gaining a better understanding of what his partner may want or need in order to stay in the relationship and how that fits with his own wants and needs; and (2) how he can feel good about himself regardless of whether he is in the relationship. We ask questions to develop his ability to be empathic, such as "Why do you think she is afraid to tell you she wants to visit her sister?" and "If you were your wife, how would you react if you were accused of lying?" We might help him begin to make choices for himself that are motivated by his desire for his own well-being, not only for getting his partner back. For example, if she is asking for space and he wants to give it to her but has a hard time controlling his urge to call her, we might say, "When you have the urge to call her, ask yourself which choice will make you feel best about *yourself* afterwards." We'd also concentrate on questions that address how he can feel best about himself until she makes up her mind: what activities he used to enjoy when he was single that he would enjoy now, how he can be a parent in a way that makes him feel like a good father, and so on.

3.   *Your bridge between two approaches offers real hope. You mention in the chapter that you want to evaluate your approach. Where does that stand?*

We gather data informally on all the couples we see, but we keep hoping to get a grant that will allow us to develop a protocol of how we work with violence in relationships that can be replicated by other people who do solution-focused work. We just finished a proposal for a comparative outcome study between a Duluth model batterers group and men seen by us with their partners, and we hope that we can get someone interested in it.

For the past ten years, Lipchik has tried to get a little financial support for her work through private and public funding sources. She has run into several problems. One is that no one wants to give money for direct services. They want to fund programs that generate help for as many people as possible and for as long as possible, not just for fifty or a hundred couples. Another is that she runs a private, for-profit agency and most grantors like to designate moneys for nonprofit agencies or universities. She has tried to hook up with nonprofits in domestic violence, but they do not want to touch research that deals with couples work because it is so controversial. They are afraid they could alienate their existing funding sources. But research funding is a problem for everyone in this field, regardless of their outlook. We will keep plugging along hoping to validate our particular approach.

References

Abbott, J., Johnson, R., Kazio-McLain, J., & Lowenstein, S. R. (1995). Domestic violence against women: Incidents and prevalence in an emergency department population. *Journal of the American Medical Association, 273*(22), 1763–1767.

Aldorondo, E., and Straus, M. A. (1994). Screening for physical violence in couples therapy: Methodological, practical, and ethical consideration. *Family Process, 33*(4), 425–441.

Archives of Family Medicine. (1992). *American Medical Association's diagnostic and treatment guidelines on domestic violence*, Vol. 1. Washington, DC: American Medical Association.

Babcock, J. C., Waltz, J., Jacobson, N. S., & Gottman, J. M. (1993). Power and violence: The relation between communication patterns, power discrepancies, and domestic violence. *Journal of Consulting & Clinical Psychology, 61*(1), 40–50.

Cantos, A., Neidig, P. H., & O'Leary, K. D. (1994). Injuries of women and men in a treatment program for domestic violence. *Family Violence, 9*, 113–124.

Colorado Standards for Intervention with Court Ordered Domestic Violence Perpetrators. (1993, November 1). State of Colorado Legislature.

De Shazer, S. (1985). *Keys to solutions in brief therapy.* New York: W. W. Norton.

De Shazer, S. (1988). *Clues: Investigating solutions in brief therapy.* New York: W. W. Norton.

De Shazer, S., Berg, I. K., Lipchik, E., Nunnally, E., Molnar, A., Gingerich, W., and Weiner-

Davis, M. (1986). Brief therapy: Focused solution development. *Family Process, 25,* 207–227.

Duncan, B., Solovey, A., & Rusk, G. (1992). *Changing the rules: A client-directed approach to therapy.* New York: Guilford.

Dutton, D. G. (1988). *The domestic assault of women: Psychological and criminal justice perspectives.* Newton, MA: Allyn & Bacon.

Feazell, C. S., Mayers, R. S., & Deschner, J. P. (1984). Services for men who batter: Implications for programs and policies. *Family Relations 33,* 17–23.

Feld, S. L., & Straus, M. A. (1990). Escalation and desistance from wife assault. In M. A. Straus & R. J. Gelles (Eds.), *Physical violence in American families: Risk factors and adaptations to violence in 8,145 families* (pp. 489–505). New Brunswick, NJ: Transaction Publishers.

Galdner, V. (1992). Making room for both/and. *The Family Therapy Networker, 16*(2), 54–62.

Geffner, R., Mantooth, C., Franks, D., & Rao, L. (1989). A psychoeducation, conjoint therapy approach to reducing family violence. In Caesar, P. L., & Hamberger, L. K. (Eds.), *Treating men who batter* (pp. 102–133). New York: Springer.

Giles-Sims, J. (1983). *Wife battering: A systems theory approach.* New York: Guilford Press.

Hamberger, L. K., & Hastings, J. E. (1986). Personality correlates of men who abuse their partners: A cross-validation study. *Journal of Family Violence, 1,* 323–341.

Hamberger, L. K., & Hastings, J. E. (1993). Court-mandated treatment of men who assault their partners. In Z. N. Hilton (Ed.), *Legal responses to wife assault: Current trends and evaluation* (pp. 188–229). Newberry Park, CA: Sage.

Hare-Mustin, R., & Marecek, J. (1990). *Making a difference.* New Haven, CT: Yale University Press.

Harway, M., & Hansen, M. (1990). Therapists' recognition of wife battering: Some empirical evidence. *Family Violence Bulletin, 6*(3), 16–18.

Hoffman, J. (1992, February 16). When men hit women. *The New York Times Magazine,* p. 24.

Holzworth-Munroe, A., & Stuart, G. L. (1994). Typologies of male batterers: Three subtypes and the differences among them. *Psychological Bulletin, 116*(3), 476–497.

Hotaling, G. T., & Sugarman, D. B. (1986). An analysis of risk markers in husband to wife violence: The current state of knowledge. *Violence and Victims, 1,* 101–124.

Jacobson, N. S., & Addis, M. E. (1993). Research on couples and couple therapy: What do we know? Where are we going? *Journal of Consulting and Clinical Psychology, 61,* 85–93.

Jacobson, N., Gottman, J. M., Waltz, J., Rushe, R., Babcock, J., & Holtzworth-Munroe, A. (1994). Affect, verbal content, and psychophysiology in the arguments of couples with a violent husband. *Journal of Consulting and Clinical Psychology, 62*(5), 982–988.

Lipchik, E. (1991). Spouse abuse: Challenging the party line. *The Family Therapy Networker, 15,* 59–63.

Malone, J., Tyree, A., & O'Leary, K. D. (1989). Generalization and containment: Different effects of aggressive histories for wives and husbands. *Journal of Marriage and the Family, 51,* 687–697.

Murphy, C. M., & O'Leary, K. D. (1989). Psychological aggression predicts physical aggression in early marriage. *Journal of Consulting and Clinical Psychology, 53,* 419–421.

Neidig, P. H., Freedman, D. H., & Collins, B. S. (1985, April). Domestic conflict containment: A spouse abuse treatment program. *Social Case Work,* pp. 195–204.

O'Leary, K. D. (1993). Through a psychological lens: Personality traits, personality disorders, and levels of violence. In L. J. Gelles & D. Loseke (Eds.), *Current controversies on domestic violence* (pp. 7–30). Newbury Park, CA: Sage.

O'Leary, K. D., Barling, J., Arias, I., Rosenbaum, A., Malone, J., & Tyree, A. (1989). Prevalence and stability of spousal aggression. *Journal of Marital and Family Therapy, 12,* 281–289.

O'Leary, K. D., & Curley, A. D. (1986). Assertion and family violence: Correlates of spouse abuse. *Journal of Marital and Family Therapy, 121,* 281–289.

O'Leary, K. D., Malone, J., & Tyree, A. (1994). Physical aggression in early marriage: Prerelationship and relationship effects. *Journal of Consulting and Clinical Psychology, 62,* 594–602.

Pan, H. S., Neidig, P. H., & O'Leary, K. D. (1994). Predicting mild and severe husband-to-wife physical aggression. *Journal of Consulting and Clinical Psychology, 62*(5), 975–998.

Pence, E., & Paymar, M. (1990). *Power and control: Tactics of men who batter.* Duluth, MN: MPDI.

Purdy, F., & Nickle, N. (1981). Practice principles for working with groups of men who batter. *Social Work Groups, 4,* 111–123.

Rosenbaum, A., & O'Leary, K. D. (1981). Marital violence: Characteristics of abusive couples. *Journal of Consulting and Clinical Psychology, 49,* 63–71.

Sherman, L. W. (1992). *Policing domestic violence: Experiments and dilemmas.* New York: Free Press.

Sirles, E. A., Lipchik, E., & Kowalski, K. (1992). A consumer's perspective on domestic violence interventions. *Journal of Family Violence, 8*(3), 267–277.

Spanier, G. B. (1976). Measuring dyadic adjustment: New scales for assessing the quality of marriage and similar dyads. *Journal of Marriage and the Family, 38,* 15–28.

Spanier, G. B., & Thompson, L. A. (1982). Confirmatory analysis of the Dyadic Adjustment Scale. *Journal of Marriage and the Family, 44,* 731–738.

Straus, M. A. (1979). Measuring intrafamily conflict and violence: The Conflict Tactics Scales. *Journal of Marriage and the Family, 41,* 75–88.

Straus, M. A., Gelles, R. J., & Steinmetz, S. K. (1980). *Behind closed doors: Violence in the American family.* New York: Anchor Books.

Strube, M. J. (1988). The decision to leave an abusive relationship: Empirical evidence and theoretical issues. *Psychological Bulletin, 104,* 236–250.

Tolman, R., & Bennett, L. (1990). A review of quantitative research on men who batter. *Journal of Interpersonal Violence, 5,* 87–118.

U.S. Department of Justice, Bureau of Justice and Statistics (1983, October). *Report to the nation on crime and justice.* Washington, DC: U.S. Government Printing Office, p. 22.

Walker, L. E. (1984). *The battered woman syndrome.* New York: Springer.

Yllo, K., & Bograd, M. (Eds.). (1988). *Feminist perspectives on wife abuse.* Newbury Park, CA: Sage.

CHAPTER FIVE

SOLUTION-FOCUSED WORK IN THE HOSPITAL

A Continuum-of-Care Model for Inpatient Psychiatric Treatment

Kay Vaughn, Bonnie Cox Young,
Denise C. Webster, and Marshall R. Thomas

The historical focus on locked inpatient psychiatric programs as the primary source of intensive treatment has been a major barrier to meeting the needs of psychiatric clients (Kiesler, 1992). The overemphasis on hospital treatment has led to unrealistic inpatient goals, underuse of aftercare resources, and prolonged, expensive hospitalizations (Nurcombe, 1988). This view of inpatient treatment is based in part on sparse scientific evidence supporting the superiority of locked hospital treatment over less restrictive forms of psychiatric care (Gudeman, Dickey, Evans, & Shore, 1985; Kiesler & Sibulkin, 1987; Turner & Hoge, 1991). In fact, hospital treatment has been shown to be detrimental for certain client populations (Nehls, 1994). In spite of growing evidence of the need for a redistribution of mental health care across a continuum of care, 70 percent of the annual mental health care dollars are spent on inpatient services (Kiesler & Simpkins, 1993).

Nevertheless, in today's managed health care market, hospital treatment is coming to be viewed more realistically as only one aspect of the total mental health care delivery system. As outpatient treatment is becoming the primary locus of care, psychiatric hospitals across the United States are closing at the annual rate of 5 to 10 percent (Lutz, 1995). To meet the demands of consumers, third-party providers, and external accrediting agencies for efficacious care, existing inpatient systems will have to undergo major change (Webster, Vaughn, Webb, & Playter, 1995), including redefining the purpose, philosophy, multidisciplinary roles, and models of delivery in the hospital setting (Harper, 1988; Santos & McLeod-Bryant, 1991; Vaughn, Webster, Orahood, & Young, 1995).

There is considerable confusion about what is considered efficacious hospitalization, in terms of both length and goals of treatment. Lengths of stay in inpatient psychiatric hospitals vary widely (Gunstad & Sherman, 1991; Nurcombe, 1988). The current national average is 17.8 days. The program we describe in this chapter has an average length of stay of 4.2 inpatient days (both locked and twenty-four-hour open settings) and 6.6 combined inpatient and partial care full-day equivalents.

The purpose of this chapter is to discuss the differences between traditional inpatient treatment and our brief, solution-focused continuum-of-care model, the Alternatives Program at Colorado Psychiatric Hospital. Those differences in treatment as well as some of the underlying philosophic differences are outlined in Table 5.1. The transition from a traditional inpatient focus to the solution-focused continuum-of-care model demands changes throughout the hospital system and in its relationship to other community support systems. In the Alternatives Program, we have incorporated solution-focused approaches in all aspects of the system, including individual, group, family, and milieu therapies; staff education; and clinical supervision (Vaughn et al., 1995; Vaughn, Hastings-Guerrero, & Kassner, in press; Vaughn, Webster, Platter, Playter, & Webb, in press; Webster, Vaughn, & Martinez, 1994; Webster et al., 1995). In this chapter we present our solution-focused, goal-oriented process for treatment planning and charting, and we discuss how the roles of various disciplines are conceptualized in our model. In addition, as background for describing keys to success, we review outcome data collected in both formal research projects and quality management activities.

Program Philosophy and Goals

An essential step in integrating solution-focused therapy into our hospital program has been the development of a multidisciplinary treatment philosophy. A shared philosophy of care is important to the success of our program because it encourages cooperation, a clear focus, and a consistent approach to brief hospital treatment. In developing our solution-focused continuum of care, we have returned repeatedly to our underlying philosophical beliefs about what clients need and about what we as health professionals value. Our treatment philosophy and goals are summarized as follows (Webster et al., 1995):

1. Treatment focuses on crisis stabilization and finding solutions to the presenting complaint, using the available client and community resources, rather than on the client's deficits or pathology.

TABLE 5.1. DIFFERENCES BETWEEN TRADITIONAL
AND SOLUTION-FOCUSED HOSPITAL TREATMENT.

Traditional	Solution-Focused
Goal: remission of disorder	Goal: crisis stabilization
Client immersed in hospital milieu	Systems oriented/community resources involved in treatment
Past/present focus	Present/future focus
Milieu observations focus on dysfunctional interaction patterns	Milieu observations focus on what is working
Rules/structure	Flexibility/guidelines
Problem-oriented charting and treatment planning	Goal-oriented charting and treatment planning
Patient adapts to system	Individualized/continuum of care
Hospital is center of patient's focus	Real world/natural environment is focus
Lengthy termination process	Discharge planning begins on admission
Physician-centered treatment model	Multidisciplinary/case management model
Psychodynamic treatment approach	Solution-focused treatment approach

2. Treatment plans include an eclectic approach that incorporates crisis management, somatic therapies, environmental support, and rapid mobilization of aftercare resources.
3. Treatment plans focus on clients' individual concerns in the context of their lives outside the treatment setting.
4. Therapeutic techniques employed include solution-focused and cognitive behavioral therapies within a systems perspective. Clients' autonomy is maximized as they are assisted in finding their own solutions, accessing resources, and focusing on their immediate goals or needs.
5. Need for inpatient hospitalization is continually evaluated, with the goal of treating clients in the least restrictive setting.

As our philosophy has evolved, we have incorporated aspects of different brief therapy approaches. Research shows that successful therapeutic approaches recognize clients as the central change agents and use a variety of interventions (Miller, Hubble, and Duncan, 1995). With attention to the need for philosophic consistency, we have integrated theories that focus on clients' worldviews, strengths, resources, and support systems. For example, we use a variety of cognitive-behavioral approaches to introduce different ways of coping (Austed & Berman, 1991; Wells & Gianetti, 1990). We ask the question posed in the interpersonal-developmental-existential (IDE) model described by Budman and Gurman (1988), "Why now?" to help develop a central focus and to understand clients' perspectives. We also incorporate assessment from a crisis intervention perspective when safety factors are a primary concern (Hoff, 1989). We emphasize a practical focus on what brought the clients into the hospital, what the clients want, and how their lives outside the treatment setting will be different when their problems are solved.

The most important addition to our program has been the integration of solution-focused approaches to treatment. Solution-focused and possibility-oriented therapies as described by de Shazer (1988a, 1988b), Friedman and Fanger (1991), and others (O'Hanlon & Weiner-Davis, 1989; Walter & Peller, 1992) have been identified for use primarily in outpatient therapy. We spent considerable time making needed modifications to address the unique needs of the inpatient setting (Vaughn et al., 1995; Webster et al., 1995). We agree with Durrant's (1993) statement that solution-focused therapy is more an attitude than a set of procedures or techniques that clinicians must rigidly follow. However, some solution-focused assumptions that have influenced the development of our central philosophy are (1) clients can make significant life changes in a brief period of time, (2) our job is to notice and highlight these changes for the clients, and (3) the real world in which clients live is more important than the artificial environment of the hospital (Webster et al., 1995). We have found that solution-oriented approaches to treatment encourage positive changes in life patterns, minimize regression, and help prevent unnecessary hospitalizations. Clients' involvement with their families, friends, work, leisure activities, and outpatient caregivers is facilitated through the flexibility of the continuum of care.

We have found that the nursing approach of Erickson, Tomlin, and Swain (1983) adds a holistic perspective to our program, as well as addressing mind/body concerns that are frequently encountered in the hospital setting. Solution-focused therapy is consistent with the aims of nursing interventions, including building clients' trust, promoting their sense of control and positive orientation, affirming and supporting their strengths, and setting health-oriented mutual goals. The development of mutual goals recognizes that clients who are hospitalized may temporarily be unable to identify a specific safety management plan. Whenever discrepancies between clients' perspectives and staff responsibilities to maintain safety are identified, an explicit negotiation is undertaken to assure the client's safety (Webster et al., 1995).

The Alternatives Program

As noted earlier, the model we have been discussing is the Alternatives Program at Colorado Psychiatric Hospital. The program operates seven days a week and is based on a flexible continuum of care that includes a crisis service, a twenty-three-hour observation component, an intensive locked setting, a twenty-four-hour open component, and partial care options. Figure 5.1 illustrates the components of this flexible continuum of care.

Reorganization of the Alternatives Program occurred in response to the prominence of managed care in the local market place, low census, and criticism from external customers that care was slow, inefficient, costly, and did not include outpatient care providers (Baker & Geise, 1992). The decision to provide a less restrictive alternative to locked inpatient treatment was based on research from an innovative program at Massachusetts Mental Health called "the Inn" (Gudeman et al., 1985). This research showed that on admission the majority of acutely ill psychiatric patients could safely tolerate open and partial settings. We made modifications to the Inn's model based on our need for a brief model that maintained continuity and allowed the same staff to treat clients across a diversified continuum of care. We wanted a model that went beyond crisis intervention to actually help clients solve the problems that brought them into the hospital.

The Alternatives Program has a thirty-bed capacity distributed among its locked, open, and partial components. Its full range of services focuses on clients' strengths and on integration of outpatient therapists, managed care organizations, work settings, families, and other external support systems. Clients can use different aspects of the program to meet their individual needs, which may require from as few as four hours to as many as twenty-four hours of care each day. All components of the program except aftercare are located in the same physical space, and the client is followed through the continuum by the same team consisting of a psychiatrist, nurse case manager, and social worker. Our program is unique in its offering of a range of acute care services unified under one treatment team within a hospital setting (Baker & Geise, 1992). Analysis of use of the components of the programs is 18 percent for intensive care only, 42 percent for twenty-four-hour open or partial care, and 40 percent for combined care.

Adolescents, adults, and geriatric clients are admitted to the Alternatives Program. Criteria for admission include destructive behavior, marked disturbance in behavior or thinking, impaired reality testing, acute and/or severe agitation, mania, or depression with vegetative signs. Locked inpatient care is considered only when clients demonstrate imminent danger to self or others and an inability to develop a realistic safety plan.

Clients can be admitted to or discharged from any component of the program based on their need and level of care required. Between admission and discharge, clients can move fluidly between intensive care, twenty-four-hour open care, and partial care. Services are provided in the least restrictive setting possible. Clients receive continuing assessment, at least once per shift, to assure use of the least restrictive level of care. The major goal of our program is to provide

FIGURE 5.1. THE ALTERNATIVES PROGRAM AT COLORADO PSYCHIATRIC HOSPITAL FLEXIBLE CONTINUUM-OF-CARE MODEL.

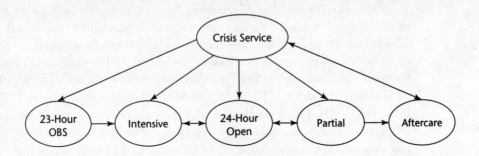

crisis stabilization in a setting that maximizes individual autonomy, interfaces with external support systems, and integrates progress made in the hospital with life outside the treatment setting.

Crisis Service

Clients are admitted to the program either through referral after evaluation by an outpatient therapist or through evaluation by our crisis service. The crisis service provides a twenty-four-hour-per-day, seven-day-per-week crisis evaluation, intervention, and referral service. Our crisis service goes beyond triage and risk assessment by providing treatment interventions at the time of contact. The goal of the crisis service is to stabilize the crisis and place the client in the least restrictive treatment setting, preferably outpatient. Our quality improvement data show that by providing solution-oriented treatment as part of the crisis service evaluation, more than 70 percent of clients seen by the crisis service remain outpatients. Our experience is that immediate solution-focused crisis intervention can prevent or shorten a hospitalization.

Twenty-Three-Hour Observation

Historically, twenty-three-hour observation services were located in the hospital's emergency department, where containment, safety, and medications were the primary tools of intervention. Crisis intervention, psychotherapy, and rapid mobilization of aftercare resources were hampered in this environment. Additionally, the client was not actively involved as part of the solution. With the primary focus on containment, care was costly and protracted. Since the Alternatives Program was reorganized, the twenty-three-hour observation component is now located in the program's locked setting. A solution-focused treatment approach is used in response to the client's chief complaint. After twenty-three hours, clients may be recompensated and discharged to outpatient therapy. However, if clients remain suicidal, homicidal, or gravely disabled, or if they require further care to stabilize their crises, they may be admitted to another part of the program: the intensive locked setting, the twenty-four-hour open setting, or partial care.

Intensive Locked Setting

The intensive component is a locked setting for clients requiring the most intensive level of care, such as seclusion and/or restraint, significant behavioral management, or complicated medical interventions. Our locked service is more flexible than traditional inpatient units in that we provide guidelines rather than rigid rules. Because of the cooperative, collaborative nature of solution-oriented approaches, the treatment team is guided by the goals of the client instead of by a unit schedule, staff expectations, or rules. This flexibility recognizes that individual clients' needs for structure and limit setting may vary drastically. For instance, in a traditional model, clients who hallucinate may be discouraged from staying in their rooms, whereas in our program we ascertain clients' unique coping strategies for dealing with their psychoses. Through discussion and observation we may learn that it is more therapeutic for them to rest in their rooms than to participate in scheduled unit activities. This respectful approach towards the client's strengths and coping strategies allows clients to incorporate *their* routine into the hospital milieu versus having to adapt to *our* routine. Milieu observations focus on anything the clients are doing that is helpful to their progress (Vaughn et al., 1995).

Nonviolent crisis intervention techniques are implemented to address violent acting out behaviors (Steiger, 1987). The philosophy of nonviolent crisis intervention is similar to solution-focused therapy in which behavior patterns are viewed as cyclical rather than constant. This approach values preserving clients' dignity and provides an opportunity for client recompensation while maintaining safety. For clients requiring increased structure, daily planning forms are available to assist them in setting goals, structuring time, and evaluating effectiveness of interventions (see Exhibit 5.1 at the end of this chapter).

Twenty-Four-Hour Open Setting

The twenty-four-hour open setting is unlocked and less restrictive than the intensive component. Clients can come and go as they wish. These clients administer their own medications and work with staff to develop their own unique safety management plans. Clients are free to participate in their usual activities, such as outpatient therapy groups, work, and other interactions in their home (real world) environment. Clients meet with nursing staff daily to formulate their goals for the day and to identify the portions of the program they plan to attend. Groups and individual meetings are available in the morning, afternoon, and evening.

Partial Care

The partial care component is tailored to the needs of clients who maintain a higher level of activity outside the hospital. Our program operates twenty-four hours a day, seven days a week because clients may require intervention and structure at times other than traditional business hours. Since the same staff treat the same clients across the continuum of care, there is no break in continuity. Clients are only charged for the portions of the program they attend. They can attend our program components during the morning, afternoon, evening, or any combination to attain their individual goals.

Multidisciplinary Roles

Our multidisciplinary staff are trained in brief, solution-oriented therapy (Vaughn et al., in press; Webster et al., 1994). The treatment team uses a multidisciplinary approach with well-defined roles for all team members. Social workers and nurses work intensively with clients and their families. With the client's permission, social workers meet with families within forty-eight hours of admission to engage them actively in generating solutions. Nursing staff lead solution-oriented group therapy three times a day, seven days a week (Vaughn et al., in press). Back-to-work evaluation and intervention on the worksite are available through occupational therapy. The attending psychiatrist provides a diagnostic evaluation and manages medications, but he or she supervises rather than performs the bulk of inpatient psychotherapy.

The Alternatives Program has two nurse case managers who treat clients across the continuum of care. Each client is assigned a nurse case manager who coordinates the client's care, including family, friends, managed care personnel, and outpatient therapists (Smith, 1994; Van Dongen & Jambunathan, 1992). The complexity of our clients' medical needs and the need to work with other medical systems makes registered nurses, preferably with master's degrees, ideal for this case management role.

The psychiatric nurse case managers maintain a holistic approach to care. They coordinate multiple systems of care, they function as the "point person" in the program, and they guide the clients through the system. In this key role, the nurse case managers work collaboratively with each client's psychiatrist to lead the treatment team. The case manager ensures that care throughout the continuum is solution-focused and appropriate for the level of care required for the client's condition.

All caregivers, including the medical director, nurse manager, nurse case managers, social workers, occupational therapist, registered nurses, and mental health workers attend morning report. All staff hear report on all of the clients across the continuum of care to ensure continuity. The goal for staff is to develop a seamless system of care. A solution-focused format is used during shift-change report. Discussion centers around the client's goals, interventions, outcomes, and recommended changes (Vaughn et al., 1995). Other purposes of multidisciplinary report include revising interventions (as needed), clarifying staff assignments, and deciding if outside consultation is necessary. Consultation is sought quickly if a client's progress is not apparent or if his or her condition is deteriorating.

Individualized Treatment Planning

The flexibility and fluidity of the program is balanced by highly focused attention to the individual needs of clients and the specificity of goals and interventions. Individualized treatment planning includes use of solution-focused assessment, client-centered treatment planning, and documentation of progress through individualized care designs and goal-oriented charting (see Exhibit 5.2 at the end of this chapter).

Solution-Focused Assessment

Crises can undermine clients' self-esteem and self-efficacy. In the midst of a crisis, it's not unusual for clients to lose track of skills they already have for dealing with difficult situations. A solution-focused assessment elicits hope and assists clients in realizing that they are capable of getting through a crisis. Table 5.2 outlines the interview format that structures our solution-focused assessment and intervention with clients (Vaughn et al., 1995).

We believe that an exclusive focus on pathology, deficits, and risk factors without evaluation and documentation of strengths, resources, and mitigating factors can put both the client and the institution at risk for unnecessary hospitalizations, increased lengths of stay, and ineffective treatment. We therefore gather assessment data concerning the problem, but we maintain a balance between history, strengths, exceptions, and the *clients'* goals. We maintain focus by continually asking two questions: What does the client want? and What risk factors have caused or prevented the client from moving to a less restrictive form of treatment? Clients are involved in evaluating their own risk factors as well as their strengths. The interview includes a purposeful transition from exploring *symptoms* to exploring

TABLE 5.2. CLIENT INTERVIEW FORMAT.

Interview Format for Clients Early in Hospitalization

Identify:
1. What brought client to hospital now
2. Criteria for discharge
3. Estimated length of stay
4. Goals and hope for the future
5. Instances of success
6. Strengths and coping strategies
7. Management/safety plan
8. Areas needing further information/education

Interview Format for Follow-Up Client Interviews

Identify:
1. What is improved
2. Details/description of improvement
3. How improvements have been made
4. Next step

strengths. Reviewing and assessing hidden strengths, coping strategies, competencies, and support systems creates a therapeutic balance between the problem and the solution (Lehnhoff, 1991).

Case Example A fifty-six-year-old white female with a history of bipolar affective disorder and substance abuse was admitted to the intensive locked setting after a suicide attempt. Her condition also required complicated medical interventions. When asked by nursing staff why she had come to the hospital at that time, she reported that her family physician recently told her she had a terminal illness and would probably die within two years. If this were not stressful enough, she had also been robbed twice in the previous few weeks while living in a shelter. She tearfully discussed her sadness, fear, vulnerability, and worry that she had to "cram thirty years of living into two" and she didn't know where to start or how to deal with it. Staff stated that they were sorry so many overwhelming things had happened and most people in this situation would have similar feelings. They also stated that a lot of people would not have had the good judgment to get help with this difficult situation. When asked how the hospital staff could be helpful, the client stated that she would like to develop specific goals to help her regain a sense of purpose so she could "go on and have hope for the future and develop strategies" to deal with her constant ruminations about death. She needed, she said, to "get over the onslaught, and get back to where I was three weeks ago." After further discussion, she agreed that she would know hospitalization had been successful (criteria for discharge) when she had safe housing, had established a specific "schedule" to deal with unsafe thoughts, and had returned to her "normal life." When asked, she described her normal life as doing volunteer activities, knitting for her grandchildren, living in her own place, and having the energy to swim, participate in physical therapy, and attend outpatient day treatment. She also talked about wanting to have a structured (9:00 to 5:00) weekday schedule that included activities she enjoyed. Staff asked if any of these things were already happening and she reported that she had moved in temporarily with a girlfriend and felt safer there. When she was asked specifically how hospital personnel could assist her in reaching these goals, she stated that help with completing application forms for housing and a home health aide would be helpful. She also requested a multidisciplinary conference to coordinate the treatment plans and medications prescribed by the numerous hospital and community physicians who were managing her medical and psychiatric problems. She felt that a second medical opinion would help her clarify her prognosis. When asked what she wanted help with first, she indicated she wanted a different, more effective antidepressant medication. With this level of specificity of goals, the treatment team was able to implement a client-centered treatment plan that was realistic and meaningful to the client.

Client-Centered Treatment Planning

Traditionally, hospital-based treatment planning has used a problem-oriented framework that is based on a client's diagnosis (medical, psychiatric, and nurse-defined deficits). Such a model emphasizes assessment of symptoms, diagnostic classification, professional treatment planning, intervention implementation, and evaluation of outcomes specific to the diagnosis. While a problem-oriented approach is still part of the medical assessment of clients, our treatment planning process also incorporates a solution-focused framework.

In client-centered treatment planning, clients' goals are the primary focus of treatment planning and interventions. A solution-focused treatment planning process emphasizes assessment of clients' goals, strengths, and internal and external resources (coping and social support) (Erickson et al., 1983). On admission, we ask "the miracle question" (If a miracle happened tonight while you were sleeping and you woke up tomorrow and the problems were solved, how would you know the problems were solved or that your life was going more the way you want?), and at the earliest possible moment, we explore clients' criteria for discharge and estimated length of stay in the hospital (Vaughn et al., 1995). Assessment also involves identification of exceptions to the clients' problems, instances of success, what the next small step toward the clients' goals might be, and what difference it will make when that small step is taken. If appropriate, friends, family, and significant others are included in identifying desired outcomes for treatment. When possible, supportive people directly contribute their observations. If this is not possible, clients are encouraged to imagine how supportive others might see the situation. Although a psychiatric diagnosis can be helpful in formulating needs for medication, safety, and level of structure, it does not necessarily contribute to understanding the client's unique situation, hopes, strengths, and abilities (Harper, 1988). In a solution-oriented framework, understanding *the client's* "diagnosis" of the presenting problem and preferred outcome is imperative to successful treatment planning.

Interventions are implemented by the client with the support of the multidisciplinary team and external resources. We seek to provide the most direct and least intrusive method of helping clients stabilize their crises, mobilize resources, and tap into strengths (Montgomery & Webster, 1993, 1994). The most pragmatic interventions incorporate the clients' value systems and facilitate mobilizing hope, maintaining progress, and preserving maximum independence (Vaughn et al., in press). Our approach gives attention to movement toward goals rather than tracking the severity of the problem (although they may be related). The flexible continuum of care assists clients in implementing small changes in their real-world setting.

Frequent evaluation of progress is emphasized throughout hospitalization. During these evaluation sessions, client progress, the difference progress has made, and recommendations for the next step are reviewed by client and staff. When progress is evident, the client can enter a less restrictive component of the program or be discharged to aftercare. Consistent with the central philosophy of solution-focused therapy, when interventions are successful they are repeated (de Shazer, 1988a). When the interventions are not successful, the process for identification of the next small step is repeated or a different approach is considered.

Documentation

When making a shift from problem-oriented to client-centered treatment, all aspects of care, including charting and treatment plan documentation, need to be modified (Erickson et al., 1983; Harper, 1988; Lehnhoff, 1991; Nehls, 1994; Nurcombe, 1988). A solution-focused approach to treatment planning reduces the inherent power hierarchy in which professional experts plan care without client participation. The client, multidisciplinary team, managed care representatives, outpatient therapist, and family members are all involved in the development of the treatment plan. All are important members of the treatment team. We feel it is important to understand the perspective of the managed care company, the outpatient therapists, and the mental health centers, as well as family or legal representatives (Webster et al., 1995). These diverse perspectives on what could constitute relevant improvement are important to know and consider in developing realistic solutions that recognize both client and provider responsibility for outcomes. Treatment planning conferences are completed within forty-eight hours of admission.

The client's goals, outcomes, and recommended changes in strategy are elicited every shift using individualized care designs and goal-oriented charting (Vaughn et al., 1995; see also Exhibit 5.3 at the end of this chapter). In a solution-focused approach there is reduced concern about compliance with the hospital's treatment plan and greater concern with the following two questions: What is the client's worldview? and What is the client willing to do? Only safety concerns require an explicit negotiation between staff and client perspectives.

Care Design

Our treatment planning documentation was revised to be consistent with a solution-oriented approach and was influenced by Zander's (1993) CareMaps™, which are based on a nurse case management model. We use a care design (our version of a CareMap™) that is based on continuity of treatment versus diagnosis of problem. The components of the care design include the client's

1. Present- and future-oriented goals
2. Strengths
3. Estimated length of stay
4. Support systems
5. Safety/management plan
6. Homework
7. Educational needs
8. Program components, identified by the client as potentially helpful (negotiated with staff)
9. Next steps
10. Scaling
11. Integration into home and community
12. Discharge concerns

The treatment plan is written in everyday language that the client can understand. The client is involved in developing the daily plan, and signs it, indicating agreement.

Goal-Oriented Charting

Nursing staff meet with each client at the beginning of each shift to determine the client's goals and plans for the next eight hours (Vaughn et al., 1995). Care designs address care over twenty-four hours, while goal-oriented charting tracks clients' goals, interventions, outcomes, and recommendations for each eight-hour shift. Frequent goal setting, changes in strategy when appropriate, and a clear focus of care are necessary to the success of a brief solution-focused approach to hospital care. Both charting and the care design reflect clients' unique observations about what facilitates movement toward their goals. Goal-oriented charting provides a systematic way to incorporate clients' goals, strengths, and resources into the treatment process. This form of charting and treatment planning ensures treatment continuity and active client participation (again, see Exhibits 5.1, 5.2, and 5.3 at the end of this chapter).

Measuring Program Outcomes

Outcome measures are particularly critical because solution-focused inpatient care is new and relatively unstudied. There are few guidelines for treatment efficacy for specific client populations. In addition, changes in clinical systems are occurring so rapidly that they outstrip the meager empirical database used to support these interventions. We need to know that we are providing a quality service. Ongoing quality improvement activities include objective measures of both clinical and financial outcomes. Since the inception of the Alternatives Program, many quality improvement activities have been completed. They have taken the form of quality improvement teams, critical incident reviews, variance tracking, client discharge satisfaction questionnaires, one-month post discharge follow-up interviews with clients and outpatient clinicians, and evaluation of staff and administrative effectiveness.

In a total quality management, solution-focused organization (Ring, 1995), the system at large is evaluated for inefficiencies as well as successes. Data about inpatient stays that exceed the norm (that is, more than five days) are evaluated to determine what situations cause delays in discharge (for example, delays related to different health provider groups, treatment, or discharge planning, and systems delays) as well as what facilitates timely discharge. Critical incidents that occur after client discharge, such as suicide attempts, violent episodes, and readmission within twenty-four hours, are reviewed.

Formal research projects have included review of the efficacy of internal versus external case managers, lengths of stay, recidivism rates pre and post reorganization, patient satisfaction, and cost reduction. For example, Baker and Geise (1992) reported results of a study involving our program one year before and after reorganization into the continuum of care model. The sample consisted of two groups of fifty-one patients each, matched for age, sex, and diagnosis. Global Assessment of Functioning (GAF) scores at admission and discharge were not significantly different for the two groups. Lengths of stay were decreased in the year following reorganization. Prior to reorganization, only 14 percent of clients left the hospital within three days of admission. After reorganization, 40 percent of the clients left all parts of the program, including partial, within three days. Prior to reorganization, 40 percent of clients left before ten days, in contrast to 90 percent after reorganization. Readmission rates did not statistically increase after reorganization. Following the reorganization, patient satisfaction was rated at 3.5 on a 4-point scale. Ninety-five percent of the clients indicated that if they required hospitalization in the future, they would return to our facility.

In an eight-year study of the Alternatives Program, five years before and three years after reorganization, Thomas (under review) confirmed Baker and Geise's findings. The study sample included two groups of 688 clients before reorganization and 675 clients after reorganization. The average cost per hospital treatment episode was $9095 prior to reorganization and $2961 after reorganization. The average length of stay before reorganization decreased from 20.2 days to 6.6 days after reorganization for all aspects of the program, an average decrease of 307 percent. Most striking, however, was the combined decrease of more than 400 percent for the diagnoses of eating disorder (from 55 to 4.5 days, or 1223 percent), anxiety disorder (from 19.6 to 3.3 days, or 598 percent), and substance abuse disorder (from 23.3 to 5.6 days, or 419 percent). In addition, depressive disorders fell from 18.1 to 6.9 days (261 percent), organic mental disorders from 16.9 to 3.4 days (239 percent), and psychotic disorders from 22.4 to 9.7 days (231 percent). There was also an impressive decrease in length of stay for adjustment and bipolar psychotic disorders, from 14.1 to 7.1 days (199 percent), and personality disorders, from 4.0 to 2.9 days (140 percent). There was no statistically significant difference in recidivism between groups before and after reorganization.

Another formal research project conducted by Thomas, Dubovsky, and Cox Young (in press) studied the efficacy of our internal nurse case managers in contrast to external case managers. Since some of our external customers provided their own case managers in addition to our internal case managers, we wondered if the addition of external case managers made a difference in length of stay. This study of a sample of ninety clients who had both internal and external case managers and of a second group of fifty-three clients who had only internal case managers found that there was no significant difference in length of stay between the two groups. The researchers compared advantages and disadvantages of both models of case management and determined that advantages for internal case managers are that they are directing from inside the organization and acting to decrease conflict with external agencies. The internal case managers have intimate knowledge of the complex hospital system and, consequently, are better able to effect change and improve efficiency in that system. The major disadvantage of internal case managers is that they have to build trust over time with agencies whose previous experiences with hospital systems have been strained. External case managers have the advantage of being more objective, since they are outside the hospital system and not influenced by such issues as bringing revenue to the hospital. Disadvantages of external case managers are that they are attempting to direct care from outside the system, therefore adding another layer of complexity and cost. Most important, their relationship with managed care systems does not facilitate shorter lengths of stay.

Keys to Success

In a brief overview of solution-focused hospital treatment it is not possible to describe in detail the many changes required to implement major shifts in treatment philosophy. We can, however, review some of the areas in which the likelihood of success in such an undertaking can be increased.

The most important key to success is applying a solution-focused philosophy to every level of the organization. This includes using solution-focused approaches to organizational problem-solving—that is, what do we want to see happen, what is possible, what's working (Durrant, 1993; Ring, 1995; Sparks, 1989). Maintaining this kind of isomorphic or parallel process means including staff from the beginning and throughout the process (Vaughn et al., in press). Developing a shared organizational vision is challenging in organizations with high staff turnover, ongoing uncertainty about market trends and job security, and constantly changing predictions about the direction of health care reform. Incorporating new employees who have not had training in our unique program or in solution-oriented therapy is a constant challenge. Annual staff retreats, ongoing education and supervision, goal setting, and reevaluation must be a priority, even with budgetary constraints. For staff to feel comfortable supporting decision making by clients, they must be helped to notice small positive changes in themselves, their clients, and their organization.

At the administrative level, there must be a strong commitment to the change in philosophy and attention to continuous quality improvement. When administrators can model the behaviors they support in others (that is, flexibility, openness to change, and noticing what is working), everyone benefits. In implementing change, administrators must maintain a broad systems perspective that considers shifting community needs, changing legislation, and unpredictable national trends. We have found that administrative support is essential for communicating our approach to care, helping us clarify what we believe, and performing research on treatment outcomes.

Maintaining continuity of care in a managed care environment requires a collaborative integrated system that actively incorporates managed care personnel in individual treatment planning and overall program development. Cooperative relationships with managed care agencies demand an interactive change process in which all parties specify their needs and negotiate decisions that reflect the primacy of client-centered care. We believe that the best client care comes from identifying multiple options and exploring the pros and cons of each decision. We specifically avoid competitive attitudes toward managed care providers and outpatient therapists. We provide information to managed care companies about our unique program, and we utilize their feedback in ongoing program development. We problem solve systems issues with them and discuss quality improvement data. Administration sets the expectation that managed care clinicians, physicians, and frontline staff are cooperatively focused on clients' needs, goals, and progress as the basis for any conflict resolution. We meet frequently with managed care companies to ascertain market trends and to confer about difficult cases. At the request of managed care agencies, we provide consultation to other hospitals to assist in implementation of brief models of care.

Our philosophy reminds us to ask frequently not only what we are doing well but also how we can improve our services to better meet the needs of the community. Marketing approaches must therefore address the specific health care needs within a particular geographic area. Ongoing data collection and analysis can help assure that approaches that are not working will be modified quickly. Even more important, research efforts will help us identify what is working, so we can do more of it.

Questions from the Editors

1. *How did you get everyone, from administrators, physicians, nurses, to frontline staff moving in the direction of solution-focused thinking?*

Administrative support and visionary leadership are essential to the successful implementation of a brief therapy model in the hospital setting. Administration supported the move to brief therapy from the beginning of the Alternatives Program and throughout the process. Administrative and physician support were facilitated by our awareness that the literature on inpatient care supported the efficacy and possible superiority of shorter term hospital alternatives models over traditional models of inpatient care. So, the model not only supported our local "market demands" but also reflected the fact that empirical data suggested better outcomes for the clients.

Involving frontline staff in planning and decision making is also important for successful problem solving. Brief therapy approaches and managed care concepts are integrated into new employee orientation, physician training, continuing education courses, and clinical supervision. Staff are encouraged to see the hospital as a complex system having numerous customers. Parallels are made between basic customer service skills and effective solution-focused care. Front-line staff acceptance and enthusiasm are imperative to the success of the pro-gram because these staff bear the culture to clients and external customers. Orientation also includes information about the change process and the need to set small, achievable goals.

We recognize that change can be difficult and that it requires everyone's hard work, creativity, and flexibility. Having a shared philosophy of care and well-defined staff roles reduces confusion and conflict. Assisting frontline staff in linking past successful therapeutic interventions to the new approach is important so that they do not feel devalued for their existing strengths as they attain addi-tional skills. Sharing quality improvement data analysis and research results with staff helps them identify what is working and assists them in taking credit for suc-cessful outcomes.

2. *What effect, if any, has the reorganization and adoption of a solution-focus had on staff (such as turnover, morale, interaction with patients, and so on)?*

Initially, staff struggled with how to integrate their previous hospital prac-tice with the new solution-focused approach. The majority of staff had been trained in long-term treatment approaches and needed education in time-limited models of care. There was no literature available to guide the implementation of solution-focused therapy in the hospital setting. Emphasizing that staff were pi-oneers of an approach that had not been adequately described for use in the hos-pital helped tap into their creativity and resourcefulness. During the initial stages of the culture shift there was significant staff and physician turnover. Some staff grieved the loss of the kinds of relationships they could develop with clients dur-ing longer hospitalizations. Now the majority of staff feel comfortable using solution-focused approaches. A recent in-house study found that our staff are pos-itive about the changes in client care. Staff reported that from first contact with clients the multidisciplinary team is now better able to focus on clients' strengths and to feel hopeful about possibilities for finding solutions. Also, clients are able to be collaboratively involved in identifying and reaching their goals. Staff also believe that the treatment team is now more creative and flexible in its approaches with clients. Predictably, staff report struggling with application of the model with highly regressed or organically impaired clients. As with other treatment ap-proaches, involuntary or "visitor clients" remain a challenge.

3. *What, if anything, about solution-focused therapy or thinking did not fit with inpa-tient work and needed to be changed or modified?*

Accepted psychiatric procedures such as eliciting a full developmental history, symptom profile, and enumeration of risk factors can create "problem-focused" interactions. We have found that listening to clients' stories and recognizing their unique risk factors allows us to individualize treatment for clients with serious and multiple problems. As in any complex system, we need to understand the diverse opinions of both the clients and those involved in providing care. Clients, health care providers, legal systems, families, and the multidisciplinary treatment team must be involved in order to provide effective and safe treatment.

We have had to modify all of our documentation systems to reflect our changed philosophy of care. Rationales for hospitalization and interventions, as well as criteria for improvement, have had to be documented in ways that facilitate communication and meet the standards of oversight agencies. While focusing on clients' strengths, we need to be able to speak the language of disease and problem-oriented medical systems (that is, DSM-IV diagnosis, medications, risk factors, and so on). In advocating for clients' best interests, we also need to acknowledge the seriousness of the problems that bring them into the hospital. In a managed care environment, safety is the main reason that a client is hospitalized. The existing literature does not adequately describe the challenge of negotiating goals with people who are experiencing severely diminished coping abilities and/or life-threatening safety needs.

We believe that therapeutic relationships have a different quality in the inpatient setting than they do in the outpatient setting. We are intensely involved with clients up to twenty-four hours a day. Many clients are in regressed states and may require somatic therapies as well as physical care and assistance with even minimal activities of daily living. Many times, clients require kindness, care, and support while they regain cognitive functioning and problem-solving abilities. Involvement of their support systems, no matter how limited, and an understanding of their baseline functioning are especially important in planning care when clients are temporarily unable to articulate their needs. The environment of the hospital also needs to be considered, with awareness that institutionalization can either impede or promote the health and welfare of clients.

References

Austad, C. S., & Berman, W. H. (Eds.). (1991). *Psychotherapy in managed health care: The optimal use of time and resources.* Washington, DC: American Psychological Association.

Baker, N., & Geise, A. (1992). Reorganization of a private psychiatric unit to promote collaboration with managed care. *Hospital & Community Psychiatry, 43*(11), 1126–1129.

Budman, S., & Gurman, A. (1988). *Theory and practice of brief therapy.* New York: Guilford.

De Shazer, S. (1988a). *Clues: Investigating solutions in brief therapy.* New York: W. W. Norton.

De Shazer, S. (1988b). Utilization: The foundation of solutions. In J. Zeig & S. Lankton, *Developing Ericksonian therapy: State of the art.* New York: Brunner/Mazel.

Durrant, M. (1993). *Residential treatment: A cooperative competency-based approach to therapy and program design.* New York: W. W. Norton.

Erickson, H. C., Tomlin, E. M., & Swain, M. P. (1983). *Modeling and role-modeling: A theory and paradigm for nursing.* Englewood Cliffs, NJ: Prentice-Hall.

Friedman, S., & Fanger, M. (1991). *Expanding therapeutic possibilities: Getting results in brief therapy.* Lexington, MA: Lexington Books.

Gudeman, J. E., Dickey, B., Evans, A., & Shore, M. F. (1985). Four-year assessment of a day hospital-inn program as an alternative to inpatient hospitalization. *American Journal of Psychiatry, 142*(11), 1330–1333.

Gunstad, M., & Sherman, C. F. (1991). A model of adolescent inpatient treatment. In C. S. Austad & W. H. Berman (Eds.), *Psychotherapy in managed health care: The optimal use of time and resources.* Washington, DC: American Psychological Association.

Harper, G. (1988). Focal inpatient treatment planning. *Journal of the American Academy of Child and Adolescent Psychiatry, 28*, 31–37.

Hoff, L. (1989). *People in crisis: Understanding and helping.* Reading, MA: Addison-Wesley.

Kiesler, C. A. (1992). U.S. mental health policy: Doomed to fail. *American Psychologist, 47*(9), 1077–1082.

Kiesler, C. A., & Sibulkin, A. E. (1987). *Mental hospitalization: Myths and facts about a national crisis.* Newbury Park, CA: Sage.

Kiesler, C. A., & Simpkins, C. (1993). *The unnoticed majority in psychiatric inpatient care.* New York: Plenum.

Lehnhoff, J. (1991). Assessment and utilization of patient strengths in acute care treatment planning. *The Psychiatric Hospital, 22*(1), 11–15.

Lutz, S. (1995, May 8). Psych hospitals fight for survival. *Modern Healthcare,* 62–65.

Miller, S., Hubble, M., & Duncan, B. (1995, March-April). No more bells and whistles. *The Family Therapy Networker,* 52–63.

Montgomery, C., & Webster, D. (1993). Caring and nursing's metaparadigm: Can they survive in the era of managed care? *Perspectives in Psychiatric Nursing, 29*(4), 5–12.

Montgomery, C., & Webster, D. (1994). Caring, curing, and brief therapy: A model for nurse-psychotherapy. *Archives of Psychiatric Nursing, 8*(5), 291–297.

Nehls, N. (1994). Brief hospital treatment plans: Innovations in practice and research. *Issues in Mental Health Nursing, 15*, 1–11.

Nurcombe, B. (1988). Goal-directed treatment planning and the principles of brief hospitalization. *Journal of the American Academy of Child and Adolescent Psychiatry, 28*, 26–30.

O'Hanlon, W., & Weiner-Davis, M. (1989). *In search of solutions.* New York: W. W. Norton.

Ring, E. L. (1995). *A pioneering guide to solution directed leadership for midlevel and front leaders.* Pueblo, CO: Parkview Episcopal Medical Center.

Santos, A. B., & McLeod-Bryant, S. (1991). Strategies for operational efficiency in a general hospital public inpatient unit. *Hospital and Community Psychiatry, 42*(1), 66–69.

Smith, G. B. (1994). Hospital case management for psychiatric diagnoses: Focusing on quality and cost outcomes. *Journal of Psychosocial Nursing and Mental Health Services, 32*(2), 3–4.

Sparks, P. M. (1989). Organizational tasking: A case report. *Organization Development Journal, 7*(4), 51–57.

Steiger, L. K. (1987). *Nonviolent crisis intervention participant workbook.* Brookfield, WI: National Crisis Prevention Institute.

Thomas, M. R. (under review). Decreasing length of stay (3.5 fold) does not increase recidivism on a university-affiliated inpatient unit.

Thomas, M. R., Dubovsky, S. L., & Cox Young, B. (in press). Lack of additional efficacy of external case management compared to utilization review for psychiatric inpatients. *Psychiatric Services*.

Turner, V. E., & Hoge, M. A. (1991). Overnight hospitalization of acutely ill day hospital patients. *International Journal of Partial Hospitalization, 7*, 23–36.

Van Dongen, C. J., & Jambunathan, J. (1992). Pilot study results: The psychiatric RN case manager. *Journal of Psychosocial Nursing and Mental Health Services, 30*(11), 11–14, 35–36.

Vaughn, K., Webster, D., Orahood, S., & Young, B. (1995). Brief inpatient psychiatric treatment: Finding solutions. *Issues in Mental Health Nursing, 16*(6), 519–531.

Vaughn, K., Hastings-Guerrero, S., and Kassner, C. (in press). Solution oriented inpatient group therapy. *Journal of Systemic Therapies*.

Vaughn, K., Webster, D., Platter, B., Playter, A., & Webb, M. (in press). Solution oriented hospital practice and supervision: Building psychiatric nursing competencies. *Perspectives in Psychiatric Care*.

Walter, J., & Peller, J. (1992). *Becoming solution-focused in brief therapy.* New York: Brunner/Mazel.

Webster, D., Vaughn, K., & Martinez, R. (1994). Introducing solution-focused approaches to staff in inpatient psychiatric settings. *Archives of Psychiatric Nursing, 8*(4), 254–261.

Webster, D., Vaughn, K., Webb, M., & Playter, A. (1995). Modeling the client's world through solution-focused therapy. *Issues in Mental Health Nursing, 16*(6), 505–518.

Wells, R., & Gianetti, V. (1990). *Handbook of the brief psychotherapies.* New York: Plenum.

Zander, K. (1993). Quantifying, managing, and improving quality, part IV: The retrospective use of variance. *The New Definition, 8*(1), 1–3.

EXHIBIT 5.1. DAILY PLANNING GOALS FOR INPATIENTS AT THE COLORADO PSYCHIATRIC HOSPITAL ALTERNATIVES PROGRAM.

University of Colorado Health Sciences Center
Colorado Psychiatric Hospital
The Alternatives Program

Daily Planning Goals

Name _____

Date _____

Schedule (Include groups, doctors/ therapists visits, etc.)	Meds
8:00 a.m.	
8:30 a.m.	
9:00 a.m.	
9:30 a.m.	
10:00 a.m.	
10:30 a.m.	
11:00 a.m.	
11:30 a.m.	
12:00 p.m.	
12:30 p.m.	
1:00 p.m.	
1:30 p.m.	
2:00 p.m.	
2:30 p.m.	
3:00 p.m.	
3:30 p.m.	
4:00 p.m.	
4:30 p.m.	
5:00 p.m.	
5:30 p.m.	
6:00 p.m.	
6:30 p.m.	
7:00 p.m.	
7:30 p.m.	
8:00 p.m.	
8:30 p.m.	
9:00 p.m.	
9:30 p.m.	

Treatment Issues to Focus On:

Goals for Today:

Actions to Meet Goals:

Outcome:

_____
Staff Signature and Title

Note: Copyright 1990 by Colorado Psychiatric Hospital, University of Colorado Health Sciences Center. Used with permission.

EXHIBIT 5.2. COLORADO PSYCHIATRIC HOSPITAL INPATIENT TREATMENT PLAN DOCUMENTATION.

University of Colorado Health Sciences Center **Colorado Psychiatric Hospital**		
Patient Goals—Day 1 Date(s) _____	**EVAL**	**Staff Orders—Day 1** Date(s) _____
Explore preliminary goals for hospitalization: Explore estimated length of stay Participate in completing data base Begin Alternative packet worksheets Complete Beck Inventory Answer Miracle Question Pt. Sig. _____ Staff Sig. RN/MHW _____		Estimate length of stay _____ Determine immediate outside supports: _____ _____ ACS _____ Assess for Intensive/Alt. program. _____ Assess for priv. level _____ Admission work: Complete Data Base Begin Alt. Packet (DP) Multidisciplinary data base Care Design _____ Rating Scale for _____ 1 = _____ 10 = _____ Advanced Directives ☐ MD orders ☐ Consents ☐ Rights ☐ Schedule PE ☐ Beck Inventory ☐ Orient to program ☐ Orient to Unit ☐ Release of information ☐ PCP _____ Schedule Case Conf. _____ Important Phone Numbers, list in kardex or data base Preliminary goals of hosp. _____ _____ Assess high risk factors—suicide, homicide, escape, abuse, substance abuse. Develop criteria for D/C _____ _____ Miracle Question _____ Critical Path _____ Signatures (Initials) _____ Prim. Nurse _____ Case Mgr. _____

EXHIBIT 5.2. COLORADO PSYCHIATRIC HOSPITAL INPATIENT TREATMENT PLAN DOCUMENTATION. (CONT'D.)

Patient Goals—Day 2 (_____) Date(s) _____	**EVAL**	Staff Orders—Day 2 (_____) Date(s) _____
Explore living arrangements following hospitalization		Meet with patient to prioritize the following and set time frames:
		Review completed worksheets
Attend groups to review and problem solve around reasons for hospitalization.		Miracle Question worksheet
11:00 Why Now Group/mgt OT Groups 1:30 Solutions 1) _____ 7:00 Choices 2) _____		Rating Scale (1–10)
Schedule meeting with family or other support system		Identify strengths
		Explore exceptions
Review completed Alt. packet worksheets with staff		FAMILY—focus of family work
Complete Miracle Worksheet		Critical Path
Explore Educational materials available		O.T. Assessment/Groups Assigned
Continue to rate self on scales and clarify behaviors at each interval (number) of the scale		OTHER:
Begin daily planning sheet		
EDUCATIONAL MATERIALS:		
		Homework Assigned:
HOMEWORK:		
Pt. Sig. _____		
Staff Sig. RN/MHW _____		

EXHIBIT 5.2. COLORADO PSYCHIATRIC HOSPITAL INPATIENT TREATMENT PLAN DOCUMENTATION. (CONT'D.)

Patient Goals—Day 3 (_____) Date(s) _____	**EVAL**	Staff Orders—Day 3 (_____) Date(s) _____
Meeting with family/support system _____ _____ Treatment Goals Continue with groups Consider outside groups _____ _____ _____ Identify old and new supports outside of hospital Educational Materials _____ _____ _____ _____ Homework: Pt. Sig. _____ Staff Sig. RN/MHW _____		INITIAL CASE CONFERENCE ELOS: _____ Goals/Time frame/Responsible team member Medications for target symptoms Family Work Need for consults Establish DX Assess priv. level and program level Additional Critical Paths Eval criteria for D/C Next Case Conference Conference Participants _____ _____ _____ _____ _____ Staff Sig. RN/MHW _____ CM _____ MD _____ SW _____ OT _____

EXHIBIT 5.2. COLORADO PSYCHIATRIC HOSPITAL
INPATIENT TREATMENT PLAN DOCUMENTATION. (CONT'D.)

Patient Goals—Day 4 (_____)	EVAL	Staff Orders—Day 4 (_____)
Date(s) _____		Date(s) _____
Treatment Goals		Meet with patient to reassess treatment goals and review progress toward goals
Educational Materials		Indicate useful staff approaches
_____		
_____		
_____		
_____		
Homework		Focus of Family work
		Reassess privs/program
Pt. Sig. _____		
Staff Sig. RN/MHW _____		CM _____

EXHIBIT 5.2. COLORADO PSYCHIATRIC HOSPITAL INPATIENT TREATMENT PLAN DOCUMENTATION. (CONT'D.)

Patient Goals—Day 5 (_____)	EVAL	Staff Orders—Day 5 (_____)
Date(s) _____		Date(s) _____
Treatment Goals		Meet with patient to reassess treatment goals and review progress toward goals
Educational Materials _____ _____ _____ _____		Indicate useful staff approaches
Homework		
		Reassess privs/program
Pt. Sig. _____		
Staff Sig. RN/MHW _____		CM _____

EXHIBIT 5.2. COLORADO PSYCHIATRIC HOSPITAL INPATIENT TREATMENT PLAN DOCUMENTATION. (CONT'D.)

Patient Goals—Day 6 (_____) Date(s) _____	**EVAL**	Staff Orders—Day 6 (_____) Date(s) _____
Complete discharge planning Utilize support systems as evidenced by: Demonstrate understanding of medication, side effects, and expected benefits. Finalize living arrangements Review treatment goals and progress toward goals. Finalize plan for follow-up care: Out-pt. therapist _____ _____ MD _____ Group _____ Attend d/c conf. Say goodbye to others. Pt. Sig. _____ Staff Sig. RN/MHW _____		DISCHARGE CASE CONFERENCE Review goals of hospitalization Complete discharge teaching, include warning signs and safety interventions Back to work/community plan Outpatient Therapist/Appt. Obtain educational materials from patient Enter discharge orders Obtain discharge rating scales and questionnaire Review risk factors Inform utilization review of discharge Verify demographic information Conference Participants _____ _____ _____ _____ Staff Sig. RN/MHW _____ CM _____ MD _____ SW _____ OT _____

Note: Copyright 1991 by Colorado Psychiatric Hospital, University of Colorado Health Sciences Center. Used with permission.

EXHIBIT 5.3. COLORADO PSYCHIATRIC
HOSPITAL PROGRESS NOTE.

University of Colorado Health Sciences Center
Colorado Psychiatric Hospital
PROGRESS NOTE

Date: _____ Time: _____   Case Manager: _____
Hospital Day: _____   Primary RN: _____
Estimated Discharge Date: ____   Legal Status:
                                  Vol —72 hr(exp. _____) —Cert
                                  Protocols: Exp: _____
                                  Restraints-Suicide-Escape-Seclusion
                                  Intensive Monitoring—Fall: I II   Attending: Room # _____
                                  Room Program: _____
                                  Medical: _____   Contracts/Ins: _____
                                  _____   Resident/ACS/UR: _____
                                  RTW OWA LGS FULL   Nursing Intensity: N: __D: __E: __

MODALITY	A P	Int. OBS ECT
		Noc Morn Aft Eve
	P A C	Inpatient Day
		ECT

Criteria for Discharge:
_____
_____

Goals for Shift: _____
_____
_____
_____

Intervention: _____
_____
_____
_____

Outcome: _____
_____
_____
_____
_____
_____
_____
_____

Recommendations/Evaluation: _____
_____
_____
_____

                                              Signature _____
Initial ____ Signature _____   Initial ____ Signature _____   Initial ____ Signature _____

CHAPTER SIX

SOLUTION-FOCUSED SUPERVISION

The Coaxing of Expertise

Frank N. Thomas

An episode of the hit television series "Northern Exposure" featured a conversation between a young filmmaker and a Native American artisan. The filmmaker was putting together a documentary to preserve the art of flute making, a painstaking process involving the creation of a ceremonial flute from a tree branch. As the sixty-eight-year-old woodcarver began to craft, the conversation turned to the philosophy of the art, and the woodcarver said, "The branch will tell me how to carve it. . . . Each piece of wood has its own shape, which you must respect. . . . In each . . . branch lies a flute; [my] job is to find it."[1]

This example defines a context for understanding the philosophy and process of solution-focused supervision as it is currently being interpreted in the field of family therapy. Based on models known as solution-focused (Berg & Miller, 1992; de Shazer, 1988, 1991; Furman & Ahola, 1992), solution-oriented (O'Hanlon & Weiner-Davis, 1989), brief (Cade & O'Hanlon, 1993; McFarland, 1995), narrative (White & Epston, 1990), competency-based (Durrant, 1993, 1995; Durrant & Kowalski, 1993; Thomas & Cockburn, in press) and possibility (O'Hanlon, 1992; O'Hanlon & Beadle, 1994) therapies, this approach to supervision is significantly different from

Note: Special thanks are due to "Chip" Chilton, Hung-Hsiu Chang, Mallika Samuel, Kristi Knorpp, and Jack Cockburn, who along with others have taught me that teachers are useless without learners.

other models of family therapy supervision. The major tenets of solution-focused brief therapy (SFBT)—curiosity and respect (Berg & Miller, 1992)—are also the primary focal points of the solution-focused supervision model in that the model seeks to coax and author expertise from the life, experience, education, and training of a supervisee/therapist[2] rather than to deliver or teach expertise from a hierarchically superior position (White & Epston, 1990). This chapter correlates some of the basic tenets of solution-oriented therapies with the supervision context to supply the underpinnings necessary for a theory and practice of solution-focused supervision.

What Therapists Want from Supervision

Very little can be gleaned from the family therapy literature regarding therapist perceptions of supervision (Gershenson & Cohen, 1978). Because of this paucity of research, Heath and Tharp (1991) examined the supervision process in an attempt to build understanding of therapists' needs, desires, and requirements in this learning system. The themes that developed from their research seem particularly relevant to the discussion of supervision models that may utilize solution-focused approaches:

1. *"We want relationships based on mutual respect."* Respect is a philosophical principle of solution-focused models of therapy (Berg & Miller, 1992), and it is fitting that a supervisory experience based on this cornerstone assumption would be in line with therapist expectations.
2. *"You don't have to be a guru."* Because the client is the expert within solution-focused models (de Shazer, 1988; Durrant & Kowalski, 1993; O'Hanlon & Weiner-Davis, 1989), an appropriate way to supervise would be to create an atmosphere of collegiality with the therapist as opposed to a traditional, more hierarchical relationship.
3. *"Supervise us or evaluate us; not both."* One of the most difficult distinctions to draw within the supervision relationship involves the evaluative process inherent in many academic, agency, and training settings. The focus of a solution-focused supervision process should be the achieving of well-defined goals set by the therapist/supervisor team; therefore, evaluation should also be a cooperative experience based on goals and change.
4. *"Assume that we're competent. We're hard enough on ourselves already."* Believing that the client has the capacity and ability to solve his or her own problems is a foundational assumption of solution-oriented therapies (Durrant & Kowalski, 1993); therefore, solution-focused supervision should likewise assume that the therapist-in-supervision is competent to bring about change when necessary, to

continue successful skills and conceptualizations, and to adjust when necessary to a more useful position, strategy, or orientation.

5. *"Tell us what we're doing right. Affirm us. Empower us."* The recognition and amplification of success are foundational in these models (O'Hanlon & Weiner-Davis, 1989; Weiner-Davis, de Shazer, & Gingrich, 1987) and should lead to a supervisory experience of empowerment based on the therapist's successes and competencies.

6. *"Listen to us. Make supervision a human experience."* Just as the therapist relies on the client to be the expert on her or his life and complaint, within this model the therapist, not the supervisor, must be the expert on the therapist's life, abilities, and experiences (Kowalski & Durrant, 1990; Walter & Peller, 1992). It naturally flows that when the supervisor listens with curiosity and respect in order to bring about change, the human factor will become primary in the relationship (Berg & Miller, 1992; George, Iveson, & Ratner, 1990). (These concepts will be discussed further later in the chapter.)

Applying these themes to a solution-focused supervision approach is not simple, nor is their implementation necessary. However, given the cooperative nature of the therapeutic model, this research offers a starting point for the creation of a supervisory relationship based on respect, competence, and cooperation.

The Concept of Isomorphism in Family Therapy Supervision

A solution orientation to supervision can be very useful when one considers an important aspect of the process: the expectations and anticipated needs of the therapist. An equally important aspect to be considered in supervision is the relationship between the supervisory approach and the model being utilized by the therapist. The most common understanding of this issue in the family therapy supervision literature involves the concept of *isomorphism*.

"As clinical training programs change, it is being discovered that a theory of therapy and a theory of training are often synonymous" (Haley, 1976, p. 170). This supervision concept is known as isomorphic, or equivalent, structures. "The word 'isomorph' applies when two complex structures can be mapped onto each other in such a way that to each part of one structure there is a corresponding part in the other structure, where 'corresponding' means that the two parts play similar roles in their respective structures" (Hofstadter, 1979, p. 49). An isomorphic relationship is not duplication or repetition; rather, it signifies an overlap and a sense of connection. According to Levinson (1972, p. 36), the "structure, or form, is constant in spite of changing content."

Within family therapy, the isomorphic structure of the supervisory relationship continues to be the most acceptable metaphor for understanding training and development. For example, within structural and strategic therapies the training task is to narrow the perception and views of the therapist toward more "contextually sensitive, systemic" orientations (Liddle & Saba, 1983, p. 5). This is achieved through goal setting, mirroring of sequences, increasing intensity, enactment, planned interventions, and other strategies inherent to these models. When supervision is organized isomorphic to these models, a hierarchical relationship between supervisor and therapist "will naturally organize" itself; it is "inevitable" (Liddle & Saba, 1985, pp. 35–36).

Perhaps the most significant "difference which makes a difference" (Bateson, 1972/1985) that is created when one formulates supervisory relationships using a solution-focused model involves this concept of hierarchy. Within the solution-oriented models, the relationship between client(s) and therapist is cooperative and respectful. Because the therapist assumes that the client both is the expert on (Berg & Miller, 1992) and has the resources to resolve her or his complaint (O'Hanlon & Weiner-Davis, 1989), the therapist seeks to discover ways to cooperate with the client's desires, definitions, goals, and language. Isomorphically, solution-focused supervision seeks to set up a cooperative, goal-oriented relationship that assumes that the therapist possesses the strength, ability, and resourcefulness to resolve a complaint and achieve training goals. It naturally follows that the supervisor is not the expert on the therapist's situation—the supervisor defines the goals, directions, and options *with* the therapist to construct a participatory experience through consensus and teamwork. Supervision proceeds as a future-oriented endeavor, setting up positive expectations and building on the unique assets of the therapist.

Some Guiding Assumptions for Solution-Focused Supervision

In supervision, it is more important to know where one begins in the process than where one ultimately goes (Cantwell & Holmes, 1995). O'Hanlon and Weiner-Davis (1989) have supplied the psychotherapy field with a set of well-formed assumptions regarding solution-focused therapy and competency-based models in general. Other chapters in this book thoroughly address solution-focused assumptions, both theoretical and clinical, which are seminal to the model; therefore, this chapter will not attempt to defend the adequacy or accuracy of the listed assumptions. Because of the isomorphic relationship between the therapy and supervision models, these assumptions have been adopted with commentary regarding how they can be understood and adapted to the supervisory experience.

Most of the assumptions discussed are derived from O'Hanlon and Weiner-Davis (1989), and they closely parallel Cantwell & Holmes's (1995) social constructionist supervision principles. Additional assumptions are noted with citations.

It is not necessary to know the cause or function of a complaint in order to resolve it. In solution-oriented models, there are no "symptoms" of underlying problems. The person is not the problem; instead, "the problem is the problem" (White, 1989). Many therapists have problem-saturated views of themselves and their therapy. Seeking a "cause" or "function" of a problem perpetuates this focus. Instead of attempting to resolve the "issue" identified by either the supervisor or the therapist, the supervisor needs to focus on what prevents the problem from being resolved in the therapist's present experience. A case example may be helpful to illustrate this concept.

Jim,[3] a therapist at the university's family therapy clinic, had a case he affectionately titled, "She Is My Mother." After Jim struggled for six months with a client who was a carbon copy of his own mother, a live consultation was arranged, which I observed from behind a one-way mirror. During a break, Jim proceeded to explain to me his connections to the client (she was the same age as his mother, she had a son with the same name as his brother, and so on), believing, perhaps, that explanation would lead to his understanding why he was stuck, and to direct change. Assuming that additional insight was unnecessary for change in the situation, the conversation focused on what Jim was doing when the treatment was progressing:

Supervisor: When in the session does she experience change?
Therapist: When I keep her on task and hold her to the topic.
Supervisor: How do you do that?
Therapist: I interrupt her!
Supervisor: Could you do more of that?

The case terminated in five weeks, with the client experiencing rapid change in her relationship to her children and husband. Jim attributed the change in the client's situation to his change in approach: doing what worked and diminishing his views on the importance of understanding his relationship to the client. He relates that he never did discover why he was stuck—he simply got unstuck.

Therapists know what is best for themselves. Because the goal of supervision is to establish a "contextual reality of competence" (M. Durrant, personal communication, October 9, 1992), this model assumes that therapists have access to the resources necessary to solve therapeutic dilemmas. It is unfortunate when supervisors become didactic before it is necessary, for the model assumes that the therapist is capable of drawing on resources to break the binds currently blocking his or her change with one case or one specific skill.

There is no such thing as "resistance" (de Shazer, 1984). The supervisor's task is to find ways to cooperate with the learning experience and style of the therapist. "Stuckness," or escalating sameness (Keeney, 1983), is often maintained collaboratively by supervisor and therapist; the supervisor's task is to discover ways to cooperate so that the therapist is free to choose new options and directions.

The supervisor's job is to identify and amplify change. The focus of supervision in this model is on solution talk, not problem talk. Because the constructivist position "believing is seeing" seems to apply (von Foerster, 1984), the supervisor is in the unique position of being able to bring attention to whatever he or she sees as relevant in the supervisory process. Paramount within this model are increasing the occurrence of successes and amplifying changes the therapist makes.

A small change is all that is necessary. Within this model, the best experience is a small success. Launching a small change will lead to a recursion of change (Keeney & Thomas, 1986). Likewise, increasing feelings of competence will lead to drawing upon different resources, which in turn will lead to additional successes and change. This "snowball" or "ripple" effect, as it has been called, is a time-tested systemic assumption in the therapy arena that begs application to supervision (O'Hanlon & Weiner-Davis, 1989).

Change is constant, and rapid change is possible. "If you assume change is constant, you will behave as if change were inevitable" (O'Hanlon & Weiner-Davis, 1989, p. 35). No supervision "problem" remains the same, nor do "problems" in supervision follow a prescripted course. The meanings, attitudes, and experiences of events are altered by time because the assignment of meaning to events requires context (Keeney, 1983). Since nothing remains the same, the responsibility of the supervisor is to locate differences that are inevitable and then to signify them. Changes in supervision may be progressive or discontinuous as the therapist develops, and the supervisor must allow himself or herself to be surprised.

Pat, an experienced therapist continuing her education by pursuing a doctorate, was exposed to the ideas of systemic perception in a clinical class. One night, while lying awake in bed, Pat cried tears of joy when she made the discovery that she could "see" systems, interactional patterns, and connections between people. This very significant change greatly accelerated her goal of working systemically with her clients—a goal she says she never would have achieved by simple progressive learning and experience. The rapid change was not anticipated, nor could it have been predicted; however, it was accepted and integrated into her learning because this model allows persons to change at their own pace and within their own limits.

Supervision should focus on what is possible and changeable. Within a solution-focused supervision experience, one should leave the impossible alone and work instead with what is possible and likely. In this regard, recognizing capabilities is more important than accentuating the intractable deficits, experiences, and beliefs of the therapist. Since one cannot undo what has been done, the supervisor should focus on what can be done next—that is, move forward with what is realizable and feasible with the therapist in the time available.

Some supervisors who implement this model may miss the "good ol' days" of meat-and-potatoes, issue-driven, pathology-defined supervision that is loaded with tears, painful insights, and arduous self-discovery. In fact, solution-focused supervision may not even feel like *real* supervision at first. However, recognizing that in the current managed care atmosphere psychotherapy supervision will go the way of psychotherapy practice, ways must be found to offer effective supervision without the luxurious time spans of the past. Helping therapists get on the right track and grow without an ongoing formal supervisory relationship may be the requirement of supervision in the twenty-first century.

There is no one "right" way to view things. Because solution-focused therapy follows a constructivist view (von Glasersfeld, 1984), "different views may be just as valid and may fit the facts just as well" (O'Hanlon & Weiner-Davis, 1989, p. 46). For this reason, it is not necessary for the supervisor to convince the therapist of the "rightness" or "wrongness" of the therapist's particular view. Rather, the supervisor's task is to develop "fit" with the therapist so that the therapist may entertain additional views (de Shazer, 1988). By so utilizing the language and perception of the therapist, the supervisor empowers the therapist with alternative and viable choices when he or she is stuck in a particular mode of thinking, feeling, or behaving.

One of the most valuable components of a solution-focused approach to supervision is the supervisor's *respectful* questioning of absolutes. Therapists in group supervision settings notice how the supervisor handles ideas, and in such a context therapists can often perceive as disrespectful the supervisor's correcting of their understanding or decisions. When supervisors ask such questions as How do you see yourself working differently in a similar situation? and What also might be true? they allow therapists to question their own conclusions with minimal threat. Consistency in questioning reified positions is essential; however, without kindness and respect, little may be heard.

Curiosity is indispensable (Berg & Miller, 1992). A genuine desire to know the opinions and perspectives of the therapist is rudimentary. The best way to expand the therapist's views and options is for the supervisor to seek to comprehend the therapist's interpretation of the complaint and to act in cooperation with this understanding. The therapist is the expert; therefore, useful knowledge begins with the therapist's knowledge. Two supervision examples may be helpful in illustrating some of these assumptions.

Keith is a middle-aged professional with years of people experience. At the first supervision meeting, he related that since he had never had any formal psychotherapy training he felt very inadequate for the tasks ahead. Keith had a full pad of paper, several sharpened pencils, and an audiotape recorder, intending to catch every drop of wisdom his supervisor had to share! After taking out a pad of paper and a pen, the supervisor turned to Keith and asked, "What strengths do you bring to this learning context?" Keith was dumbfounded! It took most of the initial session to work out how his expectations of passive learning from the "master" and the supervisor's expectations of amplifying his existing skills would fit together, creating a common goal focusing on Keith's own learning objectives and particular style. In the next few weeks, Keith set three-month goals for himself that were quite simple yet elegant: to use questions more than statements (that is, interpretations), to consistently apply the major assumptions of SFBT in 50 percent of his sessions, to read three books on SFBT, to transcribe thirty minutes of what he considered to be his best work to give himself a different view of the therapy, and to share fifteen minutes of videotape in individual supervision each week, balancing "when I blow it" with "when I'm doing well." At the end of this initial supervisory term, Keith had achieved all of these goals and had developed an effective style in the therapy room that delighted clients, colleagues, and supervisors alike. This beginning, based on cooperation and therapist motivation, laid what Keith calls a "firm foundation" for all of his future learning in the field.

Marguerite is a doctoral student with nearly fifteen years of clinical experience. Although she had rarely done any couple or family work, she brought sharp clinical eyes and ears to the supervision process. At the beginning of the supervisory relationship, her theoretical ideas were "a jumble" (her words), a "mish-mash" (again, her description) of lineal and systemic concepts that did not fit together well for her. Instead of challenging her to resolve her confusion and bringing force to bear on her nonsystemic beliefs, the supervisor simply asked her to write out her goals for the next supervision meeting. When she presented her goals the next week, she was excited by the fact that the supervisor thought she could achieve many of the aims she had set for herself. Together, they fine-tuned her goals so that both of them would know whether and when she had achieved them, working as a team with the common purpose of improving her clinical skills. From this point on, these goals were used as a focal point in supervision, carefully bringing Marguerite's sufficiency and resources to bear on the challenges she had set for herself. The result: instead of deteriorating into a debate of presuppositions each week, the supervisor and student converged to reach achievable goals that *both* were motivated to attain. Another result: Marguerite gave her best effort to move beyond the limits of her earlier learning and experience, choosing to learn a competency-based model and to apply her skills to mastering new approaches in the clinical arena.

It is hoped that these two supervision examples illustrate connections between SFBT and a supervision approach based on similar assumptions. Bringing a focus of cooperation to supervision may radically alter the supervisory process. The following sections give practical examples on implementing a solution orientation in this context.

Becoming Solution-Focused in Supervision

It is not enough simply to *know*—supervision is an inventive art, not an ivory-tower concept. Working with therapists who come with diverse experiences is a challenge for any supervisor; within this model, several ideas may guide the supervisor toward consistency with the assumptions outlined earlier. The questions that follow, which are in keeping with the solution-oriented models of O'Hanlon and Weiner-Davis (1989), Durrant (Durrant, 1993; Durrant & Kowalski, 1993; Kowalski & Durrant, 1990), de Shazer (1988), and Berg and Miller (1992), may help the supervisor (or the therapist) in the pragmatics of supervision in this model. (The categories in which the questions are organized are adapted from Kowalski and Durrant, 1990, except where noted.)

Socializing

How one introduces the supervision sets the expectations, tone, and context for future supervisory experiences. Given the assumptions identified earlier, the supervisor needs to begin applying himself or herself to the task of developing a collaborative context for supervision. The very act of joining—often called hosting (Furman & Ahola, 1992) or socializing (Kowalski & Durrant, 1990) should seek to establish and optimize a cooperative relationship.

The supervisor should inquire into subjects that are success-possible. Topics might include "good" cases, positive training experiences in the past, interests, and life experiences that the therapist brings to the supervision relationship. Here are some questions a supervisor might ask (Kowalski & Durrant, 1990):

What do you do well with regard to your therapy and supervision?

How has your life prepared you thus far for this step in your training?

How have you successfully guided your supervision in the past?

Saliency

What is important to discuss should be co-created in supervision (Berg & Miller, 1992). Seeking the therapist's personal, contextual, theoretical, pragmatic, emotional, and historical views is cardinal. Questions that may help the process include:

What would be most helpful for us to focus on?

What is the most important thing I need to know about your therapy and supervision at this time?

In maintaining a solution focus in the interaction, the following questions may be helpful:

With which types of problems (people, situations, families, and so on) do you do well?

How has your therapy improved since our last consult?

When things are better (with regard to a complaint), what are you doing differently?

Setting Goals

The questions that guide this area of inquiry should focus on the therapist's desire for change: how does the therapist wish things (feelings about therapy, behaviors, a specific case, and so on) to be different? At this point the supervisor should follow solution-focused therapy guidelines for goal development in defining achievable goals (for valuable information, see Walter & Peller, 1992).

The goals should be positively framed and as specific as possible. Further, any goal should be primarily within the control or agency of the therapist; that is, achieving one's goal should not be dependent upon "correct" client change. Also, goals should be couched in the therapist's language in a process form—that is, it should be possible to identify change and success during the course of supervision. Examples of questions to utilize include the following:

How will you know when things have improved for you?

What will be different when your therapy is better (Kowalski & Durrant, 1990)?

How will we know when it is time to move on to something new in supervision?

What will be happening differently when the issue you are complaining about is better?

The Miracle Question

One of the most important elements of goal setting involves what de Shazer and his colleagues (Berg & Miller, 1992; de Shazer, 1991; O'Hanlon & Weiner-Davis, 1989) have termed "the miracle question." By projecting the problem into the future, the supervisor asks the therapist to envision therapy without the problem and to describe activities, feelings, and perceptions without the influence of the problem. If the therapist has difficulty picturing life without the problem, asking the following questions and seeking descriptive examples of difference will allow the forming of an achievable goal:

If a miracle were to happen tonight while you were asleep and tomorrow morning you awoke to find that this obstacle was no longer a part of your life, what would be different?

How would you know that this miracle had taken place?

How would I be able to tell without your telling me?

Small Changes

Essential to the process of setting goals is understanding what small changes can be made toward the objective. As many theorists of the solution-focused model have noted, it is critical to think small to secure immediate success for the supervisee. When pursuing the goal, it is important for the supervisor to be as concrete as possible and to offer sincere compliments to the therapist when progress and change are identified. Questions in this area might include:

What will be a small sign, something that you might notice this week, that will tell you that things are looking up for you in this area (Kowalski & Durrant, 1990)?

What is a small step that you could make in the direction of the goal?

What will be the first thing I (or another person) will notice about your therapy when it improves?

Scaling Questions

One particular technique, called "scaling" (Berg & Miller, 1992), has been particularly useful with clients and translates well into the supervision process. Redefining a goal from a dichotomy (either/or, success/failure) to a range (1 to 10) allows for the discerning of small changes and the recognition of progress before finally achieving the goal. Examples of questions using this scaling technique follow:

On a scale from one to ten, with one being failure and ten being complete success, how would you rate how you're doing with your problem right now? And when you rate yourself at [one or two points higher than the therapist's response], what will you be doing differently (Kowalski & Kral, 1989)?

Since you have a pretty good idea where you stand with your problem, pay attention this week to when it is just a little better. We'll discuss what you're doing to make that happen the next time we meet.

Identifying Exceptions to Problems

Within this model of supervision, problems are defined by the therapist—the supervisor rarely identifies problems for the therapist, except in situations that require ethical and/or legal consideration before professional development (Thomas, 1992, 1995). Exceptions, according to Kowalski and Durrant (1990), are "those bits of experience, behavior, interaction, or self-perception which serve to challenge the dominant description." These are moments or events in which change has been evident to the supervisor, the therapist, or people in the therapist's context. Since exceptions are assumed to exist in any problem description in this model, the supervisor must seek to identify these exceptions and build upon them for future change. Questions might include:

I'll bet there are times when you expect the problem to occur and it doesn't. How do you explain this? How do you make that happen (Kowalski & Durrant, 1990)?

When is the problem less frequent (intense, severe)?

When is the problem just a little different?

When are you doing some of what you want to do in relation to this problem?

Making Exceptions Meaningful

Investing agency or control in the person's story is one helpful path toward change (this category was identified by Kowalski & Durrant, 1990; see also Anderson & Goolishian, 1992; Durrant & Kowalski, 1993). Questions can be formed by the supervisor that make an opening for explanation that puts solving the problem within the control of the therapist. Examples include:

[When an exception has been identified] How do you account for your ability to do this (Kowalski & Durrant, 1990)?

How did you decide to do this?

Did you know you would be able to influence your problem?

Was this easy for you to do or was it difficult?

How have you managed to decrease _____ since our last consult?

So, the problem isn't much better—what have you been doing to keep it from getting worse?

How have your mistakes, errors, and so on made you a better therapist?

What was different about you when you stood up to (changed or influenced) the problem (Kowalski & Durrant, 1990)?

What did your clients notice about you when you had an influence on this problem?

Future Orientation, or Keeping the Changes Going

The supervisor using this model is committed to amplifying positive change as the therapist experiences it. Once exceptions have been identified, the supervisor's task is to find additional exception experiences that, it is assumed, will lead to further progress toward the identified goal. Questions that relate to this concept include the following:

Let's assume you beat this problem—what will be different for you (Kowalski & Durrant, 1990)?

Now, you've got this problem on the run! What are you continuing to do this week to perpetuate the change?

All you have to do is keep up this change, right? How will you do that?

What specifically do you need to focus on doing this week to keep the problem from returning?"

Other Ideas for Implementing Solution-Focused Concepts

Accessing Therapist Resources

As with most relationships, supervision requires time and information for change to occur. Since a focus on resourcefulness is a major premise of SFBT, this supervision model works best when *both* therapist and supervisor share information that will create a strengths-based relationship. As a supervisor, I am very open about what I believe is usually helpful (and what is not helpful) in the supervision process, and my attempts to "flatten out" the seemingly inherent hierarchy of supervision have been met with equal openness from therapists.

An exercise created in a therapy context (Thomas, 1994a) has proven useful in supervision contexts as well. In the early meetings, the therapist is asked to buy a spiral-bound notebook and then to ask the following question of two or three friends or relatives who will be truthful yet kind: "What do you value about how I relate to people?" The therapist is to record each person's comments on the first sheet of paper in the notebook and bring the list to the next supervision meeting. Comments are generally one-word or short-phrase descriptions, such as "honest," "patient with children," "good listener," and "caring." At the meeting, the therapist is asked to separate those comments that "fit" (those that the therapist agrees with) from those that he or she disagrees with. Then the therapist is asked to write each comment separately at the top of the next notebook pages (so that page 2 would have "honest" at the top, page 3 would have "good listener" as a header, and so on). The supervisor then tells the therapist how to use the notebook to inform the supervisor of his or her strengths:

> During the next two weeks, I would like for you to write down examples for each and every one of these ideas. If you experience a moment of "honesty" with a client, friend, lover, or stranger, please record the particulars of that event under "honesty" in your notebook. Noting the time, place, and people involved as well as your own brief reactions or feelings will help me better know how you see yourself. If an event fits in more than one category, please feel free to place it wherever it fits. At the end of two weeks, I hope you will have a resource notebook that I can copy and return to you, and I believe this will be invaluable as we work together on accessing your strengths with people and applying them to your practice of therapy.

> This exercise can be one of the most popular activities in supervision! Therapists find it affirming and helpful in their steps toward effectively working with people in the counseling setting. One could improvise upon this theme by asking therapists to continue the notebook throughout their time in supervision, adding additional descriptions and examples as their experience in therapy broadens.

Using Presuppositional Language

Nearly everyone considered to be a major author in the SFBT area emphasizes the importance of language. Joining with therapists in their particular use of words is essential to relationship formation, and creating common understandings of experiences is certainly integral. Supervisee feedback also points to the use of pre-suppositional language as the most influential practice within this approach.

From day one, the supervisor should phrase questions and statements to include the assumption of competence. One therapist commented to me about this aspect of supervision, stating that "I knew you believed in me, even though *I* didn't believe in me!" This response was directly related to question formation. I begin every solution-focused supervision workshop (Thomas, 1990, 1992, 1995) with the question, "What do you do well?" The audience is initially pensive, but this thoughtfulness quickly segues to spirited dialogue among the members as they articulate their clinical strengths aloud and bask in the audience glow. Other questions that readers might find useful in eliciting evidence of competence include:

What do you want to *further* develop? [Assumes current development]

How did you know to do that at that moment? [Assumes prior knowledge]

What strengths would your clients say you bring to the therapy room? [Assumes positive client knowledge]

If you were to access another side of yourself at that moment, what might change (be more acceptable to you)? [Assumes flexibility, choice, and the ability to alter one's actions to create a different outcome]

What does your success in this situation say about your skills as a therapist? [Assumes that the therapist's skill was integral to the successful outcome]

I'd like your evaluation of the supervisory/learning process so far. What has been most helpful? [Assumes the therapist has valuable knowledge about the supervisory process]

The research of Swann and his colleagues (Swann, Giuliano, & Wegner, 1982) lends support to the idea that the person asking presuppositional questions will solicit information supporting the assumption from the subject, even if the interviewer knows the questions were drawn at random and are not based on what is known about the person. In addition, they found that *the interviewers come to believe in the presuppositions.* Supervisors cannot *not* be affected in a competency-based direction if they approach the supervision context in this way.

Group Supervision

In addition to utilizing this particular exercise in individual consultation, work in the group supervision setting should take much the same form. Following the assumptions outlined previously, therapists in group supervision can become "resource consultants" to each other. Andersen (1991) gives guidelines for competency-based group consultation: all statements must be positive, all observations and opinions must be stated in a tentative form, and the therapist has the right to a final response.

The meeting usually takes the following format: a therapist is scheduled to show a portion of videotape that he or she feels would be helpful to show and allow for responses from the group, all within a forty-five-minute frame. This format allows the therapist latitude in choosing to show the group examples of greater or lesser success. Following introductory comments to inform the group of the particular case, the therapist tells the group how he or she best learns in the group process. "I'd like for you to hold your questions until the end" and "Feel free to ask me to stop the tape anytime" are two ways therapists often inform the group of their learning preferences. Then the therapist shows the tape, stopping and starting it at his or her discretion. Group members are free to comment, but they are asked to restrict themselves to (1) being helpful according to the therapist's definition and (2) following the format requested by the therapist. Comments from these colleagues are usually begun with such phrases as, "I was thinking . . . ," "I wonder if . . . ," "What I saw was . . . ," and so on. A strong theme of "noticing" often emerges: "I noticed that you said . . . ," "I noticed that the client stopped . . . ," and so on. Finally, after the tape has been shown, the supervisor solicits comments from the therapist by asking the following questions:

What did you learn about your clients, your therapy, and yourself today?

What did the group contribute that was most helpful?"

What could we all do differently next time to make it better for you?

To enhance the possibilities for learning and to reinforce the positive change taking place, a videotape of the group supervision session can be made for the therapist to keep and review. This review is often useful for therapists because they can then review the particular comments and reflect on their significance in private, removing themselves from the (often) uncomfortable position of public praise, yet retaining the shared perspectives.

The value of such a format is still experimental; however, the response from therapists has been overwhelmingly positive. As one therapist confided, "It was a time for most of us when the grain of sand began to resemble a pearl. . . . It was always a place for constructive DIA-logue and informed academic support" (Chilton, 1995). Maintaining the dignity of the therapist and his or her clients is perhaps the guiding metaphor for this type of group structure. It is a simple extension of the curiosity/respect stance of Berg and Miller (1992), and it seems to support optimal learning and growth.

Goal Setting

As in SFBT (Walter & Peller, 1992), one cannot hit a target without a target. In fact, like Geertz's (1973) proverbial Mexican peasant, it would always be better to shoot a hole in the fence *first* and then paint the bull's-eye around it! In keeping with the isomorphic relationship between therapy and supervision, therapists should be goal oriented in their learning.

The maxim "If at first you don't succeed, change your definition of success" should be one's guiding principle. Three-month goals that are observable, measurable, and verifiable seem to work well with a wide range of therapist experience and personal ambition. Normally, supervisors do not participate in the goal-setting process until the therapist has written down a few goals. Then, the process of clarification involves both supervisor and therapist. Some goals may not be verifiable from the supervisor's perspective. For example, if a therapist has a goal of utilizing the SFBT model in 50 percent of his or her cases, then the therapist is in the best position to assess progress and/or need for change. Other goals may be accessible to supervisors' scrutiny and evaluation. For example, a therapist has a goal of having fifteen consecutive minutes of therapy within which he or she only asks questions. This could be verified by both therapist and supervisor via videotape or audiotape replay. The completion of certain readings could also be assessed through oral or written review in supervision. Finally, the use of one-to-ten scales or percentages gives therapists room for change without mastery. If a therapist sets a goal for himself or herself to "be consistent with the model" or "focus on client resources," then the supervisor might approach with a request for clarification: How consistent do you want to be? How do you behaviorally define "consistent"? What would be a realistic goal for the next three months—25 percent of the time? More? Less? With the therapist's first-draft goals in hand, the supervisor can guide the clarification process, creating small steps in the right direction.

Every case, question, and session can be related to the therapist's goals. Much like the emphasis placed on goal setting in SFBT (Walter & Peller, 1992), supervision goals should guide discussions and decisions whenever appropriate. For example, Bob had set a short-term goal of "holding consistently to solution-focused brief therapy assumptions 50 percent of the time." When he became stuck with a client couple, his analysis was that they were resistant and he was trying hard to change them. It just so happened that a primary problem the couple had was that each was trying to change the other! The following conversation with his supervisor took place:

Therapist: So, now that I know *what* I'm doing wrong, how do I stop?
Supervisor: Well, let's take a quick look at your goals for the semester. What did you think was important to believe about your clients?

Therapist: I need to be consistent with the solution-focused assumptions.

Supervisor: What might apply here, which of those assumptions?

Therapist: I guess it would be de Shazer's assumption that "there is no such thing as resistance."

Supervisor: OK, if you were to be more consistent with that assumption, what would change?

Therapist: I would stop viewing the couple as resistant! But that's not easy, you know!

Supervisor: It's just a habit. What perspective could you play with to get out of that stuck position?

Therapist: OK, I think I need to believe there must be a different way for me to cooperate.

At this point, the conversation moved toward Bob's change and away from labeling clients and attempting to solve the impasse with the unsuccessful approach he had been taking.

There are, of course, many therapeutic and supervisory problems that will not relate to a therapist's goals. However, utilizing the goals as a touchstone allows for constant re-vision of the entire process connecting clients, therapist, and supervisor. Focusing on this connection keeps change on track and helps in the evaluation process at the end of the contract period. Such goal watching also helps the therapist avoid trying to change everything about his or her therapy. Being goal focused allows for the spotlight to be shared, giving both the therapist and the clients center stage part of the time in the supervisory process.

Evaluation

One of the most difficult positions in professional life is the dual role of supervisor/evaluator. Critics of a "centrarchical," or cooperative, relationship in supervision often state that hierarchy must be maintained (or cannot be avoided) when the supervisor is also the one who must assess the performance of the therapist for purposes of promotion, grades, raises, and so on. There are two flaws in such a conclusion. First, dichotomous thinking (that one must either be a collegial supervisor *or* "the boss") is not only inaccurate but may also be detrimental to the supervision process. It seems that the responsibilities of evaluator always override the responsibilities of providing quality service to the public and helping therapists improve their craft. However, such an absolute hierarchical arrangement is not an inherent part of the process, and maintaining such distinctions may say more about the supervisor than it does about the context in which he or she conducts supervision.

Second, there is no intrinsic reason why supervisors cannot clarify when they are "supervisors" and when they are "evaluators." It is true that this attempt to clarify is not a unilateral move but is dependent on the meaning constructed by both the supervisor and the therapist (Bobele, Gardner, & Biever, 1995); however, initiating such a dialogue is probably the supervisor's prerogative, as attempts to co-create a relationship that maximizes value for all involved probably require some deliberateness on the part of the supervisor. Taking up the challenge from Heath and Tharp's (1991) earlier observation that therapists may want supervision and evaluation to be separate, one could begin the supervision relationship with attempts to clarify when one is supervising and when one is formally evaluating the performance of the therapist. Since we must all act on the G. Spencer-Brown imperative to "Draw a distinction!" (cited in Keeney, 1983), moving away from the secure, traditional positions that focus on hierarchy toward roles that are more fluid could effect unexpected cooperation in settings normally defined as oppositional and symmetrical.

A challenge for those defined into dual roles (such as an academic required to grade student progress) would be to experiment with alternative supervision and evaluative arrangements. Initiating mutual evaluation criteria can lead to goals that fit the therapist, the supervisor, *and* the organization. Seeking the opinions of the therapist on his or her performance keeps the supervisor consistent with the constructionist positions that brief and family therapists have espoused for decades (Anderson & Goolishian, 1992; von Glasersfeld, 1984).

Conclusions

"It is our contention that, as therapists, we have a choice about the basic 'stance' we wish to adopt. To see people in terms of pathology or to see them in terms of competence is a matter of choice rather than one of truth" (Durrant & Kowalski, 1993). This idea is vital to the practice of solution-focused or competency-based supervision—therapists must be viewed as incomplete and imperfect yet competent colleagues who seek out the supervisor in order to bring about progress toward their goals.

This model of supervision may be adapted for use with varying levels of therapist expertise. There is wide variety in perception, organization, and participation by clinicians, and varying levels of expertise should be carefully considered when applying any supervisory model (see Benner, 1984). Resting on the assumption that competence is based on experience and knowledge found in many areas of the therapist's life, solution-focused approaches to training can be adapted to fit with any therapist's level of expertise, experience, and learning style.

Future research could focus on the ways therapists respond to solution-focused supervision and the optimal approaches for differing levels of competence. Qualitative inquiries regarding "fit" between therapy and supervision models would be a substantial contribution to the field. Also, the experience of fit between the approach to supervision and the level of therapist expertise is sorely needed for both this supervision model and family therapy in general.

Portions of this model may be adopted as techniques to be utilized within most other supervision models (Thomas, 1994b; Wetchler, 1990); however, those who supervise therapists who are practicing solution-oriented therapy models should consider the quality of the fit between those models of therapeutic change and the model of supervision being utilized. The assumptions of the supervision model and the guiding questions outlined in this chapter provide a plan that creates an opportunity for fit that will hopefully optimize the supervisory experience for both the therapist and the supervisor. For this model begins and succeeds with this assumption: within each therapist lies expertise; the supervisor's job is to bring it out.

Questions from the Editors

1.   *Solution-focused and competency-based therapies are often touted as brief, short term, and time limited throughout the life cycle. Could you please say something about the typical duration and/or depth of the solution focus as applied to the supervisory process?*

I believe that supervision is isomorphic to the practice model, but not identical. Since therapists seek supervision for a variety of reasons, it would be overly simplistic to believe that a solution-focused approach to supervision would be short, long, or in between. It has been my experience that incorporating ideas of competency into a therapist's acting and knowing is dependent on his or her motivation to learn, opportunities for application, and fit with current approaches used with clients. For example, a therapist who is already fairly goal oriented in his or her therapy might take less time to work comfortably within a competency-based approach than one who has not had much practice in goal formation. And since this model is built upon assumptions of "first steps" rather than finished products, the focus of supervision is placed on the foundational ideas and behaviors one adopts more than on the character development, wisdom, and experiential knowledge one gains throughout the course of one's therapy career.

2.   *How does the solution-focused or competency-based supervisor deal with a supervisee who may be engaging in risky, unethical, or potentially dangerous behavior within the context of treatment?*

This question bubbles up at every workshop I give on this supervision model. The first thing to consider is this: within every supervision relationship, one should begin with a clear contract regarding responsibility. My degree of purposeful control in supervision is directly tied to my own comfort level, trust in the therapist's abilities, and ethics; therefore, there may be times when I become more directive with regard to behaviors (the client's and/or the therapist's) that I consider dangerous or unethical. If my contract with a therapist involves usurping the therapist's right to act independently in extreme situations (such as supervising master's students in a university clinic), I may have greater latitude in which to act than I have within another supervision situation in which the therapist is an independent, licensed professional (and I possibly have no legal right to interfere). In clinical situations the supervisor deems extreme, I suggest *posing the situation as a dilemma* and openly discussing it with the therapist. Taking as much time as needed to explain my ethical, legal and clinical opinions in an open dialogue has a much greater likelihood of creating cooperation and clinical safety than a heavy-handed, "I'm taking charge" position. In the end, I have to act according to my conscience and best judgment. However, I always try to keep Heinz von Foerster's ethical imperative in mind: "Act always so as to increase the number of choices" (1984, p. 60). In supervision, this includes choices for the client(s), the therapist, the supervisor, and the relationships between them.

3. *What role does teaching play in solution-focused or competency-based supervision?*

I have done some changing through time in my approach to teaching within supervision. I used to think that assumptions like "Clients have all the resources they need to resolve their problems" would be true in all situations. What I found is that Harry Goolishian was right: You should fall in love with an idea, but you should never marry it (personal communication, November 1989)! I feel that my least favorite option is to become didactic in the supervision setting; however, if I hold to the premise that *supervisees know what they need,* there will be times when they will seek information from me and avoiding a didactic response might be off-putting or unethical. I hold to the assumption that people change in a variety of ways, and supervisees know when reading, reflection, dialogue, critique, and teaching are the best ways in which *they* learn. I do not believe I am a repository of therapy information, so didactically disbursing knowledge is a less comfortable approach to supervision for me than it might be for others. I believe that the goals of the learner give guidance at this point. In the cooperative creation of goals, supervisor and therapist have the opportunity to negotiate how to best achieve these aspirations. Working with a learner and creating the best fit between a therapist's needs and a supervisor's talents allows for optimal use of multiple learning milieus—including teaching.

Notes

1. Copyright © 1995 by Universal City Studios, Inc. Courtesy of MCA Publishing Rights, a Division of MCA Inc. All rights reserved.
2. Throughout this chapter the term "therapist" will usually be used to designate the person traditionally known as the supervisee, learner, or trainee.
3. All names have been changed to protect the privacy of the therapists.

References

Andersen, T. (Ed.) (1991). *The reflecting team: Dialogues and dialogues about the dialogues.* New York: W. W. Norton.

Anderson, H., & Goolishian, H. A. (1992). The client is the expert: A not-knowing approach to therapy. In S. McNamee & K. J. Gergen (Eds.), *Therapy as social construction* (pp. 25–39). Newbury Park, CA: Sage.

Bateson, G. (1985). *Steps to an ecology of mind.* New York: Ballantine. (Original work published 1972)

Benner, P. (1984). *From novice to expert: Excellence and power in clinical nursing practice.* Reading, MA: Addison-Wesley.

Berg, I. K., & Miller, S. D. (1992). *Working with the problem drinker: A solution-focused approach.* New York: W. W. Norton.

Bobele, M., Gardner, G., & Biever, J. (1995). Supervision as social construction. *Journal of Systemic Therapies, 14,* 14–25.

Cade, B., & O'Hanlon, W. H. (1993). *A brief guide to brief therapy.* New York: W. W. Norton.

Cantwell, P., & Holmes, S. (1995). Cumulative process: A collaborative approach to systemic supervision. *Journal of Systemic Therapies, 14,* 35–47.

Chilton, S. (1995, August). Of monks, of dogs, and difference. *News of the Difference, 4*(2), 7–8.

De Shazer, S. (1984). The death of resistance. *Family Process, 23,* 79–93.

De Shazer, S. (1988). *Clues: Investigating solutions in brief therapy.* New York: W. W. Norton.

De Shazer, S. (1991). *Putting difference to work.* New York: W. W. Norton.

Durrant, M. (1993). *Residential treatment: A cooperative, competency-based approach to therapy and program design.* New York: W. W. Norton.

Durrant, M. (1995). *Creative strategies for school problems: Solutions for psychologists and teachers.* New York: W. W. Norton.

Durrant, M., & Kowalski, K. (1993). Enhancing views of competence. In S. Friedman (Ed.), *The new language of change: Constructive collaboration in psychotherapy* (pp. 107–137). New York: Guilford.

Furman, B., & Ahola, T. (1992). *Solution talk: Hosting therapeutic conversations.* New York: W. W. Norton.

Geertz, C. (Ed.) (1973). *Interpretation of cultures.* New York: Basic Books.

George, E., Iveson, C., & Ratner, H. (1990). *Problem to solution: Brief therapy with individuals and families.* London: Brief Therapy Press.

Gershenson, J., & Cohen, M. S. (1978). Through the looking glass: The experiences of two family therapy trainees with live supervision. *Family Process, 17,* 225–230.

Haley, J. (1976). *Problem solving therapy.* San Francisco: Jossey-Bass.

Heath, A., & Tharp, L. (1991, November). *What therapists say about supervision.* Paper presented at the American Association for Marriage and Family Therapy Annual Conference, Dallas, TX.

Hofstadter, D. (1979). *Godel, Escher, Bach: An eternal golden braid*. New York: Basic Books.

Keeney, B. P. (1983). *Aesthetics of change*. New York: Guilford.

Keeney, B. P., & Thomas, F. N. (1986). Cybernetic foundations of family therapy. In F. Piercy & D. Sprenkle (Eds.), *Family therapy sourcebook* (pp. 262–267). New York: Guilford.

Kowalski, K., & Durrant, M. (1990, October). *Exceptions, externalizing and self-perception: A clinical map*. Paper presented at the American Association for Marriage and Family Therapy Annual Conference, Washington, DC.

Kowalski, K., & Kral, R. (1989). The geometry of solution: Using the scaling technique. *Family Therapy Case Studies, 4*(1), 59–66.

Levinson, E. (1972). *The fallacy of understanding*. New York: Basic Books.

Liddle, H. A., & Saba, G. W. (1983). On context replication: The isomorphic relationship of training and therapy. *The Journal of Strategic and Systemic Therapies, 2*(2), 3–11.

Liddle, H. A., & Saba, G. W. (1985). The isomorphic nature of training and therapy: Epistemologic foundation for a structural-strategic training paradigm. In J. Schwartzman (Ed.), *Families and other systems: The macrosystemic context of family therapy* (pp. 27–47). New York: Guilford.

McFarland, B. (1995). *Brief therapy and eating disorders: A practical guide to solution-focused work with clients*. San Francisco: Jossey-Bass.

O'Hanlon, B., & Beadle, S. (1994). *A field guide to PossibilityLand: Possibility therapy methods*. Omaha, NE: The Center Press.

O'Hanlon, W. H. (1992, February). *No guru, no method, no teacher*. Paper presented at the Texas Association for Marriage and Family Therapy Annual Conference, San Antonio, TX.

O'Hanlon, W. H., & Weiner-Davis, M. (1989). *In search of solutions: A new direction in psychotherapy*. New York: W. W. Norton.

Swann, W. B., Jr., Giuliano, T., & Wegner, D. M. (1982). Where leading questions can lead: The power of conjecture in social interaction. *Journal of Personality and Social Psychology, 42*, 1025–1035.

Thomas, F. N. (1990, October). *Solution-focused supervision*. Paper presented at the American Association for Marriage and Family Therapy Annual Conference, Washington, DC.

Thomas, F. N. (1992, October). *The coaxing of expertise: Solution-focused supervision*. Paper presented at the American Association for Marriage and Family Therapy Annual Conference, Miami, FL.

Thomas, F. N. (1994a). The experience of solution-oriented therapy: Post-therapy client interviewing. *Case Studies in Brief and Family Therapy, 8*(1), 47–58.

Thomas, F. N. (1994b). Solution-oriented supervision: The coaxing of expertise. *The Family Journal: Counseling and Therapy for Couples and Families, 2*(1), 11–18.

Thomas, F. N. (1995, May). *Solution-focused supervision: Coaxing expertise*. Paper presented at the Second Annual East Coast Solution-Focused Brief Therapy Conference, Williamsburg, VA.

Thomas, F. N., & Cockburn, J. (in press). *Solution-focused pastoral counseling: Brief competency-based methods*. Minneapolis, MN: Augsburg Fortress Press.

Von Foerster, H. (1984). On constructing a reality. In P. Watzlawick (Ed.), *The invented reality* (pp. 41–62). New York: W. W. Norton.

Von Glasersfeld, E. (1984). An introduction to radical constructivism. In P. Watzlawick (Ed.), *The invented reality* (pp. 17–40). New York: W. W. Norton.

Walter, J. L., & Peller, J. E. (1992). *Becoming solution-focused in brief therapy.* New York: Brunner/Mazel.

Weiner-Davis, M., de Shazer, S., & Gingrich, W. (1987). Building on pre-treatment change to construct the therapeutic solution: An exploratory study. *Journal of Marital and Family Therapy, 13,* 359–363.

Wetchler, J. L. (1990). Solution-focused supervision. *Family Therapy, 17,* 129–138.

White, M. (1989). *Selected papers.* Adelaide, South Australia: Dulwich Centre Publications.

White, M., & Epston, D. (1990). *Narrative means to therapeutic ends.* New York: W. W. Norton.

CHAPTER SEVEN

SOLUTION-FOCUSED THERAPY WITH MANDATED CLIENTS

Cooperating with the Uncooperative

Susan Lee Tohn and Jordan A. Oshlag

Tom is a seventeen-year-old brought to treatment by his parents. When asked why he is there, he states that his parents are forcing him to go to counseling. Tom says he does not want to be in counseling. When his parents are asked why they have come, they say they want the therapist to convince Tom that he has a drinking problem.

Mental health professionals work with mandated or "resistant" clients all the time. Working with clients who are being forced to come to therapy is a complicated and often frustrating process. Use of the solution-focused model, however, makes this demanding work with mandated clients simpler and more rewarding. For our purposes, "mandated" refers to clients who have been sent or brought by someone else for treatment. This definition includes clients referred by a variety of sources, including the courts, protective service agencies, employers, employee assistance programs, schools, parents, and significant others. Mandated clients can usually be identified very rapidly during the initial contact; most therapists can spot them a mile away. When asked why they are coming to therapy, these clients typically reply, "My [parent, partner, boss, probation officer] made me come." It is not uncommon for therapists, when they hear this, to shift gears and begin preparing for a long, difficult treatment episode.

A solution-focused approach, however, allows therapists to work with mandated clients the same way they work with nonmandated clients: by *cooperating.* Applying the solution-focused model to working with mandated clients involves three steps: (1) revisiting the concepts of resistance and denial, (2) adopting the six essential components for cooperating with mandated clients, and (3) integrating the six components into the solution-focused techniques (such as the miracle question and scaling questions).

Step 1: Avoiding Resistance and Denial

Traditional therapies tend to view mandated clients as "in denial" and/or "resistant" to treatment. Discussions about resistance and denial can often be heard at clinical case conferences. Consider, for example, the following conversation:

Therapist 1: Stan is forty-five, has been married twice, and has trouble holding a job. He was referred to me by his supervisor for missing too much work. He states that the boss is just on him because of an "incident" that occurred outside of work. I have seen him four times, and think he has a drinking problem [therapist labeling the problem].

Therapist 2: Did you ask him about his drinking? [second therapist going along with this label as "reality"]

Therapist 1: Yes, both at intake and during the last session. He completely denies that he has a problem with drinking, or any other drugs.

Therapist 3: Maybe things have not gotten bad enough for him to want or need to deal with his substance abuse.

Therapist 1: Maybe.

When clients are viewed as "in denial" of a problem, the first task the therapist often undertakes is to convince the client that the problem exists, is real, and needs to be addressed. It is when therapists act on these assumptions and attempt to convince the client that resistance is often encountered. To be sure, rapport with the *referral source* (such as the spouse, the probation officer, or the supervisor) may increase, but attempting to convince the client that a problem exists does little to enhance rapport with the client. The therapist has in essence joined the same queue as many others in the client's world, by stating that there is a problem and trying to force the client to see it and do something about it. The result can be swift and immediate: the client "fires" the therapist and does not return to therapy. To increase cooperation with mandated clients, the therapist must view resistance and denial differently.

A first step when cooperating with mandated clients is to adopt the view of resistance proposed by de Shazer in his 1989 article, "Resistance Revisited." De Shazer views resistance merely as a metaphor that has outlived its usefulness:

A funny thing happens to concepts over time. No matter how useful any concept might be at the start, eventually they all seem to become reified. Instead of remaining explanatory metaphors, they become facts. That is, rather than saying, "it is *as if* the client is resisting change," once reified, people begin to say things like "the client is resisting" and eventually they begin to say that "resistance *exists* and must be sought out" [p. 228].

When resistance is viewed as merely a metaphor, it is easy to see how the therapist, not the mandated client, creates resistance. Clients do not walk into therapy resistant; they only leave that way after a therapeutic encounter. By paying close attention to their own creation of resistance, and by shifting the responsibility of cooperating to themselves, therapists can greatly reduce the number of resistant clients with whom they come into contact.

Another conceptual shift is needed in regard to resistance if the therapist is to assume a more solution-focused approach in working with mandated clients. It is essential for the therapist to move from viewing clients as resistant or in denial to viewing them as having *multiple goals*. The key to this shift is for the therapist to cooperate with the client with respect to each of the client's goals. For example, a mandated adolescent may state his or her goals as follows: "I want my teachers to get off my back, my parents to stop yelling at me, and to not have to come to therapy." When the therapist works on goals that such a client is willing to work on, the therapist is cooperating. To not cooperate with the client would be to work on the referral source's goals—to change the client's attitude, to get him to listen to his parents more and to follow the rules. We have found that by cooperating with the mandated client through use of the solution-focused approach, ultimately both the client's and the referral source's goals are met.

Step 2: Applying the Six Essential Components

There are six components to working with the mandated client in a solution-focused manner: (1) honoring the client's worldview, (2) establishing well-formed treatment goals with the client, (3) utilizing the referral source to further establish well-formed treatment goals, (4) utilizing the referral source to sustain treatment progress, (5) identifying and utilizing the client-therapist-goal relationship, and (6) helping mandated clients move toward their goals.

Honoring the Client's Worldview

Studies indicate that in treating DWI (driving while intoxicated) offenders, forcing clients to work on a goal that is not their own does not produce the desired outcome (Bradley, 1988; Ditman, Crawford, Forgy, Moskowitz, & MacAndrew, 1967; O'Callaghan, 1990; Ogborne & Glaser, 1981). In addition, in our own experience, when we try to convince clients that they do in fact have a problem (such as with drinking, acting out, or their attitude), more often than not, they "fire" us after a few sessions and do not return. To cooperate with their clients, solution-focused therapists must explore the *client's* goals for treatment. This does not mean that the therapist does not get to "the issues"; rather, the therapist starts with the client and sees where treatment goes of its own accord. Starting with the client's view of the world enhances rapport.

From the beginning of a solution-focused session, clients are encouraged to tell the therapist how they feel, who sent them, and who believes they need to change. This is very different from asking mandated clients what their problem is. When encouraged, clients tell the truth as they view it, as opposed to the party line. At first, clients may be suspicious, if in previous interactions with other service providers they have felt judged by society, friends, family, and employers. However, after the therapist shows genuine interest in a client's view of the situation, the client will begin to tell even those details that he or she knows may not be popular.

This approach enhances cooperation. This may be the first time that the client is not feeling judged (Tohn & Oshlag, 1995). It can take several exchanges of this nature for clients to begin to trust that the therapist really does care about their views. Clients also wait to see if the therapist will try to convince them to change. When the therapist does not do this, and in fact validates their views of the world, clients feel empowered. One aspect of cooperating is for the therapist to validate how difficult it must be for the mandated client to be forced to come to therapy.

Case Example Joe is a thirty-nine-year-old male with one son. He and his wife have been married for three years. It is the first marriage for both. Joe appears agitated and impatient during the beginning of the interview, as confidentiality is reviewed. Joe states that he is a manager at a plastics plant, and works long and hard hours.

Therapist: So, what brings you here today?

    Client: My wife said I have to come. She says I have a problem with my anger.

Therapist: So, it was not your idea to come? [*This helps to validate the client's view of the situation. Asking about his anger would not validate his mandated status.*]

    Client: No way, no offense. I don't think I need this. I don't beat my wife. She took out a restraining order this weekend after we had a fight.

Therapist: Okay.

    Client: She said she was scared of me. That's crap.

Therapist: So, what do you think your wife hopes will happen in therapy [*cooperating with the view that the wife wants him in therapy*]?

    Client: She wants me to control my anger, not yell so much, I guess.

Therapist: What do you want? [*Directly asking about the client's goals juxtaposes them with the wife's desires.*]

Client: I want to get back into my house. I work really hard to support her, and this is what I get.

Therapist: What will need to happen for you to be able to go back to your house [*co-operating with his worldview and accepting his goal—to get back into the house*]?

Client: I guess my wife will have to drop the restraining order. I'm sorry, I have to ask a question.

Therapist: Please [*allows the client to put his agenda first, which usually enhances co-operation*].

Client: You have not asked me if I hit my wife. How come?

Therapist: Good question. I assume if it is important for me to know, you will tell me. [*This gives the client control and respect.*]

Client: You mean I don't have to tell you my whole life story, like the couples therapist?

Therapist: Not unless you think it will be helpful in solving the current problem.

It can be very informative for the therapist and helpful to the client to follow the client's assumption and allow him or her to decide what the therapist needs to know in order to be helpful. As the conversation continued, the therapist followed the solution-focused assumption, "If it does not work, try something different" in an effort to enhance cooperation (Berg & Miller, 1992; de Shazer, 1985, 1988; Tohn & Oshlag, 1995).

Client: Huh, well, I didn't hit her. We were having a fight. She lies all the time. I caught her in this lie, and I got really mad and grabbed her shirt, but I never hit her.

Therapist: Okay. [*To maintain and enhance cooperation it is helpful to resist the temptation to elicit more details here. Doing so may be perceived by the client as the therapist judging him.*] So, you mentioned you wanted to get back into your house. What do you think your wife would say would need to be different for her to drop the restraining order so you could go home?

Client: I have to learn to control my anger and just take a walk when I get that angry. [*The client has shifted here. Through the therapist's cooperating with the client, he is now agreeing with the wife's goals and trying to find ways to accomplish them.*]

Therapist: What would it take for you to be able to do that?

Client: She would have to stop lying to me.

Therapist: So, when she stops lying, what will be different?

Client: I won't have any reason to get so mad.

Therapist: Does she lie all the time [*looking for exceptions*]?

Client: Yes . . . no, not really. Just when I'm asking her where she's going with her friends.

Therapist: So, when you are not asking her about where she is going, she is not lying?
   Client: No.
Therapist: How do you know when she is not lying?
   Client: She doesn't hesitate to tell me things, we just have a normal conversation.
Therapist: So, when she does that, what do you think she notices you doing differently?
   Client: I'm not yelling.
Therapist: Is that a sign that you are controlling your anger?
   Client: Yeah.

By adopting the client's view of the world ("What do you think your wife hopes will happen in therapy" and "What will need to happen for you to be able to go back to your house"), and by agreeing for the time being that his wife "caused" him to get angry, the therapist allows the conversation to begin to develop around the client's goals. Initially accepting a client's view of the world, and striving to understand it, is the beginning stage of cooperation. No attempt is made to convince this client that he has a problem; rather, every effort is made to help him solve the one he identifies as most salient.

A more traditional therapist might argue that by not addressing this client's history and potential tendencies toward violence, the clinician is ignoring the "real" and underlying problem. It is our contention that by cooperating with the client's view of the world, these issues are addressed more rapidly than in the traditional approach of confronting the client's assumed denial. The bases for this view are the solution-focused assumptions: (1) The therapist's job is to identify and amplify change; (2) It is usually unnecessary to know a great deal about the complaint in order to resolve it; and (3) It is not necessary to know the cause or function of a complaint to resolve it (O'Hanlon & Weiner-Davis, 1989, pp. 37–40; Tohn & Oshlag, 1995, pp. 16–18). When therapists give clients the control to choose what information they believe is relevant to solving their problems, they subtly empower these clients to take charge of solving those problems. This is a central focus of our approach. The therapist believes the assumption that clients have the resources and strengths to resolve complaints (Berg & Miller, 1992; O'Hanlon & Weiner-Davis, 1989; Tohn & Oshlag, 1995; Walter & Peller, 1992). This assumption encourages the therapist to abandon the notion that he or she knows what is best for the client. Once the therapist has begun to view the world through the client's eyes, treatment goals can be established.

Establishing Well-Formed Treatment Goals

The second component of cooperating with mandated clients is establishing well-formed treatment goals. When possible, we encourage our clients to understand what the referral source views as the goals of treatment, and how the referral source will measure progress. We often discover that clients sent by the courts, protective services, or their employer or school do not clearly understand what the referral source wants them to accomplish in treatment. We try to gain an understanding of the referral source's goals by asking our clients several questions:

> What do you think the school (referral source) wants to be different as a result of treatment?
>
> Who do you need to convince that you don't need to be in treatment anymore?
>
> How long do you think you would need to maintain these changes in order for your [referral source] to believe that you don't need to be in treatment anymore?

When working with mandated clients, we are constantly evaluating whether or not our treatment goals are "well formed" (Berg & Miller, 1992; Friedman & Fanger, 1991; Tohn & Oshlag, 1995). Following are some of the typical components of a well-formed goal:

- It should be important to the client and within his or her control.
- It should be small rather than large.
- It should be measurable by the client and the referral source.
- It should be contextual (when, where, and with whom should be known).
- It should be the presence and start of something.

A great deal of time is spent clarifying goals with clients, breaking them down into small, doable pieces, and discussing just whose goals they are. The process begins when the therapist asks a client who sent him or her to treatment and what the referring person wants the client to do differently in order for the treatment to be considered successful. By asking in this manner, the therapist gives the client the message that the therapist understands it may not be the client's goal to be in treatment but someone else's idea.

Case Example Mary is a twenty-nine-year-old female. She works for a large computer company. She states that she is single, has no children, and is college educated. Mary has been in therapy once before for relationship issues.

Therapist: What brings you here today?
Client: My boss told me I had to come.

Therapist: OK, what does your boss hope will happen as a result of your coming to therapy?

Statements such as this reveal that the client is mandated. The therapist immediately begins to think of ways to engage this client and understand her view of the situation that brings her into therapy. Since the client just stated that someone else sent her, the next step is to inquire what that person had in mind.

Client: She says I have an attitude problem, but everyone knows it's her who has the problem. Ask anyone in our department.

Therapist: I'm sure I could, but it sounds like you have a good take on the situation. How will your boss need to change in order for it to be better for you [*cooperating with the client's worldview by accepting it*]?

Client: She needs to get off my back.

Therapist: How will you know when she is off your back?

Client: She won't be looking over my shoulder all the time and critiquing my work.

Therapist: So, when she is off your back and not looking over your shoulder, what will be different?

Client: Well, I guess I will relax and do a better job. [*Notice the shift in her language, indicating the start and presence of something—both qualities of well-formed goals.*]

Therapist: Of course, that makes sense. So, what will your boss be doing differently so that you can relax more and do your job?

Client: Hum, I guess, it's hard to imagine because it's not like this at all, and who knows if she will ever change.

Therapist: I know, but let's imagine she does change. How will she be different [*an invitation to think of a nonproblem state*]?

Client: Well, she will trust that I know what I am doing, and just let me do my job.

Therapist: That makes sense. What will be some of the signs to you that she is trusting that you know what you are doing?

Client: She will give me a task and let me do it and not keep coming back to check on me.

Therapist: And what else?

Client: She will actually tell me I did a good job.

Therapist: When she does this, what will she notice different about you? [*This question helps the client shift the focus to herself.*]

Client: Like I said, I'll relax.

Therapist: What else?

Client: I'll have a better attitude.

Therapist: What do you mean?

Client: Well, I won't give her such grief.

Therapist: For example?

> *Client:* I'll do my work on time, instead of intentionally late. I'll probably not stir up so much trouble with everyone else in the department. I think we could work more like a team.
>
> *Therapist:* How will that be different for you?
>
> *Client:* I'll cooperate and feel like she respects me, so I will respect her. I'll look forward to coming to work. I'll try harder.

In this instance, the therapist is following the client's view of the world and creating a safe environment for the client to define well-formed goals. As treatment continues, the therapist will break down and further clarify the goals. As is evident at the end of this dialogue, the client is talking about what she will be doing differently. The therapist will then facilitate a typical solution-focused session, including looking for exceptions and asking scaling questions. It is vital to remember that at times the therapist and client may negotiate a well-formed goal that is "to be through with therapy." The primary goal for many clients is to stop coming to treatment. This is a legitimate goal and fits well with the solution-focused approach.

Clients who identify their goal as getting out of therapy as fast as possible require the therapist to maintain contact with the referral source. The referral source in Mary's case is of course the supervisor. For the therapist to continue cooperating with clients, the referral source must be involved in the process.

Utilizing the Referral Source to Establish Well-Formed Treatment Goals

Involving the referral source is the third component of the process of cooperation. Many times people other than the client (typically, the referral source) will be determining when the client no longer needs to be in therapy. The problem with this scenario is that clients often do everything they have been asked to do, but no one notices. Having conversations with the referring person enhances cooperation with clients and helps to clarify the goals.

It is not uncommon for a referral source to say "You will tell me when he is done," leaving the responsibility of determining goal achievement to the therapist. Another common scenario is when the referral source uses such vague criteria as "his self-esteem will be higher" or "she'll be a better employee." This ambiguity forces the therapist to assume an understanding of the referral source's goals and then convince the referral source that the client has indeed met the goals. When working to clarify the referral source's goals, it is helpful to treat the source as a client and to employ solution-focused interviewing strategies.

Case Example   Steve is a fifteen-year-old who was sent by his school counselor for treatment. The guidance counselor called the therapist to make the referral. The guidance counselor has worked for the school system for more than fifteen years and has a good working relationship with mental health professionals.

Therapist: So, what can I do for you today?

Counselor: You are going to be seeing Steve today. I wanted to give you some information about him beforehand.

Therapist: Great. Why are you referring Steve to me? [*This is akin to asking a client, "What brings you here today?" Although the guidance counselor is in a related field, it is still important to elicit her "story."*]

Counselor: Steve has been getting into more and more trouble at school recently. He has very low self-esteem. He has a very troubled home life. His parents were divorced recently. He clearly has a lot of anger and needs to deal with it in a more constructive manner. [*This is an indication of her view of the situation—she has decided that she knows why the situation is the way it is. There is no value gained in arguing or discussing this further.*]

Therapist: What kinds of things has he been doing to get into trouble at school?

Counselor: Mouthing off to the teachers, getting into fights after school. I can't remember the last time he did his homework.

Therapist: How does Steve feel about coming to therapy? [*This question helps the therapist begin to understand where the client may be coming from and how therapy was explained to him.*]

Counselor: He is not real happy about it. He had been in therapy with his family before the divorce. I'm not sure he really trusts therapists. The school did not give him a choice. It was either go to counseling or be expelled.

Therapist: What does Steve need to do in order for you and the school staff to feel that counseling has been helpful?

Counselor: Staying out of trouble would help.

Therapist: What would be some signs to you that Steve is beginning to do this?

Counselor: Maybe he would get to school on time, and stay in his classes.

Asking the last two questions in this manner serves several purposes. It gently moves the guidance counselor in the direction of clarifying what she is looking for from Steve, and begins to break this goal down into small, doable, and measurable pieces. Underlying this line of questioning is the assumption that the client—in this case, Steve—will gradually change, not that he will immediately become a model student. The therapist also encourages the guidance counselor to think about noticing and looking for these changes. This encouragement helps to ensure treatment success and cooperation with the client, by directly and indirectly asking the referral source to look for small changes in the client. This strategy reduces the likelihood that Steve will begin to change and no one will notice. When working with referral sources, some of the other typical questions that we ask are the following:

- What does the client need to do differently in order for you to know that treatment has been successful?
- What will be some of the signs to you that the client is on the right track?
- Where do you think the client needs to start to get on the right track?
- Who else do you think I should talk to in order to help this client?
- Who do you think will notice these changes?
- Who else needs to be convinced that the client is trying?
- How often does this person need to see these changes in order to be convinced the client is changing?
- What will be some of the small signs to you that the client is trying?
- How long will the client need to keep things going in order for you to believe this is lasting change and not just a "flight into health"? (This question addresses how the therapist will know that the referral source is confident in these changes.)
- How often will the client need to exhibit this new behavior in order for you to know it is true change?

When clients cannot articulate their understanding of the referral source's treatment goals, it is necessary for either the therapist or the client to contact the referral source and seek information about the goals. Our preference is for our clients to contact the referral source, but when this is not an option we will assist our clients by calling the referral source while the client is sitting in our office.

Case Example Steve came to his first session not knowing why he was sent by his guidance counselor for treatment. He is wearing blue jeans and a baseball cap associated with one of the local gangs.

Therapist: So, what brings you here today?
   Client: I'm not totally sure.
Therapist: OK. Give me your best shot.
   Client: Well, I got thrown out of class again last week, and the guidance counselor said I would have to start counseling if I want to go back.
Therapist: And you want to?
   Client: Sure. It's really dull at home.
Therapist: So, it was your guidance counselor's idea that you come to treatment?
   Client: Well, her's and my parents'.

> *Therapist:* So, what do you think your guidance counselor and your parents hope will happen to you here?
>
> *Client:* I don't know.
>
> *Therapist:* Guess. [*Often, asking a client, particularly an adolescent, to guess can help get him unstuck.*]
>
> *Client:* I'm not really sure. She just told me to go to counseling and deal with my problem.
>
> *Therapist:* What problem would that be?
>
> *Client:* My "attitude" problem.
>
> *Therapist:* So, what does your guidance counselor want to be different about your "attitude?" [*The therapist continues to ask questions from the guidance counselor's frame of reference as a means of cooperating with Steve's view of the world.*]
>
> *Client:* I'm not really sure.
>
> *Therapist:* Guess.
>
> *Client:* Well, she wants me not to talk back to the teachers.
>
> *Therapist:* Do you agree with her that this is a problem?
>
> *Client:* No, not really. I get annoyed with this one teacher sometimes.
>
> *Therapist:* So, it's not all the teachers, just one [*looking for exceptions*]?
>
> *Client:* Well, yeah, mostly one.
>
> *Therapist:* So, what would you need to do differently with this one teacher?
>
> *Client:* Just not talk back.
>
> *Therapist:* What would it take for you to do that?
>
> *Client:* If it would get everyone off my back and make it so I did not have to come here anymore, I could bite my tongue for an hour a day.
>
> *Therapist:* What else do you think your guidance counselor wants you to do differently?

Despite the fact that clients view their problems as someone else's, when the therapist cooperates, clients often begin talking about what they are willing to do to not be in treatment anymore. By clarifying what each referral source wants, we increase the likelihood that treatment will be successful.

Utilizing the Referral Source to Sustain Treatment Progress

In the effort to cooperate with clients, the fourth component is to routinely check in with the referral source and other collateral sources between each session to elicit information about any progress they have noticed. By checking in this often, the message to referral sources is that change is expected, and will, it is hoped, be noticed. Sometimes referral sources are so angry at or beaten down by clients that they do not have the ability to notice the changes or to give credit to the client for trying. In such instances, it is important to acknowledge the referral source's frustration so that the therapist can gently shift them toward noticing any changes that may occur over time. If the referral source does not notice the small changes, there is little if any hope that positive change on the client's part will be reinforced by the referral source. The following case example illustrates how *not* noticing can impede progress and, in fact, make matters worse.

Case Example Kathy is a sixteen-year-old referred to counseling by her parents. Her mother stated upon intake that she has always been a "somewhat difficult child." She is in special education, has too many loud friends for her mother's taste, and dresses "like a slob." By the end of the second session, Kathy has agreed to work on keeping her room neater as a first step in "being neater" (mother's goal) and getting out of therapy (Kathy's goal). Kathy appears for the third session wearing jeans, a shirt displaying the logo of a heavy-metal band, and boots. She appears agitated.

Therapist: So, what's been better since we last met?
    Kathy: Nothing. Things are worse.
   Mother: I agree. Things were a little better for a few days, and then Kathy started going out at night again, breaking curfew, and mouthing off. It seems like we are going backwards.
Therapist: So, Kathy, what do you think is going on here?
    Kathy: I did my part; it's her fault, talk to her.
Therapist: Can you say some more about "doing your part"?
    Kathy: Remember at the end of the last session I said I was going to keep my room neater?
Therapist: Yes.
    Kathy: Well, I did this, and no one noticed.
Therapist: What did you do that went unnoticed?
    Kathy: For three days I really tried to keep my room neat, but it didn't make any difference. No one said anything and I still had to come in at the same time. So I gave up.
   Mother: I forgot to check her room. Things have been so busy in the house lately.

It is important here to validate the daughter's efforts while not putting her parent on the defensive. The therapist could ask the parent such questions as:

So, thinking back on the week, what did you notice was different about Kathy's room?

Suppose you had noticed; how could you let Kathy know?

What difference do you think that would have made to Kathy? To your relationship?

The therapist also could have asked Kathy:

What difference would it have made if your mom had noticed?

What else would be different?

The parent and Kathy's goals are interdependent. Understanding each of their goals and how they connect with each other is the next step to successful treatment.

Identifying and Utilizing the Client-Therapist-Goal Relationship

The fifth component in cooperating with mandated clients is understanding the various triadic relationships that are possible among the client, the therapist, and the goal (Tohn & Oshlag, 1995). Utilizing these relationships helps the therapist to cooperate more effectively by providing guidelines for expectations and actions, depending on the client's relationship to a particular goal. It is important to emphasize that these relationships are goal specific. One client can have multiple goals and different relationships to each goal.

In the *customer-seller-goal* triadic relationship, the client (the "customer") knows a lot about the problem and solutions and is willing to do something about the situation. The therapist follows the client and is a good seller by working on what the client identifies as his solution. At the beginning of treatment, most mandated clients do not fall into this triadic relationship.

In the *complainant-listener-goal* triad, the client knows a lot about the problem, but someone or something else needs to change in order for the client to reach his or her goal. The therapist's job in these relationships is to cooperate with the client in the hope of finding a goal that is well-formed. Many mandated clients typically fall into this triad for at least one goal. The following case example illustrates this triad.

Case Example The client is a forty-year-old woman who came to treatment at the request of her husband. The husband stated that he is sick of hearing his wife complain about the marriage and he accused her of having an affair.

Therapist: What brings you here today?

Client: My husband is making me come.

Therapist: What does your husband hope will happen as a result of you coming to therapy?

Client: I'm not really sure. We have been having problems for a long time. He has a drinking problem. I guess right now I'm here because he thinks I am having an affair, which I am not.

Therapist: So, he is making you come here. What do you hope to get out of therapy?

> *Client:* I want you to convince my husband that I am not having an affair so he will get off my back about it.

The third triad is the *visitor-host-goal* relationship. In this relationship, the client does not see that there is a problem. When there is no problem, it is logical to conclude that no solution is needed. Some mandated clients fall into this category. It is the therapist's job to make the client feel safe and acknowledged, and to work to find a goal on which the client is willing to work.

Case Example A mother brought in her adolescent daughter for counseling because she had been diagnosed with an eating disorder. The mother already had the daughter in treatment with a physician and a nutritionist. After working with the mother and the daughter for a few sessions without much progress, the therapist finally realized an error had been made. The therapist had assumed the daughter was in the visitor relationship because she kept saying she didn't have an eating disorder. The shift in treatment occurred when the therapist began to examine this more closely. The therapist discovered that the daughter was in the visitor-host relationship for the eating disorder, but she was actually in the customer-seller relationship, desiring to get her mom off her back. The mother was in the complainant-listener relationship, wanting to convince her daughter that she had an eating disorder. Once it was clear that the daughter was in the customer-seller-goal triad, the therapist, by cooperating with the daughter's view of her situation, was able to help the client and her mother establish more well-formed goals (Tohn & Oshlag, 1995, p. 31).

Clinicians report that using these triadic relationships helps them to reduce labeling mandated clients (as complainants, for example) and emphasizes the relationship relative to the goal. Being cognizant of the triadic nature of the relationship helps the therapist to remain patient with clients and see more possibilities.

Helping Clients Move Toward Their Goals

When mandated clients view that someone else or something else needs to change first, or that the "real" problem resides in someone else, they are viewed as being in the complainant-listener-goal relationship. Many mandated clients fall into this triad at the start of therapy. When clients say, "My partner [child, probation officer] needs to change in order for me to reach my goal," we say that this client is "stuck in a box" (Tohn & Oshlag, 1995; Watzlawick, Weakland, & Fisch, 1974). Another sign of stuck clients is that they are not reporting progress and are focusing on how the problem will be solved rather than on what will be different once it is solved. The sixth and final component of cooperating with clients is to help them get unstuck and out of these boxes. Following is a case example that illustrates this concept.

Case Example Joan is a thirty-seven-year-old mother referred to counseling for "abusing" her children by the state child protective agency. The state has temporary custody of her three children. Although she is not certain, the agency worker suspects that Joan is abusing cocaine. Joan is currently on public assistance and has worked as a waitress and as a legal secretary in the past.

Therapist: So, it was not your idea to come here today?
　　Client: Yeah, right, like I would voluntarily waste my time. No way.
Therapist: So, who wanted you to be here?
　　Client: The Department of Social Services [*or DSS, a child protective service agency*].
Therapist: So, what do you think they want to have happen?
　　Client: I don't care. They just need to get off my back.
Therapist: OK.

The client's view is that in order for her to reach her goal, the agency must do something different. This client could easily be viewed as resistant or as in denial of the true problem. Using the box analogy, however, the situation is viewed as illustrated in Figure 7.1. What is in the box is not a goal but rather the client's proposed solution. The proposed solution is *how* the client thinks the problem will be solved (the agency will get off her back); this is not, however, the goal. In order to ascertain the client's goals, the therapist asks the client questions to help her move beyond this box and clarify *what* she wants. Her goal is *what* she wants, not *how* she will get it.

Therapist: OK, so, when they are off your back [*the how*], what will be different [*the what, which equals the goal*]?
　　Client: I'll have my kids back.
Therapist: What else?
　　Client: I won't have people telling me how to raise my kids, or in my business all the time [*start of more goals*].
Therapist: So, what do you think would need to happen for them to give you your kids back?

The conversation has shifted from "getting the agency off my back" to having her children returned to her. Here the therapist utilizes the technique of incorporating the client's proposed solution, "get off my back," into a question,

FIGURE 7.1. THE BOX.

Problem as Defined by Client	Proposed Solution
Agency has my children.	They should just get off my back.

which usually leads toward a goal on which the client is willing and motivated to work. This process is illustrated in Figure 7.2.

There are times when clients continue to remain in the complainant-listener-goal triad for a specific goal (for instance, to get my mother get off my back), and all attempts to challenge their assumptions and move beyond their box fail. At this juncture, the therapist begins to examine other goals. One way to accomplish this is to ask clients how they are going to manage [cope, get by] while they are waiting for the courts to change [partner to change, DSS to get off their back]. This line of questioning can often lead to finding a well-formed goal that the client is willing to address.

Case Example Bill is a thirty-five-year-old client who was mandated to therapy by a judge. He is not interested in changing his parenting style, and he wants his ex-partner and the protective service agency to let him spend time with his children unsupervised. The judge felt that Bill needed treatment to help him learn to control his anger and deal with an assault and battery charge. Bill's probation officer thinks that, based on past experience, Bill is not a good candidate for therapy, and he believes that Bill has a "flagrant thought disorder." The probation officer tells the therapist that Bill has been on medication in the past and is currently refusing to take any medication. The therapist views this client as stuck in a box; the client is waiting for others to change so he can obtain his goal.

Therapist: So, while you are waiting for your ex-partner, DSS, and the judge to change their minds, how are you going to manage?

Client: I'm not sure. I keep telling her that I wouldn't hurt the kids, but she and the DSS worker won't let me see them. So I just stopped visiting; there is no justice here.

Therapist: How was that helpful [*gently challenging the client's belief*]?

Client: Well, if they're not going to do it my way, to hell with them.

Therapist: I see. And has this worked to get them to change their minds?

Client: No.

FIGURE 7.2. SHIFTING THE CLIENT OUT OF HER BOX.

Problem as Defined by Client	Proposed Solution Viewed as a Goal by the Client (*how*)	Goal (*what*)
Agency has my children.	They should just get off my back.	To get my children back.

Therapist: Hum, that's a problem.
Client: I can wait. I do miss my kids, though.

The box this client is in is that other people—meaning his ex-partner, DSS, and the court—have not changed. At times, restating and clarifying what is in the box can help the client move beyond it while maintaining cooperation with his view of the world.

Therapist: Let me make sure I understand this. You have not been visiting your kids, in an effort to get everyone to change their minds about unsupervised visits, right?
Client: Right.
Therapist: And this has not worked so far?
Client: Nope.
Therapist: Can you think of another way to convince them to do it your way?
Client: I don't care.
Therapist: What's worse, not seeing your kids, or seeing them during a supervised visit?
Client: Not seeing them.
Therapist: What would it take for you to see your kids despite the fact that you are being forced unfairly to have supervised visits?
Client: I never thought of it that way before. [*The therapist joins him in his view that everyone else is being unreasonable. This empowers him in what feels like a powerless situation.*]
Therapist: What is going to happen when you start doing supervised visits despite the fact that it is not the just way?
Client: I could see my kids more.
Therapist: What else?
Client: The DSS worker would see that I did not hurt my kids. [*Here the client is feeling empowered by the presence of a plan. He can begin to imagine doing something that may lead him closer to his goal of unsupervised visits with his children.*]

A new goal, despite the fact that a certain condition has not changed, is a frame that works for some clients. Bill was able both to say, "The hell with them" *and* see his kids. By identifying the proposed solution (to make other people change first), the therapist was able to help the client move forward and begin to articulate a goal of wanting to see his children.

Step 3: Technical Considerations

The concepts of changing how resistance is viewed, cooperating with a mandated client's view of the world, establishing well-formed goals, involving the referral source, understanding the triadic relationships, and helping clients escape their boxes all help to enhance cooperation with mandated clients. The next step is to integrate these concepts into a solution-focused interview, utilizing the basic solution-focused components: the miracle question, looking for exceptions, scaling questions, and assigning tasks between sessions.

What Brings You Here?

In an effort to cooperate with mandated clients, the therapist employs the use of several solution-focused techniques and questions. Even when clients are known to be mandated, the therapist still opens the session with "What brings you here today?" Despite the fact that the therapist knows that the client is mandated, it is important to allow the client to tell the therapist his or her view of the reasons for coming to treatment at that moment. The primary rule of thumb here is to follow the client's lead. When the therapist does not invite clients to tell their story, he or she may erroneously assume that the clients are mandated, resistant, or in denial.

The Miracle Question

The next solution-focused technique that maintains and enhances cooperation is the miracle question (de Shazer, 1988, 1994). A tremendous amount of information has been written about the miracle question (Berg & Miller, 1992; de Shazer, 1988, 1994; Dolan, 1991; Friedman and Fanger, 1991). We prefer to state the question in the following manner:

Therapist: **Suppose** that tonight, after our session, you go home and fall asleep, and while you are sleeping a miracle happens. The miracle is that **the problems that brought you here today** are solved, but you don't know that the miracle has happened because you are asleep. When you wake up in the morning, what will be some of the first things you will **notice** that will be different that will tell you this miracle has happened?

The boldfaced sections are those that we feel are important not to change. "Suppose" invites the client to pretend that this miracle has happened. It is important not to say, "If tonight. . . ." We make the presupposition that this miracle is going to happen, and in fact already has. . . . "The problems that brought you here today" focuses the question. If instead you say, "Your problems are solved," the answers you get tend, from our experience, to be more grandiose (I'll win the lottery, have a bigger house, etc.). The third important piece is "notice." We want to be sure to include all visual, auditory, and kinesthetic responses [Tohn & Oshlag, 1995, p. 55].

One goal of the miracle question sequence is to gain and maintain rapport with clients. Another goal is for therapists to join the clients' views of the world by validating each answer and by not challenging their beliefs during the initial part of their answer to the question. The therapist may or may not ever need to challenge clients' beliefs. The therapist should be careful not to respond too quickly to comments that mandated clients often make such as, "Well, I won't be using cocaine anymore," or "I won't beat my wife anymore," or "I won't steal at work anymore." These statements can be the mandated client's attempt to see if the therapist will initially react as a social control agent, or if the therapist will listen to the client's view and truly try to understand what the client wants. A third purpose of this future-based question is to begin to establish well-formed treatment goals.

Case Example Joe, aged sixteen, and Pete, aged twelve, have been brought into therapy by their mother, Diane. Diane is a single mother, and the boys have had little to no contact with their father—until recently. Their father has been telling the boys many details about the parents' divorce, which Diane blames for many of their current problems. Diane appears distracted and anxious for the session to begin. The divorce was two years ago and has been referred to as very nasty by Diane's individual therapist. Pete is a former client who was seen for school-related issues and is very bruised on his arm and leg. Joe sits with his arms folded and a baseball cap pulled down over his eyes. The intake sheet reads, "One brother tried to kill the other—good luck!"

Therapist: So, what brings you here today?
Joe: Beats me.
Pete: She made us come [*pointing to Diane*].
Therapist: So, can I assume that the two of you would rather not be here?
Joe and Pete: Definitely.

One way to enhance cooperation with mandated clients is to be blunt and honest from the very start. By stating or asking right away, "Would you rather not be here?" the therapist is acknowledging the client's position.

Therapist: Diane, what brings you here today?

Diane: Well, Pete and Joe have been on each other a lot recently. They have never been best friends, but they recently have gotten really violent, and I am scared.

Therapist: Sounds like things have been difficult [*helps to validate her point of view without amplifying the problem*].

Diane: That's an understatement. Last week things came to a head. I was at work when my neighbor called me. When I got home the police were there. Pete and Joe got into a fight and Joe threw Pete through a wall. I mean literally through it. That's how he got those bruises. Then Pete took a shot at Joe with a beebee gun, missed, thank goodness, and hit a window. The neighbors heard it break and called the police. I know the officers, so they said if I got counseling they wouldn't file charges.

Therapist: Wow.

Diane: I know. Oh, the guns are gone.

Therapist: Good move. This seems very serious. Pete, Joe, what are your views on this?

Pete: I don't know. Can I go?

Diane: No, you cannot.

Therapist: It would help to sort all this out if you were here. How about you, Joe, anything to add?

Joe: Well, he started the fight. I didn't mean to hurt him that bad, but he took a shot at me! He was following me around like a puppy.

Diane: I was at work and Joe was in charge. That is another thing that is going to have to change. I have to work, I don't know what I am going to do.

Therapist: You said that this past week was particularly bad; how was it before that [*looking for exceptions*]?

Diane: We have been through a lot of changes lately. Their father came back to town and has been seeing them. They both seem a lot angrier since he came back and seem to be taking it out on me and each other.

This section of the interview goes on for some time. Throughout, the therapist cooperates with each person's view of the situation. Pete and Joe do not want to be in therapy, but they are each willing to say that they think the problem is the other one. Diane is very clear what the problem is and believes that Joe and Pete need to change. Through introduction of the miracle question, the intent is to shift the clients away from the problem and to begin to define some goals in which each is invested. The therapist must define these goals while continuing to cooperate with each person's view of the world. Utilizing the miracle question expedites this process.

Therapist: Let me ask all of you a question. I'll ask all of you, and Pete, you can be first to answer. [*We typically start with the youngest person in the room so that he is not overly influenced by the others' responses.*] Suppose tonight, after you leave here, go home, and go to sleep, a miracle happens and the miracle is that the problems that brought you here today are solved. The catch is that you do not know this because you are sleeping. When you wake up tomorrow, what will you notice that is different to let you know that this miracle has happened and these problems are solved?

Pete: I'm not sure.

Therapist: Think about it for a second. You wake up and the problems that brought you here today are solved. What will you notice that is different?

Pete: Maybe Joe would be nicer to me.

Therapist: What would Joe be doing differently to let you know he is being nicer to you?

Pete: Not hurting me.

Therapist: Yes, and what else?

Pete: When I tell Joe how to do something, he will listen to me. He never listens to what I have to say.

Therapist: So, when Joe is listening to you, and not hurting you, what do you think he will notice you doing differently? [*It is important to redirect the client toward the future.*]

Pete: Maybe I wouldn't bug him so much.

Therapist: Joe, what would you notice different when this miracle happens?

Joe: Pete would stop being a brat.

Diane: Joe, that's not very nice.

Therapist: So, when you don't think he is being a brat anymore, what will he be doing differently? [*The therapist is following the client's view of the world while utilizing the client's language.*]

Joe: Just leaving me alone. He is always hanging around me when I'm with my friends.

Therapist: So, when this miracle happens and he is leaving you alone, what else will you notice about him?

The therapist decides not to take this opportunity to do a psychoeducational piece about how younger siblings want to spend time with their older siblings. Launching into such an explanation at this time could break rapport and be perceived as not cooperating. The session continues with the therapist attempting to join Joe's view of the world. Only after accepting his view, that others must change first, can the therapist begin to discover what he will do differently in response.

Therapist: So, Joe, when Pete and your mother are doing all these things, what will they notice is different about you?

Joe: Maybe I would be nicer to Pete.

Scaling

Scaling questions (Berg & Miller, 1992; deShazer, 1994; Tohn & Oshlag, 1995), particularly the progress scaling question, help the therapist to cooperate in several ways with the mandated client. As mentioned earlier, the mandated client is often being asked to work on ambiguous goals imposed by other people, such as:

- His self-esteem will be higher.
- He will change his attitude.
- She will follow the rules more often.

Although the referral source typically has some ideas about what these goals mean, the use of scaling questions can help to clarify the goal for the therapist, referral source, and most important, the client. Scaling questions can also lead to defining the next step for treatment. The case example just introduced continues with the therapist's use of such questions.

Therapist: Let me ask each of you a question. On a scale from 1 to 10, 1 being when the problems that brought you here today were at their worst and 10 being when they are solved enough that you do not need to be here anymore, where would each of you say you are right now?

Joe: Three.

Diane: One.

Pete: Two.

Therapist: So, if you are at a three, one, and two, what would each of you say would be a small sign to you that things were just a little better, say half a point higher for each of you?

Diane: Hmm. . . .

Therapist: Diane, what would need to happen for you to be able to say you were a 1.5?

Diane: They would just stop fighting.

Therapist: That sounds a little higher than a 1.5. That sounds more like a 15.

In this phase it is crucial to break each step down into small goals. If the next step is too big, there is a high probability that the client will not be able to achieve it.

Diane: Maybe if they just stopped hitting each other. I got really scared the other day. They could have killed each other.

Therapist: What would be a sign to you that they were beginning to stop the hitting? What would they be doing instead (*making the goal well-formed by asking for the start and presence of something, not the absence of hitting*]?

> *Diane:* If they are going to argue, to use words, not their hands, or a gun.
> *Therapist:* Joe, Pete, what would it take for the two of you to be able to begin this?

Utilizing the scaling and next-step questions can help clarify what the referring person (Diane) is hoping to see as a next step. It is also important to continue the process with the mandated client.

> *Therapist:* Joe, what would need to happen for you to be able to say that you are a 3.5?
> *Joe:* If Pete would leave me alone, not hang around so much when I am with my friends.
> *Therapist:* So, what would be a small sign to you that this is beginning to happen?
> *Joe:* Maybe he would do stuff with some of his friends.

Although this is not a well-formed goal yet, and certainly not in Joe's control, it is a start. It can be very useful to plant the seed early in treatment that the therapist and clients will be looking for and measuring small changes. The therapist is sending the message, particularly to the mandated client (and the referral source if they happen to be in the room), that change *will* happen, and all involved must be on the lookout.

One final point on utilizing scaling questions: scaling questions help the client, therapist, and the referral source to notice and reinforce progress toward goals. This can be particularly powerful for the referral source.

Case Example A supervisor utilizes her employee assistance program to help solve a problem with an employee, Jane. Jane has been late for work on many occasions, and has been calling in sick lately. In addition, Jane has not been performing her job as efficiently as previously. The supervisor and therapist have been able to identify some well-formed goals, and the supervisor has been reporting some progress.

> *Therapist:* On a scale from one to ten, one being when the problems with Jane were at their worst and ten being when they are solved enough that she does not need to be in counseling anymore, where would you say things are today?
> *Supervisor:* I'd say a four.
> *Therapist:* What's been better to bring you to a 4?
> *Supervisor:* I think Jane is trying.
> *Therapist:* What have you noticed?

The client is presented with the opportunity to explore what she has noticed is better. The therapist then elicits as many details as possible about what the supervisor noticed was better, what she saw Jane doing differently and what difference it made.

Supervisor: Well, she is getting to work on time, and she has not called in sick at all in the past two weeks.
Therapist: Are these the types of changes you had hoped for?
Supervisor: Definitely.
Therapist: What else have you noticed that is different?
Supervisor: I think her attitude is better.
Therapist: What have you noticed that is different that leads you to that conclusion?
Supervisor: Jane smiles more!
Therapist: When you noticed these changes, what difference did it make for you?
Supervisor: Well, I'm on her back a lot less.

One final point on scaling and referral sources: therapists are often asked by referral sources if the client is just "faking" it. In these cases a variation of the confidence scaling question can be used (Berg & Miller, 1992; deShazer, 1994; Tohn & Oshlag, 1995).

Therapist: You have noticed a lot of things that are better.
Supervisor: I'm worried that it is not for real.
Therapist: How so?
Supervisor: Jane is changing, but what if she is faking it and as soon as I stop watching her so closely she goes right back to the way she was before this all started?
Therapist: This is a valid concern. Let me ask you a question. On a scale from one to ten, one being that you have very little confidence that these changes will continue and that they are for real and ten being that you have all the confidence in the world, how confident are you that Jane will continue to make these improvements and is not just faking it?
Supervisor: About a four.
Therapist: What would make you just a little more confident, say a 4.5, that these changes are for real?
Supervisor: If she were able to keep doing what she has for a while.
Therapist: How long would she need to do these things in order for you to be able to say you were a 4.5?

By directly addressing the supervisor's concerns about Jane faking it, the therapist helps the supervisor view the situation as an ongoing process. This approach helps the therapist set up criteria for "convincing" the referral source of the mandated client's sincerity.

Utilizing Tasks Between Sessions

We utilize tasks between sessions with all our clients. When working with mandated clients we find it very useful to assign tasks to the referral source as well as to the client. Since most referral sources are in the complainant-listener-goal triad, we frequently assign them notice tasks. Following are some sample notice tasks:

- Between now and the next time we meet, notice when things are just a little better between you and your student.
- I have asked your employee to work on some issues between now and the next time we meet, and I would like you to notice what he is doing differently in the next week that you would like to see more of.

To reinforce their problem-solving efforts, clients, particularly ones who do not want to be in counseling in the first place, need feedback about what they are doing well. Assigning a notice task to the referral source is the first step in this process. In order to maintain progress, clients need the referral source to notice their efforts and offer positive feedback.

Case Example A parent has been bringing her adolescent in for joint therapy. The original presenting problem was that the child was acting out at home. They have been seen for several sessions.

Therapist: So, what's been better?
    Child: I've been working really hard.
Therapist: What have you been doing?
    Child: Going to school and staying in school.
Therapist: Wow, how have you done that?
    Child: I just set my mind to it. It was worth it to get everyone off of me.
Therapist: [*To parent*] Since she has been going to school, what have you noticed is diferent?
    Parent: The house is much quieter. She is more pleasant to be around.
Therapist: What have you noticed her doing that makes her more pleasant?
    Parent: She smiles more, and has been telling me what is going on in her life.
Therapist: She has?!

When clients hear that they are doing the right thing, and when they know that the referral source has also noticed, they are more likely to continue the desired behavior. When possible, the therapist should also ask interactional-type questions (Berg & Miller, 1992; Tohn & Oshlag, 1995) to further reinforce progress made toward the goals.

Therapist: [*To parent*] So, since she has been smiling more, what has she noticed you doing differently?
    Parent: I've been smiling back. I think I've been in a better mood knowing that she is beginning to be happier.

Therapist: [*To child*] What have you noticed your mother doing differently when you
          are smiling and she is smiling more?
    Child: She trusts me more.
Therapist: What have you noticed her doing to let you know she is trusting you more?

Interactional questions also empower mandated clients to believe they can have
an impact on the situation.

Special Issues

Working with Children and Adolescents

Adolescents are often viewed as mandated clients because they rarely want to be
in treatment. They are typically dragged in by their parents, and they are tired
of everyone telling them what to do. The therapist often asks the mandated adolescent at the beginning of the session if it is his or her choice to be there. When
the mandated adolescent responds that she or he does not want to be in counseling, as a means of increasing cooperation the therapist tells the client that treatment will be as brief as possible. Adolescents are often suspicious that the therapist
is on their parents' side and trying to manipulate them. By indicating that the therapist will work on the adolescent's goals, the therapist joins the adolescent's view
of the world and validates it.

In an effort to maintain rapport with parents and adolescents, it is useful to
meet with the adolescent alone for part of the session. As with other mandated
clients, the therapist works to find a goal in which the adolescent is invested. These
typically include:

- More freedom
- More trust from their parents
- Decrease in outsiders involved in their lives
- In general, to do what they want

The therapist also meets with the parents alone. Parents are at times on their
last leg when it comes to dealing with a problematic adolescent. They are angry
and have little if any patience for working with their child. Rather, they ask the
therapist in subtle or not so subtle ways to "just fix" their child. In such instances,
it is valuable to deliberately explore exceptions to the problem as a way of empowering clients and beginning to instill hope that their situation will improve.
The therapist takes a nonjudgmental stance toward the parents. Just as it is vital

to validate the adolescent's position, it is equally important to validate the parents' position. It is helpful to ask parents the willingness scaling question in the first session to determine how much effort they are willing to put into solving the problems with their child; often they are very low on this scale.

Separating Therapeutic Issues from Mandated Reporting Issues

In today's mental health arena, clinicians are increasingly being called upon to perform functions other than psychotherapy. Following laws that mandate that the mental health professional is to report abuse or neglect, adherence to duty-to-warn requirements, and other incidences of breaking confidentiality are all part of most professionals' code of ethics and licensing requirements. It is important to utilize a clear and thorough statement of confidentiality with all clients at the beginning of treatment so that clients are well-informed of the limits of confidentiality. When working with mandated clients referred by a protective service department, the courts, parents, and other referral sources, it is important for the therapist to be as clear as possible about who gets confidential information and under what circumstances. Furthermore, it is helpful yet difficult to separate being solution-focused from any obligations around mandated reporting. When therapists are placed in a situation of having to report abuse or neglect, it is rarely viewed as "therapeutic" by the perpetrator and, at least for the perpetrator, often makes matters worse. From the therapist's perspective, reporting to a state authority that a client is abusing a child is not "solution focused." Mandated reporting does not follow the client's goals, and is not, in some cases, beneficial to the client. However, being a therapist encompasses more roles than just doing therapy. In today's changing mental health environment, therapists are being asked to do therapy, educate, advocate, and protect certain people's safety. Many of the roles that a therapist performs can be carried out in a solution-focused manner.

One method of separating these different roles is to address the mandated reporting issues with the client separately from the treatment issues. At the beginning of treatment, we thoroughly review the issues around confidentiality and mandated reporting. If an issue that the therapist is mandated to report arises during the course of treatment, we preface that discussion by saying, "This may not have anything to do with the rest of our treatment, but it is an issue that as a social worker I must address." Separating these issues allows the therapist to maintain rapport with and respect for the client.

Case Example David is a seventeen-year-old who was referred to counseling by the court for depression and issues around anger. In his third session he stated that his family had been robbed and among the articles taken was a handgun. David stated during the session that he was fairly certain he knew who had stolen the gun and he was going to get even. The session dealt with issues of safety for David and what would be gained by "getting" this other person. In the end, David was still insistent that he was going to harm this other individual, whom he had named during the session. During the consultation break, the team decided that this particular case did fall under the state's duty-to-warn laws and that confidentiality would have to be broken. Upon returning to the session the therapist informed David that he would have to call the person David was threatening and warn that person. David was visibly angry that this decision had been made and stated upon leaving that he was uncertain about returning for more sessions.

The therapist and David were able to move beyond this incident. One factor that contributed to this was David's blaming the team more than his therapist for breaking his confidentiality. Responsibility for unpopular, and in this case non-solution-focused, interventions can be given to the team as a way of preserving rapport between the therapist and the mandated client.

Another component of separating the therapeutic from mandated reporting issues is clearly defining the therapist's role with the client and the referral source and making decisions prior to starting treatment as to what the therapist is and is not willing to do.

Case Example Carol is a twenty-eight-year-old referred to therapy by the courts and to a detox program for aftercare. During the initial conversation, the probation officer stated that they would like the outpatient therapist to monitor Carol's drinking and report Carol's progress to the court. The therapist asked the probation officer just what information he would be looking for. The probation officer stated that he would want to know what and how much Carol is drinking, and after sixteen weeks he would want a formal report from the therapist stating whether Carol should get her license back. The therapist explained to the probation officer that she would be willing, with the client's permission, to report on Carol's progress in treatment; however, this might or might not involve issues of substance abuse. What would be worked on in treatment was really up to Carol. The therapist also stated that if the court really wanted to be certain that Carol was not drinking, they should do urine screens.

In summary, the assumptions and techniques of the solution-focused model provide an excellent framework for working with mandated clients. Shifting how the therapist conceptualizes resistance, coupled with techniques for enhancing cooperation, makes working with mandated clients challenging, not arduous.

Questions from the Editors

1. *What difference in outcomes have you noticed between mandated and nonmandated clients using solution-focused therapy?*

Essentially, we have noticed no difference in "outcomes" between those clients who are voluntarily seeing us and those who are mandated to treatment. However, we have noticed that since we began practicing with this model we have been more successful in our work with mandated clients. By successful, we mean that we cooperate more effectively, as evidenced by a lower dropout rate and a higher client satisfaction rating. We have also developed more cooperative relationships with referral sources.

2. *As you discussed in the chapter, working with mandated clients can create a collision of roles. What do you do with the client who simply goes through the motions of complying with the referral source but does nothing to address the original cause for the referral?*

In some cases, clients do change their behavior and never address the original cause for the referral. We think about this in two ways. First, it may be that the referral source assumed that he or she knew what caused the original behavior; however, the referral source may or may not have been correct. Also, the referral source makes the assumption that it is important to explore the cause in order to make lasting changes. We do not believe this assumption. We have worked with many clients who effectively change their behavior without spending therapy time exploring the cause of the original behavior.

Second, clients sometimes make the behavioral changes demanded by society while they are mandated to treatment, but then revert back to their old behavior when they complete probation. However, we typically encounter mandated clients who enter treatment prepared to pay lip service to the changes, but through the course of treatment they become invested in some personal goals of their own that almost always relate to the original cause for the referral. We believe that clients make this shift as a result of our efforts to cooperate and not judge them. During the initial sessions, we are careful not to preach to or confront these clients. If treatment continues without any behavioral changes, we just "sit with" these clients and listen to their complaints about the system. We sit with their frustration and try gently to explore issues they may want to address in treatment. Sometimes these clients begin faking the behavioral changes, but when they get positive feedback from other people they decide that these changes may in fact be in their best interest. In these cases, it is crucial to stay in constant contact with the referral source, encouraging that person to give positive feedback to the client.

3.   *How do you approach court-ordered clients who in the course of their work with you violate the terms for their referral to therapy? For example, you are working with a batterer. In addition to coming to therapy, the client is ordered to stop and desist from any acts of violence against his spouse. He reveals to you, after commencing work and identifying goals, that he has once again attacked his wife.*

When faced with clients who clearly are not progressing with the work they are mandated to complete, the response by the therapist is again predicated on the contract with the client and the referral source. In the above example, if the therapist and client had agreed that one of his goals was to stop all acts of violence against his spouse, his not doing so would open up a discussion. The therapist would pose questions such as, "What would you do differently next time?" "In similar circumstances how have you resisted the urge to hit her?" "What can you do in the future to avoid situations like this?"

Another component specific to working with batterers is that they need to hear that their behavior is not acceptable. When we discuss these types of issues with clients, we are clear with ourselves that we are acting as professional social workers and not as therapists. We believe that part of our role as social workers is to educate society on certain issues, but this does not always mean we are cooperating with our clients.

As clinicians we must always decide if we are willing to work with any particular client and if we can ethically work on that client's goals. There are some goals that we will not work on. For example, we would not help a client who wanted to master raping women more powerfully. We have learned to acknowledge that there are some things we cannot agree to do.

References

Berg, I. K., & Miller, S. (1992). *Working with the problem drinker: A solution-focused approach.* New York: W. W. Norton.

Bradley, A. (1988). Keep coming back. *Alcohol Health and Research World, 12,* 192–199.

De Shazer, S. (1985). *Keys to solution in brief therapy.* New York: W. W. Norton.

De Shazer, S. (1988). *Clues: Investigating solutions in brief therapy.* New York: W. W. Norton.

De Shazer, S. (1989). Resistance revisited. *Contemporary Family Therapy, 11*(4), 227–233.

De Shazer, S. (1994). *Words were originally magic.* New York: W. W. Norton.

Ditman, K., Crawford, G., Forgy, E., Moskowitz, H., & MacAndrew, C. (1967). A controlled experiment on the use of court probation for drunk arrests. *American Journal of Psychiatry, 124,* 160–166.

Dolan, Y. M. (1991). *Resolving sexual abuse: Solution-focused therapy and Ericksonian hypnosis for adult survivors.* New York: W. W. Norton.

Friedman, S., & Fanger, M. (1991). *Expanding therapeutic possibilities: Getting results in brief psychotherapy.* Lexington, MA: Lexington Books.

O'Callaghan, J. (1990). Alcohol, driving and public policy: The effectiveness of mandated A.A. attendance for DWI offenders. *Alcoholism Treatment Quarterly, 7*(4), 87–99.

Ogborne, A., & Glaser, F. (1981). Characteristics of affiliates of A.A.: A review of the literature. *Journal of Studies on Alcohol, 42,* 661–675.

O'Hanlon, W., & Weiner-Davis, M. (1989). *In search of solutions: A new direction in psychotherapy.* New York: W. W. Norton.

Tohn, S., & Oshlag, J. (1995). *Crossing the bridge: Integrating solution-focused therapy into clinical practice.* Natick, MA: Solutions Press.

Walter, J., & Peller, J. (1992). *Becoming solution-focused in brief therapy.* New York: Brunner/Mazel.

Watzlawick, P., Weakland, J., & Fisch, R.(1974). *Change: Principals of problem formation and problem resolution.* New York: W. W. Norton.

CHAPTER EIGHT

SOLUTION-FOCUSED BRIEF THERAPY IN THE SCHOOL

John J. Murphy

Solution-focused brief therapy (SFBT) offers much promise for helping professionals who are seeking a practical, time-sensitive approach to intervention for school problems. Although originally rooted in family therapy, SFBT has evolved into a versatile and widely applicable framework for conceptualizing and resolving a variety of problems. Only recently have systematic efforts to apply this approach to school problems appeared in the literature (Durrant, 1995; Kral, 1988, 1992; Molnar & Lindquist, 1989; Murphy, 1994b).

This chapter presents (1) two key assumptions of SFBT particularly applicable to school problems, (2) several case studies, and (3) special considerations for applying this approach in schools.

Two Key Assumptions

The following assumptions are particularly useful in working with school problems:

1. *Students, teachers and parents have the resources and strengths to resolve school problems.* This optimistic, competency orientation differs markedly from the deficit-based perspective prevalent in schools—namely, that students referred for services are somehow deficient or lacking in the necessary motivation or skills to change. SFBT views people as capable and adaptive, emphasizing a future-oriented focus on possibilities and solutions instead of a past-oriented focus on problems. Viewing

people as "stuck" versus "sick" expands solution opportunities by promoting interventions that build on the existing competencies and resources of students, parents, and teachers.

The importance of explicitly recognizing and accommodating client resources is supported by psychotherapy research that has indicated that *client factors* (such as competencies, resources, and unplanned events that help clients resolve problems) and *relationship factors* (such as empathy, respect, and acceptance of client goals and beliefs) contribute significantly to successful outcomes (Lambert, 1986). These factors are enhanced by the practitioner's accommodation of the unique beliefs and positions of students and others regarding the problem, its causes, and potential solutions.

In SFBT, client goals and beliefs are the primary determinants of the content and style of therapeutic conversations and interventions. For example, teachers who view a student's behavior as "manipulative and pushy" would be more likely to accept and implement an intervention accompanied by a compatible rationale (such as a "limit-setting" rationale) than to accept the same intervention presented as a way of "supporting and nurturing" the student.

The solution-focused approach does not discount the potential usefulness of traditional psychotherapy models or classification systems of psychopathology. It simply advocates that these tools be thoughtfully selected and tailored to accommodate the unique goals and position of the client instead of being used as a set of predetermined molds into which client problems and beliefs are to be fitted. From a cognitive psychology perspective, the practitioner assumes an *accommodative* rather than an assimilative position in relation to students, teachers, and parents. In other words, the practitioner adapts the language, content, and style of therapy in response to clients and their unique circumstances (Murphy & Duncan, in press).

SFBT adopts the systemic view that problems result from ineffectual interaction patterns instead of residing exclusively within the client—in this case, the student. This perspective promotes a broader range of change possibilities than the linear, diagnostic framework often adopted in schools (Wendt & Zake, 1984). The existence of intraindividual limitations (such as academic skill delays or neurological problems), and their potential impact on school performance, is not denied. However, even in these circumstances, altering the social interactions surrounding a problem may complement other treatments such as medication or modified academic instruction.

2. *A small change in any aspect of the problem situation can initiate a solution.* This assumption is based on the systemic, ecological notion that a small change in *any* part of a system (such as any person, perception, or behavior associated with the problem) can ripple into larger changes. From this perspective, "big problems" may not require highly complex, time-consuming solutions.

This assumption is highly encouraging to busy school personnel who typically do not have sufficient time to carry out extended interventions dealing with various aspects of a problem. Scheduling constraints make it very difficult to meet with parents, teachers, and students on every problem. The systemic perspective of this approach promotes pragmatism and flexibility in choosing *what* specific aspects of the situation to work on and *who* to work with at any given point, given the assumption that changes in the perceptions or actions of anyone associated with the problem may help to resolve it.

School Applications

This portion of the chapter describes and illustrates various school applications of SFBT. Different forms of service delivery are illustrated, including individual and group counseling with students, parent and teacher consultation, and a school-wide program designed to recognize and empower students' improved school performance. The case studies collectively involve students at the elementary, middle, and high school levels. Actual excerpts from school-based meetings are occasionally provided. Commentary is also included, particularly in the first case, to clarify further the process of SFBT in schools.

As evidenced in each of the case reports that follow, the practitioner collaborates with students, parents, and teachers in developing interventions. The interventions are based on two major guidelines of solution-focused therapy (de Shazer, 1991). First, if it works, do more of it; and second, if it doesn't work, do something different. Although both guidelines are operative and used interchangeably in "real world" practice, they are presented separately here for clarity.

Guideline 1: If It Works, Do More of It

A hallmark of solution-focused therapy is the recognition and utilization of *exceptions* to the problem. Exceptions are circumstances in which the stated problem does not occur or occurs less often or intensely, or that are different in other ways from problem circumstances. The solution-focused model suggests that it is often more productive to increase existing successes, no matter how small, than it is to eliminate problems directly (Berg, 1991).

Even in apparently dismal situations, exceptions usually can be discovered. For example, the student who reportedly "disrupts class constantly" and "never does any schoolwork" has probably behaved appropriately in class at one time or another, and has completed some assignments along the way. Similarly, parents who complain of having "no control" over their teenager have probably been successful in some recent situation. Once an exception is discovered, the goal is to help the student and others "do more of it."

Case 1: The Second Quarter Exception

Mark was referred for placement consideration in an alternative school for students with major behavior problems. The referral complaints focused on the following school behavior—talking out in class loudly, frequently, and without permission; refusing to complete academic assignments; and arguing frequently with peers. Mark's mother, teacher, and school principal initially reported that these problems had occurred throughout the previous school year and had been particularly evident during the last few months of the year.

The following excerpts are from the first interview with Mark and his mother in the summer preceding sixth grade.

Counselor: You mentioned taking medicine. What kind of medicine do you take?
    Mark: I don't know.
Counselor: What's it for?
    Mark: Hyper.
Counselor: Do you still use it?
    Mark: Yep.
Counselor: Does it work?
    Mark: Sometimes it does.
Counselor: What else have you found helps you hang in there in school?
    Mark: The self-esteem program.
Counselor: Mmm. Tell me about that. I'm not familiar with it.

Here the counselor adopted an "alien" or "travel agent" perspective, viewing Mark as the guide to his own world, as the one who teaches the counselor about Mark's worldview and beliefs, perceptions of the problem and solution, and so on. In effect, the counselor said: "Help me understand who you are, what you want (your goal), and what will help you get it (interventions)." This approach immediately positions Mark in an active leadership role in the process, laying the foundation for his ownership of the desired changes.

    Mark: They only had it for a month. We'd go there every Monday and they'd talk about self-esteem and they'd have these games that you play about self-esteem, and it would just cheer you up before you went back to class.

The client's perception of what has worked, or might work, toward his goal is a vital consideration in suggesting interventions and ideas that are meaningful and acceptable to him. Not surprisingly, research indicates that an intervention's "acceptability" to the client is a major determinant of its actual implementation and success (Kazdin, 1980; Reimers, Wacker, Cooper, & De Raad, 1992; Witt, Elliott, & Martens, 1984).

Counselor: If a miracle happened tonight and the problems in school that you came in here with were resolved, gone—poof—while you were asleep, what would be different when you woke up in the morning or went into school? What would be some of the first things you would notice were different about how the day would go? Mrs. S. [mother], please jump right in too.

Mark: I don't know what you mean.

Counselor: What I want to know is how we'll be able to tell when things are different, when things are improving. What will be some signs that things are on the right track?

Mrs. S.: He won't holler and scream. He won't mistreat his teachers. He won't mistreat the office staff. And I won't be called up there every other day, you know?

Counselor: Yes.

Mrs. S.: And he'll start participating in school activities and trying to get on athletic teams because that's what he likes. And his grades will be decent. I'm not saying A's or B's, but not straight F's.

Counselor: So, his grades will certainly be better than. . . ?

Mrs. S.: I'd say at least a C average.

Instead of assuming what the client will perceive as improvement, the counselor asks directly. Obtaining a clear description of what represents improvement for clients sets a collaborative tone and avoids misunderstandings that result from differences in the criteria of improvement among those involved—teachers, students, parents, counselors, and so on.

Counselor: Mark, what else will indicate to you that things are going better in school?

Mark: I don't know.

Counselor: Mrs. S., back to your statement of "he won't mistreat people," can you give me some examples of that?

Mrs. S.: He hollers and screams, he throws things. He slams the doors. He walked out of class last year.

Mark: She [*referring to the teacher*] said, "If you want to leave, leave."

Mrs. S.: It's to a point like he said, "If you want to leave, leave." I don't blame her because I know how he gets when he gets angry. The best thing to do is let him go, for the benefit of everybody else.

Counselor: Does that work for you, when you have a chance to leave the class?

Mark: [*Shrugs shoulders*]

Counselor: When you walk out of class do you come back OK?

Mark: Nope.
Counselor: Did you spend a pretty good amount of time in the office instead of class?
Mark: It was like I'd be in the office one day and in class the next day, then the office one day, class the next day.
Counselor: OK. Which did you like better—being in the office or class?
Mark: Class.
Counselor: Why?

Mark then described reasons he would prefer to be in class rather than in the office, most of which related to what he did not like about the office instead of what he did like about class. At one point, he stated, "School doesn't bother me." Following the lead of this statement, the counselor began asking Mark what he liked about school.

Counselor: What is it about school that you like?
Mark: I like math, I like spelling, I like English. I don't like social studies, science, and health.
Counselor: Math, spelling, and English. Of those three, what do you like the best?
Mark: Math.
Counselor: What is it about math that grabs you? What's your favorite thing about it?

As the interview continued, the focus shifted from descriptions of the problem and of what the student did not like to competencies, resources, and exceptions.

Counselor: Can you think of a day this year, Mark, that you stayed in class all day and weren't sent to the office?
Mark: Yea. The whole second quarter when they gave the special award. I made C's and B's.
Counselor: How would you explain that?
Mark: The teacher gave this special award.

Mark's successful academic and behavioral performance during the second quarter represented a distinct exception to the problem, and he indicated that the "special award" was an important part of this success. During the remainder of the meeting, the conversation was directed toward clarifying the details of the "special award" and other aspects of Mark's increased academic and behavioral success during the second quarter of the school year. Other questions explored what it would take from him and others to help him repeat this success at the start of the next school year. To help him effectively handle "slips" or other future challenges related to improving school performance, the possibility of relapse was discussed, along with the idea that making this change would require hard work and persistence. The interview concluded with compliments to Mark and his mother for (1) making the effort to attend the meeting in the middle of summer, (2) being committed to improving Mark's school performance, and (3) being cooperative and candid in answering numerous questions. A "homework task" was suggested to Mark and his mother in which they were asked to list anything that would help him reach his goal of improving school behavior.

Examination of school records confirmed Mark's report of behavioral and academic improvements during the second quarter, which provided an important rationale for attempting to do more of what worked upon entering the new school year. The lists provided by Mark and his mother in response to the homework task gave ample material for the collaborative development of interventions with Mark, his mother, and school personnel in a meeting just before the beginning of the school year. Interventions included adaptations of the "special award" and the self-esteem group that Mark referred to in the initial interview. These interventions were implemented in his regular school instead of in an alternative placement, with the agreement that alternatives could be considered based on his progress during the first quarter of sixth grade.

Mark's grades and behavior were significantly stronger during the first quarter of sixth grade compared to the previous year. Two interviews were held with Mark during that quarter, primarily to clarify and empower desired changes, as illustrated in the following excerpt.

Counselor: Things seem to be on track for your goal of passing sixth grade. That's a lot different than last year. What are you doing differently to make this happen?

Mark: Well, doing my work without complaining or nothing. I just listen to the teacher. Don't smart off, it just gets you in trouble. I'm tired of being in trouble. I was in too much trouble last year.

Additional questions sought to clarify specifically what Mark did, thought, said, and so on that helped him to "do work, listen, and not smart off." His willingness to continue such efforts, as well as strategies for doing so, was explored during this conversation. Mark's academic and behavioral progress was consistently maintained throughout the school year, and he was readily passed to seventh grade.

Letters, certificates, and other documents have been successfully incorporated into some solution-oriented approaches for reinforcing and maintaining progress and goal attainment (Durrant, 1995; White & Epston, 1990). I have found that students respond very favorably to personalized letters and certificates about their efforts and accomplishments. These documents can be used periodically during a case, as well as at its conclusion, as a way of assisting students, parents, and teachers in the maintenance of desired changes. I have also found it helpful to ask students who successfully change their school performance to "help me" by providing suggestions for other students wishing to make similar improvements (that is, to be one of my "consultants"). Most of the students referred for counseling are accustomed to "being helped" in school, and eagerly welcome the opportunity to help others. Many students, particularly those who have experienced a history of school difficulties, have stated that they had never considered the notion that their experiences, ideas, and skills could benefit others.

Mark was given a congratulatory letter and consultant certificate given at the end of his successful sixth grade experience. These are displayed in Exhibits 8.1 and 8.2. Mark expressed his appreciation for the letter, and eagerly accepted the invitation for membership in the Consultant Club.

Case 2: The Competent Test Anxiety Group

Four high school students (in grades ten and eleven) volunteered to participate in a six-session "test anxiety" counseling group co-led by a school psychologist and a school psychology trainee.[1] During the first meeting, students completed some basic information forms and responded to questions about what they hoped to gain from the group. Goals included improved test performance and grades, better study habits, and less worry and tension preceding important tests. Each student also identified one or more "target classes" in which they particularly wanted to improve their grades. Based on these goals, later sessions included the presentation of information and suggestions regarding topics such as relaxation and study skills, and the opportunity for students to share their personal progress and experiences related to test taking, with a solution-oriented emphasis on what they were already doing, or could do, to enhance their goals of improved test performance.

During the second session, students were asked about exceptions to test-related difficulties, using such questions as, "Tell me about a test within the last month that you did better on?" Details and conditions related to these exceptions were explored.

Most of the students initially found it very difficult to identify any exceptions. This reaction is a fairly common one in solution-focused therapy, because most clients enter therapy with a "problem-saturated" perspective (White & Epston, 1990) in which exceptions are either overlooked altogether or dismissed as insignificant by the client (de Shazer, 1991). One student said, "I thought I was doing everything wrong." Students also were asked to share ideas that they had thought of but never tried, and strategies that might be helpful even if they were not willing to try them now. To provide additional opportunities for the students to focus on what was working instead of on what was not working, they were given the following task adapted from de Shazer and colleagues (de Shazer, 1985; de Shazer & Molnar, 1984): "Between now and our next meeting in two weeks, observe and list those things that you want to continue doing that you are already doing to prepare for and take tests."

The strategies generated by the students during and following the second session fit well with "best practices" in test anxiety intervention identified in the professional literature. These ideas and strategies provided the foundation from which later sessions

EXHIBIT 8.1. CONGRATULATORY LETTER FOR MARK.

Dear Mark:

I want to congratulate you on the improvements you have made in school behavior this year.
I know it took hard work to make these improvements. I admire the fact that you hung in there and didn't give up during the tough times this year. That takes courage. Way to go, Mark!

Sincerely,
Dr. M

were structured. The sessions typically opened with variations of the question, "What's better since our last meeting?" Sessions also included didactic, information-sharing components about test preparation or performance (such as study strategies, relaxation, strategies for answering multiple choice test items, and so on).

Data on the students' test performance and grades following the establishment of the group were encouraging. Three of the four students improved their grades in target classes. Composite group data were compiled by examining the total performance of the group. The numbers of classes in which grades (1) increased, (2) remained the same, or (3) decreased also supported the usefulness of the group for students. Grades in fourteen classes increased (some as much as three letter grades, from "D" to "A"), while grades remained the same in three classes and decreased in five classes.

Students' comments following the group's termination supported the above data regarding the usefulness of the group. Statements pertinent to the solution-focused aspect of the group included the following:

> I realized that I had good ideas, even if I wasn't using them all the time.

> It was cool when we rattled off all those ideas, and I used some of those ideas.

> It was neat to get ideas from other students for a change instead of from the teacher.

> I started doing better on tests when I did the stuff I said I needed to do. It was simple.

Case 3: The *Success Stories* Movie

This case study describes a schoolwide program aimed at recognizing and clarifying specific improvements of students at an urban elementary school (Murphy, 1996). Videotaped interviews were conducted with students who made major academic or behavioral improvements during the school year. Student responses were compiled into a movie entitled *Success Stories*.

EXHIBIT 8.2. CONSULTANT CLUB MEMBERSHIP CERTIFICATE FOR MARK.

Consultant Club Membership Certificate
The Consultant Club consists of students who have made important changes in school performance, and who would be willing to serve as a consultant to Dr. M for advice on helping other students make changes.

Mark S., Consultant

_____

Dr. M., Club President

The *Success Stories* program was initiated for the following purposes: (1) to high-light specific improvements of students to help them clarify and sustain their successes; (2) to provide a permanent product and source of ideas for improving school perfor-mance for future use by school staff, parents, and students; (3) to provide a morale boost to the school staff by focusing on successes; and (4) to implement a schoolwide application of utilizing "students as consultants" within a solution-focused, compe-tency approach to interviewing.

In early May, a note was sent to all twenty teachers in the elementary school, explaining the purposes of the project and requesting the names of two students "who have successfully improved their academic work or behavior over the course of the year, even if it was only in one particular subject area or one aspect of behavior." Teach-ers also wrote a brief description of the major area(s) of improvement for each student (such as reading or classroom behavior).

Each student was interviewed individually on videotape regarding their success. Most students were asked variations of the following questions:

How did you improve your [grades, behavior, and so on] at school this year?

How are things different for you at home and school since the improvements?

What helped you hang in there this year when things got tough?

If another student asked you to help them improve their [grades, behavior], what would you tell them?

The solution-focused, competency orientation discussed earlier is evident in these questions and in the following excerpts from interviews with two students.

Second Grade Student

Interviewer: What are you doing that's different now?

Student: I'm not hollering when other people are talking, and I'm not beating up on kids like I used to when I was a little kid. And I go to my class. When I yell out and say "Teacher, Teacher" and she says, "Not right now, go back to your seat," then I raise my hand, and that's one good thing that I've been improving a lot.

Interviewer: How did you learn to do those things?

Student: My brother is the one who taught me all those things. My brother, he improved in his school, so I improved in my school. I do everything my brother does.

Interviewer: How do you manage to stay in your seat more than you used to?

Student: When the teacher's talking and picks someone else, don't get real mad and yell, "Teacher, Teacher." Wait and you'll get a turn.

Interviewer: If another second grader came to you and said, "I want to do better in school but I don't know how," what are some things you could tell him?

Student: I would tell him if you just listen to the teacher and be good in school and if you raise your hand she'll always call on you. When she's talking, you can be quiet and she'll pick you to read a book. And when you do your math, and you got it all right, and she puts "good job" on it, you put your grade back up.

Interviewer: What else?

Student: Try harder. Do your handwriting neat. If you have an attitude, stop your attitude.

Interviewer: Explain that—"stop your attitude."

Student: Stop pushing people around. Stop bossing people around.

Fifth Grade Student

Interviewer: Do the teachers treat you any differently now with better grades than they did when your grades were lower?

Student: Yea. Better.

Interviewer: How?

Student: When I had bad grades, they really didn't help me because I really didn't want to do the work, but now they're starting to help me.

Interviewer: So, the more they see that you want to do the work, the more willing they are to spend the time to help you?

Student: Yea.

Interviewer: Okay. Any other changes in the way that you're treated either at home or school now that your grades are better?

Student: I used to get a lot of detentions, but now that I'm not hanging around my old friends, I haven't got a lot of detentions.

Interviewer: Do your old friends sometimes still try to get you to hang around with them?

Student: Yea.

Interviewer: I imagine it's hard to resist the temptation. Probably hard to say no sometimes, isn't it?

Student: Yea.

Interviewer: How do you manage to do that?

Student: I just walk away.

Interviewer: What advice would you give other students to help them improve their schoolwork?

Student: Volunteer more. If you do, you'll probably feel better. Probably get better grades and get good comments.

Interviewer: What other tips would you give them on how to be with teachers to help get better grades?

Student: Okay, for number one, don't try being a teacher's pet, because it will probably annoy them. Pay attention more to the teacher. If they give an assignment you don't like, don't go [*student rolls her eyes and makes a face of displeasure*]. Just sit up to it and just do the assignment. Don't make a fuss about it.

Practical constraints, including limited access to students following the program, prevented any type of formal or empirical program evaluation. Although definitive empirical conclusions about the benefits of this experience for the students cannot be made, several students commented that the interview helped them to understand better exactly how they made the improvements. Teachers readily supported the project, as evidenced by the voluntary participation of 100 percent of the teaching staff during a very trying and demanding time of the school year—the last three weeks. The program was responsive to limited budgetary and time resources in schools in that it was inexpensive and required minimal teacher time. The tape remains at the school for future viewing by students, teachers, and parents who might benefit from the ideas and experiences documented in these success stories.

Guideline 2: If It Doesn't Work, Do Something Different

Sometimes exceptions are not provided, or people indicate a preference for a different type of intervention. In such cases, it is useful to encourage changes in the way students and others perform (that is, do) or perceive (that is, view) the problem. This strategy is based largely on the notion that persistent problems often are maintained by the very efforts intended to alleviate them (Fisch, Weakland, & Segal, 1982; Hayes & Melancon, 1989; Watzlawick, Weakland, & Fisch, 1974). As the problem gets worse, the attempted solutions are applied even more vigorously because they are thought to represent the only right and sensible approach to follow.

Consider the following example in which the teacher's "attempted solution" becomes an integral part of the problem cycle. A teacher attempts to reduce a student's disruptive behavior by scolding the student and requiring extra homework. The student's behavior becomes even more annoying to the teacher following the use of these methods. The teacher responds by scolding the student more or assigning a larger amount of extra homework. This stronger version of the same attempted solution, or "more of the same," results in similarly strong or more inventive annoying behaviors on the part of the student.

Although this example is oversimplified, it is not uncommon in schools and many other contexts that well-intentioned efforts to correct a problem actually make matters worse. In these cases, intervention is aimed at blocking the problem cycle by interrupting existing solution attempts to allow new responses to the student's behavior. This can be accomplished by changing behavior (doing) or perceptions (viewing) of the problem and its potential solution.

In *changing the doing*, people can be encouraged to alter either their usual performance of the problem itself (such as to schedule their "worrying" about a dating problem for the evening instead of doing it during class time) or their response to the problem (such as to compliment students on something, anything, first thing in the morning instead of immediately asking them for their homework assignment).

Changing the viewing involves "reframing"—that is, offering different interpretations of or perspectives on the problem. Examples of reframing include encouraging a student to view a teacher's high standards as a sign of "belief and trust in students' abilities" instead of as an indication of "dislike and anger" toward students, or encouraging a teacher to view a student's behavior as "thoughtful and reflective" instead of as "passive-aggressive and uncooperative." The following cases illustrate the process of doing something different by encouraging people to change the way they view or do school problems.

Case 4: Sometimes Less Is More

A seventh grader named Angie was described as a "constant nuisance" to the principal, teachers, counselors, and anyone else who would listen to her lengthy complaints about how other students bothered her.[2] On a typical school day, she reportedly talked to three or four staff members for several minutes at a time. After investigating the situation and finding no major support for her accusations regarding other students, the school counselor and various teachers talked with her numerous times to offer support and understanding in an attempt to discover the "real problem" underlying such behavior. Her complaints increased despite these efforts. Other than these complaints, she reportedly demonstrated adequate school performance. Angie's counselor requested consultation from the school psychologist.

Angie's teachers and counselor were identified as key "customers" for change, and their goal was to reduce the frequency of Angie's complaints. They agreed to present a message to Angie jointly in the form of a short letter:

> We've discussed how frustrated we are that we cannot give you and your complaints our closest attention when you talk to us about them during class time and in the hallways. We have an idea that will give you the respect and attention you deserve. Mrs. Smith (the school counselor) has agreed to reserve five minutes a day just for you to talk with her about anything you wish. You can report to her office immediately following fifth period on any day you choose. We're very pleased that we could arrange this for you.

Every teacher reported an immediate and marked decrease in complaining, and several said that they never heard another complaint the rest of the year. Angie met with the counselor three days the first week, and approximately once a week after that. Although some meetings included the familiar complaints, they were infrequent and less dramatic than previous complaints.

This case highlights several key features of SFBT designed to "do something different." A reduction in the frequency of complaining was the specific, concrete goal of intervention. No attempt was made to collect detailed information regarding Angie's past, family background, and personality. Instead of repeating the theme of previous solution attempts (that is, trying to uncover the "real problem" underlying the complaints), specific interactional patterns surrounding the complaints were altered by scheduling daily five-minute counseling sessions and limiting the number of school staff involved. The parsimony and efficiency of the solution-focused approach is illustrated by the intervention's simplicity and time-effectiveness, factors that are particularly germane in school settings. This intervention illustrates the important brief therapy notion that sometimes less is more. Finally, the intervention appeared to fit the nurturing position of school personnel, as well as the urgent, serious position expressed by Angie.

Case 5: To Skip or Not to Skip, That Is the Question

William, a talented student in jeopardy of not graduating due to frequent skipping of school, was regularly prodded by his parents and teachers to "be more responsible" and attend his classes. In addition to these verbal persuasion strategies, various incentive methods had been attempted, to no avail. William was referred for counseling with the school psychologist in late March.

All persons involved, including William, expressed their frustration regarding the situation and their desire to change it. His teachers and parents agreed to refrain temporarily from discussing school attendance while the school psychologist initially gathered information. In addition to its assessment function, this strategy served to interrupt existing solution attempts with a rationale that was acceptable to the teachers and parents.

The school psychologist met with William twice. William stated that his goal was to graduate, and added that he also enjoyed skipping school. Following his conversational lead, actual and potential benefits of skipping school were discussed. Questions like, "What are the disadvantages of attending school?" were employed to acknowledge his ambivalence regarding school attendance and to talk to him about this issue in a way that was distinctly different from what he was used to (which apparently was ineffective in promoting his attendance). Exceptions to the problem were explored by questions such as, "How do you manage to get yourself to school on certain days despite the strong urge to skip?" This shifted the focus of conversation from what he was not doing to what he was doing on some occasions to accomplish his goal of graduating.

These strategies were not viewed as superior to previous parent and teacher methods in an absolute sense but were used because they differed markedly from the previous solution attempts of lecturing William regarding the ill effects of skipping school, and they appeared to fit with William's position and opinions. The lectures simply had not worked, and a different approach was warranted.

William's school attendance improved from about 40 percent in January through March to 80 percent in April and May. When asked to what he attributed the change, he said that he finally realized he was just "hurting himself" and that he wouldn't graduate unless he attended school regularly. William graduated with the rest of his class in June.

Final Considerations

Several final considerations are noteworthy regarding the use of SFBT in schools. First, it is very difficult for people to "do something different" even when the strategies they are following are not working well. Molnar and Lindquist (1989) provide various possible reasons for this, including the human tendency to maintain our beliefs or attributions about a problem in the face of experiences and information that challenge those beliefs. For this reason, it is most productive to remain attentive to client beliefs throughout the intervention process, and to accommodate these beliefs in our conversations and interventions instead of trying to talk clients out of them (Duncan, Solovey, & Rusk, 1992).

By the time a problem is brought to a mental health professional within or outside the school setting, the problem typically has occurred for several weeks or even months and people are very frustrated. Teachers, parents, and students should not be immediately steered into "solution talk" or "doing something different." Often it is beneficial to provide ample opportunity for problem descriptions and information regarding the effects of the problem on their lives, while remaining alert to statements and other indicators of potential solutions. As there are no "general" or "universal" people, there are no absolute or universal guidelines for how much "problem talk" is beneficial for each particular client. This issue is discussed more thoroughly elsewhere (Nylund & Corsiglia, 1994).

The point here is that a good deal of frustration usually accompanies requests for help with school problems, and that solution-focused practitioners need to respect and accommodate this in their initial interactions with parents and teachers.

An important related consideration involves situations in which a teacher or parent holds the position "Why should *I* change when it is the child who has the problem?" This is another common and understandable position taken by parents and teachers who have dealt with challenging behaviors they view as undermining their authority. In such cases, I have found it useful to suggest the possibility that they might have a better chance of regaining their authority and control of the situation by being less predictable than they have been in responding to the problem (that is, by doing something different). The point here is twofold. First, it is important to remember Erickson's guideline to "never argue with the client" (Haley, 1986). Second, there are many roads to solutions, and practitioners are advised to respect and accommodate the unique pathways (that is, beliefs, ideas, and styles) of the students, parents, and teachers with whom they work (Conoley, Ivey, Conoley, Scheel, & Bishop, 1990).

Instead of being yet another cookbook of techniques for "fixing" students, SFBT represents a major shift in thinking about and responding to school problems and the people who experience them. This approach is well-suited for school applications.

The competency-based view of people as resourceful and capable fosters a cooperative relationship between school staff and the parents and students with whom they work. This is particularly important given the growing research base supporting the benefits of effective home-school collaboration (Christenson, 1990; Dunst & Paget, 1991; Dunst & Trivette, 1987). The pragmatic, present-to-future focus is more feasible for busy school counselors than many traditional assessment and treatment approaches requiring lengthy excursions into history and past experience. The possibility of altering difficult problems in a limited period is very appealing to school helping professionals, who typically consider time their most limited resource. The solution-focused goal of small, concrete changes in any aspect of a problem situation is more realistic for school practitioners than the highly ambitious, and sometimes vague, therapeutic goals of some other approaches. Finally, the practical assumption that people will work for change only if they perceive a need to do so helps the busy school practitioner make effective choices about who to work with toward change. Brief therapy's emphasis on working primarily with the "customers for change" also challenges the routine practice of working exclusively or primarily with students to resolve school-related behavior problems, particularly when the student does not perceive the need for change.

This chapter is not intended to cast SFBT as a panacea for school problems, or to suggest that strategies associated with more traditional approaches be abandoned. This approach, like any other, involves some potential challenges and limitations when applied to school problems.

The narrow focus on change may not be appropriate when students require considerable skill building or knowledge. For example, a student who misbehaves in math class and lacks the academic skills to perform required class assignments may be better served by interventions involving direct instruction in math skills. Amatea (1989) suggests that cases of situational discomfort in response to sudden change or trauma (such as family death, natural disasters, and so on) are not well-suited for brief therapy interventions. In addition, crisis situations such as threats of suicide or violence require specific and directive actions on the part of practitioners, regardless of a client's opinion or approval of such actions.

Other potential challenges may result from conceptual differences between solution-focused therapy and the school's typical pattern of responding to problems. The "diagnostic-remedial" intervention framework that drives student services in many schools makes it very challenging for practitioners to apply solution-focused principles and strategies. For example, a teacher who refers a behaviorally challenging student for assessment may be more interested in whether or not the student is eligible for placement in a special education class than in details regarding the child's resources, strengths, and competencies relevant to classroom intervention.

Limited practitioner training represents another potential constraint to implementing SFBT in schools. As with any approach, adequate training and supervision are required for effective practice. Training in solution-focused therapy has not been widely available in the past. However, interest in the approach is increasing along with training and supervision opportunities.

SFBT offers practitioners a practical, collaborative framework for viewing and responding to school problems. Additional empirical investigations of school applications are needed, particularly since this approach has only recently been applied systematically to school problems. As summarized elsewhere (Conoley,

1987; Murphy, 1992), however, recent school applications have been very encouraging.

Questions from the Editors

1.   *In your chapter, you list several considerations for practicing SFBT in schools. What do you regard as the major consideration and why?*

Of all the reasons for practicing SFBT in schools (and elsewhere), the most important one to me is the *respect shown to clients*—respect for their competencies, resources, opinions, and judgments. Relating to students, teachers, and parents in this way is highly pragmatic in helping them reach goals and resolve school problems. In addition, it fits nicely with the increased emphasis on collaboration in current school reform initiatives. For me, being collaborative and respectful means that I am willing to adapt my ideas and approach to the client—to "be led" by the client instead of the other way around. This potent aspect of SFBT is highly underrated, perhaps because of the attention given to some of the unique "techniques" associated with the approach, like the miracle question and prediction tasks.

2.   *School personnel are often asked to accept new therapies and programs as the answer to their problems—only to find that once they implement the supposedly innovative and different method, it falls flat. How would you set out to convince the skeptical that solution-focused therapy really offers a worthwhile way of working?*

I would start by stating that SFBT is *not* a totally "new and different" therapy (unless, of course, they were seeking a new and different therapy). As a full-time school psychologist for fourteen years, it was my search for "what works" in resolving school problems that led me to SFBT. The SFBT emphases on efficiency, clear goals, and present-future focus were very appealing to me and other school personnel, who typically have a very limited amount of time to work on each specific problem that is presented to them. My experiences in training school personnel throughout the country clearly suggest that the straightforward, pragmatic aspect of SFBT is its most appealing feature for school practitioners.

To the more esoteric skeptic, I would emphasize that many of the assumptions and practices associated with SFBT are supported by decades of psychotherapy outcome research linking successful outcomes to factors including client perceptions of the therapeutic relationship and process, and client factors (such as unique resources and spontaneous remission of problems). The SFBT approach also operationalizes specific features of various longstanding personality theories including those of Alfred Adler (1925) (such as encouraging change by "action" versus "insight," task setting, and acting "as if"), Karen Horney (1950) (such as inherent competencies and resources of personal growth), Carl Rogers (1951) (such as nonjudgmental acceptance and empathy), and George Kelly (1955) (such as constructivism).

Of course, the "real answer" to this question is that I would not try to convince a skeptic!

3. *Suppose you are asked to provide a formal evaluation of the effectiveness of solution-focused therapy in school settings. How would you go about this task?*

The process and techniques of evaluating SFBT would depend on the specific questions being asked or the purposes of the evaluation. The majority of referrals in school settings involve a request for change in the academic or behavioral performance of an individual student. In these cases, single-case repeated measures designs (such as reversal, multiple baseline designs) are useful in evaluating the effectiveness of SFBT. These designs, as compared to large-group statistical designs, are more compatible with the highly individualized, client-driven nature of SFBT. Like all other aspects of SFBT, client perceptions and judgments should be central in evaluating the effectiveness of the approach instead of occupying a "back seat" to the practitioner's opinion or to "objective data" that does not match the reported experience of clients. In schools, "permanent product" data such as report cards, conduct records, and test scores are readily available and useful in evaluating the effectiveness of interventions. For example, one might examine whether or not grades improved or disciplinary infractions decreased following the initiation of counseling or of a specific intervention. Examples of utilizing single-case repeated measures designs and permanent products in evaluating brief therapy for school problems can be found in Conoley (1987) and Murphy (1992).

Notes

1. The author gratefully acknowledges the contributions to cases 2 and 3 of Kimberly Fiser and Jacqueline Smith, who completed field practica as school psychology trainees at the University of Cincinnati under the author's supervision.
2. Descriptions of cases 4 and 5 also were included in Murphy, 1994a.

References

Adler, A. (1925). *The practice and theory of individual psychology.* London: Routledge & Kegan Paul.

Amatea, E. S. (1989). *Brief strategic intervention for school behavior problems.* San Francisco: Jossey-Bass.

Berg, I. K. (1991). *Family preservation: A brief therapy workbook.* London: Brief Therapy Press.

Christenson, S. L. (1990). Differences in students' home environments: The need to work with families. *School Psychology Review, 19,* 505–517.

Conoley, C. W., Ivey, D., Conoley, J. C., Scheel, M., & Bishop, R. (1990, March). *Practical implications of increasing the acceptability of consultation using empathy.* Paper presented at the annual meeting of the National Association of School Psychologists, Dallas, TX.

Conoley, J. C. (1987). Strategic family intervention: Three cases of school-aged children. *School Psychology Review, 16,* 469–486.

De Shazer, S. (1985). *Keys to solution in brief therapy.* New York: W. W. Norton.

De Shazer, S. (1991). *Putting difference to work.* New York: W. W. Norton.

De Shazer, S., & Molnar, A. (1984). Four useful interventions in brief family therapy. *Journal of Marital and Family Therapy, 10,* 297–304.

Duncan, B. L., Solovey, A., & Rusk, G. (1992). *Changing the rules: A client-directed approach to therapy.* New York: Guilford.

Dunst, C. J., & Paget, K. D. (1991). Parent-professional partnerships and family empowerment. In M. J. Fine (Ed.), *Collaboration with parents of exceptional children* (pp. 25–44). Brandon, VT: Clinical Psychology Publishing Company.

Dunst, C. J., & Trivette, C. M. (1987). Enabling and empowering families: Conceptual and intervention issues. *School Psychology Review, 16,* 443–456.

Durrant, M. (1995). *Creative strategies for school problems.* New York: W. W. Norton.

Fisch, R., Weakland, J. H., & Segal, L. (1982). *Tactics of change: Doing therapy briefly.* San Francisco: Jossey-Bass.

Haley, J. (1986). *Uncommon therapy: The psychiatric techniques of Milton H. Erickson, M. D.* New York: W. W. Norton.

Hayes, S., & Melancon, S. M. (1989). Comprehensive distancing, paradox, and the treatment of emotional avoidance. In M. L. Ascher (Ed.), *Therapeutic paradox* (pp. 184–218). New York: Guilford.

Horney, K. (1950). *Neurosis and human growth: The struggle toward self-realization.* New York: W. W. Norton.

Kazdin, A. E. (1980). Acceptability of time-out from reinforcement procedures for disruptive child behavior. *Behavior Therapy, 11,* 329–344.

Kelly, G. A. (1955). *The psychology of personal constructs.* New York: W. W. Norton.

Kral, R. (1988). *Strategies that work: Techniques for solution in the schools.* Milwaukee, MN: Brief Family Therapy Center.

Kral, R. (1992). Solution-focused brief therapy: Applications in the schools. In M. J. Fine & C. Carlson (Eds.), *The handbook of family-school intervention: Systems perspective* (pp. 330–346). Boston: Allyn & Bacon.

Lambert, M. J. (1986). Implications of psychotherapy outcome research for eclectic psychotherapy. In J. C. Norcross (Ed.), *Handbook of eclectic psychotherapy* (pp. 436–462). New York: Brunner/Mazel.

Molnar, A., & Lindquist, B. (1989). *Changing problem behavior in schools*. San Francisco: Jossey-Bass.

Murphy, J. J. (1992). Brief strategic family intervention for school-related problems. *Family Therapy Case Studies, 7,* 59–71.

Murphy, J. J. (1994a). Brief therapy for school problems. *School Psychology International, 15,* 115–131.

Murphy, J. J. (1994b). Working with what works: A solution-focused approach to school behavior problems. *The School Counselor, 42,* 59–65.

Murphy, J. J. (1996). *The "success stories" movie: A schoolwide application of solution-focused interviewing.* Manuscript submitted for publication.

Murphy, J. J., & Duncan, B. L. (in press). *Brief therapy for school problems.* New York: Guilford.

Nylund, D., & Corsiglia, V. (1994). Becoming solution-focused in brief therapy: Remembering something important we already knew. *Journal of Systemic Therapies, 13*(1), 5–12.

Reimers, T. M., Wacker, D. P., Cooper, L. J., & De Raad, A. O. (1992). Acceptability of behavioral treatments for children: Analog and naturalistic evaluations by parents. *School Psychology Review, 21,* 628–643.

Rogers, C. R. (1951). *Client-centered therapy: Its current practice, implications, and theory.* Boston: Houghton Mifflin.

Watzlawick, P., Weakland, J., & Fisch, R. (1974). *Change: Principles of problem formation and problem resolution.* New York: W. W. Norton.

Wendt, R., & Zake, J. (1984). Family systems theory and school psychology: Implications for training and practice. *Psychology in the Schools, 21,* 204–210.

White, M., & Epston, D. (1990). *Narrative means to therapeutic ends.* New York: W. W. Norton.

Witt, J. C., Elliott, S. N., & Martens, B. K. (1984). Acceptability of behavioral interventions used in classrooms. The influence of amount of teacher time, severity of behavior problem, and type of intervention. *Behavioral Disorders, 9,* 95–104.

CHAPTER NINE

SOLUTION-FOCUSED HOSPITAL DIVERSION

Treatment of First Choice

Judi Booker

In 1990, the parents of a college student called their local community mental health center in panic, seeking help for their son. They reported that he was slurring his words, defecating in the car, constantly interrupting them, exhibiting paranoid thoughts and behavior, and reporting auditory hallucinations. They noted that this was the first occurrence of such behavior. Had the young man been insured, it is likely he would have been hospitalized for observation, diagnosis, and medication management. Based on the symptoms, it is also likely that a diagnosis of schizophrenia would have been tendered and that the clinicians would have looked for continued signs of psychosis and dysfunction for the ensuing six months to support their suspicions.

Currently, in the private sector such treatment might be questioned by a third-party payer due to the increasing scrutiny of hospital utilization. The resulting frustration on the part of the attending psychiatrist or psychotherapist might have been conveyed to the family, giving them the message that their son was receiving second-class care.

Note: In addition to the author, therapists for the cases described in this chapter are Gary Bischof, Crisis/Detox; Lynne Daley, Emergency Services; Teresa Dyck, Crisis/Detox; Deborah Roche, New Horizons; Jo Ann Rudy, Residential; and Christopher Smith, Emergency Services. R. Jackson Dykes and Carl Hunt were consulting psychiatrists. Thanks also to Saranna Rankin for her review of this chapter.

This particular young man was fortunate to seek services from a public agency that had a family focus and a mission to treat patients within the community. He received first-rate intensive outpatient treatment, resulting in his return to college and work without a hospital stay or continuing treatment after the disappearance of his symptoms.

Hospital diversion is an active effort on the behalf of clinicians to manage a mental health emergency without psychiatric hospitalization. Successful diversion such as that which occurred in the case just presented is dependent upon three factors: the opportunity to divert, the availability of alternative treatment and risk management resources, and a supportive theoretical model. Such a model must conceptualize treatment after hospital diversion as a first choice rather than as a last resort.

This chapter examines the solution-focused hospital diversion programs of Virginia's Prince William County Community Services Board (CSB). First, the driving forces behind hospital diversion practices are summarized. Then, a brief description of CSB's diversion programs is provided. The use of solution-focused brief therapy is discussed in the context of these programs. This is followed by a discussion of some issues related to the choice of a solution-focused treatment model. Suggestions for implementing a hospital diversion function are provided at the end of the chapter.

Why Divert?

Traditionally, inpatient treatment has been used to manage risky or difficult clients requiring further observation and assessment for medication management. For psychiatrists, hospitalization is helpful to ensure medication compliance during their efforts to find the right level or mix of drugs to mitigate symptoms. It provides trained staff to monitor and report on symptom reduction and side effects. Patient management in a hospital also reduces the disruption of the psychiatrist's schedule by emergencies.

Hospitalization serves some of the same functions for a psychotherapist. With most practices built around weekly sessions, clients who must be seen more frequently can be difficult to manage. The clinician also may not want to incur the risk of managing life-threatening emergencies outside a hospital setting. In addition, when a patient is hospitalized the psychiatrist and hospital staff often make all treatment decisions with little consultation with the outpatient therapist. This can grant the therapist a respite. The hospitalization also provides a graceful opportunity to refer the client to another clinician or to the public sector after discharge.

When financial resources are abundant, there are few reasons for exploring alternative treatment settings—except perhaps the impact of repeated hospitalizations on the patient. This was a driving factor in the deinstitutionalization of the 1960s (Wylie, 1992). The policy of deinstitutionalization, in concert with the community mental health movement, led to seminal work in family-focused hospital diversion (Langsley et al., 1968).

The effect of hospitalization on the patient still remains a concern because "hospitalization may stigmatize and result in a further lowering of self-esteem and an increase in self-denigration. The impact of separation of parents from children or of increasing the likelihood of job loss must also be considered, along with the danger of inducing hospital dependency" (American Psychiatric Association, 1989, p. 1768).

In the public sector, hospital bed space has been limited since deinstitutionalization. Further, owing to concerns about patient rights, it is the law in some states (such as Virginia), that involuntary (or court-ordered voluntary) hospitalization can occur only if "there is no less restrictive alternative to institutional confinement, consistent with the best interests of the person who is the subject of the proceeding" (Department of Mental Health, Mental Retardation and Substance Abuse Services, 1992, p. 23). These constraints have led to the implementation of active hospital diversion programs in the public sector.

The economic pressures affecting the public sector have also slowly crept into the private sector. These pressures, as well as concerns for patient rights and the profit motive, have driven insurance companies, preferred provider organizations, and managed care companies to require precertification of the need for hospitalization before admission.

Few treatment options have existed outside the hospital environment, so opportunities for diversion have been limited. However, some managed care companies and health maintenance organizations are beginning to actively divert hospital patients as economic pressures increase (J. Glick, personal communication, May 1995; C. Webb, personal communication, May 1995).

A Solution-Focused Hospital Diversion Program

The Prince William County Community Services Board (1993) has a mission of providing mental health services "through a system of care that respects and promotes the dignity, rights and full participation of individuals and their families. To the maximum extent possible, these services are provided within the community." This mission is woven into the fabric of the agency.

Since the late 1970s, the agency has had a family focus (P. Haber, personal communication, August 11, 1995). This has provided a connection to an additional resource: the family. Family involvement in treatment has created opportunities for successful hospital diversion that might not have existed with a focus simply on individual pathology.

Besides outpatient services, the CSB has also set up specialized programs to provide further resources in the context of family and community. These include:

1. An active discharge planning program, the goal of which is to return those who have been hospitalized to the community quickly
2. The Residential Program, which supports those who have chronic conditions in their own or group homes
3. The Family Connections Program and Project Hope, two programs that have provided intensive treatment to families with children at risk of being placed outside the home
4. New Horizons (see Bush, 1994), a program established to provide adolescents with outpatient substance abuse treatment within the context of the family and school system
5. Emergency Services, which intervenes in mental health crises, with the goal of managing psychiatric risk in the least restrictive setting
6. Crisis/Detox, an acute care residential facility for mental health and substance abuse crises

Of special note is Crisis/Detox, inaugurated in 1989 and closed in 1993 due to severe budget cuts. It provided an alternative to Northern Virginia Mental Health Institute (NVMHI) (about twenty-five miles away) and Western State Hospital (WSH) (over one hundred miles away). WSH also housed the only residential substance abuse detox program available to the CSB.

The mission of the Crisis/Detox Program was to "provide an alternative to longer term, inpatient [treatment] out[side] of community resources; [and to] provide a quality of care which exceeds custodial maintenance, stabilization, or pretreatment preparation and instead provide[s] treatment which actively pursues solutions to clients' presenting problems" (Prince William County Community Services Board, 1991, p. 34). Crisis/Detox was unusual in that it extended significant levels of staff collaboration, which already existed. This collaboration, which was encouraged with one-way mirrors and peer supervision, was begun in the CSB in 1978 (P. Haber, personal communication, August 11, 1995). In Crisis/Detox, *solution-focused brief therapy* was the single, consistent treatment approach utilized. It was anticipated that this would facilitate staff sharing of client responsibility during intensive treatment.

Solution-focused therapy was chosen for practical and philosophical reasons. Arnold Woodruff, a strong proponent of solution-focused therapy, was CSB's mental health director at the time. Dan Blymyer, a strategic therapist, was the program coordinator. Dan was attracted to the simplicity and competency focus of the solution-focused model (D. Blymyer, personal communication, August 1995). Setting out to hire a new staff, he was in the enviable position of being able to facilitate implementation of the model by selecting staff whose views of problems and change were strength and resource based. He and the clinical supervisor, Barbara Sheer, who trained at the Galveston-Houston Family Therapy Institute, found the directness of the model helpful in training a new staff. The program's treatment model further evolved as it was influenced by the ideas of contextual residential treatment (Durrant, 1993; Menses & Durrant, 1987).

Although the Crisis/Detox acute care facility was eventually closed, its staff was integrated into the existing Emergency Services Program and has influenced the incorporation of solution-focused thinking into other programs and the hospital diversion process.

The hospital diversion process at the CSB is structured and informed by its prerequisites and by the diversion interview itself. The following sections briefly discuss these prerequisites—creating opportunity and identifying resources—and present a step-by-step format for the hospital diversion interview. Helpful ideas and techniques from solution-focused therapy are discussed and illustrated by case examples.

Opportunity

Creating opportunity is an important aspect of a successful hospital diversion program. State law, Medicaid, and public hospital policies require of the CSB that a person be interviewed face-to-face before involuntary hospitalization. This provides the first opportunity to develop alternative plans for treatment and risk management.

When the office is closed or when the treating therapist is absent, the Emergency Services program performs the evaluation. After hours, the on-call therapist conducts the interview in a safe place, such as a police station or hospital emergency room.

A second opportunity for diversion occurs when clients are temporarily detained under civil commitment laws. A CSB staff member—the treating therapist or emergency staff—must attend and coordinate the commitment hearing. This is another opportunity to explore alternatives to hospitalization. If a risk management plan is successfully developed with the client and any support system, the presiding Special Justice usually will order the client into outpatient treatment or dismiss the case.

If the client is hospitalized at NVMHI or WSH, a third opportunity for diversion is created. The CSB has an active discharge planning process (S. O'Bannon, personal communication, June 1995). The discharge planner has responsibility for all county clients at the regional or state hospitals, regardless of the outpatient therapist assigned. As soon as the client is hospitalized, the planner begins to work with the hospital staff, the client, the client's family, and the ongoing therapist to identify what change must occur so the client can return to the community.

Areas commonly explored in the discharge planning process are housing, continuing outpatient treatment (including medication management), employment, and social supports (S. O'Bannon, personal communication, June 1995). Also, based on their experience, the therapist and discharge planner can alert the hospital staff about those clients who tend to deteriorate as hospitalization lengthens, facilitating the early discharge of these patients.

Resources

When preparing for a hospital diversion interview, the clinician must be aware of the available risk management and treatment resources. Risk management alternatives include the client's family, friends, AA sponsors, or church members. Treatment alternatives are those available within the CSB or elsewhere. With the opportunity to divert and with an awareness of the resources on hand, the clinician is prepared for the interview.

The Interview

Several authors (de Shazer, 1988; Haley, 1976; Tolman, 1990) have noted the importance of structuring the first session to initiate (or complete) brief therapy productively. De Shazer (1988) and Miller (1994) have suggested specific outlines for a first solution-focused session. During the existence of the crisis/detox program, the staff modified these suggestions to fit the social control nature of the emergency interview. The modified interview, further refined in the staff's new role as emergency therapists, is presented in Exhibit 9.1. It is designed to stand alone; however, aspects of it can be included in other situations in which hospital diversion is appropriate.

Orient the Client. Orientation is an important first step. Often the identified patient has not been informed of the purpose of the interview. Other times the person might have been brought to the facility under pretense. This is a common practice when parents want help for symptomatic adolescents.

To begin the orientation, it is important to ask, "What do you understand about why you are here? This can be followed up with a statement such as, "That's right, your sister was concerned because you were talking about killing yourself

EXHIBIT 9.1. SAFETY MANAGEMENT AND HOSPITAL DIVERSION INTERVIEW.

Orient the Client

1. Ask "What is your understanding of why you are here?"
2. Orient the client by explaining the reason for the interview, based on the response to question one.

   If the client seems to have little understanding of why he is here, give a summary of what you know about the reason for the interview.

Ask About Client Concerns

3. Ask an outcome question such as:

   "What would have to be different for you to be able to manage those thoughts (or those behaviors)?"

   "What would you have to do to convince your sister you're going to be safe?"

Offer Services

4. Make an offer to assist with the client's concerns:

   "Would you like our help with this?"

   If the response is "yes:"

   a.   Outline available services.

   b.   Determine what services the client would like.

   c.   If the client has accepted treatment with you, proceed with therapy based on standard first session.

   d.   If the client declines treatment with you, take action necessary to link client to requested services.

   If the client's response is "no," proceed with safety management.

Manage Safety

5. Assess safety using scaling questions:

   "Where are you on a one-to-ten scale, where one means you have thoughts of killing yourself, a plan to do so, and intent to carry out those plans, and ten means you will be absolutely safe when you walk out of here?"

   "Where were you on the scale when you first arrived here?"

   If you feel the need for a more thorough client history related to suicidal ideation or attempts, ask the appropriate questions to assess this. If the client has attempted suicide before, follow these questions with the question:

   "What is different this time?"
6. Initiate a risk management plan if necessary, by asking:

   "What can you do to reassure others (your family, me, and so on) that you (and they) will be safe while we work on your goals?"

and so she called us for help. My job right now is to determine the best way to help you be safe while you work on solving the problems that led you to talk this way."

The orientation step is also important when, due to cultural differences, someone does not understand the significance of the interview. The emergency services staff learned this when a Korean woman was evaluated for involuntary hospitalization in a nursing home. A social worker from the Korean Community Services Agency had been engaged to interpret. She took considerably longer to translate than expected. When asked about this she stated that she often finds it necessary to give lengthy explanations about context. She also noted that she must explain the importance of answering the questions posed so that the respondents will provide appropriate information.

A thorough orientation is not only important because the client may be unaware of potential interview outcomes and may withhold valuable information, but also because it may be necessary to ensure informed consent.

Inquire About Client Concerns and Desires. Once the client understands the purpose of the interview, the therapist can ask how she can be helpful. This changes the focus of the interview, helps to transform a social control situation into a therapeutic context, or in some cases, to dissolve the perceived problem. A discussion about the client's concerns and desires provides the opportunity to understand the client's worldview and to incorporate it into the therapist's thinking.

Incorporate the Client's Worldview. When a person has been coerced into visiting the CSB, it is desirable to shift from a coercive approach into a collaborative process. An understanding of the worldview of the client (and the client's family) is necessary before this can be done. One situation in which incorporating the client's worldview made a striking difference was with the family of an adolescent girl.

Jean, a sixteen-year-old, had been brought in by her mother during the previous week because of threats of suicide. The therapist had worked successfully with the mother and daughter to extinguish the suicidal thoughts. However, the mother complained that her husband was unhappy that she had not put Jean on restriction, according to an agreement they had made. The interview session was scheduled for a time convenient to the client's father, who had been unable to attend the earlier sessions.

It became clear that the parents had agreed to new rules for Jean and had informed her of those rules and the consequences for violating them. Jean's father complained that his wife was not enforcing the rules; Jean's mother, however, felt that she had to have the flexibility to use her own judgment because she was in charge of enforcement.

The team of therapists behind the one-way mirror suggested that the therapist ask about the father's profession. When it was discovered that he installed sound systems for stage productions, he was asked what he did when his employer, who negotiates the jobs, made a mistake in specifications. The father's ensuing comments about how he had to modify "the rules" provided a context in which he could understand his wife's dilemma. This resolved the issue and contributed to a successful diversion.

As the client's concerns are understood, client goals can be elicited. These goals then provide a focus for the remainder of the work with the client.

Set Goals. In safety management situations, goal setting provides an opportunity to enhance the client's safety. This occurs through orienting the client to the future, helping the client identify small goals to support rapid success, and involving the family as part of the solution.

Questions about client goals orient the interview toward the future. As Berg and Miller (1992) have noted, one of the most important objectives a therapist can achieve in a first session is to access hope. When asked what will constitute success in therapy or in the interview, the client and family may look beyond the immediate concerns that led to the interview. This shift to the future conveys hope, which can be helpful to suicidal or homicidal clients who see no alternatives to death.

A seventeen-year-old boy, Steve, was brought to the CSB by his mother. She reported that his relationships with his siblings had become very conflictual. She was concerned because Steve, her oldest, had threatened suicide. She worked and had no leave available, and she was worried that she could not guarantee his safety. As she talked about her concerns, Steve slumped in his chair and stared at the floor. His responses to questions were minimal.

After several unsuccessful efforts to involve Steve in the session, the therapist asked his mother what a sign would be that Steve was doing better. The mother indicated that one sign would be for Steve to spend more time with the family, especially his grandfather, to whom she reported he was very close.

Steve suddenly became interested in the interview, so the therapist asked him about his relationship with his grandfather. Steve responded that he wanted to be a Navy man just like his granddad. The therapist discovered that Steve and his mother had met with a Navy recruiter and Steve had only to complete school successfully before he could enlist. He was noticeably more animated as he talked about the Navy.

The therapist asked Steve what he had to do to complete school successfully. Steve responded that his grades were good, but they suffered when he and his brothers were not getting along. Because there had been some earlier discussion about hospitalization, the therapist asked Steve how he thought that might affect his Navy career. He quickly realized that the Navy probably would not accept him with a psychiatric admission on his record.

Once Steve was clear about what he needed to do, a discussion of his responsibilities as the oldest son followed. This helped mother and son formulate a plan that included the team's suggestion that they obtain a Navy recruitment poster to help Steve remember his goals. When assessed for risk, Steve reported he no longer had suicidal thoughts.

Although sometimes the client's desired outcome is as clear as Steve's, often it is not. When a person is depressed and stuck in global or "all or nothing" thinking, taking the time and patience to listen to the client's problems may be required. Here, a question requesting more modest outcomes—one that more closely corresponds to the client's reality—can elicit small, tentative goals. Such questions could be "What is one small thing that could be different that would give you some hope?" or "When you did have hope, what did you want?"

Jaime had been seen in the agency on four occasions for poor school attendance, poor social skills, physical and verbal confrontations with family and friends, thoughts of suicide, and suspected alcohol and drug abuse. He had been hospitalized several times during this period.

Jaime lived with his grandfather but wanted to live with his mother, an unreliable parent who surrounded herself with substance abusers. When Jaime's grandfather would get frustrated with Jaime, he would threaten to give up custody to the county. Jaime then would become suicidal, complaining that he did not belong anywhere.

During one such episode, the therapist asked Jaime what small change could occur that would help him have a little hope of belonging. After some time, he replied that having his own room would help. Jaime, she discovered, had been sleeping in the living room because his mother, who had lived with them for several months, had left many of her belongings behind in the guest room.

Jaime's grandfather agreed to move Jaime's mother's possessions if Jaime would help. Hospitalization was diverted for the time being, although later Jaime was hospitalized one more time. The therapist did use this exception to help prevent later hospitalizations.

It is also important to elicit signs of change from all family members. This invites them to be part of the diversion process and part of the solution.

Brad was a fifty-year-old man whose adult children were concerned about his alcohol use. The children had jointly performed a traditional substance abuse "intervention" after reading about such measures in a self-help book. When Brad appeared at our office with his family, the family was asking that he be sent away to detox and then to a long-term residential treatment program. The children made it clear that if he did not follow through on this, they would exclude him from their lives and encourage their mother to leave him.

Brad said he would not go away for treatment. When asked what he might want from our agency, he was clear that he wanted to keep his family. The therapist used this goal to engage Brad in therapy.

The therapist then provided the family with other means of achieving their goal of Brad's sobriety. The family dropped their insistence on a residential treatment program and both Brad and his family completed treatment within thirty days. A follow-up one year later indicated that Brad was still sober and more actively involved with his family.

Offer Services. Once the client has identified goals for therapy, the next step is to outline available services. If the client accepts an offer of services, and if time allows, the remaining steps in a first solution-focused session (identifying exceptions, providing feedback, and so on) can occur. Otherwise, at the end of the interview a first therapy session is scheduled for a later date.

Ensure Safety. Once the time has been taken to develop a therapeutic relationship with the client and family, this last step occurs. The form of risk assessment at this point depends upon the clinician's understanding of the client's commitment to change. If the client's relationship to the established goals and therapy is assessed to be a customer-seller-type relationship (Berg & Miller, 1992), this step is informal. If the client's relationship is more of a complainant-listener, or especially, a visitor-host, this step is formal and detailed. Even in a visitor-host relationship, once this part of the interview has been reached, most of the factors used to assess risk (see, for example, Beck, Rush, Shaw, & Emery, 1979) have already been identified and addressed.

Ask Scaling Questions. To facilitate writing the formal risk note required by some agencies, a scaling question (Lipchik, 1988) can be used to clearly assess safety. This question helps to double check the assessment and provides a method for reporting risk and safety in the note. In addition to addressing liability, scaling helps the client to assess and examine his thinking about the situation and the future. The added clarity is helpful to the therapist and, as illustrated by the following case, to the client.

Duane, a thirty-six-year-old, is a client of the CSB's Residential Program. He lives with two roommates in a supervised townhouse. Duane's condition began before he was eighteen, and he was eventually diagnosed with paranoid schizophrenia. He came to the agency after a four-and-a-half-year stay at a state hospital. During this residential placement, Duane made slow but steady progress. He became more sociable, responded more quickly to questions, and even began initiating conversations. Recently, however, the therapist noticed that Duane's behavior was changing. He was spending most of the time in his room, not eating well, and neglecting his chores and personal hygiene. When questioned whether he was taking his medications, Duane replied "No. God told me not to." He did not remember when he had stopped taking his medications. Neither Duane's mother nor the staff psychiatrist had any success convincing him to take them again.

Eventually, Duane stopped talking. He was eating only crackers and drinking only water. He stopped cashing his checks and going on the weekly grocery run.

The therapist decided to use a scaling question to help Duane decide to start taking his medication again. She hoped that this would allow him to take control of the situation himself. Further, she was afraid that if he were rehospitalized, he, his family, and other supporters would see it as a failure and relinquish hope.

The therapist drew a scale on a sheet of lined paper and marked it from one to ten. Duane was asked to look at the scale. He looked briefly, but then turned away and would not look again. The therapist persisted, repeating her message three times. She told Duane that ten on the scale was where he was taking his medications, eating properly, taking care of his personal hygiene, doing his chores, and being more sociable. She explained that one was where he was back in the hospital, and two to three would be the point at which she would begin getting him ready to return to the hospital. She also informed Duane that his psychiatrist already believed the time had come for hospitalization, but she (the therapist) believed Duane could turn the situation around.

Although Duane still had not looked at the scale again, the therapist left the paper with him, telling him she would check with him later. The next day when the therapist telephoned and asked Duane how he was doing, he replied, "I'm taking my medicine." Duane became stable again and avoided hospitalization (J. A. Rudy, personal communication, July 1995).

In this case, the risk assessment was informal—a natural part of the relationship between the client and therapist. A more formal assessment is used when there is uncertainty about the client's relationship with therapy goals or when it is believed that the relationship is not strong.

Manage Risk. When the risk assessment is completed, the client is asked what he can do to assure everyone that he will be safe while he works on his goals. This provides the client with the opportunity to develop his own safety plan. Depending on the available alternatives and the therapist's risk assessment, an acceptable safety plan might be a promise and a handshake, a tight safety watch by family or friends, admission into a community-based intensive treatment program, or an inpatient admission.

If the client believes that hospitalization is the appropriate means for managing risk and if the therapist concurs, hospitalization is voluntary, which allows the client more control over the process. If time and context allow, discharge planning might be initiated at this point by asking, "What will be the sign that you are ready to be discharged from the hospital?"

Once a plan has been agreed upon to manage the client's safety to everyone's satisfaction (this is not always possible because of a conflict between legal constraints and other interested parties' agendas), the next steps for treatment are determined and the interview is ended.

Using a Solution-Focused Model

The solution-focused model has been helpful in hospital diversion work in three ways: addressing the coercion inherent in risk management, creating hope for clients (and therapists) who have lost hope, and clarifying the role of hospitalization in treatment. Even so, there have been difficulties implementing the model in this setting. These difficulties have surfaced in training inexperienced staff and in interfacing with other agency programs or outside providers.

Coercion

The solution-focused model has helped the staff to acknowledge that interrupting harmful or objectional client behavior is coercive. Berg's (1989) description of the *customership concept,* especially as further developed in Berg and Miller (1992), has led to an important distinction for both the staff and the clients: the purpose of the interview is usually to achieve the goals of someone other than the client. The staff acknowledges that it is being asked to carry out the state's legal and fiscal interests, or the goals of other parties who have initiated the contact.

Thus, the staff differentiates between the social control function it is asked or mandated to perform and its therapeutic role. This often facilitates the transformation of the interview from one of social control into one of therapy. By placing the social control functions at the end of the interview, the therapist can remain true to the tenet of using the client's concerns to fashion goals for therapy jointly. Once the client's goals are clear, the social control aspect can be addressed directly as the last step of the interview, thus preventing an inadvertent diversion into the issue during therapy.

This distinction has also been used to refocus sessions when the therapist is getting ahead of a client. In particular, it has been used with clients whose style is to use allusions to self-harm to convey ambivalence (or to slow the therapist down or get her attention).

Michelle had a history of self-mutilation. She provided a clue that a distinction between social control and therapy would be helpful to her when she complained early in therapy that the sessions never seemed to focus on her goals but always on safety issues. The therapist began making this distinction with Michelle by saying, "I know it is frustrating that we never get to what you want to talk about, but when you tell me you want to hurt yourself, I have to take off my therapy hat and put on my mental health police hat. Not only does the state say I can't let you kill yourself, but *I* don't want you to either."

Soon after, Michelle appeared for a session with a "Mental Health Police" hat she had fashioned from poster board—complete with black and gold antennae. From then on, the therapist had only to reach for the hat or look toward it for Michelle to become clear about her safety. Acknowledging the switch to social control was also a reminder to the therapist that she was moving too quickly and needed to listen more carefully to Michelle.

Creating Hope

In the effort to inspire hope in therapy, well-executed solution-focused therapy has an edge over other models. Its effectiveness is striking not only for clients but also for therapists. Candidates for hospital diversion often are people who have given up hope or for whom the treating therapist has given up hope of change.

Hope is the expectation of good. With the focus on the future inherent in solution-focused therapy, the therapist's main function may be that of continually collaborating with the client to find evidence of hope for the desired outcome. But to facilitate the awareness of hope, the therapist must be masterful at listening to the client.

Sonja, an eleven-year-old, was brought to therapy by her mother, who complained that if Sonja did not shape up, Sonja would have to live with her father. Sonja was not happy about this, and yet she also was very unhappy at her mother's house.

When asked what would have to be different for her to do what her mother considered "shaping up," Sonja continued to look at the floor and stated, "I gave up on that a long time ago."

The therapist, recognizing that Sonja would be unable to envision a future without hopelessness in her way, asked, "So, when you *did* have hope, what did you hope for?"

Evidently, this form of the outcome question properly matched Sonja's view, because she replied, "Mom will confide in me more, like she does with Jimmy. She'll spend more time with me and not let Jimmy get away with so much."

This reaccessing of hope provided the avenue for developing small goals agreeable to all family members. It facilitated a different kind of diversion by allowing time to see if further therapy could forestall Sonja's being sent to her father's home.

The Role of Hospitalization

As reported elsewhere (Booker & Blymyer, 1994), the CSB believes that the purpose of hospitalization is to manage clients who cannot remain safe in outpatient settings. Unfortunately, times have changed since Langsley and his colleagues (1968) suggested that very few people need hospitalization. With the breakdown of the family, the increased mobility of our society, and the many homes in which all adults must work to survive, it often is impossible to find resources for safety watches. Without facilities such as the CSB's Crisis/Detox, adequate alternatives may not exist.

Rather than hospitalizing for the convenience of the treating clinician, however, the staff of the CSB uses hospitals only when there is no alternative. Yet many people still see hospitals as a source of treatment, so we often must educate other service providers to our ideas.

As the county gatekeepers to the public psychiatric hospitals, the CSB receives calls from local private hospitals to evaluate clients for placement when a patient is about to run out of insurance. Guidelines for this type of placement are the same as for any client who presents directly to the CSB: there must be imminent risk of self-harm or harm to others or significant inability to care for self that cannot be treated in a less restrictive setting. In situations in which the hospital disagrees with the CSB's assessment, a discharge appointment is offered with the understanding that intensive outpatient services will be provided as needed to manage the risk.

There are also cases such as those described by Langsley and his colleagues (1968), "in which the hospital is endowed with magical curative powers by the patient, the family, or the doctor" (p. 49). A hint that this might be the situation occurs when outcome questions are answered with, "Tom will be in the hospital," or when at the first contact for services a request is made to hospitalize someone.

Through trial and error, the staff has learned that it is necessary to join with the client's worldview regarding hospital admission before alternatives can be suggested successfully. Sometimes, as Langsley and colleagues (1968) have noted, the client's intentions are discovered to be based on a history of hospitalization. It also may be the client's preferred recourse because a friend or acquaintance has "diagnosed" the problem and informed the client or the family that hospitalization worked for him or her or for someone else with a similar diagnosis.

Miller's (1994) distinction between *means* and *ends* has strengthened the staff's ability to think and talk about these cases. Thus, when the staff's outcome questions are answered with "June will be in a residential treatment program," questions are asked to elicit the distinction between the means of accomplishing a goal and the desired goal or ends. This might occur through some form of the question, "So, how will that make a difference?" followed at an appropriate point by the question, "Would it be okay with you if you could achieve that in some other way?" Thus, deconstruction of the client's stated goals is used to uncover the client's desired outcome. This deconstruction is important in helping to find a goal that accomplishes what the client wants within the constraints of legal, social, family, and agency interests.

Confusion of means versus ends often happens in substance abuse cases in which the popular view of treatment is that a thirty-, sixty-, or ninety-day residential program is necessary for success. Such was the case with Brad, described earlier. The family initially requested residential treatment. Brad helped his family find alternatives by refusing to agree to their means, while being clear about his desired ends: his strong desire for continuing his relationship with his children and his wife. The final success of his case was in part a result of the therapist's skillful deconstruction of the stated means to find the family's common goals.

For some clients with a history of hospitalization, however, even this distinction will make no difference. As suggested by Langsley and colleagues (1968), the staff sometimes has to surrender and focus on the length of hospitalization rather than on whether or not it will occur. For some families, hospitalization seems to be a way for the client to receive a state-subsidized and managed vacation and for the family to receive a much needed break. Focusing on the length of the stay can often reduce its cost.

Brenda, a fifty-year-old woman, had a long-standing condition. She lived with her brother's family. Periodically, she or her brother would frantically contact Emergency Services complaining of her inappropriate behavior (the nature of which was never clear).

Brenda was admitted several times to the Crisis/Detox facility. The first time, the staff worked very hard to engage her brother in treatment and to help Brenda identify therapy goals. The result was a frustrated therapist who was amazed when suddenly Brenda and her brother announced that she was ready to go home.

When asked what was different that made her ready to go home, no one could answer the question. After another episode of this, the staff realized that becoming vaguely symptomatic was Brenda's way of getting a break from her family and of giving them a break. The staff recognized that it had been working too hard to turn a visitor into a customer. For subsequent admissions, the therapist would ask Brenda at admission how many days she thought she would stay. She was always able to predict accurately, and she generally kept her stays short.

Teaching Solution-Focused Therapy

Although the solution-focused treatment model is clearly presented in many books (Berg & Miller, 1992; de Shazer, 1985, 1988; O'Hanlon & Weiner-Davis, 1989; Walter & Peller, 1992), the CSB has found some aspects of the model more challenging to teach to beginning (and sometimes even seasoned) therapists.

The issue of pacing the client is clearly discussed in Nylund and Corsiglia's (1994) article on "solution-focused forced" therapy. The CSB also has found that if the therapist forgets to pay attention to the client's verbal and nonverbal responses, the therapist may lose the client. Many clients, unfortunately, are too polite to tell the therapist this. They may report change or agree with the therapist's punctuation of change even though the identified improvements are not significant to the client.

In addition to the concerns raised by Nylund and Corsiglia (1994), some clinicians seem to misinterpret the model, believing that the therapist must provide the client with solutions. Although this misinterpretation may be an artifact of the pragmatic, problem-solving approach used in emergency work (Everstine & Everstine, 1983) or of the idea that in an emergency others must provide structure and direction for the client, it also may be a result of difficulties with the manner in which the model is presented.

The CSB has had the benefit of many in-house trainings by nationally known solution-focused theoreticians and clinicians. Nevertheless, the use of this model has still been vehemently opposed by some people in the agency. Some of that opposition is the result of people's experiences interfacing with Crisis/Detox staff (discussed shortly); however, some people have indicated (D. Blymyer, personal communication, October 1994) long after the in-house trainings that they objected to the model because they believed that "solution-focused" meant that the therapist provided the solutions.

Another issue, perhaps a developmental one, seems to be a result of having a mandated treatment model for a particular program. For some therapists, part of the process of integrating the model is a self-consciousness regarding whether their thinking or actions are sanctioned by the model. Thinking about how the model would suggest proceeding is helpful, but when it gets in the way of the clinician's own instincts, good common sense, or development of a personal style, it becomes detrimental. A simple question such as, "What do you think you should do?" often facilitates moving past this.

Interfacing with Other Treatment Models

Although the CSB is a family-focused agency, not all of its treatment programs use a solution-focused model. One outcome of the use of the model has been that clinicians view their clients positively and experience them as motivated to change. These clinicians often interface, however, with other clinicians who believe in client resistance and the necessity of assessing pathology before providing treatment. Sometimes a clinician would send a client to the Crisis/Detox program to be managed because, just like the family, the clinician was overburdened and frustrated. When the client was transferred back out for outpatient treatment, the therapist might talk enthusiastically about progress and client commitment to change. The solution-focused therapist would then be viewed as Pollyannish, inexperienced, or arrogant. An example of the impact of this shortcoming has been described by Smith and Schlechty (1994).

Just as the staff has found that pacing clients is a challenge with this model, it has also learned that pacing the clinicians with whom it interfaces, both inside and outside of the agency, is also critical. Becoming more aware of this, the staff has worked to use its language to find ways to describe clients' motivation that are more consistent with the clinician's worldview.

Suggestions for Implementing Hospital Diversion

To implement a hospital diversion program successfully, the three areas identified earlier—opportunity, alternative resources, and theoretical orientation—must be addressed. In addition to the following suggestions, those interested in implementing a program will find the work of Langsley and colleagues (1968), Langsley and Yarvis (1976), Elizur and Minuchin (1989), and Bengelsdorf, Church, Kaye, Orlowski, and Alden (1993) instructive.

The creation of opportunities to divert clients from inpatient treatment is probably the easiest part of the formula to implement. With precertification required for most hospitalizations, the insertion of a face-to-face assessment before admission and during treatment is a relatively simple procedure. It does require, however, that diversion clinicians be available twenty-four hours a day, seven days a week. Further, interview sites must be available. This may mean developing agreements with hospitals for the opportunity to interview clients in an emergency room, or having a contractual arrangement with a twenty-four-hour urgent care facility to provide space for such an interview.

To divert from hospitalization successfully, alternative resources must be developed. These might include free-standing acute care facilities such as Crisis/Detox; twenty-three-hour hospital emergency observation room stays; contracts with twenty-four-hour urgent care or other facilities, as required for bed space to be managed by on-call staff; development of volunteer homes (Polak, Kirby, & Deitchman, 1979); use of day-treatment facilities for risk management; and other resources suggested by Langsley and colleagues (1968).

One of the least costly resources to provide, and one that has a high payoff, is that of intensive outpatient services (see Bengelsdorf et al., 1993). In the private sector, intensive treatment can occur best in a group practice, with each clinician dedicating some time each week to emergency cases. The trend in the industry is toward multidisciplinary practices (Patterson & Scherger, 1995). Within this context, a common treatment orientation can provide the opportunity to share responsibility for high-risk cases, thus mitigating the emotional and fiscal impact on the individual clinician. Solution-focused therapists will do well in this regard because they focus on what is working for the client. This approach facilitates sharing treatment responsibilities because the clinician has less personal involvement in a particular method of resolving the problem.

The clinician who performs the interview should have experienced success in diverting high-risk and complex cases. He or she must be aware of the alternative risk management modalities available. The diversion specialist must be comfortable interacting with a psychiatrist as a peer and with developing collegial yet objective relationships with the psychiatrist and hospital staff to prevent an adversarial situation. Similarly, the specialist must be able to move easily between the worldviews of all the clinical specialties involved in treatment, and to balance the multiplicity of interests of those specialists, as well as those of the funding source and the client. And whatever her agreement with the decision about hospitalization, the clinician should convey it to the client in a way that supports the client's best interests.

Conclusion

To divert the maximum number of clients from hospitalization while providing high-quality service, it is necessary to view outpatient treatment as a treatment of first choice. A focus on treatment in the context of the family and everyday life facilitates such a view.

Further, conceptualizing families as part of the solution, rather than as the cause of the problem, provides opportunities for diversion. Without this focus, it is difficult to trust families to manage risk.

It is also important to stay focused on client goals associated with safety, and to negotiate goals that are small and achievable. Success with these goals can help the client find additional motivation for change and become more strongly future-oriented. As the client's orientation to the future grows, the risk of self-harm or harm to others diminishes because the client now has more to live for.

Hospital diversion is a specialty to which a solution-focused approach has much to offer.

Questions from the Editors

1. *As you "interface" with clinicians who follow different models and methods, what have you found to be most effective in bridging the gap?*

In working with clinicians who have different ideas about the goals and methods of therapy, it is helpful to remember that clients and clinicians are not so different. Both clinicians and clients want to be respected and want their ideas and concerns to be respected. Both can hear new ideas more readily when they are presented in a manner that fits their existing ideas—their worldview. Although this is sometimes difficult to do, setting aside attachment and affection for our personal ideas about therapy does more toward facilitating an honest dialogue than does prostletyzing or arguing. Solution-focused therapists have the skills to join with others and to present ideas consistent with the listener's worldview. They just have to be willing, and to remember, to use those skills.

Further, faced with a situation in which another clinician or professional (teacher, probation office, and so forth) has very strong ideas about the client and the situation, asking outcome questions such as "What will be an indication to you that she is doing better?" can be helpful. Just as it is important to help client families notice change, others who have an interest in the client's success may also need some help.

2. *You write that solution-focused therapy has much to offer hospital diversion. If you were presenting this approach to a group in charge of the "bottom line," what findings or data would you cite to support your position?*

The state of Virginia requires that the various community services boards provide treatment in the least restrictive setting available, consistent with client needs.

Thus, the state mandates hospital diversion for all its jurisdictions. Within this context, the Prince William County CSB has consistently ranked lowest in admissions per 100,000 residents among those jurisdictions that feed WSH and NVMHI, the two hospitals to which the CSB sends clients. For example, so far in 1995, the CSB has averaged 8.15 admissions to WSH per 100,000 population, compared to the average of 18.42 per 100,000 for all sending jurisdictions[1]. Comparing the peak census in both hospitals during August of 1993, 1994, and 1995, Prince William County has had 14.3, 10.5, and 11.5 admissions per 100,000 per year, respectively. The average for all jurisdictions has been 25.0, 23.4, and 21.6 for those three years[2].

Although there are many intervening variables, such as level of homelessness in the jurisdiction, availability of alternative treatment settings, and distance of residents from outpatient treatment centers, the consistently low rate of hospitalization from Prince William County can in large part be attributed to the beliefs and assumptions held by the CSB staff.

These beliefs include that clients and their families have resources and strengths rather than pathology and dysfunction, and that hospitals provide risk management but lasting treatment occurs in the context of people's everyday lives. One of the guiding assumptions is that small changes lead to more significant change and that in a crisis, a small change can make the difference between hospitalization and the ability to treat the client on an outpatient basis.

Although in the therapy room the actual style and execution of therapy of each staff member may differ, these beliefs and assumptions pervade the staff's crisis work. These values and assumptions are also foundations to a solution-focused approach.

3.   *Considering what you have accomplished in hospital diversion with a solution-focused model, what is the next step? What remains to be done?*

"If it ain't broke, don't fix it"—"If it works, do more of it" (Berg & Miller, 1992). There are several areas in which "more" can be done: developing our ideas and our staff to enhance effectiveness, increasing treatment setting alternatives, and extending our services into other settings.

Increasing the flexibility and experience of our diversion team is an ongoing process. Infusing our work with new ideas from narrative approaches, other solution-focused clinicians, and other strength- and resource-based models is encouraged through in-service training and the provision of training leave for outside training. Continuing our use of outcome studies and follow-up with clients will also increase our understanding of what is most helpful to our clients.

The major gap in our range of available treatment settings is a local acute care facility such as our former Crisis/Detox facility. Because public funding is no longer available for this program, the possibility of creating such options depends on our ability to locate other funding sources and to demonstrate to our management and board that such a facility would benefit the community. In informal discussions about reconstituting this program, we have recognized that we face a challenge without state support in justifying creation of a residential program whose success is measured by empty beds.

The success we have had in hospital diversion could be a benefit to the CSB as it is nudged into competition in the current political climate. With such uncertainty about the direction of public mental health care, positioning the agency to be competitive and to fill the hospital diversion gap that exists in the private sector could be of benefit. Whether the agency will proceed in that direction is still unclear.

Notes

1. Western State Hospital Patients in Hospital by CSB of Legal Residence, various months, 1995.
2. Western State Hospital Peak Day of On Books Census by Community Service Board 08/1993, 08/1994, 08/1995, September 1995.

References

American Psychiatric Association. (1989). *Treatments of psychiatric disorders: A task force report of the American Psychiatric Association* (Vol. 3). Washington: American Psychiatric Association.

Beck, A. T., Rush, A. J. Shaw, B. F., & Emery, G. (1979). *Cognitive therapy of depression.* New York: Guilford.

Bengelsdorf, H., Church, J. O., Kaye, R. A., Orlowski, B., & Alden, D. C. (1993). The cost effectiveness of crisis intervention: Admission diversion savings can offset the high cost of service. *Journal of Nervous and Mental Disease, 181,* 757–762.

Berg, I. K. (1989). Of visitors, complainants, and customers. *The Family Therapy Networker, 13*(1), 21.

Berg, I. K., & Miller, S. D. (1992). *Working with the problem drinker: A solution-focused approach.* New York: W. W. Norton.

Booker, J., & Blymyer, D. (1994). Solution-oriented brief residential treatment with "chronic mental patients." *Journal of Systemic Therapies, 13*(4), 53–69.

Bush, A. (1994, October). Teen substance abuse: Guiding families to New Horizons. *Family Therapy News,* pp. 25, 35.

Department of Mental Health, Mental Retardation and Substance Abuse Services. (1992). *Statutes of Virginia relating to the Department of Mental Health, Mental Retardation and Substance Abuse Services.* Charlottesville, VA: The Michie Company.

De Shazer, S. (1985). *Keys to solution in brief therapy.* New York: W. W. Norton.

De Shazer, S. (1988). *Clues: Investigating solutions in brief therapy.* New York: W. W. Norton.

Durrant, M. (1993). *Residential treatment: A cooperative, competency-based approach to therapy and program design.* New York: W. W. Norton.

Elizur, J., & Minuchin, S. (1989). *Institutionalizing madness: Families, therapy, and society.* New York: Basic Books.

Everstine, D. S., & Everstine, L. (1983). *People in crisis: Strategic therapeutic interventions.* New York: Brunner/Mazel.

Haley, J. (1976). *Problem-solving therapy.* San Francisco: Jossey-Bass.

Langsley, D. G., Kaplan, D. M., Pittman, F. S., Machotka, P., Flomenhaft, K., & DeYoung, C. D. (1968). *The treatment of families in crisis.* New York: Grune & Stratton.

Langsley, D. G., and Yarvis, R. M. (1976). Crisis intervention prevents hospitalization: Pilot program to service project. In H. J. Parad, H.L.P. Resnik, & L. G. Parad (Eds.), *Emergency and disaster management: A mental health sourcebook* (pp. 25–34). Bowie, MD: Charles Press.

Lipchik, E. (1988). Purposeful sequences for beginning the solution-focused interview. In E. Lipchik (Ed.), *Interviewing* (pp. 105–117). Rockville, MD: Aspen.

Menses, G., & Durrant, M. (1987). Contextual residential care. *Journal of Strategic and Systemic Therapies, 6*(2), 3–15.

Miller, S. (1994, April). *Solution-focused therapy.* Presentation to the Virginia State Emergency Services Conference, Virginia Beach, VA.

Nylund, D., & Corsiglia, V. (1994). Becoming solution-~~focused~~ forced in brief therapy: Remembering something important we already knew. *Journal of Systemic Therapies, 13*(1), 5–12.

O'Hanlon, W. H., & Weiner-Davis, M. (1989). *In search of solutions: A new direction in psychotherapy.* New York: W. W. Norton.

Patterson, J., & Scherger, J. E. (1995). A critique of health care reform in the United States: Implications for the training and practice of marriage and family therapists. *Journal of Marital and Family Therapy, 21,* 127–135.

Polak, P. R., Kirby, M. W., & Deitchman, W. S. (1979). Treating acutely psychotic patients in private homes. *New Directions for Mental Health Services, 1,* 49–64.

Prince William County Community Services Board. (1991). *Policy and procedures manual: Crisis/detox program.* Manassas, VA: Author.

Prince William County Community Services Board. (1993). Mission Statement. Manassas, VA: Author.

Smith, C., & Schlechty, D. (1994). Caught between two therapists: What can happen when a prescriptive approach clashes with a utilization approach. *Case Studies in Brief and Family Therapy, 8*(1), 27–35.

Tolman, M. (1990). *Single session therapy: Maximizing the effect of the first (and often only) therapeutic encounter.* San Francisco: Jossey-Bass.

Walter, J., & Peller, J. (1992). *Becoming solution-focused in brief therapy.* New York: Brunner/Mazel.

Wylie, M. S. (1992). Revising the dream: Community mental health professionals confront the realities of the '90s. *The Family Therapy Networker, 14*(4), 10–23.

CHAPTER TEN

SOLUTION-FOCUSED GRIEF THERAPY

William R. Butler and Keith V. Powers

I finally understood what life is about: it is about losing everything. Losing the baby who becomes a child, the child who becomes an adult, like the trees lose their leaves. So every morning we must celebrate what we have.

ISABEL ALLENDE (1995)

At a recent training seminar, a trainee was surprised when this chapter's authors offered to show videotapes of therapists helping clients to overcome grief using solution-focused brief therapy (SFBT). In talking with the trainee, and listening to her questions, it became apparent that she felt that grief is too sensitive an issue to address with SFBT. We asked ourselves, why would the trainee have thought this?

We had been asked this question before. Perhaps it is because of the way SFBT has been taught—as a series of techniques: "First do step 1, then step 2, then if the therapist/client relationship looks to be a certain way, suggest task A, B, or C." This is fine for learning. We must admit that the model originally appealed to us because it was very learnable. But this formula can appear uncaring, nonempathic, dry, and perhaps even unfeeling.

This may explain why people often assume that some issues like sexual abuse or grief are not suitable for SFBT. They may assume that SFBT is not nurturing or supportive enough to be helpful in working through such difficult problems—and they would be right if SFBT were really done that way. But it is not the techniques that do the therapy (Weick, 1983). It is the therapist and client that do the work. The key to SFBT is the understanding that the therapist and client make up a therapeutic system that *collaborates* on the construction of solutions. This understanding is crucial in addressing bereavement. People in the midst of deep and often overpowering grief must feel heard, understood, and supported before they are able to consider the possibility of feeling better or different (Lipchik, 1994). So, in addition to showing how SFBT techniques are used in working with grief, we feel it is imperative to emphasize attention to the basic assumptions of SFBT and to the core skills of joining, establishing rapport, and listening—or "being with the client."

Being with the Client

We agree with O'Hanlon (1993) when he says that the cornerstone of the approach is acknowledgment and possibility. The *acknowledgment* is fundamental. It is what we call "being with the client." In a sense, it is as if we place ourselves in the same location or position as the client in his or her process of dealing with the problem. It is similar to the basic Rogerian attitude of reflecting the client's feelings, accepting his or her position, and trusting his or her capacity for self-direction (Rogers, 1951). The practical expressions of this idea are the basic therapeutic techniques of listening, mirroring, paraphrasing/reflecting, summarizing, and conveying empathy through facial expressions, tone of voice, and so on.

The *possibility* side of the equation involves the therapist's presuppositional orientation toward a future time when the problems of concern are resolved. The possibility frame includes a therapeutic attitude of curiosity about how the client will solve his or her problem. The practical applications of this are the techniques of SFBT: future-oriented questions, scaling questions, amplifying of exceptions, tasks, and so forth (de Shazer, 1985, 1988; Berg & Miller, 1992; Walter & Peller, 1992).

In this chapter we illustrate how the acknowledgment/possibility paradigm, and the SFBT techniques that flow from it, can be applied to an emotionally laden issue like grief. We do this with the knowledge that once the therapist fully understands and really focuses on the client's resources, then the problem and its unique characteristics actually make little difference—because SFBT is a *model of change,* not a problem-focused model.

Acknowledgment

It is tempting simply to invite the reader to review the core skills used in any model of psychotherapy. Doing so would not serve, however, to emphasize sufficiently the importance of these skills, and it could serve to omit a crucial element of the therapeutic encounter that has been absent from most solution-focused writing: *validating the client's experience of the problem* (Durrant, 1989). The following example illustrates the importance of acknowledgment.

Case Example A middle-aged woman with a history of chronic depression was referred for therapy by her case manager at a community mental health center. The
woman had recently suffered a string of losses including the deaths of her mother and
brother, the loss of a beloved pet, and the end of a fifteen-year marriage. She also felt
the loss of her ability to work due to her chronic depression.

During the first interview the client complained about feeling increasingly depressed due to the recent losses. She also told about a long history of losses occurring
over the previous ten years (her niece had died, she had lost her job, she had filed
for bankruptcy, and so on). The therapist listened intently, reflected her feelings, and
made many empathic comments. The most important thing the therapist did, however, was to *not ask* a series of future-oriented questions. Instead, he asked questions
designed to elicit information about the client's coping skills, such as, "How did you
get through that?" and "How have you managed to keep going?" The client cried
through most of the interview and was only able to say that she somehow managed
to "keep going day by day."

In the second interview, one week later, the client again told details of her long
history of depression and loss. The therapist picked up on the theme of multiple losses
and the many years of struggle. He took out a piece of paper and drew a long line representing the past ten years. On this line he placed an X next to the spot in which each
loss had occurred. When complete, the line had over a dozen X's representing the
most significant losses. The drawing of the line and the placing of the marks was a collaborative process, with the therapist asking the client to clarify which came first and
where each mark should be placed. When the line was complete, the therapist made
the following statement to the client: "Well, Betty, it's obvious that you have been
through a tremendous struggle. And the recent loss of your mother and the end of
your marriage have been very difficult to cope with. I have seen your tears and can
hear the pain in your voice. But when I look at this long list and consider what you
have been through, I can't help but wonder—how do you keep it from getting worse?

The client looked at the therapist, paused for a moment and then began to speak.
Little by little she began to tell about beneficial actions she had taken in the past.
She still spoke about setbacks along the way, but now she included things like, "About
five years ago I felt the strong desire to return to work. And I did for about six months
until my husband was transferred."

Now the client and therapist were able to talk about how the client had gathered
her strength and returned to work. The client said that returning to work had made
her feel like her "old self." The therapist followed up by asking about her old self.
The client described herself as being able to handle "normal life stress" and as being
"able to keep myself going." The therapist asked how her old self was able to handle
stress. As the client told of things like doing needlepoint or taking walks, the therapist
took notes. During this process the client "remembered" that she had "a logical side
of myself" that would encourage her to keep going. By the end of the interview, the
client and therapist had a list of ten things that the client had done, and could continue to do, to keep herself going.

We believe that this case illustrates the importance of the process of acknowledgment. By allowing the client to fully explain her feelings, giving her the time to describe all her struggles, and validating her experience, the conversation was able to shift toward her strengths. The therapist's question about how she kept it from getting worse matched the client's experience, but it was asked after the time line was drawn that validated her many losses.

Possibilities

As stated earlier, the other side of the SFBT equation is attention to possibilities. This approach involves the basic assumption that clients have the resources to change, that they can and do have goals, and that they will have a unique process of achieving their desired goal (O'Hanlon & Weiner-Davis, 1989). The techniques of SFBT serve to facilitate this particular change process.

Much has been written about the techniques of SFBT. A complete description of these techniques can be found elsewhere (de Shazer, 1985, 1988; O'Hanlon & Weiner-Davis, 1989; Berg & Miller, 1992; Walter & Peller, 1992). The following examples are intended to show how SFBT techniques may be used in a thoughtful manner with issues such as grief. Once again, these techniques should only be used after validating and acknowledging the client's experience.

Future-Oriented Questions. The future-oriented questions of SFBT are particularly helpful in grief work. They are powerful tools that can help clients think about possibilities, because they take clients into the future when things could be better. Many times the simple act of imagining a different future can free clients from a hopeless perspective. Often these techniques can remind clients that just as they have recovered from other losses, recovery from present difficulties is also inevitable. Future-oriented questions are usually content free, so they serve to elicit clients' own goals. They enable clients to construct their own solutions, which is a key to being brief and successful with any presenting problem.

The "miracle question" is one of the interventions most closely associated with SFBT (de Shazer, 1985): Suppose that tonight you go to sleep, and while you are asleep a miracle happens and the problem you have described is solved. When you wake up in the morning, what would be different? Often we will adjust the wording of the question to fit the clinical situation. For example, the word "problem" may become "difficulty" and the word "solved" may become "different." In addition, the question is often asked slowly, with the therapist pausing at times to wait for a signal that the client understands before going on.

This question may seem disrespectful to ask of a person who has experienced a painful loss. When there has been a death, for example, we might expect the client to look at us in disgust and say, "I know I can't bring him back!" Or perhaps worse, we might expect the client to go along with the hope that we can bring their loved one back, only to be deeply disappointed when the illusion is broken. But we have not found either of these to be the case. Instead, we have found that when the therapist asks the question respectfully, after first listening to and acknowledging the client's grief, the client is usually able to answer and is often relieved to consider the possibility of some kind of emotional healing.

Case Example Mrs. Green came to treatment following the violent death of her husband. Although six years had passed, the murder still haunted Mrs. Green and her children. For most of the first two sessions, the therapist simply listened and acknowledged the family's pain. Because Mrs. Green's initial goal was to assist her children in improving their school performance, the therapist asked questions aimed at that goal. Toward the end of the second session, Mrs. Green said that she also wanted help with her immense feelings of grief. The following excerpts illustrate how future-oriented questions can be helpful in dealing with grief.

> *Client:* I just want to get past the point where any time we talk or think about it we won't have to feel so bad and cry a lot.
> *Therapist:* OK, so you want to get past this point of feeling stuck in sadness. You remember at our last visit we talked about a miracle and things being better for the children. Suppose that tonight you go to bed and while you are sleeping a miracle happens, but because you are sleeping you don't know about the miracle. When you wake up in the morning, what would be different, what would tell you that things were better?
> *Client:* That we could talk about it without crying.
> *Therapist:* And would that be the first thing you would notice? [*Mrs. Green began to cry. The therapist offered her some tissues.*]
> *Therapist:* It's hard isn't it? Who would you find it the easiest to talk with about it?
> *Client:* You mean in the family? Everyone cries when they talk about it.
> *Therapist:* So, after this miracle, that would be a lot easier? [*Mrs. Green nodded.*] What else would be different?
> *Client:* We would all be a lot happier.
> *Therapist:* The whole family?
> *Client:* Uh huh.
> *Therapist:* What would that look like?
> *Client:* It would look like we could keep his picture up, you know, and just look at it without crying. And I would be able to take the picture books out and look through them. [*She wiped tears away.*]
> *Therapist:* Look through the picture books? Who would be looking at them?

The therapist and client talked about how the entire family would be able to sit and talk and reminisce about her late husband. The therapist asked questions designed to get a detailed description of the desired future. He followed up with questions about possible interactions in the family, asking who would say what, how people would feel, and what kind of effect people would have on each other. Throughout the interview, the client struggled to answer the therapist's questions. Often she became tearful and speaking took great effort.

Therapist: What other kinds of things do you want to be able to do?

Client: I want to be able to take them to the grave site. I really want to take them, but I'm scared to. I'm even scared to go myself.

Therapist: What would be one small step toward that? I know it's a scary thought, so what would be one small step toward that?

Client: Just to get there.

Therapist: Just to get there, OK [*spoken in a soft tone*].

Client: We have planned it, you know.

Therapist: Tell me about that [*in a reinforcing tone*].

Client: I was going to take all the kids, and I was going to buy some flowers to put up there.

Therapist: Oh, that was a good idea. Had you all talked about it and kind of planned it that way?

Client: I talked with my boyfriend, John.

Therapist: John helped you plan it out and talk it over? [*Mrs. Green nodded.*] That must have been hard to think about and plan out. How were you able to do that?

Client: He just kept on—kept on asking me about it.

Therapist: That must have been scary, but you thought about the flowers—and what else did you kind of plan out? Like, how to take the kids there and talk to them and. . . .

Client: Uh huh.

Therapist: You have been trying to work on this for quite a while, and you haven't found a way to do it yet. How much would that help?

Client: It would help a whole lot.

Therapist: If you wake up after that miracle, and you are a little happier, and people are able to talk to each other more about it, I'm wondering if it will affect anything else for you. What else will be better?

Client: Just me in general—I will feel better. Be able to deal with it more.

Therapist: And if you are feeling better, just in general, what else will be better? For you I mean?

Client: I won't think about it so much.

Therapist: OK. What kinds of things will you be thinking about instead of that?

Client: Happy things that me and my kids can do together.

Therapist: Can you give me an example?

Client: We could go to the park that we used to go to.

Therapist: Oh, go to that park and enjoy it. I can picture the kids laughing. [*The therapist named all the children.*] And what else will people be doing?

Client: Just playing and having fun.

Therapist: What will you be doing when they are doing that?

Client: I'll be sitting down, looking at them, watching them.

Therapist: What will that feel like?

Client: It will feel good.

Therapist: Yeah.

Client: I will be relieved.

Therapist: Yeah, and when you are feeling relieved, and good, and happy, what will you look like?

Client: I will probably smile more.

Therapist: Smiling more. Yeah, and the kids will see that, and what will they do?

Client: My daughter will probably say, "Mom, I'm glad to see you smiling."

Therapist: So, she will even speak up about it. I see. And when your daughter mentions that you look happier, what will you say to her?

Client: I'll probably tell her thank you.

Therapist: Yeah, okay [*softly*]. And what else will be different for you and your family? Just in general.

Client: I'll feel able to move on—won't feel like we are just stuck there any more.

As the above dialogue illustrates, the miracle question can be a very helpful tool for enabling the client and therapist to consider future possibilities. In this case, the client was able to consider actions like going to the cemetery, playing with the children in the park, and looking at the family photo albums. In later sessions she was able to identify other small steps that eventually helped her move toward her larger goal of being happy.

Exceptions and Coping. Another very useful technique in SFBT is to elicit attention to exceptions. Exceptions are times when the problem of concern is either absent, not as intense, or being handled in such a way that the client feels better (de Shazer 1985, 1988; Berg & Miller, 1992). There are many useful exception questions. In grief work, the most common one is the coping question.

Simply stated, the question is: How do you cope? Or as in the earlier case: How do you keep it from getting worse? These questions do more than elicit attention to possibilities or exceptions. They also acknowledge the client's struggle. They add a focus on what the client actually does to make his or her situation bearable. Once identified, the therapist can then make comments designed to reinforce and amplify the significance of the client's actions (Berg & Miller, 1992).

Case Example The following dialogue shows the work of a therapist with a mother and family who have suffered the loss of a seventeen-year-old male family member. The teenager, named Chuck, was killed when the car he was driving struck a telephone pole. About one month later, his mother, aunt, sister, half-sister, and cousin came for therapy. The therapist used the coping question to begin to move the conversation toward client strengths. As always, the therapist did so after the clients had had an opportunity to tell about their tragic loss.

> *Therapist:* I want to ask you all a question. Here you all are together, getting this big crowd together, which is not easy to do, and everybody's here, you are all on time, the kids are pretty and dressed, how do you all cope with this? How do you keep it all together as well as you do?
>
> *Linda [the sister, age nineteen]:* I just look at it as, I would love to be where he's at. He's in the best place anybody could ever be [*crying*]. You could never wish to take that away. I can't say I wish Chuck would come back because that would be so selfish of me. I would rather be in a place where. . . .

Linda went on to explain that she believed her brother was at peace in heaven. She also felt his death may have been a blessing because after his death it was discovered that he had cancer throughout his body. The therapist made empathic comments, listened, and showed caring by his body posture and facial expressions. As this was done, the therapist also began to reinforce the idea that the family had been coping with their grief.

> *Therapist:* And so the idea that he's in a better place helps you to cope. And as much as you would like to be with him, to you it seems selfish to want that.
>
> *Linda:* I may not see Chuck for about seventy years, but I know when I go, he's going to be right there [*crying again*], showing me where everything's at. . . .
>
> *Therapist:* He's going to show you around.
>
> *Donna [the aunt]:* So we're less afraid of death. . . .
>
> *Therapist:* So that's one of the ways you cope, is that you're less afraid of death.

The therapist and the family continued to explore the family's coping methods. Donna said she felt she got strength from the notion that Chuck would want her to be strong. The therapist continued to make reinforcing comments and asked more questions to expand on the theme of coping, because such exceptions tend to be overlooked if the therapist does not emphasize them. The more time spent on such issues, the more difficult it will become for the client to discount coping behaviors.

> *Therapist:* Some of the strength to cope with all this comes from him. How about you, Tommie? How are you coping?

Tommie [the mother]:   I'm not. She [*gesturing toward Linda*] comes home from work and I'm still in bed, uh, I don't cook dinner, I don't do the dishes, I don't clean house, I don't sleep, I don't eat right, I wait up, I walk around the house, I get scared.

Therapist: Those are all normal reactions at a time like this, and really, where do you find the inner strength in spite of all this stuff, to make sure that Michelle gets to the doctor, to make sure that everybody's here today, to keep things going for the family?

Tommie: That was hard.

Therapist: Where did you get the strength to do all that?

Tommie: My family. My family, you know.

Therapist: These people [*gesturing to include everyone in the room*]?

Tommie: Uh huh.

Therapist: That's where you draw the strength?

Tommie: Yeah, I depend a lot on them. Rebecca's only two, Michelle's only seven, she's only nineteen [*pointing to Linda*], and she's only forty [*pointing to Donna, who smiles*], but between us, we'll do it.

We believe that this is a fairly typical example of how clients in grief respond to SFBT. The therapist was careful to respect the clients' experience of grief. This was accomplished by first listening and then by asking a coping question. Throughout the session the therapist both acknowledged pain and explored coping. "Between us, we'll do it" is a strong indication of movement toward possibilities.

Scaling Questions. Scaling questions are another very useful technique in SFBT. These questions can be posed in a variety of ways and for several different purposes. Most commonly they are used to measure progress, to search for exceptions, to explore future steps, or to assess motivation and/or willingness to take action.

The questions are rather simple and straightforward. They use a numerical scale and ask the client to rate his or her situation or experience with a number on the scale. One version, for example, is: "On a scale from one to ten, where one is the worst this has ever been, and ten is the best things could ever be, where are things today?" (O'Hanlon & Weiner-Davis, 1989).

As we have stated, scaling questions can also be used as another kind of future-oriented question. While the miracle question can help to clarify overall goals, scaling questions can be useful in orienting the client toward taking specific action in the near future. When done skillfully, the client becomes more and more specific (Berg & Miller, 1992). Often the client can be helped to describe smaller and smaller steps until he or she is able to perceive the possibility of some small but immediate change. For example, the therapist might say, "So, you feel like you have been stuck at around two for a very long time, and it has been very difficult to pull yourself up to two. But I am also wondering what would be a small sign that would tell you that you are moving toward two and a half? What would be a small sign that you are moving in the right direction?"

Obviously, the question itself does not guarantee successful intervention. The real work is in the follow-up to whatever the client says. In the following case examples, the therapists follow up the scaling question with more questions and comments.

Case Example In the case of the seventeen-year-old who died in the traffic accident, the therapist came to a point where a search for the clients' next small steps could begin:

Therapist: Let me ask you all, where are you on that 1 to 10 scale?

Donna: I feel, I feel good today. I feel like about a seven. I don't want to go any higher than that because it's like I was telling Tommie, it's like a depression, it's hard to shake. I mean, I feel good, and a lot of little things make me smile, or make me happy or laugh, you know what I mean.

Therapist: So, it can't get much higher than seven until you can start to laugh again, is that what you're saying?

Donna: Yeah.

Therapist: Well, what *will* be different then, when you are at eight?

Donna: That's a hard question. It's still hard for me to accept that this has happened. You know, I go from almost a kind of acceptance that this has happened, and that gives me a kind of a peace, and the next thing I know it's, like, unbelievable. Like I'm laying there on the couch or in bed thinking, "I can't believe it happened."

Therapist: Well, how will it help you if you can accept it? How will that help?

Donna: Well, it will just help me to be happy again, you know? I try to think about how we were happy before. It will be a kind of wiser but sadder happiness. I'll never know that kind of carefree, you know, like "we're so lucky nothing's ever happened to any of the members of our family" kind of happiness, you know?

Therapist: Yeah.

Donna: And thankfulness. It will be a kind of wiser but sadder happiness.

"A kind of wiser but sadder happiness." When the client begins to make statements that acknowledge *both* the pain of the loss *and* the possibility of the future, we take this as a clear sign that the process of resolving grief is moving along.

Therapist: Wow. That's very poignant the way you say that.

Donna: It's going to be hard to come to that, because I really can't be happy now— I'm not suicidal, but I'm not happy. I worry about everybody so much, I'm still mad at Chuck for him being so careless, you know [*to Tommie*]?

Tommie: Yeah.

After some talk about her relationship with Chuck, the therapist guided Donna back to what will be different at the next higher number on the one-to-ten scale.

Therapist: Are you saying that when you are at eight, you will have accepted it, you will stop wondering if it really happened?

Donna: Yeah. Even though I . . . sometimes it doesn't seem real, when Sarah is taking a nap, and I am home all alone, you know? And I'll be laying there, trying to read, or something, and then I'll think about it, you know? But it just doesn't seem real, but then, like, I know it's real because I, you know, the card, the writings in the paper, plus I just know it's real.

Donna made her goal clear, that she will know the death is real. She also indicated that at times she does know the death is real, that she has accomplished her goal sometimes. When she paused, the therapist asked the same question of her sister, Tommie.

As the transcript illustrates, the scaling question helped this family to focus on the possibilities of being happy. In this case, the resolution of their grief appears to involve their belief in God. We find this to be quite common in grief work. (We believe that SFBT is inherently respectful of people's spiritual beliefs. Because the model is focused on clients and their natural resources, people feel free to discuss their spiritual values.)

As the transcript also illustrates, the therapist tries to help the clients focus on their next steps by encouraging them to become more and more specific.

The following is an example from the case of the woman whose husband was murdered. The client had reported some progress. The therapist asked the scaling question both to reinforce the progress and to search for more specific next steps.

Therapist: Do you remember last time when I asked you that question about a scale from one to ten? Where one is the worst this has ever been and ten is some-day when things are the best they can ever be? Where are you today?

Client: About up to a seven.

Therapist: About to a seven, okay, and I think last week . . . do you remember what you said last week?

Client: I think I said a five.

Therapist: So, from five to seven, I guess talking to your sister is one of those things that helped?

Client: Uh huh.

Therapist: And what else has helped?

Client: Just seeing my kids better.

The therapist and client talked about how the client was helping her children with their school work, how she had begun to discuss her husband's death with her sister, and how much happier her children were beginning to appear. During this process the therapist made reinforcing comments designed to amplify the importance of the client's beneficial actions. Then the therapist began to search for next steps.

Therapist: Well, I know it's awfully hard work. And you are at seven now, so what do you think can get you up to just seven and a half? What do you think is the next small thing to work on?

Client: Probably if we could just discuss what happened to their father. We all have such hard feelings about it.

Therapist: Right, right. Okay. [*The therapist pauses.*] And is that a seven and a half, or is that more like an eight and a half?

Client: That's like an eight, that's where I want to get to.

Therapist: Okay, that's where you want to get to. So, what would be *between* seven and eight?

Client: Well, I guess the littlest step would be for the kids to come to me and say, "Well mama, when can we talk about this?" I think that would be good, too.

Therapist: Yeah, okay. You guys are already talking more about school work and things aren't you? And that feels good. Is that what you mean? Or do you mean, as a small step, they really need to talk about their father?

Client: Uh huh, talk about their father.

In this example the scaling question was used to measure progress, to amplify current beneficial actions, and to search for the next small steps toward the desired future. Sometimes the question is modified to measure motivation or willingness to take some specific action. For example, the therapist might say: "If I were to ask you how willing you are to talk to the children about these feelings, on a scale of one to ten, where one is 'I'm a little bit willing' and ten is 'I'm very willing,' where would you place yourself today, understanding that you are afraid?" The last phrase serves to acknowledge the fear. It conveys the idea that someone can be both afraid and still willing to face a fear.

Tasks. In SFBT, another technique is the suggestion of tasks for the client to carry out. Tasks are intended to carry the work of the therapy session into the client's real life. (A complete description of these interventions is beyond the scope of this chapter, but for further discussion see de Shazer, 1985, 1988; O'Hanlon & Weiner-Davis, 1989; Berg & Miller, 1992; and Walter & Peller, 1992.) Tasks are usually suggested at the end of the interview after the therapist has taken a break. During the break the therapist carefully considers what has transpired during the clinical interview. He or she designs a message based on what the client has said or done. Then, the therapist makes an assessment of what the client is most likely to be willing to do between sessions. If it appears that the client would be likely to take some action, then the therapist might suggest something beneficial. If it appears that the client would be more likely to think about something, then a suggestion is made that entails thinking. Sometimes clients are simply encouraged to observe their situation, or to return for another session.

Whatever the task, the message is designed around the basic acknowledgment-possibility paradigm. This is done by first making a statement that acknowledges the client's struggle. Then the therapist compliments the client by mentioning the client's strengths and assets along with any beneficial actions he or she may have taken. Finally, the therapist suggests the task and gives a rationale for it.

Sometimes tasks are developed spontaneously during the clinical interview. For example, in the case of the family who had lost their son, the therapist and family talked about special rituals that helped the family process their grief. One example was when the young man's mother told of picking up a bloodstained leaf at the scene of the accident. As the following dialogue shows, the therapist helped the mother decide what she wanted to do.

Tommie: And I remember there was a beautiful leaf, there was a beautiful leaf and it had a drop of blood on it. And it was different from the other leaves that were all bloody and smeared. It was different, it was a beautiful leaf. And it just had one drop, a single drop, right in the middle of the leaf. And I picked that up, and I remember putting it in the tool thing in the trunk of the car. And I know I want to save that.

Therapist: Well, as you talk about the things you picked up, it sounds like some of it is just sort of messy.

Tommie: Yeah.

Therapist: And at least one of them is very beautiful, and that's the leaf with that drop of blood on it.

Tommie: Um hum.

Therapist: Are there any other things beautiful enough that you want to keep besides that leaf?

Tommie: Yeah. I have some rocks that are from the base of the telephone pole.

Therapist: So, the things you want to keep are the leaf and the rocks.

Tommie: Yeah. I want to put the leaf in my jewelry box.

Therapist: That makes sense for the leaf, until you decide. . . .

Tommie: What to do.

Therapist: You know, I think what you should do is have another burial.

Tommie: That's a good idea.

Therapist: What I think you could do is maybe find a spot that would be, like, sacred to Chuck, that's around here. Maybe there's a special spot where he'd like to go. Can you think of such a place?

Tommie: He liked to go to the beach, but I'd be afraid to bury it there, I'd be afraid someone would dig it up. How about if I bury it in my yard, under a tree?

Therapist: Yeah.

Tommie: Donna and I want to plant a tree in my yard, because at my parents' house they planted a tree in the yard, all the boys, in his memory.

Therapist: Right, right! That's good.

Tommie: And then we could bury it under the tree.

Therapist: Yeah. And you have a grave up there, but you'd have a grave down here, too. And a place where, if you really needed to grieve some day, you could say a prayer, or you could have a ceremony of some kind? Are you all religious?

Tommie: I don't go to church, but we're spiritual in our own way.

Therapist: So, maybe you'd have a little prayer or a little ceremony that you could design.

Donna: Um hum, um hum, I think that's a good idea, burying it under the tree.

Therapist: And then planting a tree there. I mean have you decided you want to plant a tree there?

Tommie: Um hum.

Therapist: Well, what would happen, eventually a little bit of Chuck would be in that tree.

Tommie: Yeah. And it's got to be an evergreen tree or a fruit-bearing tree. Did you know that? This is an Indian thing, they want it to be an evergreen or a pine-cone-bearing tree, 'cause it's ever giving life.

Therapist: I see.

Tommie: Or a fruit-bearing tree, 'cause you're getting life back from the tree.

Therapist: Right, a happiness tree.

Tommie: A life-circle tree.

This is an example of how a task could be developed during a session. As the reader can see, the clients knew exactly what they needed to do. This was demonstrated when the therapist was corrected for having called the tree "a happiness tree." The therapist does assist in the construction of the idea, but it is the clients who actually take the idea, create the specifics, and personalize it to fit themselves.

As we have noted, tasks are often suggested to the client at the end of a session, after the therapist takes a break. We see the break as a way for the therapist to sit quietly and gather his or her thoughts about the client and his or her situation. Taking a break also serves to punctuate the session. For both therapist and client, it is now time to take the next step into the future.

Again, we return to the case of the family who lost the young man in an auto accident. After several more sessions of therapy, in which the family continued to make progress, the therapist delivered the following message to the family. Note how the first part of the message is acknowledgment, while the last part is possibility.

Therapist: I have been so struck by the pain you have been in, and by the hard and brave work you have been doing to struggle through it. You each care for the living as well as for Chuck, and you know the value of being as well as you can be for the benefit of the rest of your family. You have cared for one another in an exemplary fashion. Rarely have I seen people be so consistently supportive, loving, and patient. The friendships of women are often something that men can only marvel at. Your recent visit to Chuck's grave, in which you decorated it with many flowers from Tommie's yard, reminded me of something important. You, as a family, seem to benefit from rituals— planting a tree, attending a powwow, decorating where Chuck died or decorating his grave. Because this seems to have worked for you, I think you need to keep having such rituals as you need them. Some might be planned on an important date in the future. Some can be "unscheduled," like your recent visit to the grave. Any time you find yourself bogged down, you can have another ritual. This helps you to get on with life.

Process and Pacing

The reader may notice that at times the therapist continues to acknowledge difficulty while pursuing the possibilities. We believe that this occurs throughout the therapy. It is an example of what has been called a "both/and" perspective (Lipchik, 1993). So, instead of an either/or view, the therapist proposes the both/and perspective. In other words:

Acknowledgment: "You are deeply in pain and it feels like it will never end.

and

Possibility: "I wonder when things will start to feel a little better?"

When the issue is grief, it is especially important to move *at the client's pace.* Obviously, the reinforcing behaviors often associated with solution-focused therapy— smiles, exclamations, and gestures—need to be toned down for the grieving client. Any tendency for the therapist to be ahead of the client, or to minimize pain, will slow down the process and possibly result in the client dropping out of treatment prematurely.

The challenge is to really be in sync with the client. To do this, there has to be proper pacing. If the therapist is too far behind the client, there is likely to be no change, or slow change. If the therapist is ahead of the client, the result may be what many would call "resistance" (de Shazer, 1985). When the pacing is appropriate, the result is cooperation and movement toward the client's goal.

How do we know if we are working at the proper pace? If we listen closely, the client will tell us. For example:

Therapist: What you have done is really important. It took a lot of work, but you accomplished it. This may just be a turning point for you.

Client: If I'm doing so great, why can't I sleep at night?

The client's statement indicates that the therapist needs to slow down and attend to what is real for the client. This does not mean, however, that we should be afraid of going too fast. If the client never tells us to slow down, we may be going too slow!

Goals

Closely related to pacing, and equally important, is the goal orientation of solution-focused therapy. If the therapist is not paying attention to the client's goals, he or she may allow other considerations to intervene—such as preconceived ideas of how grief therapy should proceed (Kübler-Ross, 1969). Remembering that solutions are often not directly related to problems, SFBT therapists help clients achieve their goals—even if the goals would not be those chosen by the therapist.

Case Study A man in his forties came to therapy. His wife had died after a short bout with cancer. In the year following her death, he had immediately gotten involved in a disastrous relationship with another woman. A few months later he became involved in another very difficult relationship. Although he briefly mentioned the death of his wife, he really wanted to work on his relationships. The therapist and client spent five sessions addressing his current relationships. Only at the end of the fifth session did the man begin to talk about the loss of his wife.

Over the next two sessions the client and therapist talked about the loss. During these sessions an elaborate grief ritual was designed that held great significance to the client. A visit to a sacred site in a distant land was planned. This special place had held great meaning to the client's wife, and the client knew that it was the perfect location to perform a grieving ritual. The client carried special items with him to evoke his wife on the level of all five senses: a richly textured favorite scarf, a supply of her perfume, some of her favorite chocolates, several photos of her, and a cassette of her favorite classical music. He also took along a pen and writing pad to write her a letter as he experienced all these things.

When he returned from his trip, the man reported that he felt very relieved. He described the experience in great detail. He told the therapist how the letter to his wife had become soaked with tears as he cried and wrote. He resumed his therapy and revisited the issues in his relationships. After two more sessions of therapy over the next six months, he worked out his relationship issues successfully.

In this instance, it might have been tempting for many therapists to insist that the client work on his grief issues first. In SFBT, however, therapists trust the client's statements of goals. They really believe that the client truly knows what he or she needs to do. Resistance is avoided, and therapy actually proceeds quickly and more effectively.

Conclusion

The cases described in this chapter give the reader a general idea of how to proceed with cases of grief and loss. As we have discussed, we believe that the most important principle in SFBT is to be with the client. This means to listen closely, to show understanding, to be supportive, and to attend to the inner resources of the client. In many respects, it is Rogerian therapy with a twist. The twist is attention to the future and what the client knows about his or her future process. As we indicated at the beginning of the chapter, the techniques of SFBT are important but they are not the key. Instead, the key is to *validate the client's experience* while pursuing possibilities.

We must never forget that *the answer lies within*—even in difficult and challenging issues like grief. This means that the therapist must listen closely for that answer, and highlight it when it is found. As Milton Erickson taught, each client must be met on his or her own terms, and a unique treatment plan must be designed (Rossi, 1980). The easiest way to design such a plan is to let the client do it!

Questions from the Editors

1. *What is the difference between acknowledgment and more traditional notions of empathy?*

This question turned out to be very thought provoking. Originally we thought about it and answered by saying that acknowledgment is a more purposeful activity than the traditional concept of empathy. But after writing that answer, something felt unsettled. So, we pulled out an old copy of Rogers's *On Becoming a Person* (1961). Rereading Rogers turned out to be an eye-opening experience.

Rogers talks about trying to get into the person's frame of reference, trying to see the world as the client sees it, and about conveying that understanding (without judgment) to the client. According to Rogers, when the client feels heard, understood, and ready, the therapist then walks with him or her in the client's present reality, looking back on the past reality, and *helps him or her to imagine a desired future.* (We would only add that as solution-focused therapists, we emphasize co-constructing the future with the client. To be fair to Rogers, however, he does talk quite a bit about subjective and objective reality and the construction of individual reality based on the client's perceptions of the client's potential.)

Rogers talked about things that sound very familiar to the solution-focused therapist. For example:

> If, in my encounter with him, I am dealing with him as an immature child, an ignorant student, a neurotic personality, or a psychopath, each of these concepts of *mine* [italics added] limits what he can be in the relationship. If I accept the other person as something fixed, already diagnosed and classified, already shaped by the past, then I am doing my part to confirm this limited hypothesis. If I accept him as a process of becoming, then I am doing what I can to confirm or make real his potentialities (Rogers, 1961, p. 55).

Rereading Rogers has, therefore, led us to answer the question differently. There is no real difference between traditional notions of empathy and "acknowledgment." It seems that we keep reinventing the wheel, or at least renaming it. Perhaps we are doing more of what works. Or maybe we have remembered what we forgot. Or maybe the striking similarity between what works in this model and the models that preceded it is really "premodel change," not unlike the pre-session change we ask our clients about. Perhaps we should do a little more looking back toward what has worked in the past and *do more of that.*

One could say that it seems we need to know our history or we risk never being able to repeat the successes of the past. Models of therapy come and go. They get repackaged and repeated. What does not seem to change is the necessary attitude of the therapist. Again, reading Rogers is instructive. He cites some of the research from the 1950s that showed that the most important variables in the therapeutic relationship are the human qualities of the therapist.

This question really gets to the heart of why we wrote this chapter: SFBT works. It works with grief, relationships, depression, and many other kinds of problems. But it is not the model or the techniques that really matter. It is the attitude of the therapist and the interchange between the client and the therapist that is the real key.

2. *Please give some hints for knowing when to shift from acknowledgment to possibility in working with grieving clients.*

It is impossible to know in advance what the proper pace is for any individual client. It may appear that master therapists have an advance, intuitive awareness of where the client is, just as great shortstops seem to know where the ball is going before it is hit. We believe that the "masters" like Milton Erickson and Cal

Ripken are really doing what we all do most of the time. They are paying attention to feedback. We think this attention to feedback is a very learnable skill. We also believe that most therapists are much better at it than they may realize. So, the short answer is *trust your clinical judgment.*

The long answer is that if the client reverts to problem talk when the therapist attempts to move into the future, then that is probably a sign that the therapist is too far ahead. For these clients it is as though they need the therapist to understand how really difficult their problem is before they are ready for things to be different. The therapist must be willing to toss out a gambit and watch for the client's reaction. These nudges toward the future will be met with either acceptance or resistance, and the therapist must heed such feedback.

In addition, sometimes the client will initiate the move into the future. For example, the client might tell the therapist about new things done before the therapy session. The client might also begin talking with more optimism and determination. His or her body language might change, as might facial expression and tone of voice. But since these forms of feedback are ambiguous, therapists should not take it for granted that they indicate a readiness for possibility. Again, the therapist must be willing to test the waters with a small move toward the future. If the client moves with the therapist into the future, then the therapist knows the client is on firmer ground. Of course, the client may only be ready for a small amount of possibility and may then want to return to being acknowledged. The trick is to take calculated risks and to listen closely.

3.   *Is there a real difference between SFBT with grief and SFBT with other presenting problems?*

The short answer to this question is: no, there is no real difference. In a perfect world, this chapter would be unnecessary. But many therapists think that grief is a special issue. Persons ready to use SFBT with many other kinds of problems put it aside when dealing with grief (and various other problems).

Perhaps therapists think of grief and loss as more sensitive issues. Perhaps grieving persons are seen more as survivors than as co-creators of reality, and therefore are due more "TLC." These perceptions on the part of therapists, however, come more from the therapists' biases, histories, and emotions than from objective reality.

Unfortunately, we just cannot assume to know which are the intense issues for any particular client until we find out the hard way—by listening. And then we do not know which model of therapy is going to work for the client until we try one. We choose to try SFBT first. We believe that the model is helpful to most people and that it will not take long to find out if it is not helpful. If it is not, then we try something different.

References

Allende, I. (1995). *Paula.* New York: HarperCollins.

Berg, I. K., & Miller, S. D. (1992). *Working with the problem drinker.* New York: W. W. Norton.

De Shazer, S. (1985). *Keys to solution in brief therapy.* New York: W. W. Norton.

De Shazer, S. (1988). *Clues: Investigating solutions in brief therapy.* New York: W. W. Norton.

Durrant, M. (1989). Temper taming: An approach to children's temper problems revisited. *Dulwich Center Newsletter, 3,* 3–11.

Kübler-Ross, E. (1969). *On death and dying.* New York: Macmillan.

Lipchik, E. (1993). "Both/and" solutions. In S. Friedman (Ed.), *The new language of change: Constructive collaboration in psychotherapy.* New York: Guilford.

Lipchik, E. (1994, March/April). The rush to be brief. *Family Therapy Networker, 18*(2), 35–39.

O'Hanlon, W. H. (1993). Take two people and call them in the morning: Brief solution-oriented therapy with depression. In S. Friedman (Ed.), *The new language of change: Constructive collaboration in psychotherapy.* New York: Guilford.

O'Hanlon, W., & Weiner-Davis, M. (1989). *In search of solution.* New York: W. W. Norton.

Rogers, C. R., (1951). *Client-centered therapy.* Boston: Houghton Mifflin.

Rogers, C. (1961). *On becoming a person.* Boston: Houghton Mifflin.

Rossi, E. (Ed.). (1980). *Collected papers of Milton Erickson on hypnosis* (4 Volumes). New York: Irvington.

Walter, J., & Peller, J. (1992). *Becoming solution-focused in brief therapy.* New York: Brunner/Mazel.

Weick, A. (1983, November-December). Overturning a medical model of social work practice. *Social Work,* 467–471.

PART THREE

RESEARCH ON SOLUTION-FOCUSED THERAPY

CHAPTER ELEVEN

A CLINICIAN'S GUIDE TO RESEARCH ON SOLUTION-FOCUSED BRIEF THERAPY

A. Jay McKeel

What can practitioners learn from research on solution-focused brief therapy (SFBT)? This chapter summarizes research that explores or relates to the SFBT model. Studies are reviewed that report on success rates of clients completing brief therapy and SFBT. Research examining the effectiveness of solution-focused techniques is reported. Other studies are presented that describe a first session conducted by solution-oriented therapist William O'Hanlon, report on therapists' evaluations of different solution-focused techniques, and depict how clients view SFBT. The chapter concludes with a discussion of the importance of research in the future improvement of the SFBT model.

Outcome Studies

Outcome research evaluates the effectiveness of therapy. Typically, outcome studies summarize the results (outcome) of clients receiving treatment based on one model of therapy, or they compare the outcome of two or more treatment models. Following is discussion of some of the questions that outcome studies have addressed.

Note: The author wishes to thank Judy Gretsch for her comments on an earlier draft of this chapter.

Is Brief Therapy Effective?

A large body of research offers a consistent answer: yes, brief therapy can be effective for a wide range of clinical presentations, including severe and chronic problems. Studies that compare long-term therapies with brief therapies have found no difference in outcome; clients who receive brief therapy are as likely to accomplish their treatment goals as clients who receive long-term therapy (see Koss & Shiang, 1994, for a comprehensive review).

In addition to the effectiveness of brief therapy compared to longer-term approaches, two other factors suggest that brief therapy may be the treatment of choice for most clients. First, most clients come to therapy expecting it to be a brief experience. More than 70 percent of clients begin therapy expecting ten or fewer sessions to accomplish their treatment goals (Garfield, 1994; Pekarik & Wierzbicki, 1986; Pekarik, 1991).

Second, the majority of studies conducted in the past fifty years show that the median length of treatment ranges from four to eight sessions, with a clustering around six sessions (Garfield, 1986, 1994; Koss & Shiang, 1994). In both public and private mental health settings, approximately 50 percent of the adult and child clients terminate by the fifth session and 80 percent complete treatment by their tenth session (National Institute of Mental Health, 1979; Taube, Burns, & Kessler, 1984; Weisz & Weiss, 1989).

Interestingly, research has found no clear association between the therapist's model of treatment and the median number of sessions his or her clients receive. Thus, after reviewing the accumulated evidence regarding treatment length, Bergin and Garfield (1994) concluded that "almost all psychotherapy is brief" (p. 826).

Is Solution-Focused Therapy Effective?

There is not enough research evidence to be certain, but early results are promising. Two outcome studies at the Brief Family Therapy Center (BFTC) in Milwaukee found that 65.6 percent of clients receiving SFBT accomplished their treatment goals, and another 14.7 percent made significant improvement during therapy (Kiser, 1988; Kiser & Nunnally, 1990). A Swedish outcome study reported that 80 percent of clients completing SFBT accomplished their goals (Andreas, 1993). These findings are impressive, and they compare favorably to other psychotherapy outcome studies, which generally report that approximately two thirds of clients accomplish significant improvements by the completion of therapy (Rosenthal, 1983).

Although the results from the BFTC and Swedish studies are promising, the authors of those studies warn readers to view their results with caution. The studies were exploratory and have yet to be accepted for publication in peer-reviewed journals. The investigators explain that these studies had small sample sizes (Andreas, 1993, questioned only twenty-five clients), used simplistic assessments in their follow-up, and did not use a control sample (such as clients receiving treatment based on another model).

However, these favorable exploratory results of SFBT should invite other researchers to conduct well-designed outcome studies that use larger samples and employ more standard or accepted outcome instruments and measures. Well-designed outcome studies will increase the credibility of SFBT.

Is Solution-Focused Therapy Brief?

The average length of treatment in SFBT is about five sessions (de Shazer, 1991; Andreas, 1993). While this may meet popular definitions of brief therapy, this is approximately the same number of sessions found across other models of treatment (Garfield, 1994; Miller, 1994).

Two studies of SFBT describe the relationship between outcome and the number of sessions that clients receive. In de Shazer's (1991) summary of two BFTC outcome studies, he reports that 91 percent of the clients who attended four or more sessions achieved their treatment goals (the success rate in this study was calculated by combining clients who accomplished their goals and clients who made significant improvement). However, 69 percent of clients who attended three or fewer sessions reported success.

Another study examined the effectiveness of a single session of SFBT for the treatment of depression (Sundstrom, 1993). The researcher concluded that one session of SFBT promotes positive mood change but is not sufficient to treat depression.

These studies suggest a positive relationship between the number of SFBT sessions a client receives and therapeutic success. If this is so, it would match a similar trend found in studies of other models. Many studies reveal that clients are likely to experience continuing improvement until their eighth session. After eight sessions, additional treatment gains are much slower (Howard, Kopta, Krause, & Orlinsky, 1986).

Limitations of Outcome Studies

Outcome studies can provide useful information (for example, the number of sessions clients typically need to accomplish their treatment goals). Further, outcome studies may identify patterns in SFBT that can lead to improvements in the model; they may show the effectiveness of the model with particular client problems; or they may help identify which clients and problems are best addressed by SFBT. Outcome studies can also help increase the credibility of SFBT; for instance, such studies may be helpful to an agency director seeking to educate a health maintenance organization or board of directors about the effectiveness of SFBT.

Researchers, however, are increasingly realizing the limitations of outcome studies (Piercy & Sprenkle, 1990; Sprenkle & Bischof, 1994). Research will probably never demonstrate that SFBT is superior to other treatment approaches. Interestingly, fifty years of outcome studies comparing one psychotherapy approach to another show that different models produce relatively equivalent results (Luborsky, Singer, & Luborsky, 1975; Lambert & Bergin, 1994; Jacobson, 1985; Jacobson & Addis, 1993; Shadish et al., 1993).

Further, practitioners may find that outcome studies offer limited information because they do not address questions that are most useful for clinical practice. Suppose a nationwide, well-designed outcome study involving five thousand clients who received SFBT found that 73 percent accomplished their treatment goals. A practitioner might ask, "What accounts for this success? Was it the miracle question, a skeleton key homework assignment, the therapist finding ways to cooperate with the client, or some combination of these and other techniques that accounted for the change?" Or one might ask, "Do the therapists in this study do SFBT the same way I do?"

Since many therapists use a pragmatic approach to therapy—choosing strategies that fit the client and the client's goals rather than rigidly following the protocol of a single model—research that asks different research questions may be more useful for clinicians. In particular, clinicians may want to know which SFBT techniques or assumptions lead to clients accomplishing their goals, what occurs in a successful SFBT session, or what clients find useful or not useful about a SFBT session, treatment, or therapist. Such questions are more likely to be the focus of process and qualitative studies.

Process Studies

Process studies often examine the immediate or long-term impact of a particular therapeutic intervention or strategy. Several process studies have examined SFBT interventions. This section reviews process research about (1) pretreatment change, (2) presuppositional questions, (3) the Formula First Session Task, (4) client-therapist collaboration, and (5) change talk. Finally, research is presented that describes practitioner's views of different solution-focused techniques.

Pretreatment Improvement

During the first session, solution-focused therapists often ask about pretreatment improvements (de Shazer, 1985, 1988). For example, a therapist may ask a client in the initial session, "What have you done in the past couple of weeks that has made a difference in this problem?" Clinicians can feel confident about encouraging clients to do more of what led to pretreatment improvements; such suggestions can help clients feel more optimistic about their ability to resolve their problem since they will be doing more of what they have already discovered helps their situation. Because these changes were not due to therapy, focusing on pretreatment improvement encourages clients to rely less on their therapist and more on their own resources to accomplish their treatment goals.

Research shows that pretreatment improvement is common. Noonan (1973) followed clients who called for an appointment but did not show. More than a third of this group explained that they did not come to their initial session because of improvements that occurred between the time they called and the time of their first appointment. Another study found that nearly 40 percent of clients attending their first session at a university marriage and family therapy center reported *some* pretreatment improvement in their situation (Allgood, Parham, Salts, & Smith, 1995). A third study that reviewed data from 2400 clients found that 15 percent had made *significant* improvement before attending the first session (Howard et al., 1986).

Presuppositional Questions

Presuppositional questions communicate an expectation or belief. O'Hanlon and Weiner-Davis (1989) recommend that "instead of, 'Did you ever do anything that worked?' ask, 'What have you done in the past that worked?'. . . The latter [question] suggests that inevitably there have been successful past solutions" (p. 80). These questions are interventions, designed so that the client will recall information that confirms the question's presupposition.

The effects of presuppositional questions in a clinical setting were first examined in an exploratory study at BFTC (Weiner-Davis, de Shazer, & Gingerich, 1987). Clients attending their first session were asked: "Many times people notice in between the time they make the appointment for therapy and the first session that things already seem different. What have you noticed about your situation?" (p. 360). This question presupposes that noticing that "things already seem different" is common and expected. Twenty of the thirty clients answered this question by reporting examples of recent improvements in their presenting problem.

Two replications of the above study found that, when asked a similar presuppositional question in their first session, more than 60 percent of the clients reported that some specific improvement had occurred in their situation since they called for an appointment (Lawson, 1994; McKeel & Weiner-Davis, 1995). On the other hand, when clients were asked a question at the beginning of their first session that presupposed their situation had *not* changed since they had called for an appointment, 67 percent reported that their situation was the same (McKeel & Weiner-Davis, 1995).

These studies represent one goal of psychotherapy researchers: to document how clients respond to a particular technique across several studies. Replicated findings build trust in the effect or result of a technique. In this case, three studies conducted by three different investigators in different settings with a large number of clients and therapists found comparable results. Additional studies asking different presuppositional questions will further increase confidence that clients often confirm the assumptions communicated through presuppositional questions.

One issue not yet addressed by this area of research is whether presuppositional questions lead to any clinically relevant change. While clients may confirm the assumptions communicated in presuppositional questions, future research needs to establish if, how, and which clients benefit from which presuppositional questions at what time during treatment.

Formula First Session Task

De Shazer and Molnar (1984) introduced the Formula First Session Task (FFST) as the homework they typically give clients to complete between their first and second sessions. The FFST instructs the client: "Between now and the next time we meet, I would like you to observe, so that you can describe to me next time, what happens in your (family, life, marriage, relationship) that you want to continue to have happen" (de Shazer, 1985, p. 137). De Shazer suggested that the FFST promotes clients' cooperation and optimism about their situations. De Shazer also reported that when therapists follow up on the FFST during the second session, clients often describe both things they had done before the first session *and* new things that had happened since.

In an exploratory study at BFTC, therapists gave the FFST to 64 percent of eighty-eight new clients. In their second session, 89 percent of these clients who were assigned the FFST reported that something worthwhile had occurred since the first session, and 57 percent reported that their situation was better (de Shazer, 1985).

Two well-designed, randomized studies have since examined the effectiveness of the FFST. Both studies provide encouraging results. One study compared clients who received solution-focused treatment and the FFST with clients who received structural/strategic treatment and a problem-focused first session task (Adams,

Piercy, & Jurich, 1991). As predicted, the FFST enhanced cooperation; clients were significantly more likely to complete the FFST than the problem-focused task.

Further, the FFST was more effective than the problem-focused task. In clients' second sessions, 60 percent of those receiving solution-focused treatment with the FFST rated their problem as improved; only 25 percent of the clients who were receiving structural/strategic treatment and had been assigned a problem-focused task reported improvement. Clients assigned the FFST were also more clear about their goals. However, contrary to de Shazer's (1985) assertion, clients receiving SFBT and the FFST were no more optimistic in their second session than clients receiving structural/strategic therapy and a problem-focused first session task (Adams et al., 1991). An interesting finding of this study is that the FFST rather than the solution-focused approach seemed to create these differences. A third group of clients received structural/strategic treatment and the FFST. These clients responded similarly to clients receiving SFBT and the FFST (Adams et al., 1991).

A final goal of this study was to explore whether the FFST leads to better treatment outcome. The answer was no; however, these investigators point out that it is unrealistic to expect that any single intervention will strongly affect the outcome of therapy (Adams et al., 1991).

A strength of the study by Adams and colleagues (1991) is that the researchers employed three perspectives to assess improvement: those of clients, therapists, and outside observers. Strong agreement occurred among these three perspectives, increasing confidence in the study's results.

In another process study, Jordan and Quinn (1994) sought to identify the association between the FFST and several treatment variables. In this study, clients were randomly assigned to receive either problem-focused treatment that included the following first session homework assignment: "Between now and the next time we meet, I want you to watch closely, so you can describe to me next time, what happens in your (family, life, marriage, relationship) when this problem next comes up, that is, who does what before, during, and after the problem behavior" (p. 5); or solution-focused treatment in which the FFST was assigned. Clients who received SFBT and the FFST were significantly more likely to report that their problem had improved, to have greater optimism that treatment would succeed, and to describe their first session as a valuable and a positive experience. However, no difference was discovered between clients receiving the problem-focused and solution-focused task regarding the working alliance between the therapist and client.

Together these studies offer evidence that the FFST produces improvements in clients' presenting problems. One striking difference between these two studies is the impact of the task on clients' optimism: Adams and colleagues (1991) did not find that the FFST enhanced optimism, while Jordan and Quinn (1994) found that in the second session clients assigned the FFST were more optimistic about the outcome of their treatment. Additional research on the FFST could help clarify the effect of the task on the client's problem, optimism, and other issues important to treatment. Research designed to identify which clients benefit most from the FFST and when therapists should select the FFST would also be especially beneficial.

Client-Therapist Collaboration

Solution-focused authors and trainers encourage therapists to develop a collaborative relationship with their clients. In SFBT, the client sets the goal; the therapist is responsible for identifying what the client wants to achieve in therapy and then helping the client accomplish those goals (de Shazer, 1991). Solution-focused therapists are urged to take extra measures to assure that they understand and work toward the client's treatment goals, address topics relevant to the client, and respect the client's wishes about termination (Walter & Peller, 1992).

Client-therapist collaboration has received considerable attention in the psychotherapy literature. Process studies in psychotherapy have discovered that a client's sense of collaboration with the therapist is linked to session effectiveness, the client continuing in treatment, and positive therapeutic outcome (see Friedlander, Wildman, Heatherington, & Skowron, 1994, for a review of this literature). In fact, many studies show that clients' agreement with homework assignments and their sense of collaboration with the therapist are the factors most often associated with positive treatment outcome (Horvath & Greenberg, 1989).

SFBT emphasizes therapist-client collaboration, and most books about SFBT offer many strategies to help clinicians build a client-driven treatment aimed at accomplishing the goals their clients establish (see, for example, de Shazer, 1985, 1994; Furman & Ahola, 1992; O'Hanlon & Weiner-Davis, 1989; Walter & Peller, 1992). Research that examines the importance, effect, and results of these SFBT strategies on increasing collaboration will increase clinicians' confidence that these suggestions do create a client-therapist relationship that will lead to treatment success.

Solution-Talk

Words are important in SFBT. De Shazer (1991, 1994) encourages therapists to use solution-talk, or change-talk. Examples of solution-talk include a therapist asking questions about change that occurred before treatment began, amplifying or reinforcing client improvement, identifying change that the client has ignored, and asking the client to brainstorm about action they can take to improve their situation. Two studies have examined the relationship of solution-talk to short-term and long-term outcome.

In a study conducted early in the development of SFBT, Gingerich, de Shazer, and Weiner-Davis (1988) examined transcripts of first sessions in order to identify clients' responses to therapist change-talk. This investigation sought to discover whether a relationship exists between solution-talk and client change (defined as the client describing, reporting, explaining, or clarifying change; describing exceptions to the problem; or describing a change in his or her view of the problem). The study found that client changes were most likely to occur after the therapist used change-related talk.

The study discovered that SFBT therapists rarely used change-talk early in the initial session. This finding led the BFTC team to modify their first session interviewing strategy so that therapists began asking about change earlier in the session (for instance, by exploring pretreatment change, exceptions, and hypothetical solutions) (Gingerich et al., 1988).

Another study found that the amount of clients' solution-talk in the initial session was related to clients' continuing treatment. The more clients talked about solutions or goals in the first session, the more likely they were to complete therapy rather than drop out (Shields, Sprenkle, & Constantine, 1991).

Therapists' Evaluations of SFBT Techniques

An interesting research question is, "Which SFBT techniques do clinicians rate as most useful?" A survey of graduates from three SFBT training programs asked therapists about their clinical use of exception questions, the miracle question, scaling questions, and pretreatment change questions (Skidmore, 1993).

Exception questions represent the fundamental philosophy of SFBT. Such questions seek to identify when the problem does not occur and what the client does to accomplish these "nonproblem" times (Gingerich et al., 1988; O'Hanlon & Weiner-Davis, 1989). Examples of exceptions questions are "When do you two handle disagreements constructively? How do you make that happen?" "What's different about the nights you don't feel depressed?" and "When are you able to overcome the urge to drink?"

The *miracle question* is asked in the first session to help clarify the client's goal. The therapist asks: "Suppose that one night, while you were asleep, there was a miracle and this problem was solved. How would you know? What would be different? How will your husband know without your saying a word to him about it? (de Shazer, 1988, p. 5). The miracle question leads clients to describe life without the problem or problems. De Shazer reports that clients often describe concrete and specific behaviors when answering this question. This specificity helps a therapist clearly understand what the client wants to accomplish in treatment.

Scaling questions ask clients to rate their problem or any clinically relevant issue (such as confidence that their improvements will continue) on a scale of one to ten. Usually, one represents the worst the problem has been and ten represents the achievement of the client's goal. These questions are useful in monitoring progress (You were at three last week; how would you rate your situation today?), identifying intermediate treatment goals (You are at three; what will be different when you are at four?), and helping clients plan how to improve their situation (What can you do to get to four?).

Of these four questions, therapists have rated the miracle question as the most therapeutic. Scaling questions were the techniques most frequently used by these therapists, and they rated scaling questions as the best way to evaluate client progress. Therapists found that exception questions consistently led clients to report exceptions to their presenting problems and to describe what they did to create those exceptions. Finally, therapists rated pretreatment change questions as the least effective and the most difficult to implement (Skidmore, 1993).

Final Thoughts About Process Studies of SFBT Techniques

Although only a few SFBT techniques have been investigated, the existing studies have generally found that these interventions are effective. Clients often report pretreatment change, especially if clinicians ask questions that presuppose clients have accomplished improvements in their problem before treatment begins. Clients often comply with the FFST and are likely to accomplish improvements in their goals if assigned that task. Further, clinicians report that the miracle question, scaling questions, and presuppositional questions accomplish their purposes.

Clinicians will be very interested in more research that demonstrates the effectiveness and impact of SFBT techniques. As Adams and his associates (1991) remind us, studies aimed at proving that a single intervention causes a positive outcome will probably be unfruitful. However, techniques can be linked to immediate or short-term outcome. Building a collection of process studies that show if and how SFBT techniques impact the treatment process will improve the services that therapists provide to their clients.

Qualitative Research on Solution-Focused Therapy

Qualitative studies have questioned whether the books, articles, and workshops that describe SFBT match what actually occurs in solution-focused sessions. Qualitative studies do not typically use statistics; instead, researchers interview therapists and/or clients and/or report the researchers' observations of an intervention, session, or treatment.

A Single-Session Analysis of a First Session

A study by Gale and Newfield (1992) of an intake session with a married couple that was conducted by William O'Hanlon demonstrates the usefulness of qualitative inquiries. This type of qualitative research parallels the experience of viewing a videotape of an experienced clinician: the study provides information about a "real life" session, typically including transcripts of the clinician's actual wording and examples of when and how various techniques are used. In their review of a videotape of this session, the researchers identified nine categories of interventions that O'Hanlon used during the session. Five of these categories had been previously described by O'Hanlon (see O'Hanlon & Wilk, 1987; O'Hanlon & Weiner-Davis, 1989). However, Gale and Newfield discovered four categories of interventions that O'Hanlon used in the session that he had never described in his writings. These categories are:

1. *Pursuing a response over many turns.* O'Hanlon searches for a particular response and continues questioning until he gets the desired answer, no matter how long it takes.
2. *Clarifying unclear references.* O'Hanlon continues checking with the clients until he understands their statements.
3. *Modifying what he asks / says until he receives the response he is seeking.*
4. *Posing questions or possible problems and then answering those questions himself.*

This session demonstrates how SFBT "contributes to creating new 'therapeutic realities' for the clients" (Gale & Newfield, 1992, p. 163). Further, the study identifies and classifies new techniques, which can then be tested with process studies.

A question raised by this study is how consistent this session is with SFBT assumptions and principles, especially as it relates to a collaborative therapeutic alliance in which the client is the expert. In fact, after reviewing the study, O'Hanlon noted that he learned two things: that he speaks for his clients, and that he "talk[s] over the clients' talk and ignore[s] potentially unhelpful things that they say and then attribute[s] agreement to them" (Gale & Newfield, 1992, p. 163).

Client-Therapist Collaboration

As described previously, psychotherapy research has consistently found that client-therapist collaboration, such as agreement about the goals of therapy, is associated with successful treatment (see, for example, Horvath & Luborsky, 1993). SFBT emphasizes the importance of understanding and working to accomplish clients' goals.

One qualitative study discovered that solution-focused therapists can neglect this dimension of SFBT. Metcalf and Thomas (1994) asked staff at BFTC to select couples who they considered to have successfully completed treatment. The researchers interviewed these couples and their therapists about their experience of therapy. These interviews revealed sometimes striking differences in how the clients and therapists viewed their work together. The investigators found that discrepancies sometimes occurred between the couple's and the therapist's understanding about the clients' treatment goals, the therapist's role in treatment, the treatment process, and the decision to end treatment. For example, when describing a couple's termination, one therapist reported his discussion with the wife: "We agreed that she had made significant progress and I asked her if this would be a good time to stop being seen on a regular basis. She agreed" (Metcalf & Thomas, 1994, p. 58). The wife's view, however, was that the therapist said, "If I passed my driver's license I didn't need to come back. . . . I was elated but also felt like he/she pushed me out of the nest. It was like, 'you must go'" (Metcalf & Thomas, 1994, p. 58).

The Metcalf and Thomas study is not an indictment of SFBT. Proponents of the model clearly emphasize client-therapist collaboration. However, this study demonstrates that therapists sometimes have difficulty achieving the type of therapist-client relationship described in most writing about the model, even those who may be doing the writing.

On a more hopeful note, a qualitative study of SFBT therapy by Shilts, Filippino, and Nau (1994) illustrates how clinicians can develop collaborative, client-centered therapeutic relationships. This study asked clients:

1. What went on here today that you'd like to continue to see to happen?
2. Is there something that we did not do well?
3. How did [the therapist] do tonight? On a scale of one to ten, how helpful was he/she? How would you rate him/her tonight?
4. Could you give me three words, or maybe more, that would describe your experience tonight?

This study provides the responses of one client, a mother commenting on an initial family session. She told the researchers: "You know how it is. . . . You think the whole other world is so different from [how] you are. And now you have somebody else saying, 'You're good. You're communicating,' so, it's like reinforcement. So I feel better" (Shilts et al., 1994, p. 45). When this client was asked about the family's therapist, she explained, "He wasn't rushing. He took his time, and he, you know, just . . . he made me feel comfortable" (Shilts et al., 1994, p. 47).

This client reported feeling validated and comfortable with her therapist, with the result that her anxiety was reduced, which led her to feel more optimistic about her situation. In her second session, she reported several improvements in the problems for which she was seeking treatment.

Summary of Qualitative Studies

These three investigations show some of the possible benefits of qualitative studies. Studies of the clinical work of notable therapists can describe examples of existing interventions, show how and when the therapist uses certain techniques, and identify new techniques that can be included in the SFBT model. Interviews with clients can help identify how closely their experience of SFBT matches the goals of the model.

The qualitative studies discussed here also provide a "red flag," begging for dialogue on traditional SFBT assumptions about cooperation, the "client as expert," and the focus on what the client wants from treatment (Duncan, Hubble, & Rusk, 1994; McKeel & Gretsch, 1991; Shilts, Filippino, Chenail, & Rambo, 1994). Further research attention about the client-therapist alliance in SFBT will contribute to this dialogue.

Current Uses of Solution-Focused Therapy and Principles

The influence of SFBT is growing. A review of the psychotherapy literature shows that therapists are using SFBT in a wide array of settings, including schools (Metcalf, 1995), in-patient psychiatric settings (Webster, Vaughn, & Martinez, 1994), and medical settings (Webster, 1990). Further, the model is being used to address diverse clinical problems, including alcohol abuse (Berg & Miller, 1992), depression (Sundstrom, 1993), encopresis (Shapiro & Henderson, 1992), sexual abuse (Dolan, 1991), and spouse abuse (Sirles, Lipchik, & Kowalski, 1993; Popa, 1994). Solution-focused supervision strategies are also becoming common (Marek, Sandifer, Beach, Coward, & Protinsky, 1994; J. F. Keller, personal communication, June 1994; Wetchler, 1990).

A trend toward integrating solution-focused techniques and strategies with other clinical approaches also appears to be developing. For example, the psychotherapy literature describes the integration or use of SFBT in art therapy (Goldstein-Roca & Crisafulli, 1991), a common factors approach (Miller, Duncan, & Hubble, in press), experiential family therapy (Bischof, 1993), the approach of the Mental Research Institute (Duncan, Solovey, & Rusk, 1992; Eisenberg & Wahrman, 1991), Rogerian therapy (Tuyn, 1992), and twelve-step programs (Brasher, Campbell, & Moen, 1993).

This trend toward integration is supported by a survey of graduates of three SFBT training centers. The study found that while these therapists primarily used solution-focused techniques, their treatment approaches also incorporated techniques from other approaches. Consistent with the conclusions of outcome studies, many of these graduates believed that other approaches (such as Ericksonian, MRI, and cognitive-behavioral) were just as effective as SFBT (Skidmore, 1993).

Conclusions

What can clinicians learn from the current research of SFBT? The short answer: only a few studies of the model exist, but when SFBT and its techniques and assumptions have been tested, the results have generally been favorable. Outcome studies show that most clients receiving SFBT accomplish their treatment goals. While outcome studies can help clinicians understand general trends in psychotherapy (for instance, can brief therapy be effective?), outcome studies seeking to show the superiority of one model have yet to produce a convincing winner.

Process studies of SFBT techniques have found that

1. Pretreatment improvement is common. However, therapists report that exploring pretreatment change does not often lead to therapeutic progress.
2. Presuppositional questions help clients develop new views of their situation.
3. Clients typically cooperate with the FFST and report improvements in their second session.
4. Therapists find scaling questions to be an effective technique for monitoring treatment progress.
5. Client-therapist collaboration is associated with treatment success.
6. Therapists' solution-talk is typically followed by the client's report of change.

A review of research addressing SFBT reveals two critical types of relationships. The first is the relationship between research and therapeutic innovation. The second concerns the relationship between SFBT therapists and their clients.

In the 1950s, clinical research was the springboard that launched family therapy. The leaders of that young field used research to guide the development of theories and strategies. Since the mid 1970s, however, a division between researchers and clinicians has evolved, resulting in researchers seemingly publishing studies for other researchers. This has left therapists to look beyond the positivist world of multiple regressions to learn about new clinical ideas.[1] This has been an unfortunate trend.

Since the mid 1980s, practitioners have increasingly been attracted to SFBT because of the excitement of new ideas and the research support that de Shazer and others provided. The combination of the zest to innovate and the zeal to demonstrate the results of the innovations formed a productive alliance. This winning combination seems absent now. Psychotherapy needs to rediscover the dialogue and collaboration between practitioners and researchers. Clinicians are interested in research that helps them understand what works in therapy. For therapists interested in SFBT, research must be aimed at determining what outcomes are achieved by SFBT therapy, techniques, and assumptions—specifically, if and how the techniques and assumptions of SFBT help clients accomplish their treatment goals, and what techniques make treatment more effective. (Exhibit 11.1 contains a list of specific research recommendations to advance the practice of SFBT.)

The second observation of recent research regards the therapeutic relationship. Psychotherapy research consistently supports the SFBT view of the therapeutic relationship. Positive treatment outcomes are linked to therapists developing warm relationships with clients, working to accomplish the clients' goals (rather than the therapists' agendas), listening to clients, and collaborating with clients regarding significant decisions about their treatment (such as what topics will be discussed, when treatment will end, and so on). The relationship between research and innovation and the collaborative relationship SFBT encourages therapists to develop with their clients are both crucial to future growth of the approach. Loss of emphasis on either relationship will only doom SFBT to be remembered as a disembodied set of clever techniques.

Questions from the Editors

1. *Is there a contradiction between the constructivist or poststructuralist foundation of SFBT and the positivist approach of research?*

Sometimes. But this isn't a reason to avoid research. Actually, psychotherapy researchers are beginning to respond to poststructuralist critiques. The philosophical revolutions that psychotherapy witnessed in the 1980s (such as interest in constructivism, epistemology, feminism, multiple perspectives, and poststructuralism) are now influencing psychotherapy researchers. My suggestion: stay tuned. Some interesting research will be published in the next few years. Clinicians will find this new wave of research much more relevant to their practice.

2. *A clinician once told me he found research boring and difficult to understand. How do you respond?*

As I hope this chapter demonstrates, it isn't difficult to understand the results and conclusions of research studies. Frankly, I often skip the methods section of studies I read; it's like flipping to the end of a good mystery novel. I can't wait to

EXHIBIT 11.1. SUGGESTIONS FOR FUTURE RESEARCH.

The following are some general recommendations for researchers interested in conducting research that can better inform practice.

1. Pursue process research. SFBT is replete with techniques. Each of these can be investigated.

Process research is most relevant to clinical practice when the researcher explores whether a link exists between a specific intervention and changes in clients' behavior and/or cognitions. For instance, Lawson (1994) and McKeel and Weiner-Davis (1995) found that clients confirmed presuppositions about pretreatment improvement. These questions affected the clients' views of their situations (cognitive impact), but these studies did not explore whether presuppositional questions lead clients to do something different (behavioral change).

2. Always include the client's perspective.

Clients' evaluations and experiences have often been overlooked in psychotherapy research. In the past, researchers have relied too much on "objective" measures and ratings by therapists and/or outside observers. Clinicians want to know what clients find useful about treatment.

3. Pursue qualitative research.

Quantitative studies dominate psychotherapy research; however, many clinicians find that qualitative research is more clinically relevant. For a description of advantages of qualitative research and guidelines for conducting quality qualitative research, see Marshall and Rossman (1989); Moon, Dillon, & Sprenkle (1990); and Strauss and Corbin (1990).

The distinction between quantitative and qualitative research is typically a false dichotomy; most studies can be strengthened by using both qualitative and quantitative research strategies. A marriage of these two approaches will allow the consumer of research to benefit from the rich qualitative descriptions as well as to gain the information about generalizability that quantitative studies provide.

4. Use a research-and-development strategy when exploring new or previously untested interventions.

Process research typically investigates a static, unchanging intervention. For instance, a researcher may want to discover the effect of Intervention X. Therapists in this study follow the researcher's directions, using Intervention X at the end of the solution-identification stage of the first interview. The researcher decides that two hundred instances (trials) of Intervention X are necessary for the research project and waits until the research is completed before examining the data. At the conclusion of the study, the researcher discovers that the intervention did not accomplish therapeutic change; however, the researcher discovers information from the study that suggests ways to improve Intervention X.

A research-and-development strategy is appropriate for designing and improving therapeutic techniques (Bischoff, McKeel, Moon, & Sprenkle, 1995). In such a strategy, rather than waiting until the end of the study, the investigators periodically examine the data they are collecting. So, rather than conducting two hundred research trials of an ineffective Intervention X, a researcher using this strategy might evaluate the responses of the first fifty trials to detect any ways Intervention X can be improved. Asking clients, therapists, and outside consultants for suggestions about Intervention X may help discover ways to better design the task or to find a different time in treatment that is better for using the task. After another fifty trials, the new Intervention X can again be evaluated and modified as needed. This reset strategy can be used to improve Intervention X, and results of the study can describe how this version and the timing of the use of Intervention X is better than others.

5. Dismantle research.

Piercy and Sprenkle (1990) suggest that another source of information about effective therapeutic strategies is to dismantle an approach to identify its effective ingredients. This research strategy can identify which SFBT strategies are most effective and which strategies do not contribute to clients accomplishing their goals. A dismantling approach may lead to the discovery of common factors among treatment models that promote positive treatment outcome (see, for example, Miller, Duncan, & Hubble, in press). This strategy may also help clinicians understand how interventions from different models can be used together in an eclectic or integrative treatment approach.

find out how the study ended. Hopefully, as research becomes more relevant to practitioners, it will also become less boring and more user-friendly.

3. *Is research really important to SFBT?*

Early in the family therapy field, research drove innovation, leading to new treatment models and strategies (Wynne, 1983). In the beginnings of SFBT, de Shazer and his colleagues used research to explore and develop new treatment strategies (de Shazer, 1985, reports on several exploratory studies conducted at BFTC; de Shazer, 1994, reports on no new studies at BFTC). De Shazer (1985) offered a proliferation of new ideas; in his most recent book (1994), he presents transcripts of sessions that demonstrate examples of ideas that his team developed years earlier.

What new SFBT techniques have been introduced in the 1990s? Reconnecting practice with research will help the field learn more about what works in treatment, and it will provide a vehicle to generate and test new ideas that will improve the practice of psychotherapy. Since research helped the founders of SFBT to develop effective techniques, reestablishing the link between research and practice will lead other solution-focused practitioners to discover new, effective ideas to add to the model.

Note

1. One fruit of my search for research was discovering clinicians and agencies who practice SFBT and are interested in participating in research. If you are a therapist interested in participating in a study, please contact the chapter author or the book editors; we will try to link you with a researcher investigating issues that interest you.

References

Adams, J. F., Piercy, F. P., Jurich, J. A. (1991). Effects of solution-focused therapy's "formula first session task" on compliance and outcome in family therapy. *Journal of Marital and Family Therapy, 17,* 277–290.

Allgood, S. M., Parham, K. B., Salts, C. J., & Smith, T. A. (1995). The association between pretreatment change and unplanned termination in family therapy. *The American Journal of Family Therapy, 23,* 195–202.

Andreas, B. (1993, September). *A follow-up of patients in solution-focused brief therapy.* Paper presented at the Institution for Applied Psychology, University of Lund, Sweden.

Berg, I. K., & Miller, S. D. (1992). *Working with the problem drinker.* New York: W. W. Norton.

Bergin, A. E., & Garfield, S. L. (1994). Overview, trends, and future issues. In A. E. Bergin & S. L. Garfield (Eds.), *Handbook of psychotherapy and behavior change* (4th ed.) (pp. 821–830). New York: Wiley.

Bischof, G. P. (1993). Solution-focused brief therapy and experiential family therapy activities: An integration. *Journal of Systemic Therapies, 12,* 61–73.

Bischoff, R. J., McKeel, A. J., Moon, S. M., & Sprenkle, D. H. (1995). Systematically developing therapeutic techniques: Applications of research and development. In D. H. Sprenkle & S. M. Moon (Eds.), *Family therapy research: A handbook of methods.* New York: Guilford.

Brasher, B., Campbell, T. C., & Moen, D. (1993). Solution-oriented recovery. *Journal of Systemic Therapies, 12,* 1–14.

De Shazer, S. (1985). *Keys to solution in brief therapy.* New York: W. W. Norton.

De Shazer, S. (1988). *Clues: Investigating solutions in brief therapy.* New York: W. W. Norton.

De Shazer, S. (1991). *Putting differences to work.* New York: W. W. Norton.

De Shazer, S. (1994). *Words were originally magic.* New York: W. W. Norton.

De Shazer, S., & Molnar, A. (1984). Four useful interventions in brief family therapy. *Journal of Marital and Family Therapy, 10,* 297–304.

Dolan, Y. M. (1991). *Resolving sexual abuse: Solution-focused therapy and Ericksonian hypnosis for adult survivors.* New York: W. W. Norton.

Duncan, B. L., Hubble, M. A., & Rusk, G. S. (1994). To intervene or not to intervene? That is not the question. *Journal of Systemic Therapies, 13,* 22–30.

Duncan, B. L., Solovey, A. D., & Rusk, G. S. (1992). *Changing the rules: A client-directed approach to therapy.* New York: Guilford.

Eisenberg, J., & Wahrman, O. (1991). Two models of brief strategic therapy: The MRI model and the de Shazer model. *Israel Journal of Psychiatry and Related Sciences, 28,* 8–18.

Friedlander, M. L., Wildman, J., Heatherington, L. & Skowron, E. A. (1994). What we do and don't know about the process of family therapy. *Journal of Family Psychology, 8,* 390–416.

Furman, B., & Ahola, T. (1992). *Solution talk: Hosting therapeutic conversations.* New York: W. W. Norton.

Gale, J., & Newfield, N. (1992). A conversational analysis of a solution-focused marital therapy session. *Journal of Marital and Family Therapy, 18,* 153–165.

Garfield, S. L. (1986). Research on client variables in psychotherapy. In S. L. Garfield & A. E. Bergin (Eds.), *Handbook of psychotherapy and behavior change* (3rd ed.) (pp. 213–256). New York: Wiley.

Garfield, S. L. (1994). Research on client variables in psychotherapy. In S. L. Garfield & A. E. Bergin (Eds.), *Handbook of psychotherapy and behavior change* (4th ed.) (pp. 190–228). New York: Wiley.

Gingerich, W. J., de Shazer, S., & Weiner-Davis, M. (1988). Constructing change: A research view of interviewing. In E. Lipchik (Ed.), *Interviewing.* Rockville, MD: Aspen.

Goldstein-Roca, S., & Crisafulli, T. (1991). Integrative creative arts therapy: A brief treatment model. *Arts in Psychotherapy, 21,* 219–222.

Horvath, O. A., & Greenberg, L. S. (1989). Development and validation of the Working Alliance Inventory. *Journal of Counseling Psychology, 36,* 223–233.

Horvath, A. O., & Luborsky, L. (1993). The role of the therapeutic alliance in psychotherapy: Curative factors in dynamic psychotherapy. *Journal of Consulting and Clinical Psychology, 61,* 561–573.

Howard, K. I., Kopta, S. M., Krause, M. S., & Orlinsky, D. E. (1986). The dose-effect relationship in psychotherapy. *American Psychologist, 41,* 159–164.

Jacobson, N. S. (1985). Family therapy outcome research: Potential pitfalls and prospects. *Journal of Marital and Family Therapy, 11,* 149–158.

Jacobson, N. S., & Addis, M. E. (1993). Research on couples and couple therapy: What do we know? Where are we going? *Journal of Consulting and Clinical Psychology, 61,* 855–893.

Jordan, K., & Quinn, W. H. (1994). Session two outcome of the formula first session task in problem- and solution-focused approaches. *The American Journal of Family Therapy, 22,* 3–16.

Kiser, D. (1988). A follow-up study conducted at the Brief Family Therapy Center. Unpublished manuscript.

Kiser, D., & Nunnally, E. (1990). *The relationship between treatment length and goal achievement in solution-focused therapy.* Unpublished manuscript.

Koss, M. P., & Shiang, J. (1994). Research on brief psychotherapy. In A. E. Bergin & S. L. Garfield (Eds.), *Handbook of psychotherapy and behavior change* (4th ed.) (pp. 664–700). New York: Wiley.

Lambert, M. J., & Bergin, A. E. (1994). The effectiveness of psychotherapy. In A. E. Bergin & S. L. Garfield (Eds.), *Handbook of psychotherapy and behavior change* (4th ed.) (pp. 143–189). New York: Wiley.

Lawson, D. (1994). Identifying pretreatment change. *Journal of Counseling and Development, 72,* 244–248.

Luborsky, L., Singer, B., & Luborsky, L. (1975). Comparative studies of psychotherapies: Is it true that "everyone has won and all must have prizes"? *Archives of General Psychiatry, 32,* 995–1008.

Marek, L. I., Sandifer, D. M., Beach, A., Coward, R. L., & Protinsky, H. (1994). Supervision without the problem: A model of solution-focused supervision. *Journal of Family Psychotherapy, 5,* 57–81.

Marshall, C., & Rossman, G. B. (1989). *Designing qualitative research.* Newbury Park, CA: Sage.

McKeel, A. J., & Gretsch, J. C. (1991, March). *Consumer-oriented therapy*. Paper presented at the Annual Conference, Indiana Association of Marital and Family Therapy.

McKeel, A. J., & Weiner-Davis, M. (1995). *Presuppositional questions and pretreatment change: A further analysis*. Unpublished manuscript.

Metcalf, L. (1995). *Counseling toward solutions: A practical solution-focused program for working with students, teachers, and parents*. Englewood Cliffs, NJ: Simon & Schuster.

Metcalf, L., & Thomas, F. (1994). Client and therapist perceptions of solution-focused brief therapy: A qualitative analysis. *Journal of Family Psychotherapy, 5,* 49–66.

Miller, S. D. (1994). The solution conspiracy: A mystery in three installments. *Journal of Systemic Therapies, 13,* 18–37.

Miller, S. D., Duncan, B. L., & Hubble, M. A. (in press). *Escape from Babel: Toward a unifying language of change*. New York: W. W. Norton.

Moon, S. M., Dillon, D. R., & Sprenkle, D. H. (1990). Family therapy and qualitative research. *Journal of Marital and Family Therapy, 16,* 357–373.

National Institute of Mental Health (1979). Report of the work group on health insurance. In C. Windle (Ed.), *Reporting program evaluations: Two sample community mental health center annual reports* (pp. 17–85). Rockville, MD: Department of Health, Education, and Welfare.

Noonan, R. J. (1973). A follow-up of pretherapy dropouts. *Journal of Community Psychology, 1,* 43–45.

O'Hanlon, W. H., & Weiner-Davis, M. (1989). *In search of solutions: A new direction in psychotherapy*. New York: W. W. Norton.

O'Hanlon, W. H., & Wilk, J. (1987). *Shifting contexts: The generation of effective psychotherapy*. New York: Guilford.

Pekarik, G. (1991). Relationship of expected and actual treatment duration for adult and child clients. *Journal of Clinical Child Psychology, 20,* 121–125.

Pekarik, G., & Wierzbicki, M. (1986). The relationship between clients' expected and actual treatment duration. *Psychotherapy, 23,* 532–534.

Piercy, F. P., & Sprenkle, D. H. (1990). Marriage and family therapy: A decade review. *Journal of Marriage and the Family, 52,* 1116–1126.

Popa, M. S. (1994). *Couples' solutions to domestic violence: A qualitative study*. Masters thesis, Pacific Lutheran University.

Rosenthal, R. (1983). Assessing the statistical and social importance of the effects of psychotherapy. *Journal of Consulting and Clinical Psychology, 51,* 4–13.

Shadish, W. R., Montgomery, L. M., Wilson, P., Wilson, M. R., Bright, I., & Okwumabua, T. (1993). Effects of family and marital psychotherapies: A meta-analysis. *Journal of Consulting and Clinical Psychology, 61,* 992–1002.

Shapiro, L. E., & Henderson, J. G. (1992). Brief therapy for encopresis: A case study. *Journal of Family Psychotherapy, 3,* 1–12.

Shields, C. G., Sprenkle, D. H., & Constantine, J. A. (1991). Anatomy of an initial interview: The importance of joining and structuring skills. *The American Journal of Family Therapy, 19,* 3–18.

Shilts, L., Filippino, C., Chenail, R., & Rambo, A. (1994). From solution-focused therapy to client-informed research and back again. Unpublished manuscript.

Shilts, L., Filippino, C., & Nau, D. S. (1994). Client informed therapy. *Journal of Systemic Therapies, 13,* 39–52.

Sirles, E. A., Lipchik, E., & Kowalski, K. (1993). A consumer's perspective on domestic violence interventions. *Journal of Family Violence, 8,* 267–276.

Skidmore, J. E. (1993). *A follow-up of therapists trained in the use of the solution-focused brief therapy model.* Doctoral dissertation, University of South Dakota.

Sprenkle, D. H., & Bischof, G. P. (1994). Contemporary family therapy in the United States. *Journal of Family Therapy, 16,* 5–23.

Strauss, A., & Corbin, J. (1990). *Basics of qualitative research: Grounded theory procedures and techniques.* Newbury Park, CA: Sage.

Sundstrom, S. M. (1993). *Single-session psychotherapy for depression: Is it better to be problem-focused or solution-focused?* Doctoral dissertation, University of South Dakota.

Taube, C. A., Burns, B. J., & Kessler, L. (1984). Patients of psychiatrists and psychologists in office-based practice: 1980. *American Psychologist, 39,* 1435–1447.

Tuyn, L. K. (1992). Solution-focused therapy and Rogerian nursing science: An integrated approach. *Archives of Psychiatric Nursing, 6,* 83–89.

Walter, J. L., & Peller, J. E. (1992). *Becoming solution-focused in brief therapy.* New York: Brunner/Mazel.

Webster, D. C. (1990). Solution-focused approaches in psychiatric/mental health nursing. *Perspectives in Psychiatric Care, 26,* 17–21.

Webster, D. C., Vaughn, K., & Martinez, R. (1994). Introducing solution-focused approaches to staff in inpatient psychiatric settings. *Archives of Psychiatric Nursing, 8,* 251–261.

Weiner-Davis, M., de Shazer, S., & Gingerich, W. J. (1987). Using pretreatment change to construct a therapeutic solution: An exploratory study. *Journal of Marital and Family Therapy, 13,* 359–363.

Weisz, J. R., & Weiss, B. (1989). Assessing the effects of clinic-based psychotherapy with children and adolescents. *Journal of Consulting and Clinical Psychology, 57,* 741–746.

Wetchler, J. L. (1990). Solution-focused supervision. *Family Therapy, 1,7* 129–138.

Wynne, L. (1983). Family research and family therapy: A reunion? *Journal of Marital and Family Therapy, 9,* 113–117.

CHAPTER TWELVE

OUTCOME RESEARCH ON TREATMENT CONDUCTED AT THE BRIEF FAMILY THERAPY CENTER, 1992–1993

Peter De Jong and Larry E. Hopwood

The brief therapy procedures known as "solution-focused" therapy were originally developed by Steve de Shazer and his colleagues at the Brief Family Therapy Center (BFTC) in Milwaukee, Wisconsin. Publications about this work began to appear in the mid 1980s (de Shazer, 1985, 1988; de Shazer et al., 1986), with adaptations and extensions appearing soon thereafter (Berg, 1994; Berg & Miller, 1992b; de Shazer, 1991, 1994; Dolan, 1991; Furman & Tapani, 1992; O'Hanlon & Weiner-Davis, 1989; Walter & Peller, 1992). However, with the exception of some process research on specific solution-focused procedures with a limited number of cases (Adams, Piercy, & Jurich, 1991; Weiner-Davis, de Shazer, & Gingerich, 1987), solution-focused publications have been devoted to explaining and illustrating therapeutic procedures—they have given very little attention to addressing therapeutic outcomes using grouped data. Only two sources (de Shazer, 1991; Wylie, 1990) each give approximately one page to reporting the results of the same unpublished outcome study carried out at BFTC in 1988 by David Kiser (1988) and by Kiser and his colleague Elam Nunnally (1990).

Kiser's (1988) study involved contacting 164 clients six, twelve, and eighteen months after the termination of therapy. Relying on similar measurements of outcomes as those used in an earlier study at the Mental Research Institute (MRI) in Palo Alto (Weakland, Fisch, Watzlawick, and Bodin, 1974), Kiser found highly successful outcomes. De Shazer (1991, p. 162) gives this summary of the BFTC results: "We found an 80.4 percent success rate (65.6 percent of the clients met their goal while 14.7 percent made significant improvement) within an average of 4.6 sessions. When contacted at 18 months, the success rate had increased to 86 percent."

This rate of success is impressive—it is higher and indicates that fewer sessions are required than reported for MRI's form of brief therapy. MRI found a success rate of 72 percent for 97 cases, with 40 percent of clients experiencing "complete relief of the presenting complaint" and 32 percent making significant improvement. The average number of sessions for the MRI clients was seven.

Since solution-focused therapy is such a recent development, outcome research about its effectiveness is in its infancy. This chapter adds to the tiny literature on its outcomes by reporting the results of a second, more recent study at BFTC.[1] The methods and data of the study are reported here in substantial detail so that readers can reflect for themselves on their implications for the therapy's effectiveness. The study also breaks new ground by examining the therapy's effectiveness with diverse clients and across different types of client problems.

The Study Design

Historically, BFTC was an agency that offered individual and family counseling services with trained therapists from around the world. Every therapist who saw clients at BFTC used solution-focused procedures. As a result, it was an ideal setting in which to gather data about the outcomes of the approach.

The Participants

The participants in this study were the 275 clients who came for services at BFTC from November 1992 through August 1993. Most of these clients were seen by one of the ten therapists employed by BFTC. Some interviews—a small minority—were done by trainees learning solution-focused procedures, but in all cases these sessions were supervised by a BFTC therapist listening from behind a one-way mirror.

Clients knew that they might be asked to participate in an outcome study. When they first came for services, printed information was given to them indicating that BFTC would likely be contacting them in future months to ask about the usefulness of the therapy they received. Clients' signatures granted permission for future contacts for research purposes. The same procedure was used to obtain permission from clients for observation of their sessions through the one-way mirror.

At the time the data were collected, BFTC was located in an economically and racially diverse urban neighborhood and had chosen to serve a variety of clients. This diversity is represented in the data. Fifty-seven percent of the 275 clients in this study identified themselves as African American, 5 percent as Latin, 3 percent as Native American, and 36 percent as white. At the time of their first visit, 43 percent of these clients were employed, and 57 percent were not. (By far, the majority of those not employed were referred to BFTC by public welfare agencies.) Sixty percent were female and 40 percent were male. Children, teenagers, and younger adults were somewhat overrepresented among the 275 cases. In one-third of the cases, a child twelve years or younger was the identified client; in 15 percent of the cases, the client was a teenager thirteen to eighteen years old. Ninety-three percent were 45 years of age or younger.

Outcome Measurement

Two ways were used to measure outcome. The first involved using a scaling question. BFTC therapists were requested to ask clients the following question each session as a measurement of ongoing client progress: "On a scale of one to ten, where ten is 'the problem(s) you came to therapy for are solved,' and one is 'the problems are the worst they've been,' where are they now on that scale?" Therapists were also requested to record this "progress score" in their session notes, which were included in each client's file. By comparing progress scores from first session to final session for each client, we obtained our first measurement of outcome. We have chosen to call this comparison a measurement of "intermediate outcome." Therapists recorded client progress scores consistently 80 percent or more of the time.

The second way that outcome was measured involved contacting clients seven to nine months after their final sessions. The procedure here included mailing former clients a letter stating that "within a week or two someone from the Brief Family Therapy Center will be calling to ask if our services have been helpful to you." The letter also gave a rationale for the telephone survey ("We make these calls to find out how you are doing right now and to get your ideas about how we might improve our services") and stated that the interviewer would be someone other than their therapist—in fact, someone not employed by BFTC. Former clients were informed that they could ask the interviewer to call back if the call came at an inconvenient time.

Fifty percent of the former clients were reached by telephone. All those who were reached consented to be interviewed (itself a noteworthy finding). In the cases of children and juveniles, a parent or guardian was interviewed—except when those juveniles had come for services by themselves and when the parent or guardian preferred that the juvenile be interviewed. When two adults were identified as clients in the same case—such as a couple or family case—the interviewer asked to interview the first adult reached. Approximately one-third of the clients who could not be reached had changed their phone numbers to unlisted numbers, while another 25 percent of the "unreachables" had had their telephones disconnected.

The telephone survey itself included several questions intended to measure outcome. One was the same scaling question used to measure progress during therapy sessions at BFTC; another asked clients how satisfied they were with their therapy. In this analysis, the answers to two other questions were combined to form the second measure of outcome. At face value, these two questions seem to measure most directly the overall effectiveness of solution-focused procedures. They also parallel the questions used by Weakland and his associates (1974) and by Kiser (1988), mentioned earlier in this chapter. The first question is: "Overall, would you say your treatment goal was met or not met?" Clients were given the option of answering "goal met" or "goal not met." Those who answered "goal not met" were asked the second question: "Would you say there was any progress made toward that goal?" Clients were given the option of answering "progress made toward treatment goal" or "progress not made toward treatment goal." By combining the responses to these two questions, the measurement of what was called "final outcome" was obtained.

This way of measuring final outcome is consistent with the attitude toward client perceptions that underlies solution-focused therapy, in which therapists treat the client's perceptions (rather than the therapist's perceptions) as the best source of information about worthwhile client goals and strategies to address client problems. It makes sense, then, to also base the estimate of the usefulness of therapy upon client perceptions. The two questions that constitute the measurement of final outcome in this study directly ask clients for their perceptions of whether or not they got the help they wanted from their therapists at BFTC.

Results

Length of Services

The following list presents the data on the number of interviews for the 275 cases. As can be seen, 26 percent came for only one session, and more than 80 percent came for 4 or fewer sessions. The average (mean) number of sessions was 2.9. (The percentages are rounded to the nearest full percent.)

Frequency of Interviews	Number of Cases	Percentage
1	72	26 percent
2	80	29 percent

3	47	17 percent
4	31	11 percent
5	20	7 percent
6	10	4 percent
7	5	2 percent
8	4	2 percent
9	2	1 percent
10	1	0 percent
11	1	0 percent
12	1	0 percent
13	1	0 percent
Total	275	100 percent

Intermediate Outcomes

As stated, the intermediate outcome (I.O.) measurement was calculated by subtracting the progress score for the first session from that recorded for the final session. For example, a client who came to BFTC for four interviews and said "things were at two" at the first session and "at five" by the final session received a score of +3 on intermediate outcome. The following list gives the distribution of scores for this variable. These scores range from -3 to +8. Fewer cases are represented in this list than in the previous list because of incomplete data on progress scores and because clients had to come for at least two sessions for an intermediate outcome score to be calculated.[2]

I.O. Value	Frequency	Percentage
-3	2	1 percent
-2	3	2 percent
-1	8	6 percent
0	24	17 percent
1	24	17 percent
2	18	13 percent
3	27	19 percent
4	8	6 percent
5	15	11 percent

6	7	5 percent
7	4	3 percent
8	1	1 percent
Total	141	100 percent

For the sake of clarity and ease of presenting data in later sections, the data on intermediate outcome have been collapsed into three categories. Cases in which the score falls from -3 through 0 are combined into a category called "no progress." Those scores that fall from 1 through 3 are collapsed to form a category called "moderate progress," and those from 4 through 8 are combined and designated as demonstrating "significant progress." Organizing the data on intermediate outcome this way indicates that 26 percent of the valid cases showed no progress on intermediate outcome, or they worsened; 49 percent showed moderate progress; and 25 percent showed significant progress.

Final Outcomes

As stated earlier, clients seen from November 1992 through August 1993 were telephoned seven to nine months after their last interview. Among other questions, they were asked whether or not their treatment goal was met and, if not met, whether or not any progress was made toward that goal. The following list presents the results from clients' answers to these two questions. The data show that 45 percent of contacted clients said their goal for treatment was met. An additional 32 percent said that even though their goal was not met, some progress was made. Twenty three percent said no progress was made.[3]

Final Outcome	Frequency	Percentage
Goal met	61	45 percent
Some progress	44	32 percent
No progress	31	23 percent
Total	136	100 percent

Comparative Data

The outcomes of solution-focused therapy in this study compare favorably with those of other approaches. First, with regard to number of sessions, Garfield (1994) has studied the professional literature to determine the average number of sessions that clients spend with their therapists. He states that the median range across different approaches to practice is from three to thirteen sessions. The median in the present study is two. Because the research reviewed by Garfield included problem-focused approaches of one type or another, our BFTC data may suggest that clients make progress more quickly when treated with solution-focused therapy.

Lambert and Bergin (1994) reviewed a wealth of research on the effectiveness of different therapies. The clients in these studies suffered from any and all of the problems for which clients seek professional help. Some clients were severely affected, some less so. All the major therapies were represented in the studies they reviewed.

Lambert and Bergin draw two conclusions about the overall effectiveness of professional practice with clients. First, they state that *therapy is effective.* They are able to draw this conclusion because many of the studies they reviewed used both control and experimental groups. Both groups included persons with similar kinds of problems, but those in the control groups did not receive therapy while those in the experimental groups did. Comparisons of the groups consistently revealed that those receiving therapy made more progress on their problems.

Their second conclusion is that *the positive effect of receiving therapy is significant.* The data indicate that the positive effect for different psychological disorders is typically the same as or larger than that produced by medications (for example, the positive effect of antidepressant medications to treat depression). Lambert and Bergin draw this conclusion about the "effect size" of psychotherapy by comparing progress rates of clients receiving psychotherapy to persons on waiting lists and "no-treatment control comparison groups."

The data in the present study do not include comparison groups. However, some sense of the "effect size" of solution-focused therapy can be offered to the reader by reporting on the average progress scores (answers to scaling questions about progress made) at different points in the treatment process. Thus, the mean progress score for all clients at their first session was 3.4; the mean at their final session was 5.5; and at the time of the seven-to-nine-month follow-up, it was still higher at 5.8.

Lambert and Bergin (1994, p. 147) also document the positive effect of psychotherapy by stating that, on average, 66 percent of clients who receive therapy show improvement, while only 34 percent of those who do not receive therapy manage to improve on their own. Both intermediate and final outcomes for the BFTC clients studied compare favorably with the figures reported by Lambert and Bergin. Intermediate outcome data show that 74 percent of BFTC clients improved from their first to final session in therapy. The final outcome data indicate that 77 percent improved. These "success rates," as Lambert and Bergin call them, are far above those that these authors report for clients who do not see a professional, and several percentage points above the average of those reported for other, more problem-focused approaches. These differences in success rates are even more striking when the lower median number of sessions for BFTC clients (two versus six for clients served with problem-focused approaches) is factored into the comparison.

Kiser's BFTC Data

This chapter began by quoting the success rates of clients served at BFTC reported by Kiser (1988) and by Kiser & Nunnally (1990). At a six-month follow-up, Kiser found an overall success rate similar to the present study—80 percent, compared to the 77 percent we found at our seven-to-nine-month follow-up. However, a significantly larger share of the success rate in the previous studies was made up of clients who said they met their treatment goal. For example, Kiser reported that 66 percent of the BFTC clients had met their goal, compared to 45 percent of those in the current study.

Originally, the difference between the current and previous studies was thought to be due to the fact that BFTC had in the ensuing years turned to serving clients from lower socioeconomic (SES) backgrounds. A higher proportion of the clients in Kiser's data were employed and from higher social class backgrounds. As Garfield (1994) confirms after reviewing a large number of studies, clients of lower SES stop coming for services sooner. The two studies bear this out—the mean number of sessions for clients on which we have follow-up data is 3.0, while that in Kiser's and Kiser and Nunnally's studies is 4.6. And as Kiser reports, a higher percentage of clients who came for four to ten sessions reported meeting their treatment goals than those who came for fewer sessions. As a result, we thought we could reasonably expect a smaller percentage of clients in our study to fully meet their treatment goal.

In further analyzing the data, however, a modest difference in outcome by number of sessions was found in the direction suggested by Kiser's data. On intermediate outcome, 32 percent of clients who came for four or more sessions reported "significant progress"; the comparable percentage for those who came for two or three sessions was 20 percent. On final outcome, 52 percent of clients coming for four or more sessions stated they met their treatment goals, while 41 percent of those coming for three or fewer sessions stated the same. In other words, clients who came for a greater number of sessions reported higher rates of success.

Data on the average number of sessions for different categories of intermediate and final outcomes also document a modest link between more positive outcomes and more sessions. On intermediate outcome, the mean number of sessions for clients who reported "significant progress" was 4.2, for those who reported "moderate progress" it was 3.2, and for those who indicated "no progress" it was 3.5. On final outcome—a measurement more comparable to Kiser's—the mean number of sessions for clients who stated their "treatment goals were met" was 3.7, for those who indicated "some progress" it was 2.9, and for those who reported "no progress" it was 2.3.[4]

In conclusion, therefore, our data do replicate Kiser's finding that increased progress occurs with more sessions. However, no matter how the data was organized, we did not find as large a percentage of clients meeting their treatment goals at follow-up as did Kiser.

Diversity-Competent Practice

During the past decade, the field of mental health has been emphasizing the importance of therapists increasing their sensitivity to the values, beliefs, and behaviors of clients that are traceable to the reality of "human diversity" (Poston, Craine, & Atkinson, 1991; McWhirter & Ryan, 1991). Some sources have gone so far as to build their approach to practice around this concept (Axelson, 1993; Sue & Sue, 1990). These and other sources maintain that for too long that field has done its work with built-in preferences for the traits and behaviors of middle-class white culture. Such preferences have minimized or ignored the special characteristics more common among poor people, women, and persons of color. The field as a whole is now more committed than ever before to preparing therapists who are more diversity conscious, competent, and respectful.

The work currently being done in the field to foster diversity-competent practice is mainly being done within the context of a problem-focused paradigm—that is, within the context of first assessing (or diagnosing) client problems and then intervening on the basis of the assessments. Consequently, respecting human diversity is thought to be something that the expert therapist does as she or he assesses and then again as she or he intervenes. It is important, therefore, according to this view, for therapists to learn about the values, beliefs, and worldviews of different economic, ethnic, and racial groups, along with their different styles of communication and problem solving. Therapists are also encouraged to actively examine their own assumptions, biases, and ethnocentric attitudes so that these can be recognized as personal limitations for professional practice and so that steps can be taken to lessen their negative effects. Once this self-knowledge and the expert knowledge about diverse groups is acquired, the latter can be sensitively implemented in the assessment stage so that cultural traits are not misassessed as problems or deficits, and again in the intervention stage so that recommended interventions will be inoffensive and effective (Sue & Sue, 1990).

Some sources go even further in their recommendations to minimize potential diversity-based misunderstanding and conflicts between therapists and clients. They see value in matching the diversity characteristics of clients and therapists—so that women work with women, African Americans with African Americans, and so forth (Boyd-Franklin, 1989; McWhirter & Ryan, 1991).

Berg and Miller (1992a), both solution-focused therapists, have commented on the current emphases in the field regarding how best to achieve diversity-competent practice. While they agree that it is important for therapists to increase their self-awareness in this area and their awareness of the differences among diverse groups, they also maintain that it is essential not to assume homogeneity within given groups. Therapists must work with clients on an individual basis and any assumption that a particular client represents the modal person in her group "obscures the individual, internal culture of the client—a person with unique life experiences" (Berg & Miller, 1992a, p. 357).

Berg and Miller further state that solution-focused therapy is consistent both with the field's commitment to therapists becoming more diversity conscious and with the need to individualize therapeutic services. Indeed, because this form of therapy is so doggedly committed to developing goals and strategies within each client's perceptions and frame of reference, the influences of diversity are routinely and holistically integrated in individual clients.

To test Berg and Miller's beliefs about the usefulness of solution-focused therapy for achieving diversity-competent practice, data was gathered on client diversity and analyzed in relation to outcomes. The following paragraphs describe the measurements of diversity and present the findings.

Age

Information about clients' ages and other diversity variables was obtained from a client information form that clients or their guardians completed on their first visit to BFTC. When two adults came for services together—such as a couple—the couple chose one of themselves as the "identified client" for the purpose of record keeping and third-party (private insurance or Medicaid) reimbursement.

Table 12.1 presents data on intermediate outcome by different categories of age. As explained earlier, intermediate outcome is the difference in client progress measured from first to final session, and it is therefore a measurement of progress at the time of services. The table presents data only for cases in which the client is sixty years of age or younger because there were too few clients who were sixty-one

TABLE 12.1. INTERMEDIATE OUTCOME (I.O.) BY AGE.

	Significant progress (percent)	Moderate progress (percent)	No progress (percent)	Number of cases
Age 12 and Under	24	44	33	46
Age 13–18	21	58	21	24
Age 19–30	29	38	33	21
Age 31–45	27	56	17	41
Age 46–60	13	50	38	8
Total	24	49	26	140

years and older to permit analysis. The last row of the table provides the number of cases in each age category so that readers can consider the size of these categories when comparing the effectiveness of solution-focused therapy in the different categories of age diversity.

The reader can get a sense of whether or not the use of solution-focused procedures makes a difference for different age groups of clients by comparing intermediate outcome across columns within given categories. Doing so suggests that the age of the client is not related to intermediate outcome. Similar percentages of clients show significant progress for all age groupings. The only exception is for clients ages forty-six through sixty, of whom a smaller percentage (13 percent) show significant progress by their final session. This percentage is based, however, on only eight cases and hence has little influence on the overall relationship between age and outcome. When comparing across age categories for clients showing no progress, clients who are ages thirteen through eighteen and thirty-one through forty-five show a lower percentage of no progress, but the differences are not large. Overall, these data indicate that the use of solution-focused therapy in the present study was equally effective for persons of all ages.

Table 12.2 presents the data for final outcome by age. Final-outcome data were obtained by asking clients at the time of the seven-to-nine-month follow-up whether or not their treatment goal was met or not met. Those clients who responded with "not met" were also asked whether or not any progress had been made. The table shows that clients who are ages nineteen to thirty are somewhat less likely to state that their goal was met and somewhat more likely to say that no progress was made toward that treatment goal. Overall, however, there appears to be little if any relationship between age and outcome here. Consequently, *the data on age and final outcome—like those on age and intermediate outcome—suggest that solution-focused therapy was equally effective for persons of all ages.*

TABLE 12.2. FINAL OUTCOME (F.O.) BY AGE.

	Goal met (percent)	Some progress (percent)	No progress (percent)	Number of cases
Age 12 and Under	37	40	24	38
Age 13–18	42	47	11	19
Age 19–30	32	36	32	22
Age 31–45	52	24	24	42
Age 46–60	58	17	25	12
Total	44	33	23	133

Employment Status

When clients came for their first sessions at BFTC, they (or their parents or guardians) were routinely asked about their employment status. The resulting data can be taken as a rough indicator of clients' socioeconomic status. Those who were employed regularly came with authorization for services from private insurance companies; those who were not employed for the most part had their services paid for by public welfare.

The data in Table 12.3 on intermediate outcomes indicate that a somewhat higher percentage of those not employed than those employed showed no progress from their first to their final sessions, but the difference is not present in the data for final outcome (shown in Table 12.4). Here, virtually the same percentage of clients not employed and those employed show no progress (22 percent and 23 percent), although a higher percentage of the employed (50 percent) do report meeting their treatment goal than those not employed (37 percent). Overall, *the data suggest a small tendency for the employed to have better outcomes with solution-focused procedures, but essentially there is little if any difference in outcome using the indicator of socioeconomic status.*

Gender

Tables 12.5 and 12.6 present the data on outcomes for clients who are female and those who are male. Here again, the indicator of diversity does little if anything to predict the effectiveness of using solution-focused procedures with clients; *women and men show equally positive outcomes for both intermediate and final outcomes.*

Race

When "identified" clients come for their first session at BFTC, they (or their parents or guardians) are asked to complete the following question on their client

TABLE 12.3. INTERMEDIATE OUTCOME (I.O.) BY EMPLOYMENT STATUS.

	Significant progress (percent)	Moderate progress (percent)	No progress (percent)	Number of cases
Employed	22	59	19	63
Not Employed	25	42	33	76
Total	24	50	27	139

TABLE 12.4. FINAL OUTCOME (F.O.) BY EMPLOYMENT STATUS.

	Goal met (percent)	Some progress (percent)	No progress (percent)	Number of cases
Employed	50	27	23	74
Not Employed	37	41	22	59
Total	44	33	23	133

TABLE 12.5. INTERMEDIATE OUTCOME (I.O.) BY GENDER.

	Significant progress (percent)	Moderate progress (percent)	No progress (percent)	Number of cases
Female	28	46	26	81
Male	20	53	27	60
Total	25	49	26	141

TABLE 12.6. FINAL OUTCOME (F.O.) BY GENDER.

	Goal met (percent)	Some progress (percent)	No progress (percent)	Number of cases
Female	46	27	28	79
Male	44	40	16	55
Total	45	32	23	134

information questionnaire: "What race do you consider yourself/your child to be?" They are given these options: American Indian/Native American, Asian/Oriental/Pacific Islander, Black/African American, White/Caucasian, Latino/Latina/Hispanic, and Other. There were fewer than five cases for both Native Americans and Asian Americans; therefore no data is presented for these cases. Tables 12.7 and 12.8 present the outcome data gathered for the other three groups. As the data reveal, *racial groups show little difference on either of the measurements of outcomes.* What minor differences are apparent are among the Latin clients, but even this difference is small, and the Latin group itself is much smaller than the other two.

Client-Therapist Matching

As noted at the beginning of this section on diversity-competent practice, some authors see value in matching the diversity characteristics of clients and therapists (Boyd-Franklin, 1989; McWhirter & Ryan, 1991). Clinical observations of solution-focused therapy do not support this assertion, but until now we have not systematically collected data to test our observations (Berg & Miller, 1992a).

Ten therapists conducted the solution-focused sessions on which the BFTC data are based. Four of the therapists were female and four were male. Nine were white and one was Asian American. Given these therapist characteristics, we are able to examine the client-therapist "diversity mix" on gender and partially on race.

Tables 12.9 and 12.10 present the data on intermediate and final outcomes by client-therapist gender mix. The data suggest that there is little if any difference in outcome between client-therapist relationships that are homogeneous on gender and those that are not. The one noticeable exception to this generalization is in Table 12.10 on final outcome, where the rate of "no progress" is lower for those cases in which male clients were seen by female therapists (4 percent). In this sample, however, *female and male solution-focused therapists worked equally effectively with either female or male clients.*

Since only one of the ten therapists in this study was a person of color, this therapist and her cases were excluded from the analysis on client-therapist racial mix. This decision resulted in the variable of white therapists working with clients of one of three groups: African Americans, Whites, or Latins.

Tables 12.11 and 12.13 provide the data on client-therapist racial mix and outcomes. Given that there were so few Latin cases, the comparison of major interest was that of white therapists working with African American clients versus white therapists working with white clients. Table 12.11 on intermediate outcomes shows little difference on this comparison, although one might note the somewhat higher percentage of "no progress" for white therapists with African

TABLE 12.7. INTERMEDIATE OUTCOME (I.O.) BY RACE.

	Significant progress (percent)	Moderate progress (percent)	No progress (percent)	Number of cases
African American	27	45	28	78
White	21	58	21	48
Latin	43	29	29	7
Total	26	49	26	133

TABLE 12.8. FINAL OUTCOME (F.O.) BY RACE.

	Goal met (percent)	Some progress (percent)	No progress (percent)	Number of cases
African American	48	32	20	60
White	45	26	30	47
Latin	36	46	18	11
Total	46	31	24	118

TABLE 12.9. INTERMEDIATE OUTCOME (I.O.) BY CLIENT-THERAPIST GENDER MIX.

	Significant progress (percent)	Moderate progress (percent)	No progress (percent)	Number of cases
Female Client/ Female Therapist	32	46	23	44
Female Client/ Male Therapist	21	46	33	33
Male Client/ Female Therapist	27	40	33	30
Male Client/ Male Therapist	18	65	18	34
Total	25	49	26	141

TABLE 12.10. FINAL OUTCOME (F.O.)
BY CLIENT-THERAPIST GENDER MIX.

	Goal met (percent)	Some progress (percent)	No progress (percent)	Number of cases
Female Client/ Female Therapist	43	27	30	44
Female Client/ Male Therapist	47	29	24	34
Male Client/ Female Therapist	56	40	4	25
Male Client/ Male Therapist	36	36	29	31
Total	45	32	23	134

TABLE 12.11. INTERMEDIATE OUTCOME (I.O.)
BY CLIENT-THERAPIST RACIAL MIX.

	Significant progress (percent)	Moderate progress (percent)	No progress (percent)	Number of cases
African American Client/ White Therapist	25	47	28	71
White Client/ White Therapist	22	61	17	41
Latin Client/ White Therapist	43	29	29	7
Total	25	50	24	119

TABLE 12.12. FINAL OUTCOME (F.O.)
BY CLIENT-THERAPIST RACIAL MIX.

	Goal met (percent)	Some progress (percent)	No progress (percent)	Number of cases
African American Client/ White Therapist	51	37	12	49
White Client/ White Therapist	46	18	36	33
Latin Client/ White Therapist	30	50	20	10
Total	47	32	22	119

American clients versus white clients (28 versus 17 percent). Interestingly, that finding is reversed in the data on final outcome in Table 12.12. Here, the rate of "no progress" is lower for white therapists with African-American clients than with white clients (12 percent versus 36 percent). In general, these data suggest that *client-therapist racial mix was not related to outcomes of solution-focused therapy.*[5]

Conclusions

We began this section on diversity by indicating our belief that solution-focused therapy respects diversity in a more complete and holistic way than problem-focused approaches because it sets aside expert frames of reference on assessment and intervention in favor of working within clients' frames of reference. Data on problem-focused approaches were not gathered; therefore, we cannot draw conclusions about the greater or lesser effectiveness of solution-focused versus problem-focused therapy with diverse persons. However, the data that were collected do suggest that solution-focused therapy is equally effective with clients from diverse backgrounds and that client-therapist diversity mix has little or nothing to do with outcomes.[6]

Type of Problem

Problem-focused therapy is based on an assumption derived from the medical model that is rarely recognized as an assumption worthy of careful discussion and research (De Jong & Berg, in press). The assumption is that *there is a necessary connection between a client's problem and its solution,* much like the connection between a disease and its cure. Given this assumed connection, problem-focused therapies proceed as though it is necessary for therapists to first assess (or diagnose) a client's problem before attempting to intervene in (or treat) it. The field's commitment to this assumption is demonstrated by the proliferation of specialized assessment "tools" and treatment procedures.

This assumption has been progressively set aside by solution-focused therapists as the approach has developed. In solution-focused therapy, therapists use the "miracle question" to open a conversation with clients about what will be different in the client's life when the problem is solved. These conversations are intended to give clients an opportunity to develop well-formed goals within their own frames of reference. Soon after therapists began to use the miracle question, they observed that sometimes clients' answers to it seemed logically connected to their problems, but other times the answer and problem were completely unrelated. In other instances, when clients would return for a later session and begin to talk about what was going better in their lives and how they made those things happen, these successes and strengths often had nothing logically to do with their problems (de Shazer, 1988, 1991, 1994). Often, the clients were as surprised about the solutions as any problem-solving therapist might be. This was so much the case that de Shazer (1988, pp. 5–6) was led to observe that a concept of solution often precedes a definition of problem; that is, once a person figures out a solution, she or he goes back and defines (or redefines) the problem to fit the solution.

Setting aside the assumption of a necessary connection between problem and solution is a radical departure from other therapies. As a result, we wished to gather outcome data that would reflect the wisdom of doing so. In thinking about this, we reasoned that if one conceives of solution-focused work with clients as an "intervention" in traditional problem-solving terms, and if indeed there is a necessary connection between problem and solution, the solution-focused procedures should not be equally effective with all client problems. We came to this conclusion because solution-focused therapists use the same therapeutic procedures with each client—regardless of what the client might say the problem is. We tested this conclusion by analyzing intermediate and final outcomes relative to client estimates of their problems.

Client problem was measured by giving clients an extensive checklist of problems when they made their first visit to BFTC. Before they began their first session, they were asked to indicate each of the "problems that you feel apply to you." Among the problems on the list were depression, suicidal thoughts, eating disorder, job-related problems, parent-child conflict, family violence, alcohol/other drug abuse, sexual abuse, death of a loved one, self-esteem problems, blended family issues, and several more. The data were analyzed for possible relationships between any of these client self-reported problems and our measurements of intermediate and final outcomes.

The following list summarizes these data. In the interest of efficiency of presentation, a success rate on intermediate outcome and final outcome has been assessed for each type of client problem for which there were more than five cases. The success rate for intermediate outcome is a combination of the categories "significant progress" and "moderate progress"; the success rate for final outcome is a combination of "goal met" and "some progress." (The numbers in parentheses indicate the number of clients who indicated having the particular problem. The total number of cases are 141 for I.O. and 136 for F.O.)

Type of Problem	I.O. Success Rate	F.O. Success Rate
Depression	75 percent (79)	75 percent (60)
Suicidal thoughts	74 percent (34)	79 percent (19)

Anxiety	72 percent (50)	74 percent (42)
Panic attacks	80 percent (10)	50 percent (10)
Sleep problems	75 percent (59)	76 percent (49)
Eating disorder	80 percent (40)	73 percent (26)
Withdrawn behavior	67 percent (58)	80 percent (39)
Health problems	72 percent (18)	60 percent (10)
Job-related problems	84 percent (19)	80 percent (15)
Financial concerns	74 percent (43)	74 percent (31)
Parent-child conflict	71 percent (35)	76 percent (25)
Communication problems	65 percent (57)	76 percent (46)
Family violence (actual or threatened)	60 percent (20)	77 percent (13)
Sexual abuse	64 percent (11)	75 percent (8)
Physical abuse	67 percent (12)	89 percent (9)
Alcohol/other drug abuse	67 percent (12)	63 percent (8)
Marital/relationship problems	76 percent (45)	81 percent (47)
Sexual problems	72 percent (21)	89 percent (18)
Death of a loved one	72 percent (18)	79 percent (14)
Self-esteem problems	77 percent (48)	73 percent (40)
Brother/sister problems	78 percent (36)	78 percent (31)
Blended-family issues	74 percent (27)	71 percent (21)

These data suggest that solution-focused therapy was consistently successful—regardless of the type of problem or problems identified by the client. With a few exceptions—panic attacks and health problems on final outcome—the data indicate that more than 70 percent of clients showed progress on the two measurements of outcome.

These data about clients' estimates of their own problems do not support an assumption of a necessary connection between client-identified problems and client-rated improvement. Instead, they suggest that clients do not "need" specialized interventions based on expert assessments in order to make progress, at least not to the extent that they are currently emphasized in the field. Clients receiving solution-focused therapy report successful outcomes despite being exposed to the same set of procedures as other clients and without paying any attention to any assumed connection between problem and solution.

The implications of these findings are several, and potentially important. For one thing, they suggest that if the field wished to, it could greatly simplify therapist preparation. That is, the field does not have to spend the resources it currently does on conceptualizing problems, devising problem-assessment procedures and instruments, developing specialized interventions, and thereafter teaching all that content to aspiring therapists. Instead, it could turn its resources to observing more carefully how clients use personal strengths and environmental resources to make changes happen, and then to teaching new therapists how to respect and foster self-determined change in clients.

Clinical Utility

The two types of outcome measurement used in this study—intermediate and final—have distinct advantages and disadvantages for clinicians practicing solution-focused therapy who are trying to determine the effectiveness of their work with clients. The use of intermediate outcomes allows the therapist to obtain a measurement of progress from clients while they are sitting in the office. Thus, intermediate outcomes have clinical utility in that they can assist in decision making from session to session over the course of treatment. They indicate when therapy is working and they encourage client and therapist to do more of the same. They also indicate when progress is stalled and, therefore, when it is time to do something different. Intermediate outcomes, however, because they represent changes over a short period of time, may obscure gradual changes and be overly sensitive to the normal ups and downs of life. In addition, because they are obtained during the course of treatment, when clients may be inclined to overestimate desired changes, their relationship to longer-lasting effects is suspect.

Follow-up outcomes provide a better picture of overall success by assessing the effects of treatment that persist over time—well after treatment has ceased. However, without a research design that incorporates controls, one can hardly be confident that any success that is measured is indeed due to the treatment. The longer the time between treatment and outcome measurement, the greater the possibility that intervening influences rather than the therapy may have produced any gains measured. In addition, returning to the idea of using outcome results to influence ongoing treatment, retrospective studies do not afford the therapist the opportunity to use the results to influence treatment other than to invite clients who have had negative outcomes to come back for more treatment.

Whether new to the field or long-time practitioners, therapists frequently want to obtain a sense of how well their clients are doing. No matter how hard therapists try, this sense of the client's success is often directly tied to the therapist's view of their own success as a therapist, which in turn influences the enthusiasm and determination with which they carry out future therapy. Knowing how well clients are doing is also very important to agency administrators and funding sources faced with making difficult decisions about the allocation of resources. It seems to us that both groups would be keen to know more about the relationship of intermediate outcomes (measured during therapy) to final outcomes (obtained many months after termination). Data are now presented that clarify that relationship.

Table 12.13 presents data on final outcomes by intermediate outcomes. At first glance, these data suggest that the two measurements of outcome are related. When contacted seven to nine months after their last sessions, 62 percent of clients who make significant progress from their first to final session say that their treatment goal had been met in therapy. In contrast, only 23 percent of those indicating no progress during therapy stated at follow-up that their treatment goal had been met. Consistent with this pattern of relationship, while only 5 percent of those making significant progress in therapy stated at follow-up that no progress was made toward their treatment goal, 31 percent of those reporting no progress while in therapy also reported no progress at follow-up. Despite this pattern in the data, however, we cannot be confident of a relationship at this time. The number of no-progress cases on both outcome measures in Table 12.13 are too few—thirteen on intermediate outcome and ten on final outcome.

Another indicator of final outcome is the degree of client *satisfaction* with therapy once the therapy has terminated and clients have had some time to reflect on the consequences of the therapy for their lives. Client satisfaction was measured at the time of the seven-to-nine-month follow-up. As Table 12.14 shows, at first glance satisfaction appears related to intermediate outcome. However, there are too few cases of "no progress" (thirteen) and "dissatisfaction" with therapy (four) to be confident of a relationship.[7] Although it may well be that solution-focused therapists can be confident that clients who are reporting higher levels of progress during their therapy are more likely to feel satisfied with their therapy several months later, a definitive statement on this relationship will have to await further research.

Another question regularly facing therapists is when to terminate with clients. Most clients make progress while in therapy, but how much progress is enough to warrant termination? For those practicing solution-focused therapy and measuring client progress with the scaling question, a fairly dramatic break was found in the data between clients who say that "things are at about six or lower" and those who say that they are at seven or higher. (In this zero-to-ten scaling question, zero indicates "the worst the problem has ever been" and ten indicates that the problem they came to treatment for is solved.) Table 12.15 presents the data for final outcome (that is, the extent to which the treatment goal was met) by the progress score at the client's final session. Table 12.16 presents our findings on sat-

TABLE 12.13. FINAL OUTCOME (F.O.)
BY INTERMEDIATE OUTCOME (I.O.).

	Goal met (percent)	Progress made (percent)	No progress (percent)	Number of cases
Significant progress	62	33	5	21
Moderate progress	49	39	12	41
No progress	23	46	31	13
Total	48	39	13	75

TABLE 12.14. SATISFACTION WITH THERAPY AT FOLLOW-UP
BY INTERMEDIATE OUTCOME.

	Satisfied (percent)	Neither satisfied nor dissatisfied (percent)	Dissatisfied (percent)	Number of cases
Significant progress	86	10	5	21
Moderate progress	80	15	5	40
No progress	54	39	8	13
Total	77	18	8	74

TABLE 12.15. FINAL OUTCOME (F.O.)
BY PROGRESS SCORE AT FINAL SESSION.

	Goal met (percent)	Some progress (percent)	No progress (percent)	Number of cases
Six or lower	30	48	23	44
Seven or higher	74	23	3	35
Total	49	37	14	79

TABLE 12.16. SATISFACTION WITH THERAPY AT FOLLOW-UP
BY PROGRESS SCORE AT FINAL SESSION.

	Satisfied (percent)	Neither satisfied nor dissatisfied (percent)	Dissatisfied (percent)	Number of cases
Six or lower	65	28	7	43
Seven or higher	94	3	3	35
Total	78	17	5	78

isfaction with therapy at follow-up by progress score at final session. In both tables, the break is made in the progress score at final session between six and seven.
Although solution-focused therapists already give great credibility to the client's
perception of when it is best to terminate, these data indicate that therapists can
indeed be confident that clients who scale their progress near seven or higher and
at the same time state that they are ready to terminate are indeed ready to do so.[8]

Summary

Very little information about the outcomes of solution-focused therapy has been
published until now. This study done at BFTC largely confirms the findings of an
unpublished study by Kiser (1988). The major results of the present study include:

- More than three-fourths of clients receiving solution-focused therapy either
  fully met their treatment goals or made progress toward them.
- This level of effectiveness occurred over an average of 3.0 sessions.
- Solution-focused therapy was equally effective with a diversity of clients.
- Effectiveness did not vary by client-therapist gender or racial mix.
- The same therapeutic procedures were effective across a range of client-identified problems.
- Intermediate outcomes as measured by scaling client progress appear to be related to the extent to which clients believed at a seven-to-nine-month follow-
  up that their treatment goals were met, and the extent of client satisfaction with
  the therapy. In addition, higher scaling scores at final sessions were predictive of
  more positive final outcomes and higher satisfaction with therapy at follow-up.

Questions from the Editors

1. *What is or should be the role of research for the solution-focused approach, given that it
is increasingly being aligned with the highly relativistic, antiobjectivity stance of postmodern
philosophy?*

Solution-focused therapy works within the client's frame of reference, respecting the client's categories. Consequently, research about the model must somehow
do the same. This stipulation need not minimize the importance of doing research
about the model; it primarily indicates that research based on standardized, universal, scientific categories is suspected of not respecting different client "realities."
We attempted to meet our stipulation in two ways. First, we built several of our out-

come measurements around the scaling question used by therapists and clients to measure progress. The scaling question gave access to client categories because clients defined the meaning of the numbers. Second, all our outcome measurements are based on clients' rather than therapists' perceptions of progress and satisfaction with therapy. We believe that as long as the methodology respects the clients' categories, and as long as participation in the research is respectfully requested by the researchers and agreed upon by the clients, research on the model is both useful and important to do (see Rappaport, 1990, and Saleebey, 1992, for more on research consistent with a social constructivist therapeutic outlook).

2.   *What aspects of solution-focused therapy should be the focus of future research?*

Building on our last answer, we believe that those who practice solution-focused therapy should do ongoing outcome research. Where it is possible to do so and still respect client wishes and needs, we recommend using designs involving control groups. We also think it is important to do process research of two types: first, researching the placement and use of different solution-focused procedures in the therapy session—for example, gathering data on the consequences of asking the presession change question early in first sessions versus later, or the impact on client progress of frequently using indirect complimenting versus using it infrequently. Second, we must learn much more about *how* clients go about constructing and reshaping their senses of reality while in therapy. The research strategies and work of ethnomethodologists and ethnographers are important to build on here.

3.   *At this stage, what is the unique value of solution-focused therapy given that it appears to achieve roughly the same outcomes as other, more established approaches?*

Solution-focused therapy has much to offer:

- The jury is still out on solution-focused outcomes relative to other forms of therapy. Kiser's (1988) study clearly suggests more positive outcomes, and the data presented in this chapter suggest somewhat more positive outcomes than the average for other modalities.
- Data indicate that the average number of sessions for this modality is clearly lower than for others.
- By working with and respecting the client's categories and frame of reference, solution-focused therapy has wide applicability across groups of diverse persons. In this postmodern era of mixing peoples and traditions, this flexibility is increasingly important.

- Since visions and strategies for change are drawn from and constructed within the client's frame of reference, solution-focused therapy gives new and added meaning to certain core values of the profession: giving primacy to the client's interests, individualizing services, respecting client self-determination and dignity, building on strengths, and utilizing the transferability of solutions. Consistently working with client realities also serves to establish and maintain differentiation between client and therapist.
- The same solution-focused procedures can be used successfully with a large variety of client problems.
- For those therapists who can only work congruently with a modality that respects client meanings and client-defined strengths, solution-focused therapy is a breath of fresh air and a counter to burnout.

Notes

1. These results are reprinted from *How to Interview for Client Strengths and Solutions* by Peter De Jong and Insoo Kim Berg. Copyright 1995 by Brooks/Cole Publishing Company, a Division of International Thomson Publishing Inc. Used with the permission of Brooks/Cole Publishing Company, Pacific Grove, CA 93950.
2. The average number of sessions for the 141 cases on which we have data on intermediate outcome is 3.7. That this figure is higher than the 2.9 sessions for the original 275 cases is understandable because the measurement of intermediate outcome by definition excludes all single-session cases.
3. The average number of sessions for the 136 cases on which we have data on final outcome is 3.0—essentially the same as the 2.9 average for the original 275 cases.
4. The overall higher mean number of sessions for categories of intermediate versus final outcome reflect, again, that our way of measuring intermediate outcome excluded single-session cases.
5. Although strictly speaking our data do not represent a probability sample of a larger population, we did run a Pearson chi-square test on the data in each table from 12.1 through 12.12. None of the results proved to be statistically significant.
6. We collected some additional data about outcome at the seven-to-nine-month follow-ups that also supports and reinforces these conclusions. We asked former clients this question: "Overall, would you say that you are satisfied, dissatisfied, or neither satisfied nor dissatisfied with your therapy services at the center?" Of the 137 who responded, 72 percent said they were satisfied, 16 percent said they were neither satisfied nor dissatisfied, and 12 percent said they were dissatisfied. The level of satisfaction did not change when we looked separately at satisfaction level for clients of different ages, employment statuses, genders, or races.
7. Pearson chi-square tests on the data in Tables 12.13 and 12.14 indicate that the suggested relationships are not statistically significant. The reader should note that the distribution of cases on final outcome in Table 12.13 and on degree of satisfaction with therapy in Table 12.14 differ from the distributions for all clients in this study on these variables. In Table

12.13, there is a smaller percentage of no-progress cases (5 percent) than was reported earlier for all clients (23 percent). In Table 12.14, there is a smaller percentage of dissatisfied cases (8 percent) than reported in note 6 for all clients (12 percent). The reason for these differences is that the clients must have come for at least two sessions in order to receive a value on intermediate outcome, and the data indicate that those who come for more than one session are less likely to report "no progress" and "dissatisfaction" than those who come for only one session.

8. The Pearson chi-squares calculated for Tables 12.15 and 12.16 indicate that the relationships between progress scores at final session and both final outcome and degree of satisfaction with therapy at follow-up are statistically significant.

References

Adams, J. F., Piercy, F. P., & Jurich, J. A. (1991). Effects of solution focused therapy's "formula first session task" on compliance and outcome in family therapy. *Journal of Marital and Family Therapy, 17,* 277–290.

Axelson, J. A. (1993). *Counseling and development in a multicultural society.* Pacific Grove, CA: Brooks/Cole.

Berg, I. K. (1994). *Family based services: A solution-focused approach.* New York: W. W. Norton.

Berg, I. K., & Miller, S. D. (1992a). Working with Asian American clients: One person at a time. *Families in Society: The Journal of Contemporary Human Services, 73,* 356–363.

Berg, I. K., & Miller, S. D. (1992b). *Working with the problem drinker: A solution-focused approach.* New York: W. W. Norton.

Boyd-Franklin, N. (1989). *Black families in therapy: A multisystems approach.* New York: Guilford.

De Jong, P., & Berg, I. K. (in press). *How to interview for client strengths and solutions.* Pacific Grove, CA: Brooks/Cole.

De Shazer, S. (1985). *Keys to solution in brief therapy.* New York: W. W. Norton.

De Shazer, S. (1988). *Clues: Investigating solutions in brief therapy.* New York: W. W. Norton.

De Shazer, S. (1991). *Putting difference to work.* New York: W. W. Norton.

De Shazer, S. (1994). *Words were originally magic.* New York: W. W. Norton.

De Shazer, S., Berg, I. K., Lipchik, E., Nunnally, E., Molnar, A., Gingerich, W., & Weiner-Davis, M. (1986). Brief therapy: Focused solution development. *Family Process, 25,* 207–221.

Dolan, Y. M. (1991). *Resolving sexual abuse: Solution-focused therapy and Ericksonian hypnosis for adult survivors.* New York: W. W. Norton.

Furman, B., & Tapani, A. (1992). *Solution talk: Hosting therapeutic conversations.* New York: W. W. Norton.

Garfield, S. L. (1994). Research on client variables in psychotherapy. In A. E. Bergin & S. L. Garfield (Eds.), *Handbook of psychotherapy and behavior change* (4th ed.) (pp. 190–228). New York: Wiley.

Kiser, D. (1988). *A follow-up study conducted at the Brief Family Therapy Center.* Unpublished manuscript.

Kiser, D., & Nunnally, E. (1990). *The relationship between treatment length and goal achievement in solution-focused therapy.* Unpublished manuscript.

Lambert, M. J., & Bergin, A. E. (1994). The effectiveness of psychotherapy. In A. E. Bergin &

S. L. Garfield (Eds.), *Handbook of psychotherapy and behavior change* (4th ed.) (pp. 143–189). New York: Wiley.

McWhirter, J., & Ryan, C. (1991). Counseling the Navajo. *Journal of Multicultural Counseling and Development, 19,* 74–81.

O'Hanlon, W. H., & Weiner-Davis, M. (1989). *In search of solutions.* New York: W. W. Norton.

Poston, W., Craine, M., & Atkinson, D. (1991). Counselor dissimilarity, client cultural mistrust, and willingness to self disclose. *Journal of Multicultural Counseling and Development, 19,* 65–73.

Rappaport, J. (1990). Research methods and the empowerment social agenda. In P. Tolan, C. Keys, F. Chertak, & L. Jason (Eds.), *Researching community psychology* (pp. 51–63). Washington, DC: American Psychological Association.

Saleebey, D. (Ed.). (1992). *The strengths perspective in social work practice.* New York: Longman.

Sue, D. W., & Sue, D. (1990). *Counseling the culturally different: Theory and practice* (2nd ed.). New York: Wiley.

Walter, J. L., & Peller, J. E. (1992). *Becoming solution-focused in brief therapy.* New York: Brunner/Mazel.

Weakland, J. H., Fisch, R., Watzlawick, P., & Bodin, A. (1974). Brief therapy: Focused problem resolution. *Family Process, 13,* 141–168.

Weiner-Davis, M., de Shazer, S., & Gingerich, W. J. (1987). Building on pretreatment change to construct the therapeutic solution: An exploratory study. *Journal of Marital and Family Therapy, 13,* 359–363.

Wylie, M. S. (1990). Brief therapy on the couch. *The Family Therapy Networker, 14,* 26–35, 66.

CHAPTER THIRTEEN

RESEARCH ON THE PROCESS OF SOLUTION-FOCUSED THERAPY

Mark Beyebach, Alberto Rodríguez Morejón,
David L. Palenzuela, and Jose Luis Rodríguez-Arias

This chapter offers an overview of the research undertaken by the Salamanca Group over the last ten years. This research has been developed around the brief family therapy program of the Universidad Pontificia in Salamanca, where both clinical services and graduate and postgraduate training in solution-focused brief therapy are provided. This intersection of the academic and the professional, of clinical practice and training, impacts our research efforts in several ways. On the one hand, it impacts our own therapeutic practice and training procedures. Our research emerges from specific questions that at one time or another members of our team have asked themselves; the research intends to provide specific answers, or at least to generate new, useful questions. On the other hand, given that students and trainees carry out many of the research tasks, the dual focus of the program also has an immediate impact on the skills of the trainees. For instance, using a coding scheme to analyze therapeutic interaction usually has the beneficial "side effect" of sharpening certain perceptual skills in real therapy situations.

Finally, our academic environment has probably also had an effect on the kind of research we have undertaken. As this chapter shows, we are engaged in what could be described as fairly traditional research: it is nonparticipative, undertaken "from behind the one-way mirror," and, albeit naively, tries not to influence the therapeutic process it is exploring. It relies heavily on traditional scientific notions such as reliability and validity, and does not shun statistics. Within this traditional framework, however, we have clearly opted for what has been called "process research" (Kiesler, 1973; Greenberg & Pinsof, 1986), which in our view holds the greatest promise of becoming, as we like to call it, "useful" research. In other words, we are basically interested in the process of change as it unfolds during the course of therapy, especially its relationship to the interaction taking place between therapists and clients.

This interest has been translated into three different but complementary lines of inquiry, two of which we describe in this chapter. The first line addresses the *relational process* of therapist-client interaction and its association with therapeutic outcome and with various clinically significant processes such as premature termination of therapy, task compliance, and patterns of conversation displayed by novice and expert therapists. In the first section of this chapter we offer a general overview of our results and a more detailed description of one of the studies we have undertaken within this line of research. The second line of inquiry provides a *cognitive reading* of the process of change in solution-focused therapy. In the second section of this chapter we present our first results, taking into account both traditional cognitive variables and variables generated within the solution-focused approach.

The third line of investigation involves study of therapeutic conversation from the point of view not of the process but of the *content* of the dialogue. We use two different coding schemes, one derived from Sluzki's (1992) suggestions on how to research narrative transformations, and the other an adaptation of an instrument used originally at the Brief Family Therapy Center, Milwaukee, Wisconsin (Gingerich, de Shazer, & Weiner-Davis, 1987), which in our version discriminates several forms of "problem-talk" and "solution-talk." However, because we are only now beginning to get results on this third approach (Beyebach et al., 1994), discussion in this chapter is limited to the first two research projects.

Certain provisional conclusions can be drawn from this body of research, both in terms of the results we have achieved and in terms of research that remains to be done. In the last section of this chapter we offer our own considerations of these conclusions and we discuss the limitations and shortcomings of our studies and prospects for future research.

Research on Relational Communication in Therapeutic Situations

Our first line of research grew out of our interest in what de Shazer (1991) would call "therapy as a system" and, more specifically, from our curiosity about what happens *between* therapists and clients in the course of brief therapy. We wished to study this dimension without leaving the basic theoretical assumptions of our clinical work.

The relational communication approach, the "pragmatics of human communication" (Rogers & Bagarozzi, 1983; Watzlawick, Beavin, & Jackson, 1967), offered a convenient framework for this undertaking. This approach assumes that people do not relate *and* talk, but rather relate *in* talk; in other words, their exchange of messages *is* their relationship. In this view, emphasis is placed on the interlocking and reciprocal effects of each interactor on the other. Communication is considered the process by which system members define self in relation to the other and simultaneously create the ongoing nature of their relationship.

One dimension of this cyclic and recursive process is the continuous struggle to define what the rights and privileges of the interactors are. This control dimension of relational communication is best described in terms of constraint or interdependence, with symmetry and complementarity as its interactional poles. This conceptualization is consistent with the social constructionist perspective (Gergen, 1985; Hoffman, 1990), in which therapy is seen as a social construction that is recursively and constantly co-created by therapists and clients.

The relational control approach offers not only a set of premises and theoretical constructs, but also some instruments that provide a theoretically grounded and methodologically sound way of operationalizing those premises and constructs. In 1965, Sluzki and Beavin proposed a coding scheme designed to measure the relational dimension of communication. In the decades that followed, this instrument was modified by several authors (Mark, 1971; Ericson & Rogers, 1973; Rogers & Farace, 1975; Heatherington & Friedlander, 1987), until the Relational Communication Control Coding Scheme (RCCCS) and the Family-Relational Communication Control Coding Scheme (F-RCCCS) were developed. These were applied in different settings, including the study of marital couples, manager-subordinate dyads, and therapist-client interactions (Friedlander & Heatherington, 1989; Friedlander, Wildman, & Heatherington, 1991; Heatherington & Allen, 1984; Lichtenberg & Barké, 1981; Rogers & Bagarozzi, 1983).

Our group started using the RCCCS and the F-RCCCS in the coding of first sessions of brief, Mental Research Institute (MRI) style, problem-oriented therapy (Altuna, Beyebach, Piqueras, & Rodríguez-Arias, 1988; Beyebach, de la Cueva, Ramos, & Rodríguez-Arias, 1990). These studies demonstrated the ability of the instrument to discriminate between different "phases" of the interviews. The studies also produced some intriguing associations between relational control patterns in first sessions and therapeutic outcome at termination.

The picture that emerged showed that first sessions with clients who later dropped out displayed a higher degree of "competitive symmetry" (in which either the therapist or the client tried to control the exchange) and verbal conflict between therapist and client. These sessions also showed the highest incidence of question/answer exchanges. Conversely, successful cases seemed to be characterized during their first interviews by a predominance of "neutralized symmetry," (that is, by exchanges in which neither the therapist nor the client tried to control the exchange). At the same time, at a monadic level of analysis, therapists in successful cases gave more instructions and orders than in any other group of cases. An unexpected finding was that cases that eventually relapsed showed a high proportion of "submissive symmetry" in their first interviews—a type of interaction we termed "one-down hook" with too much agreement between therapists and clients.

These preliminary findings led us to undertake more specific and better designed studies in order to test, on a more solution-oriented sample, some of the hypotheses that had emerged:

1.   *Study A* examined the differences between expert therapists and trainees in terms of their relational communication in first sessions of brief therapy (de la Cueva, 1993). Therapeutic outcome at termination was also taken into account. The findings did not conform to any clear pattern, although it did become clear that there were no relational control differences between those sessions conducted by expert therapists and sessions conducted by trainees. However, a differential analysis by "phases" of the interview (the conversation before the break, or "information gathering," and the "final message" after the break, or "intervention"[1]) did show some differences. The results suggested that in successful cases the relational pattern of these two phases was different, while cases in which the conversation unfolded in a similar manner in both phases were more likely to end up in therapeutic failure or dropout.

2.   *Study B* examined the relational patterns of the intervention phase and their relationship to the clients' compliance with the homework tasks that therapists suggested (Bailín, 1995). One interesting finding was that the type of compliance, as defined by de Shazer (1985), was indeed unrelated to therapeutic outcome at termination. As predicted by solution-focused theory, clients who did comply literally with tasks or who modified them did *not* get better results than those who did not perform the assigned tasks at all or who did the opposite. There were differences, however, as far as relational communication was concerned. In particular, there was a higher proportion of competitive symmetry and of conflict triads in intervention phases after which the task was not carried out. Conversely, the highest proportion of submissive symmetry appeared in the intervention phases after which the report on the task was rated by the judges as "vague."

3.   *Study C* focused on the association of certain relational communication control patterns with continuation or dropout from therapy (Beyebach, 1993). In the rest of this section we give a more detailed account of this study.

Posing the Problem

All clinicians have been confronted with the fact that some clients with whom another appointment has been made do not show up for the interview. On other occasions, clients refuse to set an appointment for another session, even though the therapist might feel that it is appropriate. This is what traditionally has been referred to as "dropout" or "premature termination." Studies on dropping out from psychotherapy show that the incidence is certainly high, regardless of how it is measured and regardless of the context in which it is studied. In most research studies, the dropout rate is about 25 percent, and in some cases affects more than 60 percent of the patients being studied (Baekeland & Lundwall, 1975; Garfield, 1986). Additionally, most premature terminations occur at the beginning of treatment, after one or two interviews.

From the traditional psychotherapeutic perspective, dropout tends to be considered a negative phenomenon. It implies that a certain proportion of clients do not get a treatment they may have profited from, or that they quit before having benefitted as fully as possible. Some authors have pointed out that dropping out of treatment is a negative experience for most clients (Pekarik, 1983; Persons, Burns, & Perloff, 1988), reinforcing their sense of helplessness (Sherman & Anderson, 1987) and also having a bad effect on the morale of the therapist.

In contrast, for most solution-focused therapists dropout is not considered a problem. One could even argue that for brief therapists there is no such a thing as "premature" termination. After all, it is clients who have the final say concerning the pacing of the sessions and their continuation or discontinuation in therapy. For the solution-focused therapist, a client's decision not to come back to therapy might be construed as the wisest decision the client can make, even a sign of taking charge of his or her own life. In fact, research shows that quite often "dropout" is not equivalent to "therapeutic failure," and that in many cases the opposite is true. One of the reasons for dropout is that clients think they do not need more therapy because they have improved enough or have even met their goals (Buddeberg, 1987; Fiester & Rudestam, 1975; Persons et al., 1988; Presley, 1987; Stahler & Eisenman, 1987; Trepka, 1986).

Our view, however, is that dropout (understood as a client's quitting therapy without his or her therapist's agreement, regardless of the number of sessions that have already taken place) does have some negative connotations. For example, dropping out has negative financial and administrative consequences for treatment professionals (Pekarik, 1983; Persons et al., 1988; Sherman & Anderson, 1987). From a more clinical perspective, dropping out points at least to a lack of "fit" between the therapist and client. After all, we are not talking about a therapist and a client deciding that no more therapy is necessary (something that in solution-focused therapy quite often happens even after a single session), but about a therapist who fails to recognize that his or her client wants no more therapy and therefore invites him or her for additional sessions, which the client then misses. Finally, and from a research perspective, those clients who drop out and then "disappear" prevent follow-up which in turn hinders therapists and researchers from learning about their clients.

In our view, these considerations make dropping out of therapy an important research topic. However, most research on dropout from therapy has tended to assume that dropping out is essentially something associated with—and due to—certain characteristics of clients. Implicit in this assumption is that certain clients show a tendency to break off from treatment prematurely, regardless of the nature of the treatment. In this way, the influence of factors associated with the course of treatment itself or with the therapist's behavior have been overlooked, and variables such as the sociodemographic characteristics of the subjects or their psychopathology are emphasized (Baekeland & Lundwall, 1975; Bischoff & Sprenkle, 1993).

The poor balance of this type of research has led other researchers to begin to broaden their perspectives (Anderson, Atilano, Bergen, Russell, & Jurich, 1985; Dubrin & Zastowny, 1988; Duehn & Proctor, 1977; Gunzburger, Henggeler, & Watson, 1985; Hardin, Subich, & Holvey, 1988; Mennicke, Lent, & Burgoyne, 1988). Instead of focusing on variables that are static or of limited clinical relevance (demographic, contextual, and psychometric), they have underlined the fact that dropping out does not take place in a vacuum but rather in a particular context and that it is therefore necessary to also take into account the influence of therapists and their work methods. Furthermore, researchers began to take a closer look at the interactional context in which dropping out occurred.

This, then, is the approach we have taken. We have addressed the topic of brief therapy dropout not from study of the more or less intrinsic characteristics of therapists and clients but by analyzing the *interactional context* in which dropping out occurs. We have done this using a methodological approach consistent with the perspective of the pragmatics of human communication (Watzlawick et al., 1967; Rogers, Millar, & Bavelas, 1985) and using the F-RCCCS (Heatherington & Friedlander, 1987) to measure the relational control of communication taking place between therapists and clients during therapeutic sessions.

The core question of our research was *what are the differences between the communication patterns arising in brief therapy sessions after which the client continues in treatment and the communication patterns arising in brief therapy sessions after which the client abandons therapy?* This study tested a set of sixteen hypotheses that were derived from our previous studies as well as from predictions based on various theoretical premises. These hypotheses reflected both monadic and dyadic levels of analysis, as well as the "information gathering" and "intervention" parts of the interview.

In general terms, we expected the therapeutic conversations in the "continuation group" to be fluid, with the client volunteering information and the therapist giving support and producing brief statements to keep the conversation going. We further assumed that there would be fewer question-answer exchanges and fewer overlaps in this group than in the "dropout group," which would result in a higher proportion of transitional transactions in the continuation as opposed to the dropout group. In the dropout group, conversely, we anticipated that there would be less support and more overlaps than in the interviews of the continuation group. We thought that therapists and clients would engage in more question-answer patterns and symmetrical escalations. For these reasons, we predicted that there would be more competitive symmetry and also more conflict triads in the dropout interviews.

The Method

The Sample. The ninety-seven subjects in the study were sampled from cases seen over a three-year period at a private brief psychotherapy center in Salamanca, Spain. The treatment they received at the center can be described as an integration of solution-focused (Berg and Miller, 1992; de Shazer, 1985, 1988, 1991) and MRI problem-focused (Fisch, Weakland, & Segal, 1982) brief therapy approaches. Previous research by a former member of the research team (Pérez Grande, 1991) found that the overall sample had been in therapy for an average of five sessions. At termination, 71 percent of this group of clients reported either the complete disappearance of their complaints or a clear improvement. At follow-up (between six and thirty-five months after termination), 12 percent of the successful cases were rated as relapses, whereas 38 percent of the clients reported that additional positive changes had taken place.

From this population, the sample was selected following a three-step procedure:

1. Location of therapies with individual format (one therapist and one client)
2. Selection of cases of early dropout
3. Selection of a comparable group of interviews after which no dropout occurred

The definition of dropout we used, close to Garfield's (1986) recommendation, results from an exhaustive review of the diverse definitions of dropout appearing in the literature (see Beyebach, 1993). We consider dropping out (or premature termination) to be an interruption of treatment that occurs unilaterally on the part of the client without agreement by or the knowledge of the treating therapist. Dropout may occur because the client refuses to agree to another interview (despite the counsel of the therapist), because the client fails to attend an appointment (and does not ask for another), or because the client cancels a session and does not set up another one. We further define dropout to be "early" if it occurs after the first, second, or third session.

First, all of the cases with individual format in which dropout did not occur were identified. Sixteen cases were then chosen from the total number by carefully controlling a series of variables to guarantee that they were comparable to the dropout group in dimensions germane to the study. Regarding the therapists, the variables controlled were therapist's gender (male/female) and professional experience (experts/trainees). To control for possible differences in the personal styles of the therapists, each dropout case was matched with a non-dropout case treated by the same therapist. This presented no difficulty in therapies carried out by some of the expert therapists (ten of the sixteen cases). For the cases conducted by trainee therapists (five of the sixteen dropout cases), however, it was necessary to match dropout cases with those of another trainee therapist of the same gender. Finally, the gender of the client and the interview number (first, second, or third session) were also controlled.

The final sample contained thirty-two interviews, sixteen for the dropout group and sixteen for the continuation group. Owing to the design of the study, the dropout and continuation groups did not differ in the gender or experience of the therapists, the gender of the clients, or the number of the interviews analyzed. Additionally, there were no significant differences between the two groups in the age, occupation, or marital status of the subjects. Neither were there significant differences in the type of presenting problem or the basic ineffective attempted solutions (Fisch et al., 1982).

With respect to the clients' perceptions of their problems, the replies to a questionnaire administered before the first interview took place (Pérez Grande, 1991) likewise indicated no significant differences between the dropout and continuation groups regarding either the perceived severity of the problem (mean dropout = 3.61; mean continuation = 3.79; $t = .44$; $p = .67$) or its urgency (mean dropout = 4.38; mean continuation = 4.36; $t = .07$; $p = .945$). Furthermore, there were no significant differences between the groups in the number of clients who had been in therapy previously for the same problem. Logically, there were statistically significant differences between the two groups regarding the length of therapy as measured by the number of sessions received. In dropout cases, clients attended a mean of 1.7 sessions while clients in the continuation group attended a mean of 5.6 interviews ($t = 7.44$; $p < .0001$).

The Measures. We used Heatherington and Friedlander's (1987) F-RCCCS version of the RCCCS. Sufficient data exist concerning the reliability and validity of the R-CCCS and the F-RCCCS for therapy situations (Friedlander, Wildman,

& Heatherington, 1991; Gaul, Simon, Friedlander, Cutler, Heatherington, 1991; Heatherington, 1988).

Using the F-RCCCS involves three steps. The first consists of coding each intervention of the speakers (that is, each speaking turn). Each turn is assigned a three-digit code, based on speaker, format, and response mode. The first digit corresponds to the speaker (1 = therapist, 2 = client), while the second represents the grammatical format (1 = assertion, 2 = open answer, 3 = successful talkover, 4 = unsuccessful talkover, 5 = incomplete, 6 = closed question). The third digit corresponds to the response mode and refers to the pragmatic function of the speaking turn in relation to the immediately preceding one (1 = support, 2 = no support, 3 = extension, 4 = answer to open question, 5 = instruction, 6 = order, 7 = disconfirmation, 8 = topic change, 9 = answer to closed question). Thus, for example, code 123 indicates that the therapist asked an open question by which the previous speaking turn of the client was extended. On the other hand, a code of 232 indicates that the client overlapped successfully, expressing disapproval of the speaking turn of the therapist.

Once independent judges have coded each message, a set of rules are used to transform the three-digit codes into what are called "control codes." Each combination receives one of three possible control codes: (1) one-up messages (or domineering moves), which indicate a movement toward dominance in the exchange (such as questions that demand a specific answer, orders or taking the floor by overlapping); (2) one-down messages (or submissive moves) which suggest movement toward being controlled by seeking or accepting dominance of other (such as questions that seek a supportive response, or obeying an order); and (3) one-across messages (or neutralizing moves), which are characterized by a lack of movement toward control or being controlled and which have a leveling effect (such as statements of continuance, filler phrases, and noncommital responses to questions).[2]

While sounding complicated, the transformation of the three-digit combinations into directions of control is mechanical. Thus, for example, a code of 116 (or 216)—that is, an order in assertion form—always receives a "one-up" control direction. A 121 (or 221) code—that is, a message of support in question form—will always be a "one-down." An example of a "one-across" message would be a 113 code (an assertion that extends the previous message).

The third step in the use of the F-RCCCS involves passing from the monadic to the diadic level, since using the instrument creates diadic categories of control, formed by each transaction or exchange of two interventions. This is the level of analysis on which the classic constructs of symmetry and complementarity (Watzlawick et al., 1967) were described. However, the combination of *three* control directions (instead of the two initially foreseen by Watzlawick and his colleagues) permits the analysis to go beyond the traditional dichotomy and obtain a total of up to nine combinations (see Table 13.1): three symmetrical transactions, two complementary transactions, and four transitional transactions.

Table 13.2 shows an example of coded interaction, including all the coding steps.

The Treatment. The therapeutic approach used in this sample is an integration of the brief therapy models developed at the Palo Alto Mental Research Institute in Palo Alto, California (Fisch et al., 1982), and at the Brief Family Therapy Center in Milwaukee, Wisconsin (Berg & Miller, 1992; de Shazer, 1982, 1985, 1988, 1991). Basically, the approach can be described as brief therapy that focuses both on solutions and on the complaint pattern. The treatment provided during our research was not yet as purely solution-focused as our later work has become (Beyebach, 1995).

The Procedure. First, interview transcription was carried out by the first author according to the guidelines proposed by Rogers (1979). While time consuming, it does not require any kind of inference by the transcriptionist.

Then, two judges were trained to code the transcribed material with the F-RCCCS. This training was carried out according to the coding manual developed by Heatherington and Friedlander (1987) until an acceptable inter-rater reliability (Cohen's k) was achieved (Cohen, 1960). Each coder went on to code all thirty-two interviews included in the sample. The coders were blind to the hypothesis of the study. The fact that *each* session was coded by the two researchers permitted us to monitor inter-rater reliability throughout the process, ensuring that the k levels persisted at acceptable values throughout (in the case of the sample, at all times above k = .66, with a mean k of .71).

The Results

To compare the relative frequencies of the types of message and the types of transaction, the Z statistic for the contrast of proportions in two independent samples was used (Martín Tabernero et al., 1985). Table 13.3 summarizes the results obtained. (An operational description of each of the hypotheses and a more detailed report of the results obtained can be found in Beyebach, 1993.)

With respect to the analyses carried out on a monadic level for whole interviews, without distinguishing phases, the results conformed to what had been hypothesized. A significantly lower percentage of interventions were coded as support in the dropout group than in the continuation group, as well as a significantly higher percentage of nonsupport and successful talkovers. On analyzing the therapist and client data separately, it was found that for nonsupports and

TABLE 13.1. TYPES OF TRANSACTION FROM THE COMBINATION OF THE CONTROL DIRECTIONS OF TWO CONSECUTIVE MESSAGES.

Speaker 1 Control Code		Speaker 2 Control Code	
One-up	One-up Up-up Competitive symmetry	One-down Up-down Complementarity	One-across Up-across Transitory
One-down	Down-up Complementarity	Down-down Submissive symmetry	Down-across Transitory
One-across	Across-up Transitory	Across-down Transitory	Across-across Neutralized symmetry

successful talkovers the differences between both groups were due to the clients. By contrast, both the therapist and the client contributed to the difference in the proportion of support.

The hypotheses regarding the diadic level of analysis were also verified for whole interviews. In the interviews of the dropout group, a significantly higher percentage of competitive symmetry transactions (one-up/one-up) and of conflict triads (one-up/one-up/one-up) was seen than in the continuation group. The percentage of one-across/one-down transactions (neutralized symmetry) was significantly lower in the dropout group than in the continuation cases.

Analyzing by phase, the expected results were obtained for the information gathering phase of the interview. From the monadic point of view, we found that in the dropout group there were a significantly lower percentage of therapist questions and client replies than in the continuation group. There was also a significantly higher percentage of one-up maneuvers (on the part of both the therapist and the client) and a lower percentage of one-down moves (again, for both therapist and client) in the dropout group.

The hypothesis of expected differences in the proportion of domineering behavior (one-up) of the client (ab = .20; cont = .14; p< .00001) was also verified. At the diadic level, there was a significantly higher percentage of complementarity (accounted for by the question/answer exchanges) in the dropout group than in the continuation group. The hypotheses for the intervention phase were not verified, however. For example, there was *not* a lower proportion of complementary transactions in the dropout cases than in the cases of the continuation group, and the percentage of clients' one-ups was also not significantly higher during this phase of the interview.

TABLE 13.2. EXAMPLE OF CODED INTERACTON: THREE-DIGIT CODE, CONTROL DIRECTION AND TYPE OF TRANSACTION.

Dialogue	Message	Control Code	Transaction Direction
Therapist: What's better since we last met?	123	Across	
Client: My husband doesn't like therapy, you know; he is definitely not coming.	217	Up	Transition across/up
Therapist: Well, that's not really what I have asked you.	118	Up	Competitive symmetry
Client: Yes, you are right. I am sorry.	211	Down	Complementarity
Therapist: Never mind. I am sorry, I should not have interrupted you. So, he is not coming.	111	Down	Submissive symmetry
Client: Well, I guess for him there is no point in talking about these things.	213	Across	Transition down/across

In addition to verifying our hypotheses and predictions, some complementary, exploratory analyses were performed that we will only sketch here. First, we divided the dropout group into two subgroups, "successful dropout" (those cases in which the interrupted therapy had been successful and the client-therapist relationship was judged as "good" by both the client and therapist) and "unsuccessful dropout" (those cases in which the interrupted therapy had not been successful and the client-therapist relationship was judged as "bad" by the client). This categorization was done by an independent judge, combining (1) an analysis of the taped interviews, (2) the answers to a questionnaire completed by the clients before the first session, and (3) clients' answers to a semistructured questionnaire conducted during telephone follow-up.

Our hypotheses were tested on these subsamples separately. Although we expected that the hypotheses would hold for the unsuccessful dropout subgroup only, it turned out that both groups showed the same basic pattern of findings. In other words, the interactional nature of interviews followed by dropout (as opposed to interviews followed by continuation) seems to hold for different "types" of dropout, irrespective of their final therapeutic outcome or the subjective experience of the interactors.

Second, we carried out a series of markovian and sequential lag analyses (Gottman & Roy, 1990). After verifying that our sampled interaction showed markovian first-order dependency, we were able to select a homogeneous subsample

TABLE 13.3. VERIFICATION OF HYPOTHESES
FOR THE TOTAL SAMPLE.

		Dropout	Continuation	
Hypothesis 1.1 (Whole Sessions)				
Support (dyad)	DR<CO	.24	.29	p<.01
Nonsupport (dyad)	DR>CO	.0194	.0145	p<.01
Successful talkover				
(dyad)	DR>CO	.12	.10	p<.01
Hypothesis 1.3 (Information Gathering)				
Question (therapist)	DR<CO	.21	.18	p<.001
Answer (client)	DR>CO	.16	.12	p<.0001
One-down therapist	DR<CO	.24	.26	p<.05
One-up therapist	DR>CO	.25	.23	p<.05
One-down client	DR<CO	.35	.39	p<.01
One-up client	DR>CO	.20	.14	p<.0001
Hypothesis 1.5 (Intervention)				
One-down client	DR<CO	.44	.49	p<.05
One-up client	DR>CO	.19	.16	n.s.
Hypothesis 1.2 (Whole Session)				
One-up/one-up	DR>CO	.053	.037	p<.01
One-across/one-down	DR<CO	.22	.26	p<.01
Conflict pattern	DR>CO	.013	.008	p<.01
Hypothesis 1.4 (Information Gathering)				
Complementarity	DR>CO	.18	.15	.01
Hypothesis 1.6 (Intervention)				
Complementarity	DR<CO	.23	.25	n.s.

Note: DR refers to the dropout group, CO to the continuation group; n.s. = not significant.

on which to perform sequential lag analysis. This analysis showed that the pragmatic effect of the interactors' messages was the same for both dropout and continuation cases. In other words, one-across messages tended to elicit more one-across messages, while one-up and one-down messages tended to inhibit one-across messages and instead elicit one-down or one-up messages.

Discussion

For the group of sixteen interviews after which clients dropped out, fourteen of the sixteen, or the majority of, hypotheses were fulfilled. Though the differences were in the predicted direction, they are in no case spectacular. Rather, they are a series of modest, although consistent, differences that provide a certain picture of how the interaction unfolded.

The differences between the dropout group and the continuation group seem to be mainly related to the information-gathering phase. Consistent with previous findings (Beyebach et al., 1990), the data show that the "question/answer pattern" occurred with greater frequency in those interviews after which the client dropped out of treatment than in those after which the client continued in therapy. This form of interaction has also been described by Heatherington and Allen (1984), who note that "the cross-fire of questions and answers" is a type of exchange that produces a feeling of discomfort and competition between the participants. Additionally, in the interviews after which dropout took place, the client interrupted the therapist with much greater frequency (almost double), disapproved more, and gave and received less support than in the interviews of the continuation group. Essentially, the clients in the dropout group were more domineering and insistent on assuming a superior position in the communicative exchange than those in the continuation group.

From the point of view of relational control, the data suggest that therapists from the dropout group do not handle the domineering behavior of their clients adequately and have a difficult time not entering into opposition. Thus, the interviews of the dropout group show a lower proportion of transition patterns with one-down (which would indicate an easily flowing exchange and mutual support), a greater incidence of competitive symmetry, and a higher frequency of the "conflict triad" as described by Millar, Rogers and Beavin (1984). Given this result, it may be inferred that the therapist-client interaction occurring in the sessions preceding dropout has special characteristics—in particular, that the interactions are less harmonious and more conflictual than those after which treatment is continued.

Clinical Implications

Several limitations of the present study should be taken into account when interpreting these findings. First, the sample of the present study is small. In addition, all of the data included in the study were collected at a single site. It should also be remembered that the correlational design of the study and the types of analyses conducted therein never establish *causal relationships* between the independent and dependent variables under study. We cannot say, for example, that the question-answer pattern or the greater presence of conflict triads *cause* subjects to drop out from therapy, since it is possible that some third variable might be responsible for both the type of relational communication patterns observed and continuation in or dropout from therapy.

Bearing these cautions in mind, some inferences can be drawn from the data for the practice of brief therapy sessions:

1. *The question-answer pattern.* The data from this study indicate that an increase in the question/answer pattern is associated with clients dropping out of therapy prematurely. This suggests that therapists would do well to go about obtaining information without provoking the question-answer type of exchange. Of course, this does not mean that an increase in the question/answer pattern is not

the result of a client behaving in a taciturn and uncommunicative way, but rather that it is the job of the therapist to react in such a way that such situations are channeled into more effective interactional patterns regardless of how they might begin. In other words, these data suggest that it is precisely when dealing with uncommunicative clients that therapists should use some technique to prevent the interview from turning into a sterile interrogation. This may occur both through a reduction in the number of questions the therapist asks (for instance, by replacing them with other methods of soliciting information) or by the therapist engaging in some other conversational practices. For example, the data from the sequential analysis indicate that leveling messages (one-across) inhibit one-down and one-up messages (among which questions and answers are included). In fact, the emission of one-across messages elicited leveling sequences in the present study, sequences which different studies have identified as adaptive patterns of communication (Beyebach et al., 1990; Bailín, 1995; Rogers and Bagarozzi, 1983).

Among the types of messages that receive a one-across code and foster the generation of information are conversational skills usually associated with active listening (such as summarizing what the client has said, paraphrasing, extending the contents of the previous message, and so on). Another option is to promote a one-across/one-down conversation pattern (or the inverse), the greater presence of which was associated in the study with continuation in therapy. That is, once the client provides information ("one-across" extensions), use of what Hill (1985) calls minimal stimuli ("Very good," "I see," "I understand," and so forth) to continue extending the topic of conversation. In our opinion, work on stimulus-response congruence (Duehn & Proctor, 1977) supports the positive effect that this type of conversational maneuver has on both satisfaction with the therapeutic relationship and the amount of verbal interaction.

2. *The breakdown of fit: competitive symmetry and conflict triad.* Two other interactional patterns that occurred significantly more often in the dropout than in the continuation group were competitive symmetry and the conflict triad. Our data provide certain tentative ideas about how therapists can avoid these patterns. First, therapists can emit submissive messages when they experience situations of competitive symmetry. This implies introducing complementarity into the symmetry (Watzlawick et al., 1967). Second, as suggested earlier, therapists could meet competitive symmetry with the across-down pattern. This type of transaction seems to be a good way of preventing not only the appearance of sequences of competitive symmetry but also symmetric escalation.

3. *The importance of leveling maneuvers.* The previous two sections point to the possible usefulness of "one-across" maneuvers as ways both to modify the question/answer pattern and to avoid symmetric escalation with clients. In fact, it can

be suggested that these behaviors might be more useful in therapy than excessive agreement with clients, since previous studies carried out by our team suggest that the "submissive hook" (a predominance of one-down/one-down interactions) is associated with both relapse and with vague reports about compliance with homework assignments (Altuna et al., 1988; Bailín, 1995). We believe that these findings about one-across messages point to the importance of what is seemingly secondary in the psychotherapeutic process: neutral comments, "nonevents," or "nontherapy." The data indicate that sometimes what is important in therapy is precisely what tends to be overlooked—that is, the moments in which the therapist does not attempt to dominate or allow him/herself to be dominated, when no attempts are made to introduce change and no preset technique is used. In other words, what Frank (1985) and others have referred to as the "nonspecific" factors involved in the therapeutic relationship.

4. *"Listening" to the therapeutic relationship.* One of the clearest implications to emerge from the results is that therapists (and/or their teams) can use the relational control constructs to evaluate the state of the therapeutic relationship. Indeed, using the relational control constructs of symmetry, complementarity, and transition to describe the actual therapeutic conversation with clients would not only assist therapists to listen to the *content* of therapeutic conversation but also to "listen" to the *process* of that conversation (de Shazer, 1994). This in turn would enhance therapists' ability to reach a communicational "fit" with their clients (de Shazer, 1988).

Research on Cognitive Variables in Brief Systemic Therapy

Another line of research our team has pursued involves the cognitive reading of some elements of solution-focused therapy (Rodríguez Morejón, Palenzuela, & Beyebach, in press). Discussion of some theoretical background and research results follows.

Theoretical Background

We believe that an increasing amount of attention is being paid in the field of solution-focused therapy and brief therapy in general to the role of what in the classic terminology would be described as "cognitive factors" (Zeig & Gilligan, 1990; Gilligan & Price, 1993). Two important epistemological developments have likely been responsible for the increased interest in the study of cognitions (meanings, beliefs, and worldviews).

One development is the introduction of constructivism and social construction theory, both of which cast doubt on the conception of reality as something objective, unchanging, and independent of the knowing subject (Segal, 1986; Watzlawick, 1984). Within these views, reality is considered something that is created by the subject (constructivism) and meaning is considered a result of social interaction (constructionism). In therapy, such views mean that clients' meanings and beliefs gain ascendancy over therapists'. Logically, therefore, the deconstruction of those meanings and beliefs may be helpful in facilitating the generation of solutions (de Shazer, 1994).

The second development is the use of the narrative metaphor for understanding the therapeutic process (de Shazer, 1991, 1994; Sluzki, 1992; White & Epston, 1989; White, 1995). According to this approach, the material one works with in therapy can be understood as narratives—that is, stories by which people organize their construction of reality and give it coherence. Narratives can be seen as having dual functions. First, they affect the interpretation of new experiences. Second, they affect the future, since they shape people's goals and expectations, and eventually, the way people interact (Markus & Cross, 1990). By changing certain aspects of clients' stories, or the relationship between the various stories, it is possible to modify the way they construct reality, view the future, and ultimately, how they act. As researchers and brief therapists, we are therefore inclined towards a dialogical interpretation of narratives—that is, towards underlining *how* these narratives are created and modified in the course of social interaction (de Shazer, 1994; Sluzki, 1992).

Constructivism, social constructionism, and the narrative metaphor have led brief therapists to consider beliefs and meanings in addition to observable interactions. The interest in cognitive constructs is not new to brief therapy, nor to the related field of systems/family therapy. Indeed, as far back as 1983, Sluzki included cognitive concepts such as "worldviews" in the general systems paradigm and its different applications. Moreover, most therapeutic models, both of family therapy and brief therapy, refer to the importance of clients' worldviews— as something to be either modified or utilized in the process of change (Fisch et al., 1982).

This aspect has received scant scientific attention, however, within the brief therapy tradition. One possible reason for this lack of attention is that the word "cognitive" may seem synonymous with the term "intrapsychic," which for many years has been excluded from the vocabulary of brief therapy. We believe, however, that there is another way of understanding the "cognitive" and the "intrapsychic," which can indeed fit with the assumptions of brief therapy. This view of the cognitive allows us to take advantage of an enormous body of traditional cognitive research and give it meaning within a dialogical or constructionist conception of therapeutic interaction. The following pages are dedicated to outlining this conception.

Understanding Cognitions

Traditional theories frequently attempt to describe what is human on the basis of a series of internal, stable, and difficult-to-modify dispositions. Such models of human behavior are frequently unable, however, to account for the flexibility and creativity with which people adapt themselves to their environment (Mischel, 1968, 1973). For this reason, theorists began to search for more-dynamic models, units that would overcome the structural conception of reality inherent in traditional theories (Cervone, 1991).

Sociocognitive (Mischel, 1973), or cognitive-propositive units (Palenzuela and Barros, 1993; Palenzuela and Rodríguez Morejón, 1993) are two such dynamic concepts that have come to the forefront. The dynamic and fluid nature of these concepts overcome the static view of most traditional theories; they portray personality as a dynamic system in which people can be described as active, propositive agents who interact in a real and figurative sense with others and the environment and who make free and responsible decisions. These cognitive approaches make it clear that in order to understand people's behavior it is not enough to know what people "have"; one must also know what they can do and in fact do to self-regulate their behavior (Cervone, 1991). It is precisely this type of language—the language of action-oriented cognitions—that we assume and that we shall use to reflect on the intrapersonal dimension of brief systemic therapy.

A review of the cognitive-propositive literature (Rodríguez Morejón, 1994) shows that there are three well-validated variables for understanding human behavior: (1) attributions, (2) goals, and (3) expectancies. To these three variables we add a fourth: action. The relationships among the four variables can be viewed as a system (see Figure 13.1) such that any change in one may lead to modifications in the others.

The studies we address in the following paragraphs focus primarily on one of the four variables, that of *expectancies*. Expectancy can be conceived of as a multidimensional construct (Palenzuela, 1988a, 1988b, 1990, 1993; Palenzuela, Almeida, Prieto, & Barros, 1992) that includes three dimensions: (1) self-efficacy (Bandura, 1989), (2) locus of control (Rotter, 1966), and (3) success expectancies (Rotter, 1954). Self-efficacy expectancies are the estimations that a person makes about his or her abilities to put into operation a given action. Locus of control refers to beliefs of contingency-noncontingency between behavior and outcomes. Success expectancies refer to the estimated probabilities that the desired outcome will come into being.

As a way of illustrating these ideas, consider, for example, that the outcome desired by someone is that his or her problem be solved and that this person asks himself or herself about the possibilities of achieving such a solution. In this case,

FIGURE 13.1. A MODEL OF COGNITIVE SUBSYSTEMS AND THEIR RELATIONSHIPS.

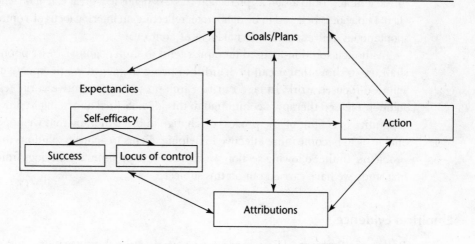

the success expectancy would be reflected in the question: What possibilities are there that my problem will be solved? Conversely, self-efficacy expectancies would be reflected in the question: Do I really feel able to solve the problem? Finally, expectancies of internal-external locus of control would appear as: To what extent is solving this problem related to what I do? A person would have an internal locus of control if they were strongly convinced that the outcomes they desire are dependent upon their actual behavior. In contrast, a person would have an external locus of control if they did not understand that the outcome might be linked to his or her own behavior.

Logically, formulating one or the other type of question and the responses given to it will largely depend on how such questions and answers interact with each other. Thus, from a narrative point of view, this process could be described as one of interacting stories, which to a certain extent shape social interaction but which are also shaped by it. From this perspective, locus of control, self-efficacy, or success expectancies might be seen as relevant "themes" of co-created narratives.

The therapy situation is one setting in which the development of such narratives takes place. In solution-focused therapy, a large part of the conversation can be described as revolving around issues of self-efficacy and locus of control—for example, questions such as "How did you do that?" and "What can you do to get up to six on the scale?" In addition, solution-focused conversation directed toward future achievements and goals can also be seen as emphasizing success expectancies. Consider, for example, the question, "How will that change when the problem is solved?" These expectancies are also an important part of the therapeutic decision-making process in solution-focused work. For example, the decision to tell clients to "do it more," or to assign a "prediction" task, depends to a great extent on whether client behavior is believed to be deliberate (reflecting an internal locus of control) or spontaneous (reflecting an external locus of control).

Although solution-focused therapists tend to shun cognitive descriptions, we shall try to show that it can be fruitful to bring the cognitive perspective into solution-focused work. In fact, our research project on cognitive variables and solution-focused therapy is committed to this idea, its final aim being to provide a "cognitive" account of the process of change in brief therapy that we hope will enable us to become more effective in helping clients to achieve solutions to their problems. In the following section we report some preliminary findings from the first study we have carried out on this subject.

Empirical Evidence

Posing the Problem. The empirical study we describe shortly explored two questions. The first question concerned the relationship between control expectancies and different clinical variables derived from solution-focused therapy (which henceforth will be referred to as solution-focused clinical variables). The second question addressed the predictive capacity of both control expectancies and solution-focused clinical variables for therapeutic outcome.

Solution-focused therapists use a variety of terms to describe their work. For example, clients are referred to as "customers" when they request from the therapist concrete suggestions for solving their problem. "Pretreatment change" is said to have occurred when families report improvements that have taken place before formal therapy has started. Special emphasis is also placed on "well-formed goals" and whether or not clients have complied with homework assignments.

As solution-focused therapists, we are also aware, however, that "customer" does not refer to an internal characteristic of a particular client's personality but rather is a label that the therapist uses to define the interactional pattern manifested during the session. This interactional perspective makes it clear that the therapist plays a decisive role in the creation of one or another type of pattern. Obviously, the skill of the therapist in establishing a therapeutic alliance will affect the style of the relationship that is established. Likewise, we could say that the appearance of pretreatment change will partly depend on the therapist's asking about such changes at the beginning of therapy, or that the achievement of clear goals will be strongly linked to the conversation developed around, for instance, the "miracle question."

We believe that the decision of the therapist to use a particular solution-focused technique depends on his or her evaluation of the expectancies inherent in the therapeutic interaction. Accordingly, we believe that it is useful to describe these techniques (client-therapist relationship type, pretreatment change, goals, and compliance with task) operationally and to relate them to control expectancies (self-efficacy, locus of control, and success expectancy).

The second aim of our research project was to test whether the client's expectancies are related to outcome of treatment. Empirical evidence suggests that clients who start therapy feeling more efficacious and in control achieve better therapeutic results (Abramowitz, Abramowitz, Roback, & Jackson, 1974; Breteler, Mertens, & Rombouts, 1990; Craig & Andrews, 1985; Foon, 1987; Scharamski, Beutler, Lauver, Arizmendi, & Shanfield, 1984; Weisz, 1986). However, all of these studies have been conducted in the domain of cognitive and behavioral therapy. For this reason, we wanted to see if the same results were true for solution-focused therapy.

Method. *Sample.* The sample used in this study was comprised of thirty-nine subjects (twenty-one females and eighteen males) who received brief therapy at a public mental health agency. The average age of the subjects was twenty-six years old (DT = 10.6) with the youngest being twelve and the oldest client being fifty-five years of age. Fifty-four percent of the subjects were unmarried, 41 percent were married, and 5 percent were divorced. Forty-eight percent of the treatments were conducted individually, 13 percent were with couples, and 39 percent were family sessions. The sample included ten subjects with diagnoses (according to the DSM III, American Psychiatric Association, 1987, used for research purposes only) of affective disorders, ten with anxiety disorders, three with somatoform disorders, eight with adaptive disorders, four with behavior disorders, three with eating disorders, and one with an education disorder.

The sample was extracted from among the total population of clients who sought care and were seen by the therapist at the center between 1992 and 1993. In a previous study of this population, 10 percent of the clients dropped out after the first session and 80 percent of those who continued beyond the first session were rated (by independent judges) as successful cases at termination (Fontecilla, Ramos, and Rodríguez-Arias, 1993). The average number of sessions was five and the average length of each session was thirty-three minutes.

Measures. Control expectancies were measured at two different levels of specificity/generality using two different instruments (Rodríguez Morejón, 1994). The Generalized Expectancies of Control Scale (GECS), a shortened version of Palenzuela's (1990) Generalized Expectancies of Control Scale, is composed of nine items, three for each of the three expectancy dimensions. As indicated by its name, this scale measures expectancies at a maximum degree of generality. Examples of the items include: "In general I feel very capable" (self-efficacy), "How my life will go depends on how I act" (locus of control), and "I am convinced that I will be successful in life" (success expectancies).

The second instrument used in the study was the Specific Expectancies of Control for Problem Solving Scale (SEC-PS). This scale also contains nine items with the same distribution as the previous instrument. As the name implies, this instrument is useful for assessing the expectancies of the subjects concerning the solution of the concrete problem that initially led them to seek therapy. Some examples of the items are: "I feel able to confront this difficulty" (self-efficacy), "That I will be able to overcome this problem is closely linked to what I do" (locus of control), and "I believe that in the end this problem will be solved" (success expectancy). Both scales have been subjected to rigorous analyses in both clinical and nonclinical samples and have proved to have satisfactory psychometric properties (Palenzuela, 1990; Rodríguez Morejón, 1994).

The solution-focused variables under consideration in this study were categorized by the therapist in charge of the cases using standardized procedures. For example, the therapist categorized the relationship with the client as being a "customer-type relationship" when the client answered the question, "To get what you want, would you be willing to do anything I ask you to do?" affirmatively and unhesitatingly. This question was asked of the client immediately preceding the break prior to the first session intervention. Similarly, the therapist assessed pretreatment change by asking the client, "From the time when people ask for consultation to when we can see them, some time usually elapses. Many people tell me that during that time things have gotten better. What have you noticed?" The therapist considered that the client's goals for therapy were "well-formed" when the client was able to state at least one behavioral sign of future improvements; if not, the goals were deemed vague. Assessment of compliance with homework assignments was made in the second session based on client report.

A panel of independent judges blind to the hypotheses of the study were used to assess treatment outcome. These judges listened to audiotapes of the first and last sessions of treatment and assigned the subject to the success group when there was behavioral evidence of change (the client spoke of his or her complaint in the past tense or indicated that she or he had reached most of the goals set), or when both the client and therapist talked favorably about the complaint and agreed that no further therapy was necessary.

Treatment. Treatment was delivered by the same therapist for the entire sample. The type of therapy can be described as basically solution-focused with an emphasis on pretreatment change, exceptions to the problem, and the negotiation of well-formed goals. On occasion, the therapist utilized more problem-focused interventions such as introducing small changes in the pattern of the complaint (see, for example, O'Hanlon & Weiner-Davis, 1989) or even trying to change the basic ineffective attempted solutions of the client (Fisch et al., 1982).

Procedure. Baseline measures were taken of the three control expectancies before treatment was initiated. With the exception of assessing compliance with the homework task, all of the solution-focused variables were assessed by the therapist on the break preceding the intervention of the first interview. Treatment outcome was evaluated after the termination of therapy.

Results and Discussion. The correlations between control expectancies (specific and generalized) measured before treatment and the clinical variables are shown in Table 13.4. We found the following significant relationships: (1) pretreatment changes showed a significant, positive correlation with generalized locus of control and self-efficacy; and (2) compliance with homework assignments after the first session was significantly and positively correlated with generalized locus of control. Regarding specific expectancies, there were also some significant, positive correlations: (1) specific expectancies correlated with customer-type relationship and with well-formed goals; and (2) specific success expectancies also correlated with the customer-type relationship. Figure 13.2 offers a graphic plot of the relationships.

Relationship type. The clients who in the judgment of the therapist established a customer-type relationship showed stronger expectancies that their problem would be solved than those who did not, no differences in other cognitive variables being observed. This is an interesting finding since, based on solution-focused theory, we had originally expected that this clinical variable would be related above all to locus of control. The reader will recall that "customers" have traditionally been viewed as those clients who see themselves as part of the solution and who want to do something about the complaint (de Shazer, 1988). In the light of these findings, however, it seems more important to measure clients' expectancies that the problem will be solved than their overall willingness to do something about their problem.

A possible explanation for this finding might be the operation of a third, mediating variable—for example, the client's trust in the therapist. It is possible that our method of evaluating the type of client-therapist relationship contained the implicit question, "How much do you trust me?" Conversely, it seems logical to assume that, to the extent that clients trust the therapist to help them solve their problems, clients' expectancies that the problem will indeed eventually be solved should increase.

Pretreatment change. In the study, subjects who reported improvement prior to the formal initiation of treatment showed a greater generalized internal locus of control and, moreover, a greater generalized sense of self-efficacy. These findings can be interpreted in two ways: (1) subjects scored higher in self-efficacy and showed a more internal locus of control because they had already started to

TABLE 13.4. CORRELATIONS BETWEEN COGNITIVE VARIABLES AND CLINICAL SOLUTION-FOCUSED VARIABLES.

	Customer (N=35)	Pretreatment Change (N=39)	Goals (N=35)	Task Compliance (N=39)
Generalized expectancies				
Global index	.09	.44**	.29	.03
Self-efficacy	−.07	.33*	.19	.08
Locus of control	.20	.53***	.30	.32*
Success expectancies	.08	.23	.21	.12
Specific expectancies				
Global index	.36*	.25	.35*	.21
Self-efficacy	.32	.10	.24	.26
Locus of control	.06	.278	.31	.26
Success expectancies	.36*	.26	.31	.03

*p<.05

**p<.01

***p.001

Note: For all solution-focused variables there are two categories. For "customer" and "pretreatment change" there are "yes/no"; goals can be clear or vague; and compliance with tasks can be literal or not. In any case, the first element is 0 (no, no, vague, not literal) and the second element is 1. Biserial Puntal** correlation was used. "Global index" is the summatory of the three expectancy variables.

Source: Rodríguez Morejón, A., Palenzuela, D. L., & Beyebach, M. (1996). Copyright 1996 by Editorial Fundamentos. Used with permission.

experience improvements, or (2) subjects began to improve without the help of the therapist precisely because they felt more capable and because they believed that what happens to them depends on their own behavior.

We are inclined to believe the second interpretation—that is, that clients who believe they are more capable and who anticipate contingency between their behavior and the desired outcome are more likely to experience and report pretreatment change. The reasoning on which we base our belief is that if increases in the two types of expectancy were a consequence of pretreatment change, then the increases should be more apparent in the specific rather than the generalized expectancies. Recall that generalized expectancies are by definition more global and stable (Rotter, 1990) whereas specific expectancies are more specific and modifiable (Bandura, 1989). Our research has established, however, that quite the opposite is true.

Additionally, pretreatment change is a phenomenon that is constructed in the conversation that occurs during the session. As such, pretreatment change only

FIGURE 13.2. BISERIAL PUNTAL CORRELATIONS BETWEEN CONTROL EXPECTANCIES AND CLINICAL VARIABLES.

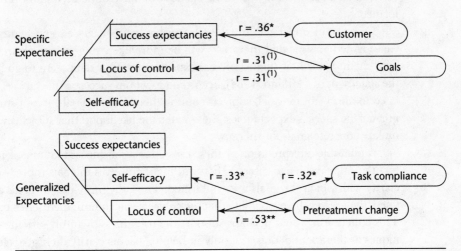

Note: [1]p<.06; *p<.05; **<.01.

Source: Rodríguez Morejón, A., Palenzuela, D. L., & Beyebach, M. (1996). Copyright 1996 by Editorial Fundamentos. Used with permission.

begins to be relevant to the client after talking about it with the therapist. Since on most occasions pretreatment change is not considered relevant by the client before therapy has begun, it is hard to conceive that it would be responsible for the increase detected in generalized expectancies. For these reasons, the most parsimonious interpretation of the data is that people who *a priori* tend to describe themselves as capable (high generalized self-efficacy) and as being able to affect outcome through their behavior (internal locus of control) are more likely to engage in effective solution attempts that when discussed with the therapist during the session are then construed as pretreatment change.

Goals. The research also found that well-formed goals were related to specific control expectancies. In particular, subjects who in first sessions were able to establish concrete goals tended to have higher scores on specific locus of control and on specific success expectancies. Negotiating well-formed goals should be thought of as a process that occurs when clients feel that solving their problems will depend on themselves, and when clients have high hopes that their problems will be solved.

The relationship between locus of control and well-formed goals can be interpreted in two ways: (1) having well-formed goals makes people feel that achieving their goals will depend on themselves, or (2) the more responsible people feel for future changes, the more well-formed their goals will be. In this case, we do not find any advantage in favoring one position over the other. The practical outcome is that it might be helpful to use therapeutic techniques that promote a more internal locus of control with those clients who have difficulty establishing well-formed goals.

One way of understanding the relationship between success expectancies and well-formed goals is that therapists will be more likely to generate clearer goals with clients who show higher success expectancies. Our data seem to go beyond the statement of Garland (1984), according to whom success expectancies are related to the extent to which subjects commit themselves to goals. In our study, the greater the success expectancies, the greater the likelihood that subjects will formulate concrete goals for therapy.

A plausible interpretation of these crossed relationships is that one of the factors that may influence subjects' committing themselves to goals is precisely the clarity with which the goals are established. Thus, the more clearly goals are defined, the greater the probability that the subjects will commit themselves to them. This conclusion would perhaps support the usefulness of future-oriented techniques as therapeutic tools, not only in helping clients clarify their goals for psychotherapy but also in promoting commitment to achieving those goals.

Compliance with tasks. Finally, the results of this study show that people who fulfilled homework assignments tended to have an internal locus of control. These findings seem to contradict the work of Foon (1989), since in our study it was precisely those subjects who believed that outcome depends on their own behavior who complied with the prescriptions of the therapist. We believe, however, that no such contradiction exists. The results of the present study can be interpreted in two different ways: (1) that subjects with an internal locus of control feel that outcome depends on what they do, or (2) that subjects with an internal locus of control allow the therapist to decide what they have to do to begin the change process. Whatever the reason, the important finding is that clients with an internal locus of control believe that *they* must "act"—even if guided by the therapist.

In summary, the study showed that clients who establish a customer-type relationship are those who trust the therapist most and whose success expectancies are therefore higher. In addition, the study found that clients who score highest on internal locus of control and self-efficacy tend to show improvements before therapy as compared with those scoring lower. Also, those clients who establish clear goals are those with higher success expectancies with respect to the problem and with established beliefs that the solution to the problem depends on their own behavior. Finally, the study found that subjects who comply with homework assignments have a higher internal locus of control.

Predictors of Therapeutic Outcome

To determine whether any of the three measures of expectancy were related to treatment outcome, a logistic regression with treatment outcome (success/no success) as the dependent variable and the initial generalized measurements of self-efficacy, locus of control, and success expectancies as independent variables was conducted.

Only one of the three variables, locus of control, was significantly related to treatment outcome (R = .276, p < .01). In this regard, subjects with an internal generalized locus of control were three times more likely to have a successful treatment outcome. Locus of control continued to predict outcome even when the effects of other cognitive variables (self-efficacy and success expectancies), sociodemographic variables (age, gender), and clinical variables (customer-type relationship, type of goals, compliance with homework assignments, and treatment format) were controlled. Only pretreatment change seemed to decrease the predictive value of locus of control. Indeed, in this study, pretreatment change was also significantly related to treatment outcome (R = .261, p < .05). Specifically, subjects displaying pretreatment change were four times as likely to finish therapy successfully (Rodríguez Morejón, 1994). By contrast, the presence of clear goals increased the likelihood of a successful therapeutic outcome by a factor of two.

From a constructivistic, nonessentialistic point of view, the predictive capacity of pretest general locus of control is an intriguing finding. After all, the results of this study imply that treatment outcome is largely dependent on features that clients show before therapy begins.

We prefer to emphasize a more interactional view of the process. Consider, for example, that people who show a more internal locus of control on pretest get better therapeutic results because they tend to have actively searched for and developed solutions on their own before therapy starts. If the therapist then highlights and amplifies these pretreatment changes during the first session, the probability of therapy being successful increases. In addition, the active solution-searching behavior of these clients leads them to accept and follow the suggestions they may receive from their therapist, complying literally with the tasks they are given.

Results from other studies further caution against viewing locus of control as a static quality of clients. These results show that locus of control is variable and becomes more internal over the course of successful therapy (Rodríguez Morejón, 1994).[3] This lends support to the notion that the task of solution-focused therapists is to foster situations in which clients experience a better sense of control over their own lives.

Clinical Implications

Many implications for clinical practice can be drawn from the results of this study. However, given that this is the first study of its kind, the data should be treated with caution. For this reason, the generalizations that follow are probably best considered tentative suggestions or working hypotheses that require further research to establish their veracity.

First, the data point out that the three cognitive variables we studied show some association with solution-focused clinical variables. This association might allow a "solution-focused reading" of these fairly traditional variables and, vice versa, a cognitive reading of solution-focused concepts. Such a reading might help brief therapy practitioners recognize the value of cognitive research for the practice of brief therapy. Clinical ideas such as "promoting expectations for change," "positive blame," and "doing what works" are not unlike more-scholarly variables that have been studied for decades by cognitive researchers.

A second relevant finding is the predictive ability of pretreatment change. Our data suggest that generally speaking it might prove especially useful to focus on pretreatment changes in the first session of therapy. More specifically, the data may even lend some provisional support to the idea that discussing pretreatment changes with our clients may be more helpful in terms of therapeutic outcome than working on goals in first sessions. To be sure, the data have moved our own clinical practice in first interviews away from a heavy emphasis on the miracle question (and other future-oriented techniques) and toward pretreatment change (Rodríguez Morejón & Beyebach, 1994). Our training procedures have also moved in the same direction.

Third, the strong relationship between locus of control and treatment outcome lends indirect support to the idea that one task of solution-oriented therapists is to foster a sense of control in their clients. In other words, our data indicate that while it may be good for clients to discover what works, it might be even better for them to discover that they can *make it work*. The results could also be used to predict those clients who will not succeed in solution-focused therapy. In this regard, those clients whose self-description reflects an external locus of control or with whom the therapeutic conversation fails to increase an internal locus of control may be more likely to experience failure in solution-focused therapy. In our opinion, this possibility certainly warrants further investigation.

Finally, the results of the present study also emphasize the importance of well-formed goals. In particular, the results lend support to the idea that the construction of well-formed goals helps to enhance commitment to the process of therapy. They also point to the usefulness of fostering a more internal locus of control when there are difficulties in getting a clear description of goals ("So how will you do that?"), and vice versa, resorting to goal-related questions as a way to enhance internality.

In summary, the results of this research project provide some empirical support for three basic practices of solution-focused therapy; namely, amplifying pretreatment change, negotiating well-formed goals, and empowering clients by giving them credit for change. All of these practices were found to be related to therapeutic outcome at termination.

Conclusion

We have tried to provide an empirical account of certain therapeutic processes from three very different perspectives: (1) the relational aspect of communication, (2) cognitive variables, and (3) solution-focused theory and practice. We hope we have shown the utility of using such divergent approaches in evaluating solution-focused work.

Overall, the research reported in this chapter provides some empirical support for the idea that certain solution-focused topics of conversation (pretreatment change and goals) are indeed relevant to treatment outcome, and that certain ways of approaching these topics (certain patterns of conversation) are related to both continuation in therapy and compliance with therapeutic tasks. This suggests that it is not only useful in therapy to focus on certain topics, but it is also useful to do so in a prescribed way (that is, both content and conversation process do matter).

Moreover, our results provide a certain empirical underpinning for some of the central tenets of solution-focused therapy. For example, they point to the relationship of pretreatment changes and clear goals to therapeutic outcome, as well as to the negative effect of confronting clients. They also provide support for solution-focused therapists' commitment to promoting clients' internal locus of control.

In addition, the results confirm that compliance with tasks is best understood in relational terms and that therapy can be successful even when the clients do not comply with the tasks they are assigned (Bailín, 1995). Finally, the data provide some new, tentative guidelines for clinical decision making. For instance, they suggest that in general focusing on pretreatment changes might be more productive than working on goals. They also suggest the importance of what others have called nonspecific factors in therapy, and that too much agreement with clients might be less productive than previously thought.

We certainly expect that future research along these lines would improve and clarify these findings. In this regard, we suggest that future studies not only consider outcome at termination but also at follow-up. We also believe that some of the tentative conclusions we have drawn should be subjected to a more focused research process. Specifically, it would be interesting to study the immediate impact of certain conversational practices or therapeutic techniques on the variables we studied. This should be done at different moments of the therapeutic process in order to obtain a more accurate account of the process of change as it unfolds over time. At the methodological level, statistical procedures such as sequential lag analysis, and research paradigms such as event-analysis, seem to us to be the most promising for future research. They would help us to keep research connected to theory, training, and clinical practice.

Questions from the Editors

1. *Given the constructivist leanings of some solution-focused thinkers, there has been a bias against empirical research. Could you please comment?*

We think that, in fact, this bias not only reflects the impact of constructivist and constructionistic thinking in our field, but it is also closely linked to the general distrust between researchers and clinicians that has existed almost from the beginning of psychotherapy research. We might even say (but we do not) that the narrow-minded reading of constructivistic ideas has simply provided an elegant alibi to those clinicians who dislike the idea of conducting research or of submitting their practices to it.

In our view, constructivism and constructionism should not cast doubts on the possibility of doing meaningful empirical research. They should, however, make us wonder what kind of research we want to call "empirical" and what kind of research is meaningful for clinicians who describe themselves as constructivists or constructionists. We think we should not dismiss empirical research as a futile academic exercise but should try hard to find (or develop) research practices that fit into our theoretical models.

2. *What are you investigating in your present research?*

We are studying the shifts from problem-talk to solution-talk and vice versa using a coding scheme we have adapted from earlier research by Gingerich and associates (1987). At the same time, we are taking a closer look at the shifts that occur *within* problem-talk. For this we are using a measure developed by Sluzki (1992).

3. *How do researchers deal with a model like solution-focused therapy that keeps changing and evolving over time?*

On first thought, we might say "badly." Indeed, the gut feeling is—and we think it is a feeling shared by many researchers—that research is always lagging behind clinical practice, always trying to catch up in vain with the developments that take place in the therapy room. On second thought, however, it turns out that things are not so negative. In our view, the changes in the solution-focused model have not been so radical as to invalidate the present research efforts. Certain techniques or specific practices have kept on evolving, but the basic theoretical assumptions have stayed stable. Therefore, one way to deal with the research-practice time lag is to keep the research focused not on specific techniques but on those more general aspects of the approach—elements like the therapeutic relationship, communication processes, cognitive changes in the course of therapy, and so on. Finally, we should say that it is a good thing that the approach continues to evolve and change—not only on the basis of clinical and theoretical developments but also on the basis of research. That is what we hope we are accomplishing with our work.

Notes

1. These denominations are certainly inaccurate, because we see any therapeutic interaction as intervention. Although it might be more accurate to talk about the "conversation" and the "final message" parts of the interview, we will stick to the shorthand "information gathering" and "intervention," which we have used in previous publications.

2. It should be stressed here that the pragmatic conception of control is different from the classic notion of "power." Accordingly, the following should be taken into account. First, relational control is always an *interpersonal* phenomenon, codefined by the interacting participants. Therefore, it is not a property of individuals but rather of social systems (Rogers-Millar & Millar, 1979). In other words, a subject may propose a given manner for defining his or her relationship with another person, but it is the response of the latter (and the new response of the former, and so on) that determines the form the relationship will take at each moment. One may therefore state that it is not possible to determine a relationship *unilaterally*. Conversely, relational control is best understood as a *constriction*. In other words, all messages within an interpersonal context somehow constrain or limit the communication options of the other speakers. A message given to A (who we should remember proposes a certain definition of the relationship) "obliges" B to position himself or herself with respect to A (to accept that definition or to propose another) and may limit the options of B, who in turn will impose a certain constriction on the next message of A, and so on successively. The implication underlying this form of control is that different maneuvers of control may be equally controlling and that a "one-down" message may be as controlling—or even more so—as a "one-up" message.

3. This study showed that on comparing prepost measures, clients who at termination of treatment were rated therapeutic successes showed significant increases in their specific self-efficacy and specific internal locus of control. Conversely, clients in the "no change" group did not show any changes in these variables.

References

Abramowitz, C. V., Abramowitz, S. I., Roback, H. B., & Jackson, C. (1974). Differential effectiveness of directive and nondirective group therapies as a function of client internal-external control. *Journal of Consulting and Clinical Psychology, 42,* 849–853.

Altuna, A., Beyebach, M., Piqueras, R., & Rodríguez-Arias, J. L. (1988). La relación terapéutica en primera entrevista de terapia sistémica: Análisis por fases [Therapeutic relationship in first session of systemic therapy: Phase analysis]. In M. Beyebach and J. L. Rodríguez-Arias (Eds.), *Terapia Familiar: Lecturas-I* [Family Therapy Readings, I] (pp. 97–116) Salamanca, Spain: Kadmos.

American Psychiatric Association. (1987). *Diagnostic and statistical manual of mental disorders, third edition.* Washington, DC: Author.

Anderson, S. A., Atilano, R. B., Bergen, L. P., Russell, C. S., & Jurich, A. P. (1985). Dropping out of marriage and family therapy: Intervention strategies and spouses' perceptions. *The American Journal of Family Therapy, 13,* 39–54.

Baekeland, F., & Lundwall, L. (1975). Dropping out of treatment: A critical review. *Psychological Bulletin, 82,* 738–783.

Bailín, M. C. (1995). *Estudio sobre el cumplimiento de prescripciones en un modelo de terapia sistémica* [Prescription compliance in systemic therapy]. Unpublished doctoral dissertation. Salamanca, Spain: Universidad Pontificia.

Bandura, A. (1989). Regulation of cognitive processes through perceived self-efficacy. *Developmental Psychology, 25,* 729–735.

Berg, I. K., & Miller, S. D. (1992). *Working with the problem drinker: A solution-focused approach.* New York: W. W. Norton.

Beyebach, M. (1993). *Relación terapéutica y abandono en terapia sistémica breve* [Therapeutic relationship and dropout in brief systemic therapy]. Unpublished doctoral dissertation, Universidad Pontificia, Salamanca, Spain.

Beyebach, M. (1995). Avances en terapia breve centrada en las solucione [Advances in solution-focused therapy]. In J. Navarro Góngora & M. Beyebach (Eds.), *Avances en terapia familiar sistémica* (pp. 157–194) Barcelona, Spain: Paidós.

Beyebach, M., de la Cueva, F., Ramos, M., & Rodríguez-Arias, J. L. (1990, June). *Relational communication control in first interviews of systemic therapy.* Paper presented at the International Communication Association Annual Meeting, Dublin, Ireland.

Beyebach, M., Macías Sánchez, P., Abad López, A. M., Arribas de Migues, F. J., Díez Méndez, A. B., Pérez Mateos, I., & Rodríguez Morejón, A. (1994, November). *El impacto de la supervisión en vivo sobre la conducta de los terapeutas en formación* [The effect of live supervision on the in-session behavior of trainees]. Paper presented at the XV National Conference on Family Therapy, Vitoria (Spain).

Bischoff, R. J., & Sprenkle, D. H. (1993). Dropping out of marriage and family therapy: A critical review of research. *Family Process, 32,* 353–375.

Breteler, R., Mertens, N., & Rombouts, R. (1990). Motivation to change smoking behavior: Determinants in the contemplation stage. In L. R. Schmidt, P. Schwenkmezger, J. Weinman, & S. Maes (Eds.), *Theoretical and applied aspects of health psychology.* London: Harwood Academic Publisher.

Buddeberg, C. (1987). Behandlungsabbruch: Erfolglose Kurztherapie? [Interruption of treatment: Unsuccessful brief therapy?] *Praxis der Psychotherapie und Psychosomatik, 32,* 221–228.

Cervone, D. (1991). The two disciplines of personality psychology. *Psychological Science, 2,* 371–377.

Cohen, J. (1960). A coefficient of agreement for nominal scales. *Educational and Psychological Measurements, 20,* 37–46.

Craig, A., & Andrews, G. (1985). The prediction and prevention of relapse in stuttering: The value of self-control techniques and locus of control measures. *Behavior Modification, 9,* 427–442.

De la Cueva, F. (1993). *Análisis de primeras entrevistas de MRI mediante el Sistema de Codificiación del Control de la Comunicación Relacional* [Analysis of first interviews of MRI therapy with the Relational Control Communication Coding System]. Unpublished doctoral dissertation, Universidad Pontificia, Salamanca, Spain.

De Shazer, S. (1982). *Patterns of brief family therapy.* New York: W. W. Norton.

De Shazer, S. (1985). *Keys to solution in brief therapy.* New York: W. W. Norton.

De Shazer, S. (1988). *Clues: Investigating solutions in brief therapy.* New York: W. W. Norton.

De Shazer, S. (1991). *Putting difference to work.* New York: W. W. Norton.

De Shazer, S. (1994). *Words were originally magic.* New York: W. W. Norton.

Dubrin, J. R., & Zastowny, T. R. (1988). Predicting early attrition from psychotherapy: An analysis of a large private-practice cohort. *Psychotherapy: Theory, Research and Practice, 25,* 393–408.

Duehn, W. D., & Proctor, E. K. (1977). Initial clinical interaction and premature discontinuance in treatment. *American Journal of Orthopsychiatry, 47,* 284–290.

Ericson, P. M., & Rogers, L. E. (1973). New procedures for analyzing relational communication. *Family Process, 12,* 245–267.

Fiester, A. R., & Rudestam, K. E. (1975). A multivariate analysis of the early dropout process. *Journal of Consulting and Clinical Psychology, 43,* 528–535.

Fisch, R., Weakland, J. H., & Segal L. (1982). *The tactics of change: Doing therapy briefly.* San Francisco: Jossey-Bass.

Fontecilla, G., Ramos, M. M., & Rodríguez-Arias, J. L. (1993, November). *Evaluación de resultados en terapia familiar breve* [Outcome research in brief family therapy]. Paper presented at the XIV National Conference on Family Therapy, Santiago de Compostela, Spain.

Foon, A. E. (1987). Review: Locus of control as a predictor of outcome of psychotherapy. *British Journal of Medical Psychology, 60,* 99–107.

Foon, A. E. (1989). Mediators of clinical judgment: An exploration of the effect of therapists' locus of control on clinical expectations. *Genetic, Social and General Psychology Monographs, 115,* 243–266.

Frank, J. D. (1985). Therapeutic components shared by all psychotherapies. In M. J. Mahoney & A. Freeman (Eds.), *Cognition and psychotherapy.* New York: Plenum.

Friedlander, M. L., & Heatherington, L. (1989). Analyzing relational control in family therapy interviews. *Journal of Counseling Psychology, 36,* 139–148.

Friedlander, M. L., Wildman, J., & Heatherington, L. (1991). Interpersonal control in structural and Milan systemic family therapy. *Journal of Marital and Family Therapy, 17,* 395–408.

Garfield, S. L. (1986). Research on client variables in psychotherapy. In S. L. Garfield and A. E. Bergin (Eds.), *Handbook of psychotherapy and behavior change* (3rd ed.). New York: Wiley.

Garland, H. (1984). Relation of effort-performance expectancy to performance in goal-setting experiments. *Journal of Applied Psychology, 69,* 79–84.

Gaul, R., Simon, L., Friedlander, M. L., Cutler, C., and Heatherington, L. (1991). Correspondence of family therapists' perceptions with F-RCCCS coding rules for triadic interactions. *Journal of Marital and Family Therapy, 17,* 379–393.

Gergen, K. (1985). The social constructionist movement in modern psychology. *American Psychologist, 40,* 266–275.

Gilligan, S., & Price, R. (Eds.). (1993). *Therapeutic conversations.* New York: W. W. Norton.

Gingerich, W. J., de Shazer, S., & Weiner-Davis, M. (1987). Constructing change: a research view of interviewing. In E. Lipchik (Ed.), *Interviewing.* Rockville, MD: Aspen.

Gottman, J. M., & Roy, A. K. (1990). *Sequential analysis: A guide for behavioral researchers.* New York: Cambridge University Press.

Greenberg, L. S., & Pinsof, W. M. (1986). Process research: current trends and future perspectives. In L. S. Greenberg & W. M. Pinsof (Eds.), *The psychotherapeutic process. A research handbook.* New York: Guilford.

Gunzburger, D., Henggeler, S., & Watson, S. (1985). Factors related to premature termination of counseling relationship. *Journal of College Student Personnel, 26,* 456–460.

Hardin, S. I., Subich, L. M., & Holvey, J. M. (1988). Expectations for counseling in relation to premature termination. *Journal of Counseling Psychology, 35,* 37–40.

Heatherington, L. (1988). Coding relational communication control in counseling: Criterion validity. *Journal of Counseling Psychology, 35,* 41–46.

Heatherington, L,. & Allen, G. J. (1984). Sex and relational communication patterns in counseling. *Journal of Counseling Psychology, 31,* 287–294.

Heatherington, L., & Friedlander, M. L. (1987). *Family relational communication control system coding manual.* Unpublished manuscript. Psychology Department, Williams College, Williamstown.

Hill, C. E. (1985). *Manual for the Hill counselor verbal response category system.* Unpublished manuscript.

Hoffman, L. (1990). Constructing realities: An art of lenses. *Family Process, 29,* 1–12

Kiesler, D. J. (1973). *The process of psychotherapy.* Chicago: Aldine.

Lichtenberg, J. W., & Barké, K. H. (1981). Investigation of transactional communication relationship patterns in counseling. *Journal of Counseling Psychology, 28,* 471–480.

Mark, R. A. (1971). Coding communication at the relationship level. *Journal of Communication, 21,* 221–232.

Markus, H., & Cross, S. (1990). The interpersonal self. In L. A. Pervin (Ed.), *Handbook of personality theory and research.* New York: Guilford.

Martín Tabernero, M. F., Fernández Pulido, R., & Seisdedos Benito, A. (1985). *Estadística inferencial: Manual de prácticas para las ciencias de la conducta* [Inferential statistics: Manual for the behavioral sciences]. Salamanca, Spain: Universidad Pontificia de Salamanca.

Mennicke, S. A., Lent, R. W., & Burgoyne, K. L. (1988). Premature termination from university counseling centers: A review. *Journal of Counseling and Development, 66,* 458–465.

Millar, F. E., Rogers, L. E., & Beavin, J. (1984). Identifying patterns of verbal conflict in interpersonal dynamics. *The Western Journal of Speech Communication, 48,* 231–246.

Mischel, W. (1968). *Personality assessment.* New York: Wiley.

Mischel, W. (1973). Toward a cognitive social learning reconceptualization of personality. *Psychological Review, 80,* 252–283.

O'Hanlon, W. H., & Weiner-Davis, M. (1989). *In search of solutions.* New York: W. W. Norton.

Palenzuela, D. L. (1988a). *Control personal: Un enfoque integrativo-multidimensional* [Personal control: An integrative-multidimensional approach]. Unpublished manuscript.

Palenzuela, D. L. (1988b). Refining the theory and measurement of expectancy of internal versus external control of reinforcement. *Personality and Individual Differences, 9,* 607–629.

Palenzuela, D. L. (1990, November). *Midiendo las expectativas generalizadas de control: primeros datos* [Measuring the generalized expectancies of control: preliminary data]. Paper presented at the VIII Congreso Nacional de Psicología, Barcelona, Spain.

Palenzuela, D. L. (1993). Personal control: an integrative-multidimensional approach. In D. L. Palenzuela & A. M. Barros (Eds.), *Modern trends in personality theory and research* (pp. 87–108). Porto, Spain: APPORT.

Palenzuela, D. L., Almeida, L., Prieto, G., & Barros, A. M. (1992). Estudio transcultural de la escala expectativas de control percibido (ECP) [Transcultural study of the expectancies of perceived control scale]. *Memoria Final de la Acción Integrada entre España y Portugal* (66 B), Universidades de Salamanca-Minho, Salamanca-Braga.

Palenzuela, D. L., & Barros, A. (1993). Modern trends in personality theory research: An introduction. In D. L. Palenzuela & A. M. Barros (Eds.), *Modern trends in personality theory research* (pp. 9–27). Porto, Spain: APPORT.

Palenzuela, D. L., & Rodríguez Morejón, A. (1993). Cognitivismo y personalidad: un análisis histórico-epistemológico [Cognitivism and personality: A historical-epistomological analysis]. *Revista de Historia de la Psicología, 14,* 417–426.

Pekarik, G. (1983). Follow-up adjustment of outpatient dropouts. *American Journal of Orthopsychiatry, 53,* 501–511.

Pekarik, G. (1985a). Coping with dropouts. *Professional Psychology: Research and Practice, 16,* 114–123.

Pekarik, G. (1985b). The effects of employing different termination classification criteria in dropout research. *Psychotherapy, 22,* 86–91.

Pérez Grande, M. D. (1991). Evaluación de resultados en terapia sistémica breve [Outcome research in brief systemic therapy]. *Cuadernos de Terapia Familiar, 18,* 93–110.

Persons, J. B., Burns, D. D., & Perloff, J. M. (1988). Predictors of dropout and outcome in cognitive therapy for depression in a private practice setting. *Cognitive Therapy and Research, 12,* 557–575.

Presley, J. H. (1987). The clinical dropout: A view from the client's perspective. *Social Casework: The Journal of Contemporary Social Work, 23,* 603–608.

Rodríguez Morejón, A. (1994). *Un modelo de agencia humana para analizar el cambio en psicoterapia: Las expectativas de control en terapia sistémica breve* [A human agency model to analyse the change in psychotherapy: The expectancies of control in brief sistemic therapy]. Unpublished dissertation, Universidad Pontificia de Salamanca.

Rodríguez Morejón, A., & Beyebach, M. (1994). Terapia sistémica breve: Trabajando con los recursos de las personas [Brief systemic therapy: Working with resources]. In M. Garrido & J. García (Eds.), *Psicoterapia. Modelos contemporáneos y aplicaciones* (pp. 241–289). Valencia, Spain: Promolibro.

Rodríguez Morejón, A., Palenzuela, D. L., & Beyebach, M. (in press). Un modelo cognitivo para analizar el cambio intrapersonal en terapia familiar sistémica [A cognitive model for the analysis of interpersonal change in systemic family therapy]. In A. Espina (Ed.), *Terapia familiar: clínica e investigación.* Valencia, Spain: Promolibro.

Rodríguez Morejón, A., Palenzuela, D. L., & Rodríguez-Arias, J. L. (in press) La relación de colaboración en terapia sistemica breve: un analisis desde las expectativas de control [The collaborative relationship in brief systems therapy: A control expectancies analysis]. In A. Espina (Ed.), *Terapia familiar: clínica e investigación.* Valencia: Promolibro.

Rogers, L. E. (1979). *Relational communication control coding manual.* Unpublished manuscript.

Rogers, L. E., & Bagarozzi, D. A. (1983). An overview of relational communication and implications for therapy. In D. A. Bagarozzi, M. Jurich, & R. W. Jackson (Eds.), *Marital and Family Therapy* (pp. 48–78). New York: Human Sciences Press.

Rogers, L. E., & Farace, R. V. (1975). Analysis of relational communication in dyads: New measurement procedures. *Human Communication Research, 1,* 222–239.

Rogers, L. E., Millar, F. E., & Bavelas, J. B. (1985). Methods for analyzing marital conflict discourse: Implications of a systems approach. *Family Process, 24,* 175–187

Rogers-Millar, L. E., and Millar, F. E. (1979). Domineeringness and dominance: A transactional view. *Human communication research, 5,* 238–246.

Rotter, J. B. (1954). *Social learning and clinical psychology.* Englewood Cliffs, NJ: Prentice Hall.

Rotter, J. B. (1966). Generalized expectancies for internal versus external control of reinforcement. *Psychological Monographs, 80*(1), 609.

Rotter, J. B. (1990). Internal versus external control of reinforcement: A case history of a variable. *American Psychologist, 45,* 489–493.

Scharamski, T. G., Beutler, L. E., Lauver, P. J., Arizmendi, T. A., & Shanfield, S. B. (1984). Factors that contribute to post-therapy persistence of theapeutic change. *Journal of Clinical Psychology, 40,* 78–85.

Segal, L. (1986). *The dream of reality.* New York: W. W. Norton.

Sherman, T. R, & Anderson, C.A. (1987). Decreasing premature termination from psychotherapy. *Journal of Social and Clinical Psychology, 5,* 298–312.

Sluzki, C. (1983). Process, structure, and world views: Toward an integrated view of systemic models in family therapy. *Family Process, 22,* 369–376.

Sluzki, C. (1992). Transformations: a blueprint for narrative changes in therapy. *Family Process, 31,* 217–230.

Sluzki, C.E., & Beavin, J. (1965). Symmetry and complementarity: An operational definition and typology of dyads. In P. Watzlawick & J. H. Weakland (Eds.), *The interactional view.* New York: W. W. Norton.

Stahler, G. J., & Eisenman, R. (1987). Psychotherapy dropouts: Do they have poor psychological adjustment? *Bulletin of the Psychonomic Society, 25,* 198–200.

Trepka, C. (1986). Attrition from an out-patient psychology clinic. *British Journal of Medical Psychology, 59,* 181–186.

Watzlawick, P. (1984). *The invented reality.* New York: W. W. Norton.

Watzlawick, P., Beavin, J., & Jackson, D. D. (1967). *The pragmatics of human communication.* New York: W. W. Norton.

Weisz, J. R. (1986). Contingency and control beliefs as predictors of psychotherapy outcomes among children and adolescents. *Journal of Consulting and Clinical Psychology, 54,* 789–795.

White, M. (1995). *Re-authoring lives: Interviews and essays.* Adelaide, Australia: Dulwich Centre Publications.

White, M., & Epston, E. (1989). *Narrative means to therapeutic ends.* Adelaide, Australia: Dulwich Centre Publications.

Zeig, J. K., & Gilligan, S. G. (Eds.). (1990). *Brief therapy: Myths, methods, and metaphors.* New York: Brunner/Mazer.

CHAPTER FOURTEEN

WHAT WORKS IN SOLUTION-FOCUSED BRIEF THERAPY

A Qualitative Analysis of Client and Therapist Perceptions

Linda Metcalf, Frank N. Thomas, Barry L. Duncan,
Scott D. Miller, and Mark A. Hubble

The study of client and therapist perceptions of treatment and change has a long and rich history in psychotherapy research. Treatment and change *process* has been traditionally and most extensively studied under the rubric of the client-therapist *relationship*. Research demonstrates that client perceptions of the relationship are the most consistent predictor of improvement (Gurman, 1977; Horowitz, Marmar, Weiss, DeWitt, & Rosenbaum, 1984; Patterson, 1984).

More recently, client/therapist perceptions have been studied in terms of the *alliance*. Building upon earlier Rogerian conceptualizations of the relationship, the alliance includes both therapist and client contributions and emphasizes the collaborative partnership of the therapist and client in achieving the goals of therapy (Marmar, Horowitz, Weiss, & Marziali, 1986). The alliance research reflects more than a thousand findings (Orlinsky, Grawe, & Parks, 1994). An illustrative example is a study by Bachelor (1991). She found that clients' perceptions of the alliance yield stronger predictions of outcome than therapists' perceptions, and that from the client's view the most salient factors in producing change are *therapist-provided warmth, help, caring, emotional involvement, and efforts to explore material relevant to the client.* From therapists' perspective, the strongest determinants to improvement are *client participation, a perceived sense of collaboration, and positive client characteristics.*

The superiority of client perceptions in predicting success supports the claim that the client is the better judge of what contributes most to change (Marziali,

1984). Clients are arguably in a better position to witness therapist performance and determine the value of the therapist's approach because their appraisal is less likely to be influenced by well-defined theoretical views (Murphy, Cramer, & Lillie, 1984).

While considerable research identifies what clients and therapists see as responsible for success in psychotherapy, no research has specifically addressed client and therapist perceptions regarding solution-focused brief therapy (SFBT). This chapter presents a qualitative study (Metcalf, 1993) that addresses (1) differences in perceptions of treatment and change process between therapists of a SFBT orientation and their clients, and (2) differences between SFBT assumptions and what therapists actually do. The chapter addresses the important issue of whether or not we do what we say we do, and more importantly, what clients perceive as effective. Client and therapist perceptions of SFBT are also discussed in light of the existing process-outcome literature. The results of this qualitative study affirm many findings of psychotherapy research, and both affirm and challenge the assumptions and practice of SFBT.

Method

This project adapted methodology from the field of nursing because of its extensive utilization of qualitative research to better serve patient needs. Ethnographic interviews focused on discovering the meaning of the experiences of six cohabiting couples, ages twenty-five to sixty-five, and their therapists at the birthplace of SFBT, the Brief Family Therapy Center (BFTC) in Milwaukee, Wisconsin. The BFTC was chosen because of its consistency in therapist training and supervision, and arguable "purity" in theory and application. The couples participated in the study based on their therapists' opinions that they had terminated therapy successfully, and the couples' confirmation of this conclusion. The therapists volunteered for the study and had practiced from a SFBT orientation for at least two years. The therapists were under the supervision of the clinical director.

The method of sample selection was purposive (Bogdan & Biklen, 1982). Couples who successfully terminated were intentionally selected in hopes that it would shed light on what factors contributed to the favorable outcome, from both client and therapist perspectives. Client and therapist perceptions of such factors could add to, support, or refute SFBT theory, thus enhancing the understanding of what makes SFBT effective.

The research procedure consisted of collecting data through separate interviews with couples and their therapists. Interview questions were void of theoretical or therapeutic terminology in an attempt to obtain fresh descriptions of treatment and change process (Field & Morse, 1985). Questions began at a general and superficial level, and increased in depth and specificity as relationships within the data (domains) were identified (Spradley, 1979). Some questions were prepared in advance while others were formulated based on answers given by the respondents. To further category development, the study employed an analytical, constant comparative approach to the data based on the stages proposed by Turner (1981).

The central interview question to the couples was "What was it that occurred in the therapy process that you found the most helpful? The central question to the therapists was, "What did you do in the therapy process that seemed to help change occur?"

Results

The results of these interviews are organized in three sections based on identified common themes. The quotations are from interview transcripts. Data were chosen according to coding similarities and are representative of other data obtained in the study. The three sections are (1) the therapist's role and what actually happens in SFBT, (2) the reasons clients sought therapy and termination, and (3) how change occurs.

The Role of the Therapist: What Really Happens in SFBT?

To explore the therapist's perceptions of his or her role and of what actually happens in the treatment process, the following questions were asked:

What exactly is it that you do, from your point of view?

What do you see as your role when you meet with people in this setting?

Can you describe for me what usually happens in a typical visit with a couple from the time it starts until it finishes?

If I sat in the back of the room during those early visits and watched both you and your client, how would you have described to me what was going on?

The following questions were asked of couples to investigate how the couple viewed the role of their therapist and the treatment process:

What did you see as [the therapist's] role while she or he met with you?

Can you describe for me what it was like to come to your first visit?

Can you describe what usually happened in a typical visit with [your therapist] from the time it started until it finished?

If I sat in the back of the room during those early visits and watched both you and [the therapist], how would you have described to me what was going on?

Results. Following is a list of the contrasting descriptions of the therapist's role provided by therapists and couples. These perceptions revealed the most marked differences between clients and their therapists in the study.

Therapists	*Couples*
Consultant	Mediator
Asked scaling questions	Friend
Paraphrased	Outsider
Looked for strengths, resources	Sounding board
Listened	Said what would work
Didn't participate unless asked	Savior
Gave ideas	Guide
Highlighted competencies	Made suggestions

Therapists were generally seen as more active and directive by the clients than by the therapists. Five of eight categories identified with clients spoke to the therapist's active role in terms of providing guidance or suggestions, ranging from "mediator" to "savior." In contrast, only one of eight categories that emerged from therapist interviews reflected a directive or advice-giving therapeutic stance ("Gave ideas").

The following list displays categorically consistent responses regarding perceptions of what actually happened in therapy:

Case	*Therapist Couple*
They come in and we consult together.	We talked and he/she focused on me.
Work together to achieve objectives	I sat and babbled about my fears.
I talk about the mirror . . . team . . . find a way to dialogue.	He/she said "I'm impressed." Pointed out false attitudes.
I take a break.	He/she made a difference.

After the initial session I ask what is
better, what is improved and we
spend the majority of the session
trying to identify what caused it
and reinforcing it.

He/she jumbled it all up so
I could get it straight.

He/she set me up for success.

He/she taught me a scheme.
I don't usually give suggestions.

The team made suggestions.
He/she made suggestions.

The therapists stated that listening, collaborating, observing and reinforcing strengths, and *not* making suggestions were parts of the process of therapy. Four out of six couples indicated that the therapist reinforced their strengths. Three out of six couples perceived that the therapist made active suggestions.

The therapists' and clients' responses to the process of therapy were similar to each other in their descriptions of reinforcement, listening, and focusing on the client. However, similar to the earlier discussion of the role of the therapist, clients perceived their therapists to be more directive than the therapists perceived themselves. Clients perceived the process as characterized by suggestions, pointing things out, and teaching. Not one of the participant therapists noted that making suggestions, directives, and teaching were part of what actually happens, although one therapist noted that suggestions are not usually given. Keep in mind that despite the differences in perception, all six cases were successful by client and therapist standards.

Comparison of Results with SFBT Assumptions. The clients' perceptions of the therapists' role differed significantly from the therapists' self-description and the philosophy of SFBT. SFBT discourages giving suggestions or assuming an expert role. Therapist perceptions of their role were consistent with SFBT assumptions. Consider the following statement by Berg and Miller (1992, p. 7): "Assuming an atheoretical, nonnormative, client-determined posture . . . allows the mental health professional to relinquish the role of expert or teacher in favor of the role of student or apprentice." Also, de Shazer (1995, p. 272) asserts that "there is no need for a therapist to overwhelm clients by making lots of suggestions or by inventing novel tasks." Therapists' perceptions of their role were clearly "theoretically correct" and ranged from listening to highlighting competencies, with only one category of responses reflecting a directive role.

With regard to treatment process, or what actually happens in therapy, de Shazer (1991, p. 122) writes: "The majority of a solution-determined therapeutic conversation is spent in . . . three interrelated activities: (1) producing exceptions, (2) imagining and describing new lives for clients, and (3) 'confirming' that change is occurring, that clients' new lives have indeed started." Only one therapist's and client's description can be construed to fit these three activities. However, these activities become more apparent when couples and therapists are asked about change.

Why Clients Sought Therapy and Termination

Both therapists and couples were asked for their views on why the couple sought therapy and how termination occurred. The following questions were asked of the therapist regarding a particular couple:

> Can you tell me what was said by the couple as to their reasons for coming to see you?
>
> Who decided the visits should stop and that working together was completed?

If [the therapist] responded that the couple decided to terminate, the following question was asked: Did you agree with them?

The following questions were asked of couples regarding the reason for entering therapy and termination:

> Looking back at the visits, why did you initially decide to meet with [the therapist]?
>
> What went on in the visits when you presented your reason for coming here?
>
> How did it occur that you stopped coming to see [the therapist]?

If the couples responded that the therapist terminated them, they were then asked: Did you agree with him or her?

Results. The following list compares the views of couples and their therapists regarding why the couple sought therapy. Perhaps predictably, therapists used therapeutic jargon, speaking of symptoms, disorders, dysfunctions, and discord, while clients gave more down to earth descriptions. In essence, the content of the reasons given for seeking services were similar, but the language utilized was clearly different, with therapists relying on professional jargon rather than clients' own language.

Case	Therapist	Couple
A	There was a divorce . . . multiple relationships . . . a death. . . . The mother was worried about how the death impacted her son.	It was an emergency treatment for me when I brought my son. I was concerned about my son— his out of control behavior. I needed to be apathetic.
B	The female had physical and depressive symptoms . . . a panic disorder . . . she was agoraphobic. Marital dicord . . . she said her body was attacking her.	The panic disease. . . . We talked about stressors too. . . . We had a lot of family stressors. . . . That was about it. . . . The son and his problems. . . .
C	They were having marital difficulties, and were not getting along like they had before.	To try to stay together. . . . We weren't talking to each other like we should and couldn't come together.
D	Childhood experiences with an alcoholic parent that he related in his mind with the problems he had with his family. . . . He wanted insight. . . . He had violent, angry outbursts and had destroyed something and it shocked him.	Just particular life events catalyzed the action on my part. . . . A crisis precipitated it. . . . I had trouble with what I thought were inappropriate outbursts at my kids and I wanted some help. . . . I really wanted out of it.
E	She said both of the kids were hyperactive and had behavioral problems . . . it involved more her relationship with her boyfriend. . . . She thought her relationship was in trouble . . . her anger. . . .	I wanted to figure out what the problem was. . . . We had a lot of negative people who were into our relationships. . . . Problem with anger and emotional problems. . . . I have a terrible temper.
F	Tension . . . sadness . . . he didn't want to keep hurting her and she took the sexual dysfunction personally . . . she was depressed and devastated.	Our doctor suggested counseling here. . . . Said it was Christian based and not generic. . . . We were good friends and didn't have the intimate parts of our lives in order.

The following list compares the responses given by therapists and couples to questions about termination. The list reveals that four of six couples perceived the therapist as deciding when termination was necessary.

Case	Therapists	Couples
A	I suggested to mother that they needed to take a break over summer since school was over . . . School-related issues . . . I think she agreed. . . . I got a call later and I told her I didn't think it was a therapy issue. . . . She agreed.	It was the therapist's decision. He/she said, "It sounds like you're doing well." He/she said that ——— didn't need to come back and I was torn. . . . I wanted my son to have someone to talk with. . . . I still have difficulty with him.
B	We agreed that she had made significant progress and I asked her if this would be a good time to stop being seen on a regular basis. She agreed.	He/she said if I passed my driver's license I didn't need to come back. . . . I was elated but also felt like he/she pushed me out of the nest. It was like "you must go."
C	They decided they didn't need to come back. . . . They thought they could do it on their own.	We had limited visits. He/she said the problem was not that severe. We didn't come to the last session and he/she didn't contact us.
D	We started spacing the sessions out. . . . I suggested that he take time to work this through for the insights were going to continue to occur. . . . I framed the change as a continual process. He agreed.	He/she left it open to me but I think he/she felt that I had accomplished what I needed to accomplish.
E	Things were at a 9 for him and an 8½ for her. They decided to leave the next appointment open. It was their choice. They felt things were resolved.	I had to stop because I changed jobs and the insurance dropped I told him/her that we would try it on our own and call if we needed him/her.
F	They decided to stop. They said change takes time. They brought it up. They went to a marriage class . . . he said he would call us.	We had only 3 visits (HMO) so we said, "OK, we'll take three." After those three we figured out what we needed to get on track. I don't think we asked him/her.

Some couples expressed apprehension and disappointment when therapy was terminated by the therapist. One couple reported that they were left with unresolved issues. A striking difference in perception is present between clients and their therapists regarding termination. Therapists tended to believe that the decision was agreed upon, while many clients felt it was unilaterally the therapist's call.

Comparison of Results with SFBT Assumptions. On the topic of accepting the client's reasons for therapy and termination, de Shazer (1991, p. 57) states: "If therapists accept the client's complaint as the reason for starting therapy, therapists should, by the same logic, accept the client's statement of satisfactory improvement as the reason for terminating therapy." Also: "At BFTC no limit is set on the number of sessions. . . . Therapy ends when the client meets his or her goals for therapy (pp. 157–158). Finally, Berg and Miller (1992, p. 102) state: "Empowerment of the client starts with honoring and following his lead in deciding what is important to him."

These quotes point to the conclusion that the client is in charge of the definition of the complaint and the criteria for termination. Inconsistencies between the messages contained in the quotes and client perceptions in this study were notable. First, the therapists' language differed significantly from the clients' presentations of their reasons for seeking therapy. Utilization of the client's language is a basic tenet of SFBT, as well as other brief approaches. The therapists' use of pathological terminology also deviates from the philosophy of SFBT.

Perhaps a more glaring inconsistency, from the vantage point of the client, was the therapists' perception of a collaborative termination. The therapists' responses were consistent with SFBT assumptions, but the clients' perceptions of termination revealed a far less mutual process in which some clients felt pushed out, disappointed, or as if the therapist thought they should stop therapy. It could be speculated that therapist anxiety about length of treatment contributed to misperceiving clients' apprehensions about ending treatment.

The Change Process: What Worked in SFBT

Couples and therapists were asked questions regarding what they considered to be influential factors in creating change. The following question was asked of the therapists: What actions do you think occurred on your part that influenced the couple to change? The following question was asked of the couples: What went on in the time that you met with [the therapist] that you feel influenced you to change?

Results. The following list presents a representative set of responses to the questions addressing the process of change:

Case	Therapists	Couples
A	I validated the mother and helped her think about what she wanted. . . . Separated the kids from mom . . . helped her figure out her goals . . . empowered her.	He/she and the team told us some very positive things we were doing to resolve conflict. He/she was positive and reminded us of things we had forgotten about ourselves.
B	I believed she could do it . . . found strengths she had through questions.	He/she mixed up things she said and asked "why?" He/she helped her be less "perfect." He/she told us about himself/herself.
C	I reinforced . . . spent some time looking at what they had done to cause the improvements. I may have punctuated the experience for them.	He/she made us think a little more before we did stuff . . . through his/her suggestions, and the group's (team).
D	I did positive blame. . . . I gave him all the credit for the changes made. . . . I just showed up. . . . I just punctuated it.	I think dumping it initially and getting it out in the open. His/her self-disclosure about being ———helped. He/she said I felt strongly about things. . . . like love. He/she asked "what's better?" He/she focused on what I did right.
E	I looked for differences that made a difference . . . listened, focused on what worked and made them feel better.	Pointed things out in a different way. . . asked me to think how it was when the negative thought's not there. . . . Praised us.
F	I asked them to notice what was going on that they wanted to continue and which one was changing. . . . Scaling questions.	He/she helped us see that we got along better than we thought. We learned our recreational life was lacking. . . . He/she gave us a neutral place to come . . . gave us a map.

While four of six couples and their therapists held different perceptions of the change process, many similarities also emerged from the interviews. Similarities included amplifying strengths, praising, noticing differences, and focusing on what worked. Differences revolved around therapists' mention of techniques (separated the kids from mom, positive blame, scaling questions), as opposed to clients' mention of relationship factors (allowing to dump, therapist self-disclosure, and affirmation).

Comparison of Results with SFBT Assumptions. The SFBT approach is based on the assumption that change is so much a part of living that clients cannot prevent themselves from changing (de Shazer, 1985). Clearly the therapists' perceptions of the change process were consistent with this assumption. Therapists largely attributed change to noticing exceptions, pointing out differences, and focusing on what works, as well as reinforcing and complimenting client competencies and successes. Clients also noted the positive nature of therapists' comments and the focus on what worked, but five of six couples noted relationship factors as well. Only two of the therapists mentioned relationship-oriented factors.

Discussion

The results of this qualitative study are largely supportive of SFBT, which views change as a constant, empowers clients' existing resources, and encourages clients to seek their own solutions through the investigation of prior successes. However, the results of this study also indicate that the therapists at BFTC who participated in this project take a more directive role than indicated in the written work of de Shazer (1985, 1991, 1995) and of Berg and Miller (1992). In addition, the results show that participant therapists tended to recast client complaints into pathological jargon. Finally, from the arguably more objective perspective of the client, termination was far less collaborative than SFBT assumptions suggest. Despite these inconsistencies, all of the couples included in the study perceived therapy to be meaningful and helpful.

Based on the information presented in this study, an increased focus on clients' language and description of the reasons for seeking therapy might satisfy the model's tenet of utilizing the clients' language and frame of reference for therapy. In addition, termination should be openly discussed and the client given choice regarding the continuation of therapy.

What Makes Therapy Successful? How Does SFBT Fit the Data?

The factors that contribute to what works in therapy are client (40 percent), relationship (30 percent), and placebo and technique (15 percent each) (Lambert,

1992). What works in therapy may be thought about as a pie (Miller, Duncan, & Hubble, in press). The main ingredient to any pie is the filling, be it chocolate, custard, rhubarb, or lemon. There is little point to the pie without it. Eating a pie without filling is like doing therapy without the client, without a dependence on the client's resources. One could argue that SFBT is effective for this very reason. Perhaps more than any other approach, SFBT seeks to highlight competencies and empower strengths and successes. Depending on client resources was a consistent theme among clients and therapists in this study. Two therapists described their role as looking for and reinforcing client strengths; five of six therapists attributed change to some form of highlighting client resources and successes. According to thirty years of research about what makes therapy successful, maybe SFBT is on to something.

The next most important aspect of what works is the relationship or common factors that compose the crust or container for the filling of the pie. The relationship contains clients comfortably while allowing their resources to take center stage. The crust is the structure and context that allows the filling to be appreciated. The client-therapist relationship has consistently been viewed, by researchers and clinicians alike, as a significant factor in favorable outcome (Bordin, 1979; Duncan, Solovey, & Rusk, 1992; Marziali, 1984; Miller, Hubble, & Duncan, 1995; Miller et al., in press; Rogers, 1957).

According to psychotherapy research on client perceptions, therapists' contributions toward helping clients achieve favorable outcomes is made mainly through empathic, affirmative, collaborative engagement with the client (Orlinsky et al., 1994). Looking at client perceptions of change in the current study only reinforces the existing literature. Five of six couples attributed change to some form of relationship or therapist contribution. Clients tend to attribute success to such qualities of the relationship. Four of the couples mentioned some variation of the therapist emphasizing what they were doing right, their positive qualities, or what researchers call "affirmation." Affirmation is defined as acceptance, nonpossessive warmth, or positive regard. Orlinsky and colleagues (1994) reviewed ninety findings that indicated that the client's perception of therapist affirmation is a significant factor in promoting a positive outcome. SFBT points out successes, compliments clients, and thinks highly of clients' abilities to solve their problems. Here again, the data indicate that SFBT may be on to something.

The pie's visual presentation, aroma, and aroused expectations constitute the placebo factors, which are those aspects of change accounted for by the client's knowledge of being in treatment and hopes for improvement. To finish the pie metaphor, technique can be understood as the meringue. The meringue enhances the appearance of the pie and may embellish its taste, but cannot stand on its own, lest it run and lose its shape and definition. Without the rest of the pie to give it form and substance, the meringue is nothing but fluff, devoid of any value in isolation of the rest of the pie. Indeed, without the client's resources and the relationship to give intervention something to attach to and provide meaning, technique adds little to the process of change. In spite of all the emphasis on technique in solution-focused therapy, *only one of six clients in the current study mentioned the therapist's suggestion as being influential to the change process.* Perhaps the effectiveness of SFBT can be attributed less to miracles and techniques and more to its assumptions that support accommodating, affirming, and honoring client competencies. Psychotherapy research, as well as this small qualitative study, points to such a conclusion.

Implications for Future Study

This study, although small and limited in scope, is a step in the right direction. Therapist and client views of therapy provide valuable information which to date has been lacking—not only related to SFBT but also other postmodern, narrative, or constructive therapies. It is recommended that future studies explore client and therapist perceptions of these approaches to see if client perceptions can be utilized to encourage more effective and meaningful therapy. SFBT and other related approaches have evolved to the point that model advancement and credibility will likely be most promoted by research.

SFBT has also matured to the point where it is possible to evaluate what is effective about the model and what is not. Such an evaluation may be difficult because of the possibility that client and relationship components may be more powerful than technical aspects of the approach. The strength of SFBT may lie in its ability to empower and enhance client and relationship factors. SFBT may indeed influence the field more through its philosophy of treatment than through its interventions; SFBT seems to offer something to which clients respond favorably. SFBT will only expand its influence by connecting itself to what makes it successful, from both the larger context of psychotherapy research and the clients' perspective.

Questions from the Editors

1. *What are the limitations of this study?*

Qualitative studies, by design, provide in-depth information from a small number of participants about a topic area, rather than large-scale generalizations. The major limitation, therefore, is the great caution required in generalizing the results. Generalizing the results is also limited by the reliability of the instruments used. Since the researcher *is* the instrument in qualitative studies, reliability is always questionable. Finally, the sampling was not random; selection was purposeful, which of course enabled successful cases to be studied.

2. *Are there any other interpretations of your major findings?*

One other interpretation comes to mind regarding the findings of therapist directiveness, and the clients' perceptions of premature and therapist-determined termination. A common misunderstanding about SFBT or any approach is that it consists of a group of techniques that have some intrinsic value separate from the client and the therapeutic relationship. Therapists in this study seemed to rely more on technique and less on the client's perspective. SFBT is a way of thinking, a respectful philosophy that depends on client resources and viewpoints for success. Techniques cannot work without such a reliance on the client, and a connection to the client's favorable evaluation of the treatment process. Techniques, even great ones like the miracle question, have no inherent value.

3. *What future research do you recommend?*

Client perceptions of SFBT should be a focus of research, particularly client perceptions of the alliance. It is our hunch that research will find that clients will rate the alliance in SFBT very favorably because of SFBT's client-directed assumptions, thereby predicting positive outcomes. In addition, we would like to see research become more in line with SFBT philosophy by emphasizing what is *useful to clients,* as opposed to the more "medicalized" emphasis on what is *effective in treatment.*

References

Bachelor, A. (1991). Comparison and relationship to outcome of diverse dimensions of the helping alliance as seen by client and therapist. *Psychotherapy, 28,* 534–549.

Berg, I., & Miller, S. (1992). *Working with the problem drinker.* New York: W. W. Norton.

Bogdan, R., & Biklen, S. (1982). *Qualitative research for education.* Needham Heights, MA: Allyn & Bacon.

Bordin, E. S. (1979). The generalizability of the psychoanalytic concept of the working alliance. *Psychotherapy, 16,* 252–260.

De Shazer, S. (1985). *Keys to solutions in brief therapy.* New York: W. W. Norton.

De Shazer, S. (1991). *Putting difference to work.* New York: W. W. Norton.

De Shazer, S. (1995). *Words were originally magic.* New York: W. W. Norton.

Duncan, B., Solovey, A., & Rusk, G. (1992). *Changing the rules: A client-directed approach to therapy.* New York: Guilford.

Field, P., & Morse, J. (1985). *Nursing research: The application of qualitative approaches.* Rockville, MD: Aspen.

Gurman, A. S. (1977). Therapist and patient factors influencing the patient's perception of facilitative therapeutic conditions. *Psychiatry, 40,* 16–24.

Horowitz, M., Marmar, C., Weiss, D., DeWitt, K., & Rosenbaum, R. (1984). Brief psychotherapy of bereavement reactions: The relationship of process to outcome. *Archives of General Psychiatry, 41,* 438–448.

Lambert, M. (1992). Psychotherapy outcome research. In J. C. Norcross and M. R. Goldfried (Eds.), *Handbook of psychotherapy integration* (pp. 94–129). New York: Basic Books.

Marmar, C., Horowitz, M., Weiss, D., & Marziali, E. (1986). The development of the Therapeutic Alliance Rating System. In L. Greenberg and W. Pinsof (Eds.), *The psychotherapeutic process: A research handbook* (pp. 367–390). New York: Guilford.

Marziali, E. (1984). Three viewpoints on the therapeutic alliance: Similarities, differences, and associations with psychotherapy outcome. *Journal of Nervous and Mental Diseases, 172,* 417–423.

Metcalf, L. (1993). *The pragmatics of change in solution-focused brief therapy: Ethnographic interviews with couples and their therapists.* Unpublished doctoral dissertation, Texas Woman's University, Denton, Texas.

Miller, S., Duncan, B., & Hubble, M. (in press). *Escape from Babel.* New York: W. W. Norton.

Miller, S., Hubble, M., & Duncan, B. (1995, March/April). No more bells and whistles. *Family Therapy Networker,* pp. 53–63.

Murphy, P., Cramer, D., & Lillie, F. (1984). The relationship between curative factors perceived by patients in their psychotherapy and treatment outcome. *British Journal of Medical Psychology, 57,* 187–192.

Orlinsky, D., Grawe, K., & Parks, B. (1994). Process and outcome in psychotherapy. In A. E. Bergin & S. E. Garfield (Eds.), *Handbook of psychotherapy and behavior change* (4th ed.) (pp. 270–375). New York: Wiley.

Patterson, C. H. (1984). Empathy, warmth, and genuineness in psychotherapy: A review of reviews. *Psychotherapy, 21,* 431–438.

Rogers, C. R. (1957). The necessary and sufficient conditions of therapeutic personality change. *Journal of Consulting Psychology, 21,* 95–103.

Spradley, J. (1979). *The ethnographic interview.* New York: Holt, Rinehart, and Winston.

Turner, B. (1981). Some practical aspects of qualitative data analysis. *Quality and Quantity, 15,* 225–247.

THE EDITORS

Scott D. Miller is a therapist, trainer, and lecturer on solution-focused brief therapy. He directed Alcohol and Drug Treatment and Training Services and was a member of the research and training team at the Brief Family Therapy Center in Milwaukee, Wisconsin, for three years. He continues to conduct research on the practice of brief therapy and specializes in treating the homeless mentally ill and other traditionally underserved populations. Miller conducts workshops and training in the United States and abroad, and is known for his humorous and engaging presentation style. He has presented to many professional audiences including the American Psychological Association, the American Society of Clinical Hypnosis, the International Congress on Ericksonian Approaches to Hypnosis and Psychotherapy, and the International and National Associations of Social Workers. He is the author of numerous articles, and coauthor of *Working with the Problem Drinker: A Solution-Focused Approach* (1992, with Insoo Berg), *The Miracle Method* (1995, with Insoo Berg), *Finding the Adult Within: A Solution-Focused Self-Help Guide* (1995, with Barbara McFarland), and the forthcoming *Escape from Babel: Towards a Unifying Language for Psychotherapy Practice* (with Barry Duncan and Mark Hubble) and *Psychotherapy with Impossible Cases: Efficient Treatment of Therapy Veterans* (with Barry Duncan and Mark Hubble).

Mark A. Hubble earned his degrees from the University of Maryland and Arizona State University. As a postdoctoral student, he completed the clinical psychology internship at the Norfolk Regional Center and the Northern Nebraska Comprehensive Mental Health Center. He is a graduate of the prestigious Postdoctoral Fellowship in Clinical Psychology at Menningner in Topeka, Kansas, and is a member of the editorial advisory board of the *Journal of Systematic Therapies*. In the past, he founded and directed the Brief Therapy Clinic of the Counseling and Testing Center at the University of Missouri, Kansas City; served as a contributing editor for *The Family Therapy Networker*, and served as a member of the faculty of the Dayton Institute for Family Therapy in Centerville, Ohio. Known for his witty and thought-provoking presentations, Hubble has broad experience in teaching and training practitioners from various disciplines. He is a frequent presenter at regional and national meetings. In recent years, he has been an invited member of the faculty for the Family Therapy Network Symposium, held annually in Washington, D.C. In October 1992 he presented at the Fiftieth Anniversary Conference of the American Association of Marriage and Family Therapy, and in March 1993 he lectured at the Annual Convention of the American College Personnel Association. Hubble has published in several professional journals. In 1988, a synopsis of his doctoral research was reported in *Psychology Today*. In 1992, he was the senior author of "The Limits of Setting Limits on Mental Health Services," a paper appearing in *Medical Interface*, a major periodical of the managed health care industry. He is coauthor with Scott Miller and Barry Duncan of *Psychotherapy with Impossible Cases: The Efficient Treatment of Therapy Veterans* and *Escape from Babel: Toward a Unifying Language in Psychotherapy Practice* (both in press). He has been interviewed for articles in *USA Today*, *Psychology Today*, *The Family Therapy Networker*, and *Glamour*.

Barry L. Duncan is a therapist who has had more than fourteen thousand contact hours with clients. He is in private practice in Port St. Lucie, Florida, and is an adjunct faculty member at Florida Atlantic University and New York Institute of Technology, Boca Raton campus. Duncan received a B.S. in psychology from Wright State University (WSU) in 1980 and the Doctor of Psychology degree from the WSU School of Professional Psychology in 1984. He is a former president of the Ohio Division of the American Association of Marriage and Family Therapy (AAMFT), and is an approved supervisor of AAMFT. Duncan has published more than thirty-five articles and chapters and six books. Most recently, he coauthored *Escape from Babel* (in press, with Scott Miller and Mark Hubble) and *Psychotherapy with Impossible Cases* (in press, with Scott Miller and Mark Hubble). Duncan has appeared on "Oprah" and Gary Collins's "The Home Show," among others, and has also been featured in *Psychology Today*, *USA Today*, and *Glamour*.

THE CONTRIBUTORS

Mark Beyebach is a psychologist and professor of family therapy in the Department of Psychology at the Universidad Pontificia de Salamanca in Spain. With colleagues he has been conducting research on solution-focused and other brief therapy for the better part of ten years.

Judi Booker is a clinical supervisor at Prince Williams County Community Services Board, Virginia. She is an AAMFT supervisor in training and has written other articles related to the application of solution-focused therapy with special treatment populations.

William R. Butler practices and teaches solution-focused brief therapy at the Brief Therapy Center of Psychotherapy Associates of Ghent in Norfolk, Virginia.

Peter De Jong is currently the director of social work at Calvin College, where he also teaches courses in interviewing skills and individual and family practice. He also trains in solution-focused therapy at public and private agencies. He has several years' experience doing individual, couples, and family therapy and has written *How to Interview for Client Strengths and Solutions* (in press, with Insoo Berg).

Barbara S. Held is professor of psychology at Bowdoin College, Brunswick, Maine, and has a private psychotherapy practice.

Larry E. Hopwood received his Ph.D. in molecular biology in 1971 from Washington University in St. Louis, Missouri, and his M.S.W. in 1990 from the University of Wisconsin at Milwaukee. He is currently the site director for one of the United Behavioral Systems clinics in Milwaukee, Wisconsin, where mental health and substance abuse treatment is provided for the Medicaid population. He was formerly the director of training at the Brief Family Therapy Center in Milwaukee and the executive director of Problems to Solutions, a Milwaukee clinic based in a shelter for the homeless. His interest in research stems from a twenty-year previous career as a radiation biologist. Hopwood often teams up with Scott Miller to provide advanced training and consultation in solution-focused therapy.

Anthony D. Kubicki has been a domestic violence advocate since 1985. He has worked at Sojourner Truth House, a shelter for battered women and children, for a decade. Tony developed and coordinates the Batterers Anonymous-Beyond Abuse Program (BA). To date, more than four thousand men who have hit the women they say they love have come to BA to attempt to eliminate their violence. He has also played an integral part in developing Milwaukee's coordinated community response to domestic violence and its mandatory arrest for domestic violence law. For the past ten years he has sat on the city of Milwaukee's Common Council Task Force on Sexual Assault and Domestic Violence, and he is presently an advisor to the State of Wisconsin Governor's Domestic Violence Council subcommittee, commissioned to set standards for domestic violence programs.

Eve Lipchik is co-owner of ICF Consultants, Inc., in Milwaukee, Wisconsin. From 1980 to 1988, she was a full-time member of the Brief Family Therapy Center in Milwaukee, where she codeveloped the solution-focused brief therapy model. She developed an interest in domestic violence in 1980, when asked to consult at the original Sojourner Truth House in Milwaukee. In 1981, when the Sojourner Truth House was reorganized and the Milwaukee Women's Center was founded, she became clinical and program consultant. In addition to teaching, training, writing, and clinical practice, Eve has spent the last fourteen years applying SFBT ideas to the development of a clinical protocol for couple domestic violence treatment that could stand the test of empirical evaluation and thereby become an accepted option for treatment.

Linda Metcalf is a licensed Marriage and Family Therapist in private practice in Arlington, Texas. She is a lecturer at the University of Texas at Arlington and an adjunct professor at Texas Christian University in Fort Worth, Texas. She is the author of *Counseling Toward Solutions* (1995), on which she lectures nationally, as well as the author of several articles on brief therapy.

A. Jay McKeel is a professor in the marriage and family therapy program at St. Thomas University, Miami, Florida, and has a private practice. His current research interests include how clients' and therapists' expectations affect treatment outcome; strategies to enhance client-therapist collaboration; and the research and development of therapeutic interventions. He is completing his Ph.D. at Purdue University.

Alberto Rodríguez Morejón is a psychologist and professor of family therapy at the Universidad Pontificia de Salamanca, Spain. He is the coordinator of the master's degree program in solution-focused and brief systemic therapy.

John J. Murphy is assistant professor in the Department of Psychology and Counseling at the University of Central Arkansas. He has worked for several years as a full-time school psychologist and as a high school teacher. Murphy trains school personnel and other professionals throughout the country in solution-focused brief therapy. He maintains a private practice dealing primarily with school-related problems of children and adolescents. He is currently coauthoring a book on brief therapy for school problems with Barry L. Duncan.

Jordan A. Oshlag is codirector of Solutions, a private practice group specializing in solution-focused therapy, and on the staff of the Family Counseling Center in Fitchburg, Massachusetts. Oshlag works extensively with adolescents and adult populations in a variety of settings. He trains professionals in solution-focused brief therapy both nationally and internationally. In addition, Oshlag is on the adjunct faculty at Boston University School of Social Work, and a consultant to mental health professionals in utilizing computers in clinical practice. Oshlag is coauthor of *Crossing the Bridge: Integrating Solution Focused Therapy into Clinical Practice* (1995, with Susan Tohn).

David L. Palenzuela is a psychologist and a professor at the Universidad Pontificia de Salamanca, Spain. He has been instrumental in developing instruments to measure expectancies of control, success, and self-efficacy in clinical and nonclinical settings.

Jane E. Peller is codirector of Consultations, a practice and training center for solution-focused personal consultation in Chicago, and assistant professor in the Department of Social Work at Northeastern Illinois University, Chicago. She conducts workshops in training throughout the United States and is coauthor of the popular *Becoming Solution-Focused in Brief Therapy* (1992, with John Walter).

Keith V. Powers practices and teaches solution-focused brief therapy at the Brief Therapy Center of Psychotherapy Associates of Ghent in Norfolk, Virginia.

Jose Luis Rodríguez-Ariàs received his Ph.D. in Psychology from the Universidad Pontificia de Salamanca in Spain and is a psychologist at Centro de Salud in Laredo, Spain. He is interested in the development of brief therapy techniques for specific client problems.

Dvorah Simon is staff psychologist and clinical assistant professor of rehabilitation medicine at the Rusk Institute for Rehabilitation Medicine, New York University Medical Center. She has conducted several research studies involving the application of solution-focused approaches to persons with brain injury. Dvorah maintains a small private practice in Manhattan. Her proudest achievement is the creation of a newsletter for therapists working in solution-focused and other collaborative traditions, the *News of the Difference.*

Frank N. Thomas is associate professor in the Family Therapy Program at Texas Woman's University in Denton, Texas. A graduate of Texas Tech University, Thomas has written extensively on competency-based approaches in therapy and supervision and presents both nationally and internationally. He is also on the adjunct faculty at Brite Divinity School, Texas Christian University, and serves as a clinical supervisor in pastoral counseling training. Thomas directed the annual conference of the Texas chapter of the American Association of Marriage and Family Therapy (AAMFT) for ten years, as well as AAMFT's first Summer Institute. His video *Solution-Oriented Supervision: The Coaxing of Expertise* is a part of AAMFT's Supervision Videotape Series™. Thomas's first book, tentatively entitled *Strength Upon Strength: Competency-Based Approaches,* written with Jack Cockburn, is scheduled for release in 1996. His second book, coauthored with Thorana Nelson, is tentatively entitled *102 Tales from Family Therapy* and is scheduled for release in 1997.

Marshall R. Thomas is director of Psychiatric Emergency, Acute Care, and Inpatient Services at Colorado Psychiatric Hospital. He is assistant professor of Psychiatry at the University of Colorado Health Sciences Center School of Medicine. He is also on the faculty of Denver Institute for Psychoanalysis and the University of Denver Graduate School of Professional Psychology. Thomas has been principal investigator for numerous studies of psychiatric interventions, including the impact of managed care on treatment outcomes. He is published widely on mood disorders, psychiatric delivery systems, and psychopharmacology.

Susan Lee Tohn is co-director of Solutions, a private practice group specializing in solution-focused therapy. Tohn works with couples, adolescents, and families using the solution-focused model. She provides training for and consultation with management teams, mental health organizations, hospitals, and managed care organizations, and presents to professional audiences both nationally and internationally. Tohn is an adjunct faculty member of Boston University School of Social Work. In addition, she sits on the Provider Advisory Council of American Biodyne, a division of Medco Behavioral Care. She is coauthor of *Crossing the Bridge: Integrating Solution Focused Therapy into Clinical Practice* (1995, with Jordan Oshlag).

Kay Vaughn is psychiatric clinical nurse specialist for Colorado Psychiatric Hospital and volunteer faculty for University of Colorado Health Sciences Center School of Nursing. She received her M.S. degree in Psychiatric Mental Health Nursing from Texas Women's University. She is author of numerous publications on utilizing solution-oriented approaches with hospitalized psychiatric clients. She has presented to many professional audiences, including the International Society of Psychiatric Consultation Liaison Nurses, Colorado Society of Clinical Nurse Specialists, Second Annual East Coast Conference on Solution-Focused Therapy, and the Department of Psychosocial Nursing, University of Washington. She has consulted with numerous health care organizations on applying solution-focused therapy to hospital settings.

Denise C. Webster is associate professor at the University of Colorado Health Sciences Center School of Nursing. As coordinator of the graduate program in psychiatric nursing, she developed a program preparing graduate students in the use of brief therapy interventions for a wide variety of client populations. She received her Ph.D. in nursing science from the University of Illinois. Webster is published widely in the areas of women and mental health, women's health, and health-oriented brief therapy approaches.

John L. Walter is co-director of Consultations, a practice and training center for solution-focused personal consultation in Chicago. He conducts training throughout the United States and abroad, and is coauthor of the popular *Becoming Solution-Focused in Brief Therapy* (1992, with Jane Peller).

Bonnie Cox Young is director of Psychiatric Patient Services for Colorado Psychiatric Hospital. She is volunteer faculty for University of Colorado Health Sciences Center School of Nursing and School of Medicine. She received her

Master of Nursing Science (Nursing Administration) from University of Colorado Health Sciences Center School of Nursing. She has authored publications on outcomes, nurse case management, and brief therapy. In addition to professional presentations, she has provided consultation to a variety of managed care organizations on innovative inpatient program development.

NAME INDEX

A

Abad López, A. M., 330
Abbott, J., 66, 96
Abramowitz, C. V., 319, 330
Abramowitz, S. I., 319, 330
Adams, J. F., 256–257, 260, 268,
 272, 297
Addis, M. E., 97, 254, 269
Adler, A., 202, 203
Ahola, T., 128, 136, 149, 258, 269
Aitkin, R., 51, 61
Alden, D. C., 222, 226
Aldorondo, E., 75, 81, 96
Allen, G. J., 301, 312, 332
Allende, I., 228, 247
Allgood, S. M., 255, 268
Almeida, L., 316, 333
Altuna, A., 301, 314, 330
Amatea, E. S., 200, 203
Andersen, T., 9, 26, 142–143, 149
Anderson, C. A., 303, 334
Anderson, H., 9, 16, 19, 26, 139,
 146, 149
Anderson, S. A., 304, 330
Andreas, B., 252–253, 268
Andrews, G., 319, 331

Angie, 196–197
Arias, I., 98
Arizmendi, T. A., 319, 334
Armantage, J., 44n
Arribas de Migues, F. J., 330
Atilano, R. B., 304, 330
Atkinson, D., 280, 298
Austad, C. S., 101, 117
Axelson, J. A., 280, 297

B

Babcock, J. C., 89, 96, 97
Bachelor, A., 335, 348
Baekeland, F., 303, 304, 330
Bagarozzi, D. A., 301, 313, 334
Bailey-Martiniere, L., 44n, 51, 61
Bailín, M. C., 302, 313, 314, 327,
 330
Baker, N., 103, 112–113, 117
Bandura, A., 316, 322, 330
Barké, K. H., 301, 332
Barling, J., 98
Barros, A., 316, 333
Bateson, G., 10–11, 12, 26, 48, 53,
 61, 131, 149
Bavelas, J. B., 304, 334

Beach, A., 263, 269
Beadle,. S., 128, 150
Beavin, J., 46, 62, 301, 312, 332,
 334
Beck, A. T., 215, 226
Bengelsdorf, H., 222, 223, 226
Benner, P., 146, 149
Bennett, L., 66, 98
Berg, I. K., 6, 29, 31, 42, 44n, 46,
 52, 61, 96–97, 128, 129, 130,
 131, 134, 136, 137, 138, 143,
 149, 156, 157, 158, 170, 174,
 176, 177, 182, 186, 203, 213,
 215, 217, 221, 225, 226, 229,
 231, 234, 236, 239, 247, 263,
 268, 272, 281, 285, 288, 296,
 297, 305, 308, 330, 339, 343,
 345, 348
Bergen, L. P., 304, 330
Bergin, A. E., 252, 254, 268, 269,
 278–279, 297–298
Berman, W. H., 101, 117
Betty, 230–231
Beutler, L. E., 319, 334
Beyebach, M., 6, 299, 300, 301,
 302, 305, 308, 311, 313, 314,
 322n, 323n, 326, 330, 333

359

SUBJECT INDEX

For information and training on solution-focused brief therapy please contact:

Brief Therapy Consortium
P.O. Box 578264
Chicago, IL 60657-8264
(312) 404-5130
email: 72203.1131@compuserve.com